Financing Economic Development

THE INDONESIAN CASE

BOOKS FROM THE CENTER FOR INTERNATIONAL STUDIES
PUBLISHED BY THE FREE PRESS

HANDBOOK FOR INDUSTRY STUDIES
Everett E. Hagen

CHANGING IMAGES OF AMERICA: A Study of Indian Students' Perceptions
George V. Coelho

THE JAPANESE FACTORY: Aspects of Its Social Organization
James C. Abegglen

INDUSTRIAL CHANGE IN INDIA: Industrial Growth, Capital Requirements, and Technological Change, 1937-1955
George Rosen

THE PASSING OF TRADITIONAL SOCIETY: Modernizing the Middle East
Daniel Lerner, with Lucille W. Pevsner

THE RELIGION IN JAVA ("Modjokuto" Series)
Clifford Geertz

CHINA'S GROSS NATIONAL PRODUCT AND SOCIAL ACCOUNTS: 1950-1957
William W. Hollister

INDUSTRIAL GROWTH IN SOUTH INDIA: Case Studies in Economic Development
George B. Baldwin

AMERICAN BUSINESSMEN AND INTERNATIONAL TRADE: Code Book and Data from a Study on Attitudes and Communications
Raymond A. Bauer and Ithiel de Sola Pool, eds.

OVERSEAS CHINESE NATIONALISM: The Genesis of the Pan-Chinese Movement in Indonesia, 1900-1916
Lea E. Williams

FINANCING ECONOMIC DEVELOPMENT: The Indonesian Case
Douglas S. Paauw

OTHER BOOKS FROM THE CENTER FOR INTERNATIONAL STUDIES

THE DYNAMICS OF SOVIET SOCIETY
W. W. Rostow, Alfred Levin, and Others, Norton, 1953; Mentor Books, 1954

THE PROSPECTS FOR COMMUNIST CHINA
W. W. Rostow and Others, Technology Press and Wiley, 1954

NINE SOVIET PORTRAITS
Raymond A. Bauer and Edward Wasiolek, Technology Press and Wiley, 1955

AN AMERICAN POLICY IN ASIA
W. W. Rostow and Richard W. Hatch, Technology Press and Wiley, 1955

MOSCOW AND THE COMMUNIST PARTY OF INDIA
John H. Kautsky, Technology Press and Wiley, 1956

A PROPOSAL: Key to an Effective Foreign Policy
M. F. Millikan and W. W. Rostow, Harper, 1957

FRANCE DEFEATS EDC
Daniel Lerner and Raymond Aron, eds., Praeger, 1957 (published as LA QUERELLE DE LA C.E.D., Armand Colin, 1956)

THE ECONOMICS OF COMMUNIST EASTERN EUROPE
Nicolas Spulber, Technology Press and Wiley, 1957

SOVIET EDUCATION FOR SCIENCE AND TECHNOLOGY
Alexander Korol, Technology Press and Wiley, 1957

INDONESIA'S ECONOMIC STABILIZATION AND DEVELOPMENT
Benjamin Higgins, Institute of Pacific Relations, 1957

FORGING A NEW SWORD: A Study of the Department of Defense
William R. Kintner, with Joseph I. Coffey and Raymond J. Albright, Harper, 1958

SCRATCHES ON OUR MINDS: American Images of China and India
Harold R. Isaacs, John Day, 1958

THE INFLATIONARY SPIRAL: The Experience in China, 1939-1950
Chang Kia-Ngau, Technology Press and Wiley, 1958

THE AMERICAN STYLE: Essays in Value and Performance
Elting E. Morison, ed., Harper, 1958

ALLOCATION IN SPACE: Production, Transport and Industrial Location
Louis Lefeber, North-Holland, 1958

JAPANESE POPULAR CULTURE: Studies in Mass Communication and Cultural Change
Hidetoshi Kato, ed. and trans., Tuttle, 1959

THE HUMAN MEANING OF THE SOCIAL SCIENCES
Daniel Lerner, ed., Meridian Books, 1959

A CHINESE VILLAGE IN EARLY COMMUNIST TRANSITION
C. K. Yang, Technology Press, 1959

THE CHINESE FAMILY IN THE COMMUNIST REVOLUTION
C. K. Yang, Technology Press, 1959

BLOC POLITICS IN THE UNITED NATIONS
Thomas Hovet, Jr., Harvard, 1960

THE STRUCTURE OF THE EAST GERMAN ECONOMY
Wolfgang F. Stolper, Harvard, 1960

POSTWAR ECONOMIC TRENDS IN THE UNITED STATES
Ralph E. Freeman, ed., Harper, 1960

THE UNITED STATES IN THE WORLD ARENA
W. W. Rostow, Harper, 1960

THE QUESTION OF GOVERNMENT SPENDING: Public Needs and Private Wants
Francis M. Bator, Harper, 1960

The Center for International Studies
MASSACHUSETTS INSTITUTE OF TECHNOLOGY

Financing Economic Development

THE INDONESIAN CASE

by Douglas S. Paauw

Introduction by Benjamin Higgins

The Free Press, Glencoe, Illinois

Printed in the United States of America

Library of Congress Catalog Card Number: 60-9583

Second Printing, September 1961

For my Mother and Father

CONTENTS

LIST OF TABLES

FOREWORD

Dr. Paauw's report on financing Indonesian development is the first major product of the field research done by the Indonesia project of the Center for International Studies, Massachusetts Institute of Technology. My "interim report" on *Indonesia's Economic Stabilization and Development*, published by the Institute of Pacific Relations, reflected the author's experience as Monetary and Fiscal Adviser to the Indonesian government in 1952 and 1953 as much as his subsequent work with the Indonesia project. It started as a data paper for an IPR conference, and it was still essentially a data paper as published; it reviewed briefly the Indonesian government's measures for stabilization and development from 1950 to 1957 and presented some economic analysis of these policies and some of the political and sociological background. Our report on *Stanvac in Indonesia*, published by the National Planning Association, was a case study of the role of foreign enterprise in Indonesian development. It was deliberately restricted in size and scope, and it made considerable use of both source materials prepared by others and results of the project's own field research. Dr. Paauw's book, on the other hand, is based almost exclusively on his own field work in Indonesia and his subsequent deliberations. It is thus the first book-length publication which is entirely the outcome of the project's own undertakings.

Four more such publications are planned: Professor William Hollinger's study of the balance-of-payments aspects of Indonesian development; Elizabeth Pelzer's study of Batak entrepreneurs; Professor Everett Hawkins' study of entrepreneurship and labor relations in Java; and a final volume synthesizing all the research of those who have been associated with the project. In addition, the results of the Indonesia Field Team's sociological and anthropological studies in East Central Java will be published as a separate set of monographs.

Rightly or wrongly, it has been the project's policy to publish the parts prior to the whole. The reason is simple enough: the final volume will draw on all the work of the project, and it will therefore be convenient to have the detailed studies in print when this final volume appears. The trouble with this policy, obviously, is that each separate part in turn reflects the collective knowledge and analysis of the project, which is not yet in print. For example, Dr. Paauw's book, while essentially self-contained, can be better appreciated against the whole background of economic, political, and social analysis which informs it. This background material will not be presented in full until the final volume is published. Only there shall we attempt to analyze the reasons for Indonesia's failure to achieve high living standards for her people despite a resource endowment much more favorable than is found in most underdeveloped countries. The economic, political, and sociological factors which encourage or impede economic development, and suggestions for future development policy, will also be set forth in this final volume.

The same problem will arise, in greater or lesser degree, with the other monographs in this series. For this reason, it has seemed desirable to include in this first volume of the series a chapter which will serve as a general introduction to the whole series. We provide therein some major facts concerning Indonesia's economy, politics, and social structure, with a limited amount of analysis, and some anticipation of conclusions which can be fully documented only in the final volume. For students of economic development and finance who do not have any special knowledge of the Indonesian scene, the Introduction provides background material in summary form.

Benjamin Higgins, Director
Indonesia Project

Cambridge, Massachusetts
May 1959

PREFACE

In this preface I wish to present my views on issues not explicitly covered by the data and analysis presented in the text. It has been my purpose in treating the subject matter of this book to attempt to present the data and analysis which follows as objectively as possible. Although I have consistently felt sympathy for and a certain amount of identification with the new Indonesian Republic, I do not wish to be construed as taking a position on issues which are essentially Dutch-Indonesian controversies. In particular, I am not interested in making a value judgment about a currently popular drawing room question, "Who got Indonesia into this mess?" Any nation which finds itself in the throes of a major social revolution is likely to have difficulties; it is unrealistic to attribute all of these difficulties to a colonial heritage or, alternatively, to the ineptness of the political leaders upon whom responsibility is thrust by independence.

The colonial society was one form of social organization, the new Republican society another. Neither is wholly good or wholly evil. Which is more desirable for Indonesia is not our central concern. We are concerned with this general question only to the extent that it has implications for Indonesia's present and future capacity to finance economic development.

The first nine years of Indonesian independence have yielded little in the way of national integration. There has been much backing and filling on political issues as well as on the formulation of economic goals and their realization. Some Western observers have concluded from this that American aid and understanding have produced so little in the way of concrete progress in Indonesia (and elsewhere) that we had best keep our valuable resources to ourselves.

The first point that should be made as a rejoinder to this mistaken view is that it represents a misunderstanding of the dynamics of Indonesian society and the potential impact of a very meager volume of United States aid. Basically, the long-run development of Indonesia as a member of the world community will be determined by the expression of powerful domestic forces which were unleashed by independence. The force of nationalism is dominant in Indonesian social dynamics; it appeared early in the present century, but colonial restraint prevented leadership groups from arising to use it as a weapon for changing the *status quo*. Nationalism took firm root during the Japanese occupation, and it was later harnessed to unite Indonesians in their struggle for independence. Since independence, however, Indonesia has largely failed to mobilize this same force for constructive social change. The leadership has placed too much emphasis upon essentially revolutionary goals—"sweeping away the vestiges of colonialism"—and too little upon national integration. From the perspective of long-run social change, however, such a radical shift in national goals could hardly have been expected in a short span of time; and prognostication about the long-run prospects for Indonesian society on the basis of less than a decade's record is both unfair and unrealistic.

Looking further into the basic makeup of Indonesian society, one can find much evidence to justify an optimistic outlook. Democracy, a sense of fair play, and concern for social justice appear to be firmly rooted in traditional Indonesian society. In the villages on the myriad islands, programs of common welfare and reconciliation of opposing views through voluntary methods (gotong rojong and musjawarat desa) are basic characteristics of social organization. In many areas of Indonesia, local involvement with economic change has produced a vigorous expression of new energies since independence; and a host of local development programs has been one of the most positive features of Indonesia's post-independence economy. These basic values, which apparently will remain dominant in Indonesia for a long time, do not, however, point to the evolution of a capitalistic economy as we understand the term in the West. The society's new economic goals, formulated by a small but articulate elite, have been pronounced in their anti-capitalistic tone; virtually all political parties view capitalism as a short-run evil to be accepted where it now exists only as a stepping-stone to the eventual creation of a cooperative economy. Indonesian leaders envisage their goal as a society with enough socialism to avert concentration of economic power in private hands, but with enough "cooperativeness" to promote the expression of individual abilities. These economic goals, as in India, are not inconsistent with building a fully democratic political framework, and only strong external forces are likely to subvert the internal leadership into compromise with an authoritarian system.

When independence was achieved in 1949, Indonesia was unique as a newly independent country: there was little polarization between wealthy groups with political power and a populace oppressed by feudal authority. No single group combined national political power with vested interests in the colonial economy, and there was no great problem of an aristocratic landed class wielding its economic power to political advantage. There were, indeed, local aristocratic groups such as the *prijaji*; but more often than not, membership in such a group was regarded by Indonesians as a political liability rather than an advantage. To the extent that wealth and income were unequally distributed, it was largely a cleavage between low-income Indonesians and higher-income minorities or foreigners. Indonesian economic and political stake in the *status quo*, therefore, has not been, and is not likely to be, an important obstacle to social and economic progress. The redress of economic power and wealth between Indonesians and non-Indonesian groups, however, has probably diverted the attention of the ruling elite from attacking more fundamental economic problems. It is even possible that excessively nationalistic redistribution programs have begun to foster a tendency toward the kind of social and economic stratification which might hamper progress. What has been achieved during the past few years, however, has not altered the basic fact of a relatively equal distribution of poverty among Indonesians.

Perhaps because of this fact of shared poverty, Indonesians have placed great emphasis upon the spread of education and literacy; whatever its cause, this emphasis has been another important feature of the new Indonesia. Progress in raising the literacy rate has been dramatic, though perhaps not as great as Indonesian statistics claim. Local interest in education has called forth considerable local sacrifice in providing educational facilities. The desire for literacy and rudimentary learning has been the solid core around which the revival of local development programs, discussed in Chapter 7, have rallied mass support in many of the Indonesian islands. This general concern for education, and the fruits it has already borne in raising the literacy rate, must be counted as a strong point in the case for optimistic prognostication.

Establishing preconditions which may eventually lead to rapid economic growth requires, first of all, that these highly diversified but positive forces be brought to bear upon the problems of economic backwardness through the formulation and mass communication of unambiguous social goals. Among the social goals essential for progress, the necessity to convey to all Indonesians a sense of national purpose must be accorded first place. The fundamental problem of unity—a problem which was dramatized by the outbreak of civil war in 1958—concerns the _conditions_ and _terms_ on which the interests of local loyalties are to be subsumed in the interest of a unified Republic. Indonesian leadership, after successfully dealing with the most disruptive military and political aspects of the 1958 revolt, has finally begun to show some willingness to recognize the legitimacy of local opposition to unification by extension of central power. If the way to effective negotiation between Central Government and the dissident local groups throughout the archipelago can be further opened, the outlook for integrating Indonesia into a social and political unit will improve. There has been little sentiment among the dissidents for separation from the Republic. Resistance has focused upon the issue of obtaining from Central Government concessions to local autonomy which are not inconsistent with unification under one national government.

A second important precondition for national economic development is the acceptance of the concept of _national_ development as a widely supported social goal. There is no basis for believing that Indonesians are not aware of the desirability of economic development. During the last few years, local programs to promote the more effective use of local economic resources have been adopted with widespread popular support throughout Indonesia. In contrast to this encouraging tendency, however, the National Development Plan has languished in Djakarta. The issues raised by the Plan—its allocation of investment resources, its potential effectiveness in raising real income per capita, and its financial feasibility—have exercised the minds of a small group of planners in Djakarta, but elsewhere the Plan has been overlooked in favor of local development programs. These paradoxes are obviously symptoms of national disunity, but yet one cannot fail to see favorable prospects for linking local plans and the interest they excite to a national program through the same processes of compromise which are necessary for political unity. If a formula to achieve a substantial degree of coordination can be devised, a National Development Plan may serve to promote political unity and to produce economic results which will be helpful in overcoming local disaffection.

The struggle to reap expected gains from independence over the past nine years appears to have yielded rather meager results. The important preconditions for the progress of Indonesian society toward social, economic, and political integration have been neglected in the emphasis upon rooting out the vestiges of colonialism. Perhaps little more could have been achieved in a country saddled with the limitations which Indonesia inherited along with independence. Indonesia's population of 85 million consists of a wide diversity of ethnic groups scattered about thousands of islands, with little modern precedent of social or political cohesion. It would be unfair to overlook the fact that the new Republic confronted massive political and economic problems. Indonesia possessed few advantages promising rapid progress. Its educated elite, capable of providing national leadership, was very small—perhaps numbering less than 300. Education and experience had generally been denied to all but a few select candidates. There was little or no foundation for political unity among the numerous ethnic groups, and Indonesians believe that the Dutch encouraged fragmentation of the economy. The facts seem to support the Indonesian presumption that foreign minorities were encouraged to fill important political and economic roles which the Dutch themselves did not wish to fill. Colonial income distribution statistics lend some support to this position. Whatever the merits of the Indonesian views on these matters, it seems clear that Indonesian leadership was ill-equipped to permit a graceful transition from colonial administration to self-government.

Viewed from this perspective, the performance of the Indonesian Republic during the past nine years hardly warrants harsh and negative criticism. However irrational _Benteng_ and anti-Dutch programs might appear from the viewpoint of economic progress, they may have been an inevitable reaction to a particular kind of colonial experience. Even the overzealous attempts to centralize political control beyond the capacities of a severely handicapped administration acquire some logic in the context of a fragmentized political and economic setting, especially in view of the Indonesian conviction that decentralization was a tool for preserving colonial control.

This is not an indictment of Dutch colonial policy in Indonesia, and it is not a blanket statement of approbation for the Indonesian policies which have sought to complete the domestic "revolution" while adopting an outward pose of neutralism. The point which deserves emphasis is that Indonesia's performance since independence has been an almost inevitable aftermath of independence. If this interpretation has merit, events in Indonesia during the past nine years provide no basis for concluding that the United States should refrain from extending economic assistance to promote Indonesian development. If any one lesson is to be learned from recent Indonesian experience, it is that we must avoid inheriting the special kind of hostility toward the West and its institutions which Indonesia's colonial history generated. United States policies which remind Indonesians of their long colonial status are likely to produce irrational and unfortunate responses. If this posture can be avoided, our contribution to the growth of a free society with great capacity for leadership in the Free World may prove to be significant.

Indonesia's post-independence struggle to build a society free from what Indonesians regard as colonial restraints has involved great economic costs. Efforts to remove Dutch political and economic influence, to transfer strategic economic roles to Indonesians from the Dutch and their supporting minorities, and to create unity by centralism and force have yielded little more than inflation and continued economic stagnation. The path to economic instability was widened by overambitious economic programs in the early years of independence—programs which sought to reshape what Indonesia's leaders considered the warped structure of a "colonial economy" and to replace foreign enterprise with a large and vigorous class of indigenous entrepreneurs. At the time of this writing, the eagerness with which surrealistic and irrational programs have been adopted in the past seems to have diminished, and the time for a sounder approach to Indonesia's social problems may be at hand. What has gone before, however, has made the restoration of economic stability a precondition for undertaking a comprehensive program for economic development. The domestic political crisis of 1958, which was met with resolute military action, led to the last in a series of costly post-independence efforts to bring political integration and economic welfare by quick and dramatic means. This action—regardless of its merits—has produced an unprecedented budget deficit in a country which had used deficit financing extensively. It has further accelerated the pace of inflation, a condition which has threatened Indonesian economic progress throughout the short history of the Republic.

Indonesia today seems to be on the threshold of undertaking a general reappraisal of its post-independence domestic and foreign policies. Central Government has shown a new willingness to make concessions on the issues which precipitated rebellion. On the question of communist infiltration into government, recent cabinet changes have strengthened the position of noncommunists. Prime Minister Djuanda has announced efforts to bring greater economy to Central Government administration and to increase fiscal allocation to areas outside Java. This has been accompanied by a plan to permit localities to retain a share of their foreign-exchange earnings.

A fresh attitude toward the United States and other Western countries is also apparent. A New York Times correspondent close to the situation in Indonesia has reported that:

> To bolster it through the difficult times ahead the Government hopes for new foreign credits and other economic aid, particularly from the United States. . . . Its foreign policy is still predicated on nonalignment with either the Communist bloc or the West, but the outlook is for at least more cooperative relationships between Jakarta and the West than there have been. (Tillman Durdin, "Indonesia Facing Many Problems," July 20, 1958, p. 6b.)

Despite the alarm which many Westerners have expressed about political instability in Indonesia, and the threat of an imminent communist takeover in particular, Indonesia is still an uncommitted nation with many influential leaders receptive to closer relations with the West.

Indonesia requires external economic assistance to cope with her massive economic problems, and the present signs seem to indicate a preference for dealing with the West in solving these problems. The determination of Indonesia's top leadership to pursue a sound development program, once stability has been achieved, also appears to have become more firm. The Prime Minister's recent statements reflect a sense of awareness of the necessity for adopting a national development program which will serve to provide incentives for local cooperation and thus promote progress toward national unity.

The climate produced by deepening domestic crises in Indonesia perhaps offers to the United States an opportunity to adopt a more positive posture in Indonesia. We have argued that a favorable prognosis for Indonesia's development rests basically upon the expression of strong democratic elements which appear to be rooted in Indonesian society. Yet the United States can do much to foster the growth of a free democratic society in Indonesia. If, indeed, our motives are no more than seeking to promote the growth of a stable Indonesian democracy and the development of a sound, expanding economy, Indonesians are likely to welcome an aid program large enough to have significant impact on the conditions for progress. Demonstration that American economic assistance is available without strings and in sufficient quantity to contribute significantly to the solution of Indonesia's own immediate and longer-run problems would go far toward reviving Indonesian respect for the United States.

Perhaps the most important conditions for the progress of underdeveloped countries toward the goals expressed in the United Nations charter—"to promote social progress and better standards of life in larger freedom"—are the preservation of independence in domestic political decisions and a general feeling of self-respect for national integrity. Genuine neutralism for newly independent countries is not far from the realization of these conditions, and this brand of neutralism cannot be construed to conflict with United States interests. If there is any dominant American interest in the future of newly independent but underdeveloped countries, there can be little doubt that it is in the preservation of these conditions.

The American diplomatic and aid representation in Indonesia has been effective in maintaining relatively good relationships with the Indonesian government in the atmosphere of misunderstanding which has prevailed in recent years. The climate of uncertainty amid which American representatives have been forced to work has, by and large, not been of their own making. The limitations to cooperative relationships between Indonesia and the United States have been matters of broader United States foreign policy: the posture we assume toward the major uncommitted countries in general. The present residue of good will toward the West is, in large part, a product of careful and intelligent work of our representatives in Indonesia. The diplomatic basis for enlarged American economic contributions to Indonesian development is firm, and our much maligned aid program has—in the case of Indonesia—already paid off handsome dividends in spite of the comparatively small sums we have seen fit to allocate to Southeast Asia's most important nation.

Douglas S. Paauw

Lake Forest, Illinois
January 12, 1959

ACKNOWLEDGMENTS

An author's acknowledgments are seldom adequate. Brief mention in print seems ridiculously small compensation to people who have given freely of themselves to indulge a research worker. Yet failure to mention as many as possible of those who have assisted me would certainly reflect callousness.

My first and greatest debt is owed to the Center for International Studies, and to its Director, Dr. Max F. Millikan. From this organization I received support for the research behind this volume, continual encouragement, and consistent cooperation in producing the manuscript. I should like to single out the Director of the Indonesia Project, Dr. Benjamin H. Higgins, for special recognition. Much of what I have learned about Indonesia, and many of my conclusions, emerged from Dr. Higgins' critical but friendly comments. Many errors in judgment have been removed from print because of his constant rereading of my material; many that remain are a reflection of my obstinancy. I am grateful to the Center for invaluable editorial advice and assistance rendered by Mr. Richard W. Hatch.

I am indebted for intellectual stimulation provided from many seminars at the Center for International Studies, generous criticism from its Senior Staff, and fruitful association with other members of the

Center's Indonesia Project. Much of my background on Indonesia is a joint product created in large part by my colleagues, Guy J. Pauker, William C. Hollinger, Mr. and Mrs. Clifford Geertz, Mr. and Mrs. Karl Pelzer, and many others.

I acknowledge gratitude to those who made my trip to Indonesia possible and pleasant: Dr. George B. Baldwin, then Assistant to the Director at the Center for International Studies; Mr. William Jones, the Center's former business manager; and Mrs. Priscilla Bruggeman, who was inimitable in surmounting the problems raised by international research.

In Indonesia, the way for my research could not have been more pleasant or easier. I should like to express gratitude to the National Planning Bureau for providing an unusually cooperative atmosphere and for opening many doors to information which proved helpful to my study. I should like to mention in particular the cooperation of Dr. Djuanda, formerly Director of the National Planning Bureau, and Ali Budiardjo, the present Director, as well as encouragement and help from the Planning Bureau's foreign staff: Douglas Dean, Edgar McVoy, Leon Baransky, and others. The Indonesian staff of the Planning Bureau perhaps taught me more about Indonesia than I learned from any other source. Sadli, Widjojo, Suhadi, Sie Kwat-soen, Sujono, Sisman, and many others gave freely of their time to tutor one unlettered in Indonesian economics.

Indonesian government officials were, without exception, cooperative and helpful. R. A. Kartadjoemena, formerly Director of Revenues, Oey Beng-to of the Bank Indonesia, Soetikno Slamet of the Ministry of Finance, and others too numerous to mention provided materials and information on each of my many visits to their offices. I shall not forget the graciousness with which I was received by officials who were undoubtedly overburdened with many pressing and important duties.

Several friends have read most or all of the present manuscript and have done much to improve it. In this category, I should like to express gratitude to John Paul Meek of the Federal Reserve Bank of New York, M. Sadli of the University of Indonesia, Sumitro Djojohadikusumo, William C. Hollinger, Ann Willner Berger, Surjo Sediono, and many of the people who have been associated with the Center for International Studies. For the imperfections that remain, I alone am responsible.

The herculean task of typing several drafts of the manuscript fell mainly to Mrs. Priscilla Bruggeman. I appreciate her painstaking efforts to produce excellent intermediate copies of this work. I am also grateful for careful typing assistance provided by Mrs. Edna Keller, Mrs. Marjorie Ryon, and Mrs. Helen Hurd of Lake Forest College.

I am deeply indebted to Mrs. Ada Espenshade Wrigley of the U.S. Bureau of Foreign Commerce for her cooperation in placing materials at my disposal. I have the conviction that Mrs. Wrigley has an unusual degree of respect for academic research and that she has a unique formula for helping bewildered academicians make use of voluminous government materials.

I have found the Library of International Relations in Chicago to be an unusually excellent source of materials. I wish to convey my gratitude to Miss Eloise ReQua and Miss Jean Statham of this fine library for their interest, cooperation, and encouragement. I also wish to thank Mrs. Joan Wilts of the Lake Forest College Library for assisting me in obtaining materials.

I am grateful to Lake Forest College for assistance at a task which must seem somewhat peripheral to the _raison d'être_ of a small liberal arts college.

I should like to acknowledge permission to reproduce in part material previously published in the Far Eastern Quarterly, Economic Development and Cultural Change ("Financing Economic Development in Indonesia," Vol. IV, January 1956), Ekonomi dan Keuangan Indonesia, and the Internationale Spectator (published by the Netherlands Institute of International Affairs). I also appreciate permission to use material originally prepared for the Indonesia volume produced by the Human Relations Area Files at Yale University.

Finally, my greatest debt of gratitude is due my wife, Kaye, for her constant encouragement and patience.

Douglas S. Paauw

Lake Forest, Illinois

January 12, 1959

INTRODUCTION

by Benjamin Higgins

INTRODUCTION

Indonesia is not a country which, like India, for example, is united by a strong central government with a development plan commanding wide support among both elite and electorate. The financial problem is not simply one of deciding how to raise the internal revenue and foreign exchange required for an agreed development plan. On the contrary, the Indonesian problem is to obtain enough agreement among leaders, political parties, and peoples of different regions and groups to permit the execution of any effective development plan. In the Indonesian case, the mobilization of financial resources for development—if it is accomplished—will be the symbol of successful mobilization of human resources, among leaders and people alike, behind a development plan. Perhaps more than anywhere else, financing economic development in Indonesia means prior solution of deep-seated and complex political, sociological, and economic problems. To fully appreciate Dr. Paauw's analysis and the recommendations arising from it, some knowledge of these broader problems is necessary. It is the purpose of this Introduction to provide such knowledge for the general reader.

Economic Problems

Indonesia is confronted with an unhappy combination of poverty and instability. Underlying both is the badly distorted structure of the economy. In order to denote the special character of this distortion, we refer to it as "technological dualism."

Poverty

The basic economic problem in most underdeveloped countries is to raise total production faster than the population grows. For many of them, a "big push" is necessary if the growth of income is to exceed population growth by enough, and for long enough, to assure cumulative expansion.* In very few countries is the need for a "big push" more obvious than in Indonesia. For, while Indonesia today is relatively well off among Asian countries, with a per capita income of about $100 per year, this per capita income is apparently lower than it was in 1939, is probably lower than it was in 1929, and perhaps even lower than it was in 1889 or 1819. There is no clear evidence that it is currently rising; such symptoms of prosperity as appear are those of a speculative inflationary boom that does a few people good and many people harm.

Considering the range and abundance of the country's resource base, Indonesia's failure to show significant economic progress cries aloud for explanation. The population is large—about 85 million; but relative to the area of the country, the population is not so great as in some other Asian countries. For example, the average population per square mile

*For a presentation of the theory and facts underlying this formulation of the development problem, see Benjamin Higgins, Economic Development: Problems, Principles, and Policies, Norton, New York, 1959, especially Part IV.

for the whole country is lower than in the Philippines, where per capita income is about 60 per cent higher than in Indonesia. True, over three-fifths of the population are crowded onto the one small island of Java, making that the most densely populated large area in the world, with nearly eleven hundred people per square mile. This extreme population density, however, is made possible by Java's rich volcanic soil and its assured rainfall, which together permit two or three crops a year throughout much of the island. Indonesia as a whole is a fertile land, with near self-sufficiency in foodstuffs (of which the most important are rice, cassava, and maize) and with great plantation industries—rubber, copra, coffee, tea, sisal, tobacco, pepper, teak, and others.

The country also has abundant hydroelectric power potential in some areas, and a wide variety of mineral resources. Of the latter, petroleum has become most important since the war. Tin and bauxite are also found in significant quantities. There are deposits of gold and silver, iron, coal, manganese, nickel, diamonds, copper, sulfate, lead, and zinc.

In earlier writings we have made the point that Indonesia is not quite so "rich in natural resources" as some Indonesians think. The quantity and quality of some of these resources is not impressive in relation to the size of the population, and the quantity and quality of some others are not thoroughly known. The most promising source of hydroelectric power (the Asahan Valley) is not ideally located relative to the present geographic distribution of population and raw materials, while other regions with dense populations and larger supplies of raw materials are power poor. Nevertheless, there can be no doubt that in comparison to most of her neighbors Indonesia is blessed by nature.

Indonesia's failure to develop economically since achieving independence is not altogether the fault of the Indonesian leadership. It can be explained in part by the two decades of bewilderingly rapid change after 1939 and the three previous centuries of relative quiescense. The Indonesians inherited from the Dutch a badly distorted economy, with exports concentrated on a few commodities highly sensitive to the vagaries of the world market, with no indigenous Indonesian financial, trading, or transport sector, and with little processing of domestic raw materials within the country. The Dutch also left Indonesia with per capita incomes in the peasant agriculture sector, where most Indonesians earn their livelihood, under $50 per year, with illiteracy near 90 per cent (probably higher than in 1600), and with no such cadre of trained civil servants and business executives as the British left behind in India. Then came the war, Japanese occupation, revolution, independence, eight stormy years of internal struggle for power, and civil war. These twenty years of turmoil left Indonesia with impaired plant, equipment, and transport facilities, loss of foreign expertise of every kind, sadly depleted foreign-exchange reserves, chronic and accelerating inflation, intensified political conflict, and deepening and spreading disillusionment.

Instability

Indonesia provides a picture of a highly regionalized economy devoted mainly to production of food and raw materials. This kind of limited economic development was what Dutch policy encouraged. Since the transfer of sovereignty, public policy has placed more emphasis on industrialization; but the government's efforts to expand small industries have not as yet met with striking success. There has been some expansion of small industrial enterprises, mainly outside the government program, but not enough to alter the country's balance-of-payments position.

Indonesian exports are more highly concentrated today than ever before. The composition of exports has changed since 1938—or 1929—but Indonesia has not succeeded in reducing the degree of concentration in her export industries. In 1928 rubber accounted for 24.8 per cent of the total value of exports, while the two next most important products (sugar and petroleum) accounted for 23.1 per cent and 9.1 per cent respectively of the total. Thus these three products together were responsible for slightly less than half the total value of exports. In 1955 rubber alone accounted for over 45 per cent of the total value of exports. Petroleum and petroleum products accounted for 23 per cent, and tin for 6 per cent of the total. Thus three products account for three-quarters of the total value of exports. If seven other leading plantation products are included, the total value reaches nearly 95 per cent of total exports.

On the import side, textiles remain the major item. In 1955 textiles and textile raw materials accounted for over one-quarter of the total value of imports. Other major imports were rice (3.6 per cent), paints and dyes, fertilizer, paper and cardboard, iron and steel, automobiles and trucks, bicycles, and industrial machinery.

Indonesia's normal balance-of-payments position is an unhappy one for an underdeveloped country: an export surplus combined with a large deficit in invisibles and an uncertain capital inflow. The result is an unfavorable balance of payments whenever prices of principal exports drop. The marginal propensity to import is high, and from Dutch times until now the government has found it necessary to impose import restrictions, which have recently become very severe.

Thus trade, money income, and employment outside the rural sector are heavily dependent on a narrow range of raw materials and foodstuffs. As a consequence the Indonesian economy is a highly unstable one. Few countries in the world suffered a more violent collapse of monetary income during the depression of the 1930's than the Netherlands East Indies. Similarly, with the boom in strategic materials during the Korean war, Indonesia enjoyed a balance-of-payments and budget surplus. From mid-1952 to mid-1954, however, Indonesia was losing reserves of gold and foreign exchange more rapidly than any country covered in International Monetary Fund reports, and it suffered serious budget deficits.

In August 1954 the Indonesian government resorted to the escape clause in the statutes of the Bank Indonesia, permitting the Bank to suspend its 20 per cent legal reserve requirements "in extraordinary circumstances." During the latter part of 1955 and 1956, with rising export prices, the Indonesian economy recovered somewhat. The reserve position improved and the legal reserve ratio was restored; but the reserves were protected by import restrictions so severe that "bottleneck" unemployment appeared, some semi-luxuries were available only in the black market, and prices of others rose to levels several times as high as they were a few years earlier. The black market value of the rupiah in 1956 was about one-third of its official value—the biggest spread between black market and official rates among members of the International Monetary Fund.

In July 1956, following another drop in export prices, the government was compelled to suspend reserve requirements once again. This time there was no saving recovery of export earnings. In April 1957 imports were suspended altogether, except for government orders, capital goods, and certain special transactions. In May it was announced that imports would be gradually resumed, starting with industrial raw materials; but at the same time a bill was introduced permitting suspension of reserve requirements for another six months. Finally, with the crushing losses of reserves during the rebellion of 1957 and 1958, when exports dropped by about two thirds, the Bank Indonesia statutes were revised to eliminate formal reserve requirements altogether.

The Indonesian budget has been in chronic deficit since 1952. The deficit rose from Rp. 2.0 billion in 1953 to Rp. 3.6 billion in 1954. The 1956 figure was Rp. 2.8 billion, but in 1957 the deficit reached new record heights. As a consequence of the swelling deficit, the note circulation increased by nearly 50 per cent between mid-1957 and mid-1958 and continued to soar thereafter. The inflation which had long been endemic became epidemic. By the middle of 1958 the cost of living was rising by 3 to 4 per cent per month.

Inflationary tendencies were aggravated by reduced domestic production and by further cuts in imports, which were in turn necessitated by the loss of foreign-exchange earnings. Rice imports, despite the concentrated effort to achieve self-sufficiency in rice, exceeded 700,000 tons or 10 per cent of total requirements in 1958. Rice imports alone cost Indonesia some $75 million annually. On the other hand, estate production has held up remarkably well. Tin exports dropped moderately, and petroleum exports continued despite the interruption of Caltex operations. Smallholders' rubber, which has become more important than estate rubber since independence, fell far below the 1957 level. Exports of smallholders' products in general were Rp. 687 million in the first half of 1958 as compared to Rp. 1,711 million for the same period of 1957. The losses through the barter trade,* which even in 1957 cost the government some $100 million in foreign exchange ($60 million on Central Sumatra exports alone), were running at still higher rates in the first half of 1958. By the end of September the Bank Indonesia reserves were down to 7 per cent of the note circulation, as compared to the former legal ratio of 20 per cent. Imports of luxuries were cut out altogether, and imports of semi-luxuries and even some necessities were drastically curtailed. The black market rate for the dollar reached eight times the official rate.

Technological Dualism

The "dualistic" nature of the Indonesian economy has long been noted. Some of the Dutch writers sought to explain this dualism in sociological terms. In our view, the explanation of dualism, which is a phenomenon common to many underdeveloped countries, lies in economic, technological, and demographic rather than in purely cultural factors.†

Certainly the Indonesian economy can be divided into two quite distinct sectors. The "industrial" sector, consisting of plantations, mines, oil fields and refineries, large-scale manufacturing, and transport, trade, and finance associated with these activities, is capital intensive; the capital-job ratio is high; and man-hour productivity is also high. In this sector technical coefficients (ratio of land and capital to labor) are relatively fixed—or at least are regarded as such. Engineering techniques are largely Western, and mechanized production processes are used rather than labor-intensive ones. (If the managers of mines, manufacturing industries, and plantations are so convinced

*"Barter trade" is the Indonesian euphemism for exchange of smuggled exports for smuggled imports.

†See Higgins, op. cit., especially Chapters 12, 14, and 16.

of the superiority of mechanized techniques that they do not seek labor-intensive ones, the possibility that alternative methods may be available does not alter the economic situation.)

The other sector consists of peasant agriculture and small or cottage industry, and trade, transport, and finance associated with these activities. Here technical coefficients are variable; output can be produced with a wide variety of combinations of labor with land and capital. Because labor is relatively abundant and cheap and capital is scarce in this sector, labor-intensive techniques are chosen and man-hour productivity is extremely low.

How did this unbalanced structure develop? Answering this question will be a major purpose of the project's final volume. Here we can present only a brief summary. The main point is that "dualism" resulted from the special form of industrialization by foreign enterprise after the Napoleonic wars. Until about 1820 the entire country was given over to smallholders' and peasant agriculture, with no marked difference in technique from one sector or region to another. The population of Indonesia was small—about 10 per cent of its present level, with less than 5 million people on Java and perhaps 3 million in the Outer Islands. Land was therefore relatively abundant. There was no serious population pressure anywhere in the country, and, while standards of living were not high, there was little real hardship.

After the brief interlude of British rule during the Napoleonic wars, the Dutch colonial administration in Indonesia gradually shifted to plantation agriculture. Some decades later the development of the mining, petroleum, and processing industries began.

Industrialization seems to have brought an initial increase in the per capita incomes of Indonesians. However, instead of leading to permanent improvement in Indonesian living standards, the initial increase in incomes was rapidly offset by accelerated population growth. The higher incomes afforded subsistence for greater numbers. Moreover, the shift in policy brought Indonesians in closer contact with Western civilization; industrialization meant settlement by Europeans. Efforts were made to raise levels of health and to maintain peace and order among the Indonesians, who were previously rather given to fighting each other. Death rates dropped. It may also be—although this is less clear—that improved health and nutrition raised fertility rates. The form of development, centered as it was on plantations, mines, and oil fields, all producing raw materials for export, brought more _industrialization_ than _urbanization_; the checks on family size brought by urban industrialization of Europe and the new world were less effective in Indonesia. The net effect was that the total population increased over fourfold in some three generations.

The sector of the economy in which new investments were being made was totally incapable of absorbing the increase in population which it generated. For the plantation, industry, oil, and mining sector was land and capital intensive; technical coefficients either were, or were assumed to be, relatively fixed. The increased numbers inevitably led to a return flow into the peasant-agriculture and small-industry sector, where technical coefficients were relatively variable and opportunities for obtaining a living still existed within the village structure. With abundant labor and scarce capital—and in Java, scarce land as well—production methods in this sector became highly labor intensive.*

*Even in the Outer Islands, there is now no obvious superabundance of fertile, easily cleared, readily cultivatable land. And in recent decades population growth in the Outer Islands has been nearly as rapid as it was in Java during the late nineteenth century.

Eventually labor became redundant in this sector (marginal productivity fell to zero), and the growing population merely swelled the ranks of the disguised unemployed (static or dynamic). Per capita incomes in this sector returned to the subsistence level.

Technological progress was confined largely to the capital-intensive sector. Meanwhile, in the labor-intensive sector, the rate of population growth far exceeded capital accumulation. More recently, trade union activity and government policy have established industrial wage levels which, low as they are, are sometimes high relative to the marginal productivity of labor. This situation further aggravates the tendency to use labor-saving devices in the industrial sector wherever possible.

On the other hand, there is no incentive for groups of individual farmers or small enterprises to introduce labor-saving but capital-absorbing innovations in the rural sector. A technology that will raise man-hour productivity without net investment has yet to be discovered.* Nor is there any incentive for labor _as a group_ to increase its efforts since the labor supply is already redundant. Thus methods remain labor intensive, and levels of technique, man-hour productivity, and economic and social welfare remain low in the peasant-agriculture and small-industry sector.

Solution of both the economic and political aspects of the problem is made more difficult by the fact that the two sectors conform roughly to two regions, Java and the Outer Islands. The main development of plantations, mines, and oil fields took place on the Outer Islands, especially Sumatra, Kalimantan, and Sulawesi; the big growth of population took place where the soil was most fertile and best suited for

*Even manpower training programs usually require some investment in tools and equipment. See _ibid._, pp. 668-676.

growing foodstuffs, and where most of the people already were—Java. Employment in cottage and small industry is also highest in Java.

Here then is a country in which two-thirds of the population are crowded on one relatively small island, engaged mainly in the production of foodstuffs or simple handicrafts and small-scale manufacturing for home consumption, and dependent on imports for textiles and other essential items of consumption; while the other third of the population is scattered through an enormous area in which there are some highly efficient large-scale industries producing mainly for export. With such a discrepancy in economic conditions, it is small wonder that there are stresses and strains between Java and the Outer Islands.

Requirements for Development

Since the Indonesian economy is still essentially stagnant, the basic economic problem there is to generate a "take-off" into sustained economic growth. Stabilization will be easier, and the balance-of-payments problems more tractable, when a change in structure and higher productivity have been achieved. Meanwhile capital, entrepreneurship, technical and managerial skills, and foreign exchange are all bottlenecks that must be broken—as in most underdeveloped countries.

The Indonesian problem is even less tractable than others, however, because of the extreme form which technological dualism takes there and its relation to the regional structure of the economy. Some increase in output can still be obtained on Java through fertilizer and seed selection; these may still give a "breathing spell" of a few years. Then the Javanese rural economy in its present form will be simply unable to absorb further Javanese population growth without falling standards of living. Once the "breathing spell" is over, increases in man-hour productivity in Javanese agriculture will be obtainable only through a shift to more extensive and more mechanized agriculture.

In short, solution of the Javanese problem requires that somewhat more than the 300,000 families added each year to the Javanese population be absorbed elsewhere in the economy—into industries in Java or in the Outer Islands, or into extensive agriculture in the Outer Islands. Such a program will be expensive. Providing, say, 400,000 jobs a year in any of these ways would take 4 to 8 per cent of national income—just to absorb Javanese population growth without a fall in per capita output. Bringing significant increases in per capita income will require much more in the way of new investment, as shown in Dr. Paauw's first chapter. The obvious lines of development are the creation of middle-sized import-replacing industries on Java (where the market is) and carrying further the processing of export products of the Outer Islands (aluminum, tin smelting, pulp and paper, petroleum refining, etc.).

The Scale of the Plan

Indonesia's Five Year Development Plan (Garis-Garis Besar Rentjana Pembanguman Lima Tahun, 1956-1960) was prepared by the National Planning Bureau and presented to the Cabinet in May 1956. It was subsequently approved by the Cabinet, but it did not obtain formal Parliamentary approval until 1959.

The plan called for investment over the first five years of Rp. 30 billion, of which Rp. 12.5 billion represented Central Government outlays. It was hoped that community development would reach proportions equivalent to an investment of Rp. 7.5 billion, the balance to come from private enterprise. Net investment was to rise from 6 per cent of national income to 8 per cent during the first five years, as compared to the pre-plan level of about 5 per cent. With an incremental capital-output ratio of 2.0:1 and an estimated population growth of 1.7 per cent, this program would yield an annual increase in national income of 3 per cent and a per capita increase of 1.3 per cent. Forty per cent of the increase in income was to be recaptured for further investment, leaving 60 per cent for improvement in the current standard of living. Of the central government's development budget, 13 per cent was allocated to agriculture, 25 per cent for power and irrigation, 25 per cent for industry and mining, 25 per cent for transport and communications, and 12 per cent for education, welfare, and information.

The plan has never been published in English and is not readily available even in Indonesian. A summary translation of the plan is provided in Appendix A to give a general indication of its scope and nature to those who do not have ready access to the document as a whole. However, in discussing the problems of Indonesian development and its financing, both Dr. Paauw and I have thought it unwise to confine ourselves to the published plan. One reason is that the period covered by the plan is now nearly over; the significant questions now relate to the scale, scope, and composition of the <u>second</u> plan. Another reason is that the plan was never executed because of both the government's absorption with the problem of unification and the high cost of the anti-Dutch campaign and the rebellion in terms of foreign exchange, managerial talent, and energy of the nation's leaders. A third reason is that in our view—a view supported below—the plan was not adequate to launch a take-off into sustained growth in Indonesia even if executed in full. Dr. Paauw has therefore conducted his discussion mainly in terms of the kind of development program he thinks is really needed and the financial problems associated with the execution of such a plan.

The size of the investment budget in a development plan is the product of three factors: the targets that are set with regard to the rise in per capita income (or in employment); the estimated rate of population growth; and estimates of the incremental capital-output ratio (ICOR) or of the incremental capital-job ratio. We will discuss each of these factors in turn.

Targets

It is of course the responsibility of the government of an underdeveloped country to select its own target with respect to the growth of per capita income. The degree of ambitiousness in this respect necessarily reflects political and administrative considerations as well as economic and technical ones. However, it is possible to state a few principles regarding targets on the basis of general knowledge of the process of economic growth.

First, the target for increase in total output must be high enough to assure that it will exceed the growth of population and bring at least some measurable and noticeable increase in per capita income. It follows that the target for growth of output must exceed the estimated growth of population by enough to offset probable errors in the estimates. Second, in a society which has not experienced economic growth for generations, the target increase in per capita income must be high enough to bring significant changes in attitudes toward technological progress, propensity to save, supply curves of labor and entrepreneurship, and the like so as to launch a cumulative process of technological improvement, rising productivity, and rising standards of living.

The target set forth in the First Five Year Plan does not meet these requirements. The estimates of capital requirements for launching cumulative growth in Indonesia in Chapter 1 below suggest that the capital requirements for a "take-off" in Indonesia amount to some Rp. 12-15 billion per year. The same conclusion seems to have been reached by the National Planning Bureau; the plan is designed to achieve sustained growth only in the course of the fourth five-year period. The First Five Year Plan calls for net investment of only Rp. 6 billion per year, or 6 per cent of national income. This target does not seem high enough to meet either of the two requirements set forth above.

The plan speaks of the "sacrifice" of the current generation for Indonesia's future. In fact, however, the Indonesian development plan involves neither a sacrificial effort for one generation nor an early take-off into steady growth. Only 40 per cent of the expected small increase in per capita income (1.3 per cent) is to be recaptured for future investment, and 60 per cent is to be made available for higher consumption. Thus no "belt-tightening" is called for; on the other hand, an increase in per capita consumption of three-quarters of one per cent per year, starting from the present low level, will not in itself generate enthusiasm for the plan.

Perhaps the authors of the plan felt that in a society that has been essentially stagnant for generations (if not actually declining) it does not matter much whether cumulative growth starts now or in twenty years. However, in the present plan the achievement of steady growth in twenty years depends on the increase of investment from 6.0 per cent of national income in the First Five Year Plan to 8.5 per cent in the Second Five Year Plan, 12 per cent in the third five years, and an average of 16 per cent in the Fourth Plan; by the end of the Fourth

Five Year Plan, investment is supposed to be running at 20 per cent of national income.* These increases in investment are so small that with existing imperfections of national income statistics it would be very hard to tell whether year-by-year goals are being attained or not; yet even these modest goals require a more rigorous fiscal policy—and thus some enthusiasm for the plan. A stagnant economy is like a stalled car; leaning on it with gradually increasing weight is unlikely to get it started. It needs "a big push." The present plan will not change parameters enough to bring new attitudes, new behavior patterns, and the like.

For all these reasons, further delay in launching cumulative growth should be avoided if at all possible. The revolution injected a dynamic into Indonesian society, and every effort should be made to direct this outburst of energy toward economic growth. If too much time is allowed to pass without a major developmental effort, this dynamic may be lost.

If the modesty of the plan represents a political judgment of what is possible at this stage, it would be brash indeed for any outsider to criticize it on these grounds. If it is based on the experience of such countries as India (the scale of the investment budget and the ICOR are the same as in the Indian First Five Year Plan), however, it represents a misapplication of this experience. Indonesia starts from a much higher per capita income and a much broader resource base than India, and can accordingly start with a more ambitious program than was entailed in the Indian First Five Year Plan. It is our conviction, reached through sociological and political as well as economic analysis, that every effort should be made to accelerate the expansion of developmental investment.

*See the Statistical Appendix for a comparison of this original growth model with the revised model of August 1957.

Population Growth

The estimates with respect to population growth seem reasonable enough, and it is a strong feature of the plan that it allows for some initial rise in the rate of population growth as a consequence of the present age distribution, public health measures, and the possible positive impact on fertility of a new wave of industrialization. However, the margin of error allowed in the plan is so small that a population growth of 2 per cent in the first five years (instead of the estimated 1.7) and an ICOR of 3 (instead of the estimated 2) would mean that the present plan would bring no rise whatsoever in per capita income even if the plan were carried out completely in all sectors, including the private-investment and local-government sectors. It is therefore of obvious importance that demographic studies be undertaken to determine more accurately the present and probable future rates of population growth. Meanwhile, it is safer to plan for the _highest_ rate of population growth to which a high degree of probability can be attached.

It must also be recognized that the result of further research may be a conclusion that, given the limitations on the scale of investment in the near future, an active population policy, designed to reduce fertility at least enough to offset expected reductions in death rates, will be a _sine qua non_ for economic growth. The inclusion of population experts in the team of foreign experts in the National Planning Bureau presumably reflected a recognition of this possibility; but the plan includes no discussion of this problem. The dramatic drop in birth rates in Japan, the initial results of research in India, and the initial results of research in Indonesia undertaken by the Institute of Economic and Social Research in Djakarta suggest that an active policy with regard to population can be effective. Even such measures as keeping girls in school to the age of sixteen or seventeen might influence birth rates significantly. However, the subject clearly merits further study.

At one stage of the discussion of the development plan it was thought that an ambitious transmigration program might provide relief for population pressure on Java. The discussion of transmigration in the present plan indicates that this approach to the population problem has been abandoned. It is our view that this course was the correct one; the whole experience with organized resettlement, both in Indonesia and in other countries, suggests that it is not a solution to the problem of finding productive employment for the annual additions to the Javanese population. With the total cost of resettlement running at Rp. 10,000 to Rp. 15,000 per family,* resettling, say, three hundred thousand families a year, so as to absorb the whole of the Javanese population growth, would require a budget of Rp. 3.0 - 4.5 billion—considerably more than the total development budget of Central Government as proposed in the present plan.

On the other hand, it should be recognized that the population problem at this stage of Indonesian development <u>is</u> a Javanese one; and the use of a simple average population growth for the entire country, together with a single ICOR for estimating capital requirements, may result in a target that is quite unrealistic when it is considered that nearly two-thirds of the population growth takes place on the one small island of Java. (Current <u>rates</u> of growth, however, are higher in the Outer Islands than in Java.) The costs of absorbing the population growth into productive employment are much higher than they would be if the existing population were evenly spread throughout the country.

*This figure was given by Dr. Sie and Dr. Pelzer. The official figures for 1953 and 1954 are lower.

In arriving at over-all targets, capital-job calculations as well as capital-output calculations should be made. The present plan includes no estimates of capital-job ratios.

The ICOR

Dr. Paauw shows in his first chapter that the ICOR of 2:0 used as a basis for calculation in the first five years is almost certainly too low, especially in the light of the composition of the plan, which is rather heavily weighted toward high-ICOR projects. As was pointed out in my article in Ekonomi dan Keuangan Indonesia, January 1957, there is no record of ICORs this low except during postwar reconstruction periods. Indonesia suffered a good deal of destruction and disruption of economic life during the war and revolution. The ICOR of 1.5:1 implicit in the Planning Bureau's estimates of national income in the past few years may be plausible, considering the amount of rehabilitation and reorganization required and the opportunities for capital-cheap increases in agricultural output through introduction of fertilizer, seed selection, repair of irrigation systems, replanting of abandoned land, and the like. It is also possible that in Indonesia the "reconstruction period" in this sense should have lasted five years after the transfer of sovereignty.

It would be very risky, however, to count on the "bargain-counter" phase lasting five years more. Some opportunities for capital-cheap increases in output—such as removing squatters from plantation land—still exist. The possibilities of raising output of foodstuffs by increased use of fertilizer and better seed are not altogether exhausted. But in calculating an aggregate ICOR for the economy, it is the proportion of new investment going into capital-cheap projects that counts, not the proportion of total income or employment now in the labor-intensive sector. The three sectors accounting for three-quarters of the central government's investment budget—transport and communications, power and irrigation, and industrialization—can have very high ICORs indeed, probably averaging above 4:1. Private investment is also likely to be rather capital intensive. The community development sector can of course be capital cheap, but it is only one-quarter of the total and may not bring much permanent increase in national income in a country like Indonesia, where lack of access roads, irrigation systems, and the other kinds of social capital that can be provided on a community self-help basis are not the major bottlenecks. Given the sectoral allocation of the investment budget, it is hard to see how the ICOR could average as low as 2:1.

If there were opportunities for substantial increases in per capita output in the peasant-agriculture sector, one might be more optimistic about the size of the aggregate ICOR. In Indonesia, however, the possibilities of capital-cheap development are limited by the special nature of the problem of Java. Fragmentation of holdings in Javanese peasant agriculture has gone as far as it can go and still support families at a subsistence level. The increase in Javanese population of nearly one million persons per year must be taken care of elsewhere in the economy.

It is our understanding that the selection of this low ICOR was based partly on Indian experience under the First Five Year Plan. However, as the following table shows, even the Indian Second Five Year Plan seems somewhat less capital intensive than the central government sector of the Indonesian plan, and the first Indian plan was less capital intensive than the second. Of course, the Indian plan incorporates the community development program, which is perhaps the least capital intensive of all, while the figures given for Indonesia relate to the central government sector alone. On the other hand, the private investment sector in Indonesia is likely to have extremely high capital-output ratios if the projected level of private investment is achieved. For the only way in which private investment of Rs. 10 billion (say, $500 million) could have occurred in the five years covered by the First Plan is through a large-scale inflow of foreign capital. Capital has been attracted only to such highly capital-intensive projects as petroleum and mining; in the less capital-intensive plantation sector, there may have been a net capital outflow.

It is unlikely that Indonesia will enjoy an ICOR lower than that experienced under the second Indian plan, which seems to be running at about 3.5:1. If this figure were used for Indonesia instead of 2, the present plan would bring no improvement in per capita income in the first five years even if executed in full and if the population growth does not exceed the estimated 1.7 per cent per year.

Ultimately, of course, the use of ICORs derived from the experience of any other country is always somewhat dangerous. Here is another area in which further research should be undertaken. It would be desirable to estimate ICORs both by sectors and by regions. The aggregate ICORs should than be calculated according to the sectoral and regional distribution of the investment budget. For example, there is some reason to suppose that the ICOR may be lower in Java than in the Outer Islands since the "infra-structure" (or social capital) is more highly developed on Java than elsewhere in the country. Java is clearly better off than the Outer Islands for railroads, and it is somewhat better provided with shipping and airways. It is probably better provided

THE STRUCTURE OF INDONESIAN, PHILIPPINE, AND INDIAN DEVELOPMENT PLANS

	Indonesia	Philippines	India*
Total net investment in per cent of national income	6	10.6	9.0
Public net investment in per cent of total	55	40.0	60.0
Private net investment in per cent of total	45	60.0	40.0
Current expenditures of Central Government in per cent of GNP	12	7.3	
. . .			
Structure of public investment (per cent)			
Agriculture	13	8.5	11.8†
Irrigation	11	8.0	7.9
Industry and mining	25	23.0	18.5
Transport	25	25.0	28.9
Public works (and other)	--	12.0	4.3
Public utilities (power)	14	16.0	8.9
Social development	12	7.5	19.7
	100	100.0	100.0

*Second Plan.

† Includes community development.

Sources: Five Year Plans.

with roads as well. While some Javanese roads have fallen into disrepair, their improvement would be less costly than the construction of new roads in Sumatra and Kalimantan. However, this is precisely the sort of question on which more detailed research needs to be done.

The Structure of the Plan

An obvious weakness of the present plan is that only the investment of the central government can be regarded as in any way assured. Nothing approaching a "plan" now exists either for the community development sector or for the private investment sector.

It is true, of course, that detailed targets with respect to investment and output in these sectors can be rather meaningless. On the other hand, if the projected investment in these sectors—nearly 60 per cent of the total—is really to be carried out, a great deal more attention must be paid to policies to guarantee that the estimated level of investment will in fact be reached in each of these sectors. The community development sector needs much more detailed planning with regard to types of project and personnel than has been possible for the First Five Year Plan. The private investment sector needs a clear delineation of policies designed to encourage and direct private investment.

Foreign investment, mining, and petroleum laws have now been passed by Parliament. However, the questions of land policy, squatter policy, monetary policy, and tax policy designed to direct and encourage private investment so as to assure the required level and structure of investment for the achievement of targets set forth in the plan clearly need a good deal more research.

Closely related to the sectoral structure is the regional structure of the plan, which has political as well as economic importance. It is obvious that there is at present a disequilibrium among the major regions of Indonesia, and that both political stability and balanced growth would seem to require the achievement of some regional equilibrium.

For this reason, Dr. Paauw has devoted special attention to problems of regional and local finance.

From a purely economic point of view one might favor investing in the Outer Islands, where opportunities are best, and redistributing income so as to maintain the Javanese rural population despite a growing volume of disguised unemployment among them. It is highly doubtful whether such a course is politically feasible. Tension between the Outer Islands and the central government is already severe, the centrifugal forces already strong. The people of the Outer Islands, where per capita output is relatively high, are already restive; they feel that they are contributing too much to the support of the Javanese and would be better off economically on their own. The Javanese population must be provided with jobs as well as incomes. Moreover, Javanese productivity and incomes must not be too obviously below those of the Outer Islands; otherwise the Javanese will tend to use their superior political power to obtain concessions which the populations of the Outer Islands will bitterly resent. True, rich and poor groups exist in every society and yet societies survive; but it must be remembered that the major islands of Indonesia are really countries unto themselves. Each has its own history, culture, language, and racial characteristics. They have never before been governed by the same laws administered by the same central government at the same time; the Dutch did not choose to govern that way, and none of the many empires of the pre-Dutch era covered the whole country or maintained tight centralized control over the areas they did cover.

Thus the plan must provide both jobs and substantial increases in income for the Javanese. Achievement of this goal will require some increase in the average size of holding in peasant agriculture to permit mechanization wherever it is suitable to the terrain. Thus development will require the removal of some peasants from the land of Java; the number of people transferred to other islands or absorbed into industry must exceed the annual additions to the Javanese population. And neither transmigration—which involves difficult clearing of jungle or of alang-alang grass as well as transportation—nor providing industrial employment is truly capital cheap.

Moreover, as we saw above, Indonesia has a balance-of-payments problem. Solving it will require expansion of exports as well as development of import-replacing industries. Import replacement may be capital cheap as industrialization goes; textile manufacture, for example, can be fairly labor intensive and still be efficient. However, the fields in which Indonesia's prospects for increased exports are brightest—petroleum products, aluminum, tin products—are capital intensive in the extreme.

All these factors suggest an ICOR considerably higher than 2:1 even for the first phase of the Indonesian development plan.

The Political Background of the Current Development Problem

Indonesia's problems of economic stabilization and development are imposing enough to make the most courageous of statesmen quail. Even with all the obstacles to be overcome, however, a country with Indonesia's resource base could have made progress if its leaders had been united behind an agreed economic policy. Instead there was disagreement even on the kind of social and economic system Indonesia should have, and a feeling that particular economic policy issues should be left unresolved until the over-all pattern was chosen. The disagreement is reflected in a constitutional crisis of a sort which has become familiar enough to us in Europe: no single party has commanded enough parliamentary support to form a government by itself, and the shifting coalitions have never agreed long enough to give the country political stability. Out of this sort of situation, proposals for more unified leadership—termed by President Sukarno "democracy with leadership" or "guided democracy"—are bound to arise, as they have recently done in France. The problem in Indonesia, however, is even more complex than in Europe and can be understood only against the background of Indonesia's special political history.

The Problem of Unification

The struggle for freedom—from outside invaders and from each other—is not just part of Indonesian history, it is part of Indonesian life. Indian princes invaded parts of Indonesia at least as early as 500 A.D. Indonesian kingdoms fought China and Ceylon as well as India, and also spent a good deal of time and energy fighting each other.

From the eighth to fourteenth centuries, when the Indonesian Hindu civilization was at its height and the great Hindu-Bhuddist movements were built, two empires predominated: the Shrivijaya empire of South Sumatra and the Singosari empire of East Java. The latter was powerful enough to defeat a large invading army sent by Kublai Khan, the Chinese potentate, in 1294. In the latter part of the fourteenth century, thanks largely to the administrative and military skill of the great Prime Minister of the East Javanese empire, Gadja Mada, the two empires were united into one, the empire of Madjapahit. From its capital in East Java the Madjapahit empire spread its control over much of what is now Indonesia, which was perhaps more truly "united" than at any time until the Indonesian Republic was established in 1949—if then. Even today many Indonesians confronted with the problem of determining national goals take refuge in the past glories of Shrivijaya and Madjapahit.*

The Spread of Islam

Indonesia was one country in which Islam was spread more by faith than by the sword; but rebellious princes found the conversion to Islam a convenient rallying cry in their fight for freedom from "Madjapahit Imperialism." Perhaps the empire would not long have survived the deaths of Gadja Mada and King Hayam Wuruk anyhow; but the spread of Islam hastened its dissolution. Hindu refugees escaped to Bali, where they helped to preserve the Hindu culture. Unable to inflict decisive defeats on the Indonesian sultans, the Portuguese were no match for the British and Dutch once the latter decided to move into the Indies, opened to them by the defeat of the Spanish Armada in 1588. With the establishment of the English East India Company in 1600 and the Netherlands East India Company two years later the fate of the Portuguese was sealed, although it took another half century to drive them from the Indies altogether.

The Gradual Extension of Dutch Control

To understand present-day Indonesia it is important to realize that the Dutch had scarcely completed their conquest of the islands when the Japanese drove them out. Anyone who imagines a prewar Netherlands East Indies with a tightly knit administration, maintaining law

*See Guy J. Pauker, "Indonesian Images of Their National Self," The Public Opinion Quarterly, Vol. XXII, No. 3 (Fall 1958).

and order throughout the entire archipelago, has a completely false picture.

Java was the first of the major islands to be completely subdued. Having come to an agreement with the British in 1824, the Dutch set about consolidating their hold on Java. They met immediate resistance in Central Java, which spread to become "the Java War," lasting five years.

The Minangkabau people of southwestern Sumatra continued fighting until at least 1835; traveling in the Minangkabau area even today one sees little evidence of Dutch penetration. The Bataks in North Sumatra held out longer, and the Atjinese gave trouble from beginning to end. The actual legal position of Atjeh was undetermined until the British agreed to Dutch occupation of the region in 1871. Actual fighting began in 1873 and continued throughout the rest of the century, to the financial and political embarrassment of the government.

The forbidding interior of Kalimantan the Dutch did not even try to conquer. The coastal towns and the main river centers were easy prey, but the Dutch were content to leave the rest of the island to the primitive tribes who roamed the swamps and jungles. In Sulawesi (Celebes) under the Dutch as well as today, the predominantly Christian area of Minahasa gave little trouble; but the intensely Moslem peoples to the south, the Maccassarese and Buginese, fought hard for their independence, and it was not until 1910 that they abandoned their war against the Dutch. Bali, so attractive to the Dutch from the beginning that two of de Houtman's men jumped ship to stay there, resisted until the eve of World War I. The last major act of rebellion was also the most dramatic: the Sultan of Klungkung and his retinue commited mass suicide by marching in full regalia, armed only with spears, into the Dutch guns.

The Principle of "Indirect Rule"

"Unification" of Indonesia under the Dutch was therefore a very short-lived affair. Even for this short interval the archipelago was not unified in the sense of having a closely integrated administration with the same laws and regulations enforced uniformly throughout the land. Perhaps because they feared the rise of that very Indonesian nationalism which was to be their ultimate downfall, the Dutch preferred to administer their colony on a regionalized basis. There were eight governors, one for each major region; these were divided in turn into residencies, assistant-residencies, and districts. But the system did not stop there. Even in 1940 the system of "indirect government" prevailed. The laws and regulations were administered through the local rulers, who were "advised" by the appropriate NEI official. In Java four sultans were retained, controlling 7 per cent of the area of the island; but there were also 70 "regencies" nominally under a local ruler. Outside of Java there were 266 Indonesian states, varying in size and wealth from Solo (Surakarta), whose Susuhunan spent $1,000,000 a year from government subsidies, to tiny principalities. There were also Indonesian _bupatis_, or district officers, and Indonesian _lurahs_, mayors, or village chiefs.

Thus when the Republic of the United States of Indonesia was established in December 1949 it was not a matter of the new sovereign Indonesian government taking over from the Dutch a country united under a single strong administration, the laws and regulations of which were recognized throughout the archipelago as the law of the land. The people of the outlying islands had known the Netherlands East Indies government, if they knew it at all, through their local governor or regent. Many of them were reluctant to acknowledge the right of any government in Djakarta to rule their lives, especially a government which they considered to be dominated by "Javanese Imperialism."

As in the United States after the American Revolution, unification is a major problem of the infant republic today. But the problem confronting Indonesia is much greater than the one that was faced by the United States in 1776, for the American republic then consisted of only thirteen colonies huddled together on the Atlantic seaboard. The Indonesian problem is similar to what would have been faced by the American government if Louisiana, Texas, California, and the mid-Western states had all come into the Union at once, with their different historical backgrounds, interests, and languages, instead of being added to the Union over the course of two centuries.

Continuing Importance of the Fight for Independence

The Declaration of Independence was made by Sukarno on August 17, 1945; but it was not until December 27, 1949 that sovereignty was transferred after much bloodshed. The length and bitterness of the Indonesian struggle for independence colors Indonesian attitudes toward the West and Western institutions even today. Economic (including financial) policies which seem obviously desirable to outsiders may fail to be adopted if branded as "Western" by the opposition. The reluctance to return to a federal constitution, which seems to be recommended by Indonesia's geography and sociology, because of its association with Dutch "divide-and-rule" strategy, is another example of the barrier to current decision-making imposed by the cultural impact of the revolution.

The Internal Struggle for Power

Success in the struggle for independence did not lead to a unified effort to improve the lot of Indonesians but to an internal struggle for power. Between the establishment of the unitary state in 1950 and the general elections of November 1955 fifteen coalition governments, each with several parties represented in the Cabinet, held office. The elections showed that these cabinets were actually broader in their representation than they need have been; it turned out that only four among the dozens of parties were important in terms of popular support. The Nationalist Party (PNI) received 8.4 million votes. The big Moslem party, Masjumi, received 7.9 million votes but, because of the system of proportional representation, has the same number of seats in Parliament as the PNI (57). The third biggest party is the Nahdatul Ulama (NU), with 45 seats, an orthodox Moslem party at once more conservative and more nationalist than the Masjumi. The Communist Party (PKI) comes next, with about 20 per cent of the popular vote and 39 seats.

While all four of these parties follow the neutralist path, there are important differences among them with respect to attitudes toward foreign economic relations which influence their development policies. Equally important differences exist between factions within the same party. Most obviously split is the PNI, with its extremist and moderate factions, the former leaning far toward the PKI in their sympathies and the latter being essentially anti-Communist and pro-Western. A government controlled by Masjumi and right-wing PNI, with a strong majority and the assured support of the people, could probably move to the extreme Western end of the "neutralist" spectrum and thus seek and obtain substantial foreign aid and investment. It might even move openly into the Western camp. But the Communists and left-wing PNI now represent nearly half of the electorate, and no government has yet dared to announce open opposition to this large and unified sector of public opinion, especially in view of the sympathies within every party for the neutralist approach. Consequently all governments have been restrained in their efforts to obtain technical and capital assistance in large quantities.

All political parties in Indonesia announce themselves as being anti-capitalist—by which is really meant being anti-colonial, anti-imperialist, and anti-materialist, rather than opposed to private enterprise. Until public opinion changes a good deal, it will not be possible for any Indonesian government to move completely away from the neutralist foreign policy, or even to embrace a domestic policy of vigorous encouragement to private enterprise, and stay in power.

Elections in the cities of Djakarta, Surabaya, Bandung, and Semarang showed the same trend. In Java it now seems clear that the Communist Party has a plurality. But it is in Java alone, where over two-thirds of the total population live, that the local elections of 1957 showed a strong trend toward the Communists. The Communist Party now controls the provincial assemblies of Central and East Java. In the West Java assembly the PKI and smaller left-wing parties combined have only one less member than the Masjumi.

The struggle between Communists and anti-Communists in Indonesia is aggravated by two factors. First, it has its counterpart in the struggle between the President and the Cabinet (except for the two Ali Sastroamidjojo and the present Djuanda governments, which have tended to avoid open conflict with the president) for *de facto* control of the government. According to the Provisional Constitution of 1950, Sukarno is supposed to be a president only in the old-style French sense—a signer of bills, a layer of cornerstones, and an appointer of Cabinet *formateurs*. Sukarno has never been content with this role, and his popular following is such that it has never been necessary for him to accept this modest interpretation of his function. At the same time, he has always resisted taking formal responsibility in the sense of subjecting himself and his policies to the vote of the electorate or even of the Parliament.

Secondly, the Communist versus anti-Communist split is almost completely a Java versus Outer Island split. Moreover, the growth of Communist strength has solidified opposition to communism. The Nationalist Party itself has decided to cooperate with the Communists in the National Parliament but to collaborate with the Masjumi in those regional assemblies where the Communists have an absolute majority. Similarly, the strength of the opposition from the Moslem parties is increased by Communist gains.

Finally, the Communist versus anti-Communist struggle is reflected within the army. The majority of the army leaders are strongly anti-Communist and perhaps even pro-Western. As such they have found themselves in frequent conflict with their Commander-in-Chief, President Sukarno. However, it appears that within the army, especially in West Java, there are some Communist sympathies as well.

The inherent explosiveness of this situation is apparent. Only the extraordinary capacity of the Indonesian people for getting along with people of opposite views—according to the ancient tradition of gotong rojong and musjawarat desa (which Sukarno has translated as "mutual assistance and to settle problems by discussion, not by imposing settlement"), which are basic features of village "rice-roots democracy," prevented the explosion from occurring before 1958—and it is not clear that the real explosion has yet taken place. What is clear is that the political situation is one which greatly restricts any government's freedom of movement in the field of fiscal policy.

Economic Development and Political Development

The polarization of political opinion is closely related to the wide and deep disappointment over the economic effects of independence. The "revolution of rising expectations" takes a somewhat different form in Indonesia from that found in other underdeveloped countries. Indonesia had a real revolution, and many Indonesians believed "Merdeka" would automatically bring prosperity in its wake. For many Indonesian villagers the freedom to be won through revolution was less political independence than freedom from hard work, freedom from poverty, freedom from taxes, and freedom from the local Chinese moneylender. When these freedoms failed to follow independence, nationalist leaders, workers, and peasants alike began to talk of "completing the revolution." If we are still poor, the argument went, it is because the revolution is not finished; the Dutch are still with us, running the plantations, the mines, the oil fields, the shipping and air lines, and the banks. Those lackeys of the Dutch, the Chinese, are with us too. Only when we have driven them all out will we enjoy the prosperity expected from the revolution.

Against this view the "pragmatists" argued—correctly but unconvincingly—that in the short run driving out the Dutch and Chinese could only make Indonesia poorer still. For some years the only concrete measures for "completing the revolution" were restrictions of trade in certain commodities to Indonesian importers—the so-called "*benteng* system." The one clear-cut result of this system was to drive some Chinese entrepreneurs from trade into productive enterprise, which developed the economy a bit but had little impact on the distribution of income and power. By 1956 the revolutionary fire seemed dead to many observers; in fact it was smouldering underneath the surface.

Since no government succeeded in directing the energies released by revolution into concrete development programs, they broke out at the end of 1957 in the seizures of Dutch properties.

While Indonesian opinion is divided on the desirability of ejecting the Dutch and nationalizing their properties, all governments and all parties have expressed themselves in favor of "converting the colonial economy into a national economy." The concept of a "national" economy has differed from party to party and from leader to leader; indeed only the Communists have had a clear idea of what a "national" economy would be. Relatively few Indonesian leaders have had the bright vision of a growing economy, which would become "national" as the United States, Canada, and Australia have become "national" and as India and the Philippines are now becoming "national"—not by driving the foreigner out but by following policies which would assure an increasing domestic share in new investment.

All parties also have paid lip service to the national goal of "organizing the economy along cooperative lines," which was written into the Provisional Constitution; but this goal also has lacked clear definition. For some leaders it has meant an extension to national economic policy of the principles of rice-roots village democracy—*gotong rojong*, *kertja sama*, *ramah tamah*, and *musjawarat desa* (roughly, mutual assistance, working together, a family-like society, and search for unanimity); but what this would mean in terms of specific development projects, or monetary, fiscal, and foreign-exchange policies, has not been spelled out. For other leaders the "cooperative society" was defined in 1930's-European fashion as the "middle way" between communism and unbridled monopoly capitalism. For them extension of the cooperative way to the national economy has meant simply organizing more and bigger cooperatives—credit cooperatives, producers' cooperatives, marketing cooperatives. They have seemed to take it for granted that the European cooperative and Indonesian village communalism were the same thing in spirit. The idea that a cooperative can be as ruthlessly exploitative in intent as a corporation, if not more so, seems to have occurred to few Indonesian leaders.*

Thus, although independence brought no agreement on concrete social goals, there was from the beginning agreement that Indonesia was not to be developed on "capitalist" lines. Rugged individualism, free competition, and private enterprise had few enthusiastic backers. They were associated in the minds of most Indonesians with imperialism, colonialism, materialism, and a ruthlessly exploitative, ferociously competitive, "devil-take-the-hindmost" approach to social organization. Indonesians did not want such "capitalism." So what was the economic and social system to be? No one but the Communists was quite sure. Meanwhile, it was considered necessary to avoid making decisions on concrete issues—such as what to do with the North Sumatra oil properties taken over, but not formally confiscated, from Shell Indonesia—lest the decisions prove inconsistent with the ultimate definition of social and economic aims.

*Actually, the modern corporation with its widely diffused ownership, its old-age, sickness, and life insurance, its guaranteed annual wages, its five-year wage contracts with escalator clauses, its profit-sharing arrangements, and trade union participation in management may come closer to the spirit of cooperation than some forms of cooperative organization.

In one way, of course, a corporation can never conform to the Indonesian conception of communal life; decision-making can never be entirely dependent on achieving the appearance of unanimity. Decisions must be based—at least occasionally—on majority opinion. For example, if trade unions are accorded minor representation in the management it is out of the question to postpone or avoid all decisions on which differences of opinion between the trade union representatives and the ownership representatives still prevail. See Benjamin Higgins, "Hatta and Cooperatives: The Middle Way for Indonesia?" _The Annals_, July 1958.

Similarly, while everyone agreed that the political system was to be "democratic," they also agreed that it was not to be democratic in the ordinary "Western" sense. No one but the Communists wanted a "People's Democracy." It was to be an "Indonesian" democracy, reflecting the spirit of gotong rojong and musjawarat desa and rejecting—as Sukarno put it—"the principle that 50 per cent plus one is right." But what exactly did this mean? No one was quite sure—at least until President Sukarno assured the people, the Parliament, and the Constituent Assembly that it meant diluting the power of the political parties and a return to the 1945 Constitution, making him a new-style French president instead of an old-style French president. Meanwhile, it was felt that "as the twig is bent so is the tree inclined." No new institutions should be set up or legislation passed that might prejudice the final outcome.

With such confusion regarding ultimate goals, much time and energy of national leaders was dissipated in fruitless debate at the ideological level while pressing economic issues absorbed the attention of only a handful of leaders in the agencies concerned—the Bank Indonesia, the Ministry of Finance, the National Planning Bureau, the Industrial Development Bank. Such questions as "Where can we find capital for development projects? How can we best protect our dwindling foreign-exchange reserves? Should we reintroduce a land tax? Should we develop Asahan or increase hydroelectric capacity in Java?" could never be answered in terms of economic effectiveness alone. At some point they always ran into an ideological or nationalist issue. Whenever the choice was between an effective stabilization or development policy and satisfying nationalist sentiments, nationalism won. When government energies were directed toward economic matters at all, it was to meet pressing short-run stabilization needs—not long-run development requirements.

The continuing paralysis led to increasing disillusionment with the parliamentary process as a way of getting things done. In the case of Sukarno, this disillusionment found expression in his proposal for "guided democracy"—or "democracy with leadership," to use the translation preferred in Indonesia. It also led to the growth of communism, a natural response of peasants and workers to disappointment over the failure of "Merdeka" to bring the expected prosperity. These trends in turn aggravated the growing discontent in the Outer Islands, culminating in the declaration of a Revolutionary Government, with headquarters in South Sumatra, in February 1958. From a military view the rebellion is already over, but guerrilla warfare continues and the leaders still fight a propaganda war from outside the country.

To describe the rebellion as an "anti-Communist revolt" is too simple. Certainly the rebel leaders were eager to see Indonesia develop on non-Communist lines; but there was not a single member of the Communist Party in the legal Indonesian government and communism could still be fought by constitutional means. The desire for increased regional and local autonomy was one major motive. There was also an urge to build upon the "growing points and leading sectors" in the Outer Islands, in order to launch an effective development program, and the wish to rid the government of the abuse of party politics and incompetence. But mainly the rebellion reflected disillusionment with the democratic process, in part caused by the lack of effective development policy.

The Indonesian Economy in 1958

During 1958 economic conditions in Indonesia reached their lowest ebb since the collapse of the Korean war boom early in 1952. The rebellion was the major contributing factor. Others were the continuing fall in prices of major exports and the disruption of banking and transport through the government's assumption of the management, and subsequent nationalization, of certain Dutch enterprises and the departure of thousands of Dutch managers and technicians. Together these developments brought increased budget expenditures, reduced tax revenues, diminished foreign-exchange earnings, delays in the development program, and general deterioration.

In an earlier publication, Dr. Paauw has described the situation as follows:

> Indonesian experience in 1957 and 1958 presents an almost classic example of the economic ramifications of political instability. But there is more to the recent Indonesian story. Deteriorating economic conditions during the past several years have aggravated deep-seated political tensions. Behind this vicious circle of political and economic instability lie more fundamental forces associated with general social revolution. These forces, which smouldered during the last decades of colonial rule, were unleashed to react upon Indonesian society by the struggle for independence and its ultimate achievement. The response of Indonesia's overburdened political elite to forces precipitating economic and social change may or may not have contributed to reducing the Indonesian economy to its present extremity. In any case, the economic policies which the Indonesian government pursued seem to be, in large part, a function of the social and economic transformation in which Indonesia found herself and the backgrounds of the elite as participants in this great drama. The events of recent months may perhaps be viewed as a particularly acute stage in this transformation. The short-run consequences of these events can be superficially described, but their longer-run impact upon the shape of Indonesian society cannot yet be perceived clearly.
>
> The national crisis precipitated by the anti-Dutch actions of 1957 was merely a prelude to the greater threat of national dissolution posed by outright rebellion of dissident provinces. Resolute and apparently successful military action against the dissident

groups now appears to be one of the most far-reaching events in recent Indonesian history. Its impact upon an economy already in disequilibrium—a subject which is discussed below—has been so grave that immediate and dramatic measures are needed to prevent per capita income from falling below tolerable levels.*

The impact of the revolution is clear enough from the figures. When he first assumed office in the middle of 1957, Finance Minister Sutikno Slamet hoped to keep the 1958 budget deficit down to Rp. 1.5 billion. By the time the year began the estimate was already up to Rp. 3.5 billion, and at the time of writing it appeared that it would exceed Rp. 9 billion before the year was out. The growth of the deficit can be explained partly from the revenue side; the head tax on foreigners has been disappointing as to yield, and the rebellion led to some loss of revenues. The main factor, however, was the cost of fighting the rebellion. Prime Minister Djuanda has estimated the total cost of the insurrection, including loss of output as well as increased military expenditures, as more than Rp. 3.5 billion. To return to Dr. Paauw:

> Throughout the first three months of 1958 inter-island trade continued in a state of paralysis, causing warehouses to be crammed with goods awaiting shipment and extreme local price variations among even adjacent markets. [Economist Intelligence Unit, Three Monthly Economic Review of Indonesia, No. 24, May 1958, p. 8.] Even as late as August, export products in some areas were piling up, awaiting local transport. Indonesia was reported to have lost foreign exchange reserves at the rate of Rp. 400 million in the first quarter of 1958, reducing the cover ratio to about 9 per cent. [Ibid., p. 8.]
>
> As the costs of military operations against the rebels began to mount during the second quarter of 1958, the economic situation became more desperate. Imports were recurrently halted,

*"The High Cost of Political Instability in Indonesia, 1957-58," Internationale Spectator, November 1958, pp. 523-524.

and critical local rice shortages began to appear. In outlying areas dependent upon inter-island shipping reports of starvation arose as late as August. On Java the most serious problems were reported to be "malnutrition from diet deficiencies or disease." [New York Times, August 3, 1958, p. 18.] Essential production had continued to decline as late as the third quarter, and the government found itself obliged to allocate scarce foreign exchange reserves to import a record quantity of rice.

Behind these symptoms of economic disintegration lay the effects of war inflation upon the economy. Military operations had raised government expenditures well above levels of recent years (perhaps Rp. 30 billion in 1958 compared to about Rp. 18 billion in 1956). By August the government seemed to accept the prospect that the 1958 budget deficit would reach Rp. 10 billion. Meanwhile, the subject of the 1959 budget was mooted in Djakarta, projecting an unrealistically small estimate of total expenditures of Rp. 21 billion. Even so, the Finance Minister, Sutikno Slamet, declared that a 1959 deficit of Rp. 8 billion "can hardly be avoided," but simultaneously admitted that "the main problem is to eliminate or at least abate the inflationary threat to avoid an even larger deficit." [Antara (New York edition), August 28, 1958, p. 4.] He further confirmed that in 1958 state revenues had decreased while expenditures had increased. It was estimated that budget receipts would reach Rp. 13 billion in 1959 despite the fact that they had totalled Rp. 15.7 billion as early as 1956. The inflationary implications of these projections scarcely need emphasis. The submitted budget almost seems to represent an admission by Indonesia's senior financial official that the fiscal reorganization which is a *sine qua non* for breaking the inflationary spiral is unthinkable in present conditions.*

As noted above, the pace of inflation showed a marked acceleration during 1957 and 1958; creeping inflation gave way to galloping inflation. The price index for nineteen foodstuffs in Djakarta (1953=100), which stood at 157 in December 1956, was 244 in December 1957 and 275 in September 1958.

*Ibid., pp. 547-548.

Inflationary tendencies were aggravated by reduced domestic production and by further cuts in imports, which were in turn necessitated by the loss of foreign-exchange earnings. Rice imports, despite the concentrated effort to achieve self-sufficiency in rice, exceeded 700,000 tons, or 10 per cent of total requirements, at a cost of $75 million. Estate production held up remarkably well, but smallholders' rubber, which has become more important than estate rubber since independence, fell far below the 1957 level. Moreover, the losses through the barter trade, which even in 1957 cost the government some $100 million in foreign exchange ($60 million on Central Sumatra exports alone), were higher still in 1958. Total exports dropped from Rp. 3 billion in the third quarter of 1957 to Rp. 1.8 billion in the first quarter of 1958. The balance-of-trade surplus of Rp. 925 million in the former period had all but disappeared in the latter, despite curtailment of imports from Rp. 2.1 billion to Rp. 1.7 billion. With the usual large deficit on services account, the result was a severe drain on foreign-exchange reserves.

Thus 1958 will go down as a black year in the economic history of the infant Indonesian Republic. Yet it may also become known as a turning point, Indonesian leadership having been forced by the rebellion to put economic stabilization and development at the top of the agenda. In fact, during 1957 and 1958 the Indonesian leadership learned four valuable lessons:

1. Political stability and economic development are not two separate problems. No government can let economic development wait while it maneuvers to keep in power. On the contrary, the basic political struggle—a struggle between outer islands and center, and between Communists and left-wing Nationalists on the one hand and

moderate-rationalists on the other—cannot be resolved without a program of economic development. The essence of such a program must be measures that will feed and clothe the Javanese while building on the growing points and leading sectors of the Outer Islands; the problem of providing jobs for Javanese outside the overcrowded peasant-agriculture sector must be tackled in the second phase of the program.

2. Raising Indonesian incomes requires making the pie grow; redividing the pie—even redividing it between Indonesians and foreigners—is not enough.

3. Communist parties are not easy to utilize for non-Communist purposes. Both the Nationalist Party and President Sukarno are considerably less enthusiastic now than they were a year ago about collaboration with the Communist Party.

4. Government by _mufaket desa_—the unanimous opinion of the village—doesn't really work at the national level. A central government cannot just postpone awkward decisions on which there is no unanimous agreement. Certain basic decisions must be made _now_: on the responsibilities of the new National Planning Board, on the scope and content of a new development plan, on the allocation of powers between the central and regional governments. If for no other reason, the growing impatience and growing power of General Nasution and the army command would make decisions on these matters urgent. As Dr. Paauw puts it:

> In aggravating the economic situation the national emergency of 1958 may have improved conditions for the expression of effective national leadership. The emergency provided the opportunity for a virtual takeover of important economic and political functions by military authorities. The extension of army influence is quite apparent in Djakarta, in outlying

> provinces, and even in village affairs in many areas. Most significant, perhaps, is the new role of the army in supervising operations in the vast network of firms recently taken over from the Dutch. The economic implications of this new force in Indonesian society cannot yet be evaluated, but it is clear that the new network of military control will affect economic performance in the immediate future, perhaps even in the long run.*

President Sukarno chose the first anniversary of the formation of the National Front for the Liberation of West Irian to state that economic development is even more important at this stage of Indonesian history than the gaining of sovereignty over West Irian, and to stress the need for leadership in the economic field. The proposed constitutional reforms, whatever may be one's view of them in terms of political philosophy, should improve the capacity of the central government to make the decisions needed to launch economic growth. Returning to the Constitution of 1945 means that the President becomes the *de jure* as well as *de facto* head of government, choosing the Cabinet and assuming responsibility for its program. The revamping of Parliament to make half of its members representative of functional groups, while reducing the number of political parties represented by the other half, should facilitate and accelerate parliamentary approval of administration programs. If at the same time substantially greater authority is accorded to the regional and local governments for the raising and spending of funds for development purposes, Indonesia may at last be in a position to launch an effective program of economic development. Some progress has already been made in this direction. Underlying Dr. Paauw's study is the assumption that further progress is possible, and that a solution of the political problems impeding economic growth will be found in the near future.

***Ibid.*, p. 524.

The true importance of Dr. Paauw's study of financing Indonesian development emerges from this analysis of the Indonesian problem. In making the decisions and undertaking the measures needed to <u>finance</u> economic development in Indonesia, the government will also be making the decisions and undertaking the measures needed to overcome <u>all</u> the obstacles to economic development, including the political and sociological ones as well as the economic and administrative ones.

Benjamin Higgins

Cambridge, Massachusetts
May 1959

Financing Economic Development

THE INDONESIAN CASE

1

CAPITAL REQUIREMENTS AND ABSORPITVE CAPACITY

Before we proceed to study Indonesia's capacities for financing economic development, we must have some idea of the size of the job to be done. In Indonesia, as in most underdeveloped countries, data are too scanty to permit accurate estimation of capital requirements. Nevertheless, the methodology and data now available give results which show the rough order of magnitude of the capital which is needed for economic growth. We supply these estimates on the assumption that rough approximation is preferable to complete ignorance. In this chapter, then, we attempt to provide estimates of the size of the development program, as measured by investment requirements, which Indonesia needs to reach reasonable growth objectives. In later chapters we proceed to examine the feasibility of financing these requirements.

We must recognize, however, that the ability to supply resources to "finance" the capital requirements for development is a necessary but not sufficient condition to insure economic progress. Financial resources must be transformed into productive capital equipment. Once installed, the new plant and equipment must be operated efficiently to provide the increased output which is the chief objective of economic development. In other words, financing economic development must

Table 1

ILLUSTRATIVE SEQUENCES OF (NET) INVESTMENT REQUIREMENTS FOR DIFFERENT OBJECTIVES

(Million Rp.)

	1	2	3	4	5		
Year	Independence of Imports	Maintaining Per Capita "Food and Necessities"	Maintaining Per Capita "Other Goods"	Increasing Per Capita All Goods 2 Per Cent Per Year	Compensating for Half of 1953–1955 Cut in Imports over 5 Years	Combination 1 + 2 + 5	Combination 1 + 4 + 5
1956	881.500	4,506.975	786.375	12,457.018	410.000	5,798.475	13,748.518
1957	881.500	4,547.796	798.171	12,643.873	410.000	5,866.296	13,935.373
1958	881.500	4,643.418	810.144	12,833.531	410.000	5,934.918	14,125.031
1959	881.500	4,713.069	822.296	13,026.034	410.000	6,004.569	14,317.534
1960	881.500	4,783.765	834.630	13,221.424	410.000	6,147.021	14,512.924
1961		4,855.521	847.149	13,419.745		4,855.521	13,419.749
1962		4,928.354	859.856	13,621.041		4,928.354	13,621.041
1963		5,002.279	872.754	13,825.357		5,002.279	13,825.357

Source: Extract from Eugene Grasberg, Indonesia's Investment Requirements, Center for International Studies, Massachusetts Institute of Technology, Cambridge, 1955, Table 6, p. 29.

take account of the demand for capital as well as the supply. The ability of a society to make productive use of financial and real capital, whether mobilized through private or state channels, is limited as well as its ability to accumulate it. In the latter part of this chapter, therefore, we raise the question as to whether or not Indonesia's entrepreneurial resources are adequate for the task of organizing and managing the real resources of production which the financial mechanism makes available.

Total Capital Requirements

Grasberg's Estimates

We begin with estimates of the amounts of capital required to reach alternative developmental objectives in Indonesia.* These estimates, a product of research at the Center for International Studies, Massachusetts Institute of Technology, are primarily the result of pioneering work by Dr. Eugene Grasberg, whose study, Indonesia's Investment Requirements, was published in 1955.[1] Recent changes and some additional evidence have prompted us to make some adjustments.

Grasberg's basic results are presented in Table 1. They comprise estimates of the amount of annual investment required to meet a number of specified growth objectives, some of which appear to be close to those which Indonesia has incorporated in her development plans. It is clear that the main economic objectives of Indonesia's development

*These estimates, as well as all financial data presented in this section, will be given in terms of Indonesia's currency unit, the rupiah (Rp.), at its average 1952–1955 value. The effective rates, however, are considerably higher, the export rate being about double the official rate and import rates roughly varying between 100 and 600 per cent of the official rate.

program are, first, maintaining the existing level of per capita output and, second, adding whatever increases are consistent with the performance of the economy.* Grasberg emphasizes that the magnitude of both tasks will be increased by continued growth of Indonesia's population. The annual rate of population growth which may be expected during the early years of development has been placed at 1.5 per cent. This estimate appears to be conservative. Indonesia's Five Year Plan (1956–1961), announced by the National Planning Bureau† in May 1956, is based on an annual population growth of 1.7 per cent, with expectations of 2 per cent after another decade. (See Appendix A.)

Indonesia's plans also include moving toward self-sufficiency in the production of goods which are now produced domestically but the current output of which falls short of domestic requirements. The Indonesians hoped by 1960 to attain self-sufficiency in the production of food, with very slight increases in caloric intake per capita.[2] On the basis of Indonesia's 1951–1956 balance-of-payments data, realization

*Equally important, however, are the political objectives of Indonesia's postwar plans, which have sought to establish greater economic independence vis-à-vis advanced Western countries and the fostering of Indonesian business and entrepreneurial groups.

†In preparing the Five Year Plan, the National Planning Bureau functioned as Indonesia's basic planning agency. It was responsible for coordinating specific plans submitted by various ministries into a national investment budget. During the years in which the Five Year Plan was prepared, Ir. Djuanda was the Director-General of the Bureau, aided by Deputy Director-General Ali Budiardjo. The National Planning Bureau reported to the National Planning Board, made up of nine Cabinet ministers. Ir. Djuanda was secretary to the Planning Board and later became the Minister of National Planning, a post created during the second Ali Sastroamidjojo Cabinet. This ministry became responsible for coordinating all development activities of the Indonesian government. Benjamin Higgins has described Ir. Djuanda, the present Prime Minister, as the "chief architect of the five-year development plan." Benjamin Higgins, Indonesia's Economic Stabilization and Development, Institute of Pacific Relations, New York, 1957, p. xxii. For further details of Indonesia's planning organization prior to 1957 see this same source, pp. 40–47.

of these objectives might have provided a small surplus in the current account for strengthening Indonesia's weak gold and foreign-reserves balances. Unfortunately, the economic aftermath of the recent seizure of Dutch holdings and the 1958 rebellion has aggravated Indonesia's balance-of-payments problem and has forced the Indonesians to accept delays in achieving self-sufficiency in food supplies.

Grasberg's estimates further provide for replacing one-half of the reduction in supplies of nonfood essential goods which occurred during the 1952-1955 period of foreign-exchange stringency. This aim may be achieved by increasing export earnings to provide foreign exchange to finance additional imports, or by developing import-replacing industries. In either case, additional investment will be required. Grasberg feels that the replacement of these goods, the total value of which amounted to about Rp. 1,000 million annually, is "undoubtedly . . . essential to a minimum standard of living."[3] It should be added that many of the essential imports eliminated in the years of stringency are indispensible as both incentive and supporting goods for a development program.

In the light of recent developments, Grasberg's estimate must be regarded as much too low. During 1957 and 1958, foreign-exchange receipts outside Java, the major source of foreign-exchange earnings, were seized by outlying provinces.[4] Foreign-exchange reserves have fallen far below the already low level on which the Grasberg estimate was based; moreover, Indonesia's foreign-exchange earning capacity has been reduced by the anti-Dutch campaign. Petroleum exports had fallen by 25 per cent in the year preceding August 1958, and tin exports were down by 40 per cent. Combined, these exports produce about one-third of Indonesia's export earnings. In addition, "the now idle rubber, tea, coconut, and coffee plantations seized from the Dutch last December are more often than not being reclaimed by the jungle."[5] The value of total exports has since shown substantial recovery; but it is clear that maintaining export earnings at their pre-rebellion level will require investment in capital rehabilitation and management training. If the goal of replacing import cuts is to be realized during the next several years, this investment requirement might have to be three or four times as great as Grasberg's estimate (Rp. 410 million per year).

The objectives for which estimates of capital requirements have been computed by Grasberg may be summarized to include:

1. Maintenance of per capita supplies of all goods and services at pre-planning (1954-1955) levels.

2. Eliminating imports of food and reducing fiber imports by 25 per cent within five years (which is tantamount to avoidance of further balance-of-payments deficits and rebuilding the country's foreign-exchange reserves).

3. Compensating, over a five-year period, for one half of the 1952-1955 reduction in nonfood essential imported goods.

4. Increasing per capita supplies of all goods and services by 2 per cent per year.

Grasberg's calculations, presented in Table 1, suggest that the first objective, maintenance of per capita supplies of all goods and services in the face of population growth, would require net annual investment averaging approximately Rp. 5.4 billion over the first five years. If objectives 2 and 3 (reduction of imports of food and fibers and replacing one half of essential import goods cuts) are added, total net investment requirements would rise, by Rp. 1.3 billion annually, to Rp. 6.7 billion. In the Indonesian situation in 1959-1961, however, realization of these objectives will probably raise capital requirements by Rp. 2.5 to Rp. 3 billion per year. Since these objectives will be reached in five years, investment requirements will then fall by a similar amount.

If, however, the development goals include objective 4, raising per capita supplies of all goods and services by 2 per cent per year, net investment outlay required would rise steeply. The total annual investment requirement would have to be more than doubled, the differential between that required to reach the first three objectives and all four being an average of Rp. 7.4 billion annually. Thus Grasberg's results suggest that, over a five-year period, average annual investment requirements to raise per capita income each year by 2 per cent would rise from the Rp. 6.7 billion for reaching the first three objectives to about Rp. 15.5 billion.*

Capital requirements of this order of magnitude would suggest that over 15 per cent of Indonesia's national income would have to be devoted to net investment to provide per capita output increases of 2 per cent. This would indicate considerably more than a doubling of present investment rates.†

The Present Situation

In our opinion, however, the Grasberg results placed capital requirements at the upper range of realistic estimates for the pre-1956 situation. The choice of the incremental capital-output ratio (ICOR) is the most important and most controversial problem in the empirical

*Rp. 5.4 billion to maintain per capita consumption, plus Rp. 2.5 to Rp. 3 billion to obtain self-sufficiency in food, reduce fiber imports, and replace essential imports reductions, plus Rp. 7.4 billion to raise per capita supplies of all goods and services by 2 per cent.

†Our estimates place net investment during 1951-1955 at about 6 per cent of net national product. See Chapter 2.

estimation of capital requirements. Grasberg has chosen to work with conservative ICORs—4:1 for agriculture and 4.5:1 for industry—to avoid the danger of making the task of financing development appear misleadingly easy.[6] A slight change in the assumed ICOR brings substantial differences in results. This suggests that the choice should be made with greatest caution and with awareness of the geographical area and pattern of development concerned.

The evidence on capital-output ratios, in Indonesia as elsewhere, is still far from satisfactory. One conclusion, however, appears to be emerging from the scanty empirical research which has been done: the ratio varies greatly depending on the stage of economic development and the basic endowments of the economy. Available evidence suggests that Indonesia would be favored by both conditions. Indonesia lies in the Southeast Asian tropics and has access to geographical frontiers. A recent area survey by the United Nations suggested that evidence in the Southeast Asian countries pointed to an aggregate ICOR of 2.5:1, a figure which the Economic Commission for Asia and the Far East employed to compute capital requirements for the area as a whole.[7] A leading Indonesian economist has chosen to work with ICORs of 2.5:1 for agriculture and 3:1 for industry, suggesting that the figure (aggregate ICOR = 4:1) from the United Nations, Measures for Economic Development of Underdeveloped Countries (1951), "should be considered somewhat high for Indonesia."[8]

We have chosen, therefore, to modify Grasberg's results by selecting an aggregate ICOR of 3.5:1, which appears to have as much empirical support as the higher United Nations figure of 4:1.[9] The Indian First Five Year Plan suggested an ICOR of 3:1, and experience with the Indian Second Plan suggests a figure nearer to 3.5:1. Ratios averaging near 3.5:1 have been used by several experts for empirical estimates of capital requirements.[10]

Indonesia's present Five Year Plan is based on an estimated ICOR of 2:1, rising to 4:1 for the Fourth Five Year Plan. The general principle of allowing for a rising ICOR as "bargain-counter" projects are exhausted and emphasis on industrialization is increased is a good one; the question is only whether there are enough bargains left to justify an ICOR as low as 2:1 even in the first phase of the development plan, given the pattern of investment proposed.[11]

In the Introduction to this volume, Benjamin Higgins pointed out that there is little reason to expect an ICOR as low as the Indonesian Five Year Plan has projected. The National Planning Bureau's ICOR of 2.1:1 is based on the belief that the relationship between increased investment and the growth of national income was about 1.5:1 during the rehabilitation years of 1950-1956. The experience of these years, however, suggests that Indonesia was successful with development activities only where a low ICOR was possible and demands on organizational and entrepreneurial resources were negligible.[12] It is only in the essentially rehabilitative, capital-cheap projects—fertilizer, irrigation repair, replanting, and the like—that increases in output have been gained. During this period, recurrent failure prevented the Indonesians from making an all-out effort to promote the growth of output in those sectors where capital requirements were higher.[13] Yet such a comprehensive effort is precisely what the Five Year Plan calls for. It is clear, therefore, that the plan itself, if it is to be successful, must represent a shift of emphasis from capital-cheap projects to more capital-intensive investment, which has been neglected during the pre-plan period. The plan allocates only 13 per cent of the entire development resources to agriculture, and even in this sector a significant share is to be devoted to bringing new acreage under cultivation. (See Appendix A, p. 391.) One would expect to find a higher ICOR in such activity than the 1.5:1 ratio which the National Planning Bureau reports for the 1951-1955 period, when agriculture provided most of the output gains.* Three-quarters of the plan's investment resources are to be devoted to three sectors with characteristically high ICORs—transport and communications, power and irrigation, and industrialization. In these sectors the ICOR cannot be expected to be below 4:1. The remainder of the plan's investment budget (12 per cent) is allocated to education, welfare, and information. While there is little evidence on the positive effects of such investment on output, it is clear that investment in health, education, housing, and similar projects has a long gestation period and that dramatic output results cannot be expected over the course of a short-run planning period.

Moreover, Indonesia has a serious balance-of-payments problem which has been greatly aggravated by economic independence in the Outer Islands and the exodus of Dutch nationals. Solving it will require expansion of exports as well as development of import-replacing industries. Import replacement may be capital cheap as industrialization goes; textile manufacture, for example, can be fairly labor intensive and still be efficient. The fields in which Indonesia's prospects for increased exports are brightest, on the other hand—petroleum products, aluminum, tin products—are capital intensive in the extreme.

*This low ICOR apparently resulted from the failure to measure capital formation accurately. It is suggested in the next chapter that the Planning Bureau estimates of capital formation suffer from lack of complete statistical coverage and, perhaps, from an arbitrarily chosen but unrealistically low allowance for capital consumption.

All these factors suggest an ICOR higher than 2:1 even for the first phase of the Indonesian development plan. It may be that we have underestimated the number of "bargain-counter" projects still available. Certainly Indonesia's National Planning Bureau is in a better position than the author to evaluate investment opportunities—we can only express our honest doubts. On the other hand, we have chosen the minimum supportable estimate of annual population growth. The Planning Bureau uses a figure of 1.7 per cent where we are using Grasberg's estimate of 1.5 per cent, and it may be that current rates of population growth are already as high as 2.0 per cent. Moreover, we must reckon with the possibility that successful development—including improved public health and higher incomes—will bring with it a new spurt in population growth. The Planning Bureau allows for a gradual increase in population growth to 2.0 per cent in fifteen years. The Javanese have shown a capacity for extremely high rates of growth in the past—approaching 3 per cent—as an aftermath of economic development; why should they not do so again? It may turn out that our estimate of ICOR is too high; it is more probable that our estimate of population growth is too low. The capital requirements we suggest may prove to be of the right order of magnitude because of these compensating errors.

With an estimated ICOR of 3.5:1, then, Indonesia's net investment requirements for the first year of a development program would be modified as indicated in Table 2. Investment required in the first year (a) raising output to provide increased per capita consumption (2 per cent), (b) reduction of imports of food and fibers over five years, and (c) compensating for recent cuts in imports of "other necessities" amounts to between Rp. 12.7 and Rp. 13.2 billion. This amounts to a slight reduction in Grasberg's estimate, even with much heavier capital

Table 2

INDONESIA'S INVESTMENT REQUIREMENTS FIRST YEAR OF A DEVELOPMENT PROGRAM

(Million 1952 Rp.)

Objective	Grasberg Estimate		Revised Estimate*	
1. Restoring supplies per capita of all goods and services to 1954–1955 levels:				
Food	3,099.6		2,646.0	
Other necessities	1,407.4		1,094.6	
Other goods and services	786.4		611.6	
		5,293.4		4,352.2
2. Eliminating food imports and 25 per cent reduction in fiber imports (over five years)	881.5		2,500.0 to 3,000.0† (items 2 and 3)	
3. Compensating for reduction in imports (over five years)	410.0			
4. Increasing per capita consumption of all goods and services by 2 per cent	12,457.0		10,242.5	
5. TOTAL (objectives 2, 3, and 4)		13,748.5		12,742.5 to 13,242.5

*Assuming an aggregate ICOR of 3.5 : 1 rather than Grasberg's 4 : 1 for agriculture and 4.5 : 1 for industry.

†The sizable increase in capital requirements for achieving these objectives takes account of the effects of recent Outer Islands dissidence and nationalization of Dutch properties.

Source: For Grasberg estimate, see Table 1; for revised estimates, see text.

requirements to compensate for import cuts because of recent events which will certainly reduce Indonesia's ability to earn foreign exchange. Over a five-year period, average annual net investment necessary to achieve the foregoing objectives would be between Rp. 12.75 and Rp. 13.25 billion rather than Rp. 14 billion as estimated by Grasberg.* In terms of investment rates, this would point to the necessity of investing about 13 per cent of net national product. It is interesting to note that this is about the rate of investment necessary to raise a country to the stage of a "growing economy" in Rostow's analysis.[14] In terms of Indonesia's recent economic performance, investment requirements of this order of magnitude would involve at least doubling the present estimated rate of net investment.

Unfortunately, the problem is not this simple. The problem of meeting investment requirements for development in Indonesia is complicated by existing financial and budgetary disequilibria. Perennial budgetary deficits and the expansion of private credit have brought Indonesia repeatedly to the brink of unrestrained inflation.[15] Aggregate demand has been steadily expanded while it has failed to produce accompanying increases in output. There is considerable evidence suggesting that inflationary policies have had little stimulating effect on investment. Inflationary price rises in important sectors of the economy have interfered with the government's ability to transfer resources to its development activities as well as to its current expenditures.[16] These disappointing results prompted the former Governor of the Bank Indonesia, Sjafruddin Prawiranegara, to make a plea for the curtailment of

*It should be emphasized that these requirements are estimated in terms of the pre-rebellion value of the rupiah, when net national income was about Rp. 100 billion.

inflationary finance in Indonesia:

> First and foremost, every effort is to be made to curb the inflationary factors, since the near future is causing very great concern in monetary respect. Any expansion of total outlays, either in the Government or in the private sector, interfering further with the equilibrium to the value of the volume of goods and services becoming available in the same period of time, even though they are investment expenditure, should be avoided. Only increased investment expenditure attended with reduced consumptive spendings can be deemed justified.[17]

By late 1958 the situation had worsened. In his 1958 report, M. D. Dris, the United Nations fiscal expert who prepared a study of the tax system for the Indonesian government, described the problem of inflation in these terms:

> The notorious inflation evident for many years past inevitably leads to complicated regulations which consume much of the time and energy of individuals capable of productive work; it gives rise to pernicious trafficking and speculation; it imperils the existence of economically sound concerns and discourages investment in projects not likely to bring immediate returns. Whatever restrictions the authorities may impose, it is bound to lead sooner or later to an increase in the cost of living, higher wages and economic upheaval. Apart from the use of means such as the balancing of the budget and a strict curb on budgetary and extra-budgetary expenditures (an important factor in inflation) taxation can and must play an effective though secondary part in soaking up surplus money in circulation or at least in preventing its increase.
>
> These imperious and urgent needs call for taxation policies that will bring about or help to bring about three essential aims: a rapid large-scale increase in the volume of receipts from taxation; a faster development of concerns likely to contribute directly or indirectly to increasing foreign currency reserves; and last but not least a halt to monetary inflation.[18]

The problem of financing economic development in Indonesia, therefore, is one of transferring resources to the production of investment goods without continuing to expand the level of aggregate demand. With regard to capital requirements this means that a part of the real savings which can be mobilized from the domestic economy or abroad must be devoted to achieving economic stability, a precondition for development. The former Governor of the Bank Indonesia called attention to this important reality as the First Five Year Plan was being released. "In Indonesia," he wrote, "a different and more complicated situation has to be faced. The country is already in a state of monetary dis-equilibrium resulting from the financing of budget deficits by inflationary means. If at this time large investment schemes are floated, which might well produce equilibrium-disturbing forces, the existing inflationary tensions will increase even more. . . . My point is to draw attention to the problem of financing which unfortunately is more difficult to solve on account of the already existing monetary dis-equilibrium."[19]

The budgetary deficit, the primary stimulus to the expansion of aggregate demand and rising prices, must be reduced and perhaps even eliminated. Deficits averaged between Rp. 2.5 and Rp. 3 billion in the pre-rebellion years, but rebellion and the continuing security problems have led to much larger deficit spending. Net investment of 13 per cent of net national product might meet the estimated requirements for a take-off into steady growth; but financing this investment without inflation will require either cuts in current government spending or provision of total financial resources—private savings + taxes + foreign capital—of somewhat more than this amount. In other words, total <u>financial</u> requirements include provision for restoring equilibrium between aggregate demand and output.[20] This would raise total financial requirements by at least Rp. 2.5 billion, bringing the total minimum to 15 per cent of national income. This estimate, made before the unfortunate events of 1956 and 1957 occurred, must now be regarded as conservative. The taking over of Dutch firms and the repair of damage done by the rebellion have increased the burden on Central Government. The new expenditures resulting from these events must be eliminated and the tax losses recovered before economic stabilization will be feasible.

Foreign Capital Requirements

There are two major reasons why foreign capital will be necessary to complement the domestic financing of development. First, a developing economy must import some capital goods, but the foreign component of a country's total capital formation may well lie beyond its foreign-exchange earning capacity. This appears to be the case in Indonesia. Secondly, the financial burden which a development program of adequate magnitude imposes may be beyond the total savings capacity of the country concerned. In Indonesia, where financial requirements for achieving economic stability must be added to those of development, this consideration too seems to emphasize the need for a certain amount of foreign financing (outright aid and grants, public and private loans and investments).

In an economy with an underdeveloped industrial structure an important share of the physical capital goods for development, and, in the case of Indonesia, of the raw materials for industrial production, must in the short run be obtained from abroad. We know little about the required foreign trade ingredient of capital formation in countries at the stage of Indonesia's development, but a preliminary estimate may be ventured on the basis of Indonesia's own experience and estimated requirements for its development program.

Figures published by the Indonesian Planning Bureau indicate that the ratio of capital-goods imports to gross investment averaged 29 per cent for the five years 1951-1955.[21] The import component of government investment, however, averaged 37.5 per cent while that for the public and private (capital-intensive) sectors combined averaged about 37 per cent. On the basis of these data, the Planning Bureau has projected foreign-exchange costs at 37.5 per cent of additional investment during the Five Year Plan period.[22]

This estimate, too, should perhaps be regarded as unduly favorable. If investment allocation follows the contours of the Five Year Plan, the pattern of investment will be more capital intensive than during the pre-plan period, and prosecution of the plan will rely more heavily upon the import of capital equipment which is not locally available. However, if the Planning Bureau's estimate is accepted, the import component of the additional capital required to raise output by 2 per cent (Rp. 7 billion) would reach some Rp. 2.6 billion annually (about U.S. $220 million). Over the first five-year period the new investment is assumed not to add to requirements for replacement. Thus additional foreign-exchange costs refer to additional <u>net</u> investment only. While the import component of additional investment accomplished by the private sector may be somewhat lower than for the public sector, this advantage is offset by the favorable import-component ratio employed.

It appears clear that foreign-exchange requirements of this order of magnitude will remain beyond the foreign-exchange earning capacity of the Indonesian economy over the period of a short-run development program (e.g., five years), thus underlining the need for foreign capital in financing the development program. Since 1952 the Indonesian government has strictly limited the use of foreign exchange for the import of consumer goods; and the ability to import capital equipment and raw materials has been a very real limit to expanding investment and domestic output. By 1954 it was apparent that the import of consumer goods could not be reduced further without reductions in the supply of basic necessities in the economy. In fact, in that year the National Planning Bureau felt that "there are limitations that [sic] can be achieved in the consumption sector [of the import accounts]; after a certain point further reductions in supplies being increasingly difficult to bear. Therefore, to achieve the required decrease in foreign exchange expenditure some reductions in the productive sector [of the import account] were unavoidable."[23] Even so, the import of consumer goods was reduced 33.33 per cent below the 1953 level.[24] On the other hand, the ability of the economy to earn significantly greater amounts of foreign exchange in the short run is extremely doubtful, barring fortuitous rises in world prices for Indonesia's major exports. In 1956 Indonesia's export earnings fell by approximately Rp. 600 million. An attempt to increase imports to the pre-1953 level without increasing exports caused a loss of Rp. 1.1 billion in gold and foreign-exchange reserves. Reserve losses of this magnitude cannot be accepted in the future. At the end of 1955 Indonesia's gold and foreign-exchange reserves totaled Rp. 2.7 billion. By early 1958 they had fallen to Rp. 1.2 billion. Since the end of 1951, when gold and foreign-exchange reserves were at their postwar high of Rp. 6.2 billion, Indonesia's average loss of reserves has been nearly Rp. 700 million.* Yet, during this period, import and foreign-exchange controls were, by and large, stringent. The short-run danger implicit in this situation is that a serious slump in demand for Indonesia's exports might deprive Indonesia

*See Chapter 9, Table 42.

of even the present minimum supplies of imported consumer and capital goods. Rebuilding the country's foreign-exchange reserves to near Rp. 2.5 billion must, therefore, become a paramount objective for both stability and development. The recent takeover of Dutch enterprises will undoubtedly reduce Indonesia's foreign-exchange earnings over the short run considerably more than it will reduce claims against these earnings for profits, pensions, and similar transfers. Indonesia's recent balance-of-payments situation suggests that herculean efforts are needed to provide export earnings to maintain imports at the 1953-1955 levels (about Rp. 7 billion per year in terms of pre-rebellion rupiah value) without a complete loss of gold and foreign-exchange reserves. The introduction of an export certificate system in 1957 to increase exporters' proceeds by approximately 100 per cent has failed to increase export earnings.[25] It seems safe to conclude that the import of capital goods for an expanded development program cannot be financed from increased export earnings alone or by providing foreign exchange from further reductions in the present levels of imports of consumer goods or raw materials for domestic industrial production.

The empirical study of Indonesia's financial capacities in later chapters points to the same conclusion. Anticipating later conclusions, it appears that the maximum domestic capacity for financing development might reach about Rp. 13 billion annually. This falls short of providing resources to meet the estimated capital requirements by about Rp. 2.5 billion.

At the pre-rebellion level of government expenditures (about Rp. 20 billion per year gross), the government was operating at an annual budgetary deficit averaging about Rp. 2.5 billion. The 1958 budget deficit was about Rp. 9 billion. If, however, military expenditures can be reduced as domestic security is gradually re-established, and tax yields can be raised to their previous levels, budgetary experience before 1957 suggests that the deficit could be trimmed to approximately Rp. 2.5 to Rp. 3 billion. Foreign resources in the amount of Rp. 2.5 billion, therefore, should be considered as a minimum needed to eliminate the greater part of the peacetime deficit.* It can be seen, however, that the government should make efforts to reduce its nondevelopment expenditures below their pre-1957 level since even a balanced budget is likely to produce inflationary pressures.† The relatively high level of public consumption expenditures throughout the period since 1950 indicates that national efforts to restore stability through more stringent controls over expenditures should be capable of producing reductions in collective consumption adequate to offset the inflationary pressures implicit in a balanced budget. It is important to note that even balancing the budget will require access to outside resources in the amount of Rp. 2.5 billion, and that the program suggested here calls for stringent public expenditures policies designed to produce what would, in effect, be a budgetary surplus, including the foreign resources. It is clear, therefore, that access to foreign grants or other foreign economic assistance in the amount of Rp. 2.5 billion is a minimum condition for financing economic development with relative domestic price stability.

In short, total net investment requirements to achieve the objectives of stability and development approximate Rp. 15.5 billion; and the

*For further discussion of this point see Chapter 9.

†The inflationary effects of a balanced budget would be equal to the amount of government expenditures (or tax collections). If, for example, the marginal propensity to consume (as a fraction of net national income) is 4/5, the required surplus to produce no inflationary pressures would be one in which tax revenues exceeded expenditures by 1/4 (i.e., the budget would have to show a ratio of government expenditures to tax collections of only 4/5).

economy appears to be capable of supplying about Rp. 13 billion in domestic savings through the program outlined in later chapters. Unless external funds in the amount of about Rp. 2.5 billion are made available, a development program of the size indicated by the estimate of Indonesia's capital requirements would require continued inflationary financing which would jeopardize both the economy's stability and development. This is tantamount to concluding that a program large enough to provide cumulative growth would fail without substantial external financial assistance—even though maximum domestic mobilization were undertaken.

Our conclusions on Indonesia's investment requirements, measured in terms of the pre-rebellion rupiah value and assuming a pre-rebellion budgetary situation, may be summarized as follows:

1. The development program will require expenditures for investment in foreign exchange as well as in local currency. The foreign-exchange component has been estimated to approximate 37.5 per cent of the new investment added by the development program.

2. In rough terms, this program would call for additional (net) investment expenditures over and above pre-rebellion levels totaling (at the minimum) about Rp. 7 billion, with Rp. 4.5 billion spent domestically and Rp. 2.5 billion spent abroad.

3. Investment requirements for the developmental objectives presented above are estimated in terms of <u>net</u> rather than <u>gross</u> investment. This is done on the assumption that depreciation of new capital facilities will not produce an added investment problem in the early years of the development program. The Indonesian economy is now providing for depreciation of existing facilities and, above and beyond this, a

positive rate of net investment which provides growth of output at approximately the rate of population growth. The financial capacity referred to here provides for reductions in consumption of some categories of goods. In some cases this will allow existing capital facilities to be transferred to developmental objectives; in others it will result in lower depreciation costs for the economy as a whole as luxury-producing capital equipment becomes idle. On balance, therefore, we believe that depreciation of new development facilities can be met from these resources and need not impose further investment requirements.

4. The total amount of additional resources which might be mobilized domestically approximates Rp. 7.3 billion per year,* while additional foreign resources in the neighborhood of Rp. 2.5 billion are required. This would permit virtual elimination of the anticipated budget deficit (given restoration of security) in addition to financing the required investment outlays.

5. The additional Rp. 7.3 billion in domestic resources will represent about Rp. 4 billion in tax-enforced reductions in consumption, Rp. 2 billion from reductions in Central Government transfer payments (subsidies) to local governments, and the balance (about Rp. 1.3 billion) from the mobilization of presently unemployed resources made available by local fiscal processes without involving payments in money. Increased money expenditures from these resources may eventually generate some inflationary impact upon the economy as they are spent for investment. Assuming that the marginal propensity to consume is less than 1, and that private investment will not fall as a result of the in-

*This estimate anticipates conclusions from later chapters; see Chapter 8 in particular.

creased taxes, the increase in government expenditures will somewhat exceed the reduction in private spending.

6. Mild inflationary pressures, thus generated, might be helpful in facilitating the transfer of resources to development activity as the economy begins to move forward, and if the development program begins with stable price conditions.

Entrepreneurship and Capital Absorptive Capacity

The problem of financing economic development concerns the ability to mobilize resources for capital formation on a scale adequate to expand output per capita. Although our study emphasizes this problem, we must recognize that there is nothing automatic about transforming financial resources into output-increasing investment. In fact, Indonesian experience since the transfer of sovereignty in 1949 suggests that the country's prospects for development may hinge more on its capacity to provide effective entrepreneurship than on its capacity to mobilize financial resources. The problem of entrepreneurship may be viewed either as one of demand for capital or as one of supplying enough intangible—primarily human—capital to complement savings and real capital.*

The problem of entrepreneurship in its Indonesian setting has many overtones—political, ethnic, social, and economic. Recognizing the importance of this problem, the Indonesian government's economic

*The problem referred to here is partly that of lack of inducements to private demand for capital formation, a problem that received emphasis by Ragnar Nurkse in Problems of Capital Formation in Underdeveloped Countries (Basil Blackwell, Oxford, 1953). It also refers to the scarcity of entrepreneurial skills capable of putting capital to productive use even where profit inducements exist. The question of entrepreneurship and incentives is discussed in Chapter 7.

programs during the pre-plan period were predominently efforts to spark Indonesian entrepreneurship. These programs have come to be known as the Benteng movement. Its purpose has been the fostering of Indonesian enterprise by largess of capital, credit, and positions of special privilege.

The Indonesian presumption that the chief obstacles to indigenous entrepreneurship have been lack of credit and capital and an inferior competitive position vis-à-vis foreigners is questionable. Former Finance Minister Sumitro called attention to this fallacy even before the Benteng movement reached its zenith:

> In reference to capital expenditures I cannot fail to make the following remark. There is a widespread assumption in this country that many problems would soon be solved if only the necessary equipment—machinery and other capital goods—were available.
>
> The rush for making rather indiscriminate commitments for the purchase of capital goods can partly be traced to such belief. We have experienced to our bitter disappointment, however, that capital equipment purchased resulted in actual capital loss just because no account was taken of the organizational preparations and skills required to generate capital expenditures into really productive results.
>
> I would consider for the next five years the problem of human investment of equal importance as capital investments, if not more important.[26]

In 1954 the University of Indonesia's Institute of Economic and Social Research undertook a penetrating study of the results of the government's Benteng and developmental efforts. One of the major conclusions emerging from that study was that the rather general failure of development efforts was traceable to the quality of entrepreneurship rather than the shortage of capital or credit. Startling as it may seem, the report charged that entrepreneurial bottlenecks were as pronounced within the ranks of the prime mover—the government—as they were among the complementary elites the program sought to stimulate to productive activity. It was observed that:

> In many cases . . . lack of equipment was not the most serious bottleneck. Equally serious, if not more so, was the lack of skills in general, and the critical conditions of public administration in particular. We have dealt in our report mainly with segments of administration directly concerned with industrial programs. But it is fair to state that similar conditions prevail in other branches of government. It was a fundamental cause for a considerable waste of resources. Immediate improvement of our public administration is a precondition for satisfactory implementation of future economic and financial policies. We refer not only to the government but also to government controlled or government sponsored enterprises, banks, credit agencies, etc. [27]

Indonesia's experience in attempting to foster the development of an indigenous entrepreneurial class through its *Benteng* programs is a most dramatic example of the fallacy that supply of capital and credit will create their own demand. With development objectives in the background, the *Benteng* program sought as its first goal the growth of an Indonesian business class to replace existing Dutch and Chinese firms. Once this end was achieved, it was the purpose of the Indonesian economic planners to use the new Indonesian entrepreneurial class as the vehicle of economic development. Behind this procedure lay the belief that colonial rule had had a suffocating effect on indigenous Indonesian enterprise while it had fostered the entrepreneurial activity of the Dutch and minority groups, particularly the Chinese. Indonesian planners foresaw a great entrepreneurial response from Indonesian nationals to the removal of colonial restraints and the provision of special privileges, credit, and capital. Before the *Benteng* program had been long under way, more sober Indonesian observers saw that it was failing to generate an Indonesian entrepreneurial class and that, a fortiori, it was failing to expand output. Former Vice President Hatta was quoted as saying that:

> Indonesian traders, under the guise of national economic development, have obtained privileges which have cost the country tens if not hundreds of millions of rupiah while the suffering of the whole society increases.[28]

The Governor of the Java Bank (now the Bank Indonesia) observed that the government's attempts to foster an Indonesian foreign-trading class had provided little effective enterprise, the multiplication of firms, and "big, quick and easy profits." He concluded that "the present course of affairs . . . must be considered with great concern."[29]

Indonesia's economic leadership employed the same methods in their Urgency Industrialization Plan, begun in 1951. This program, too, attempted to unleash Indonesian enterprise in many industrial activities, both large and small scale. In the field of small-scale industrial development the government sought to take advantage of existing Indonesian enterprise. The strategy to be employed here was one of infusing physical capital and deficit-financed credit to expand the size and output of firms in these industries. The results of the program, up to mid-1954, revealed once again the failure of administration and enterprise. The government was unable to distribute capital and credit at the rate it had anticipated; even so, small-scale enterprises became saturated with more than they could absorb, and much of the assistance went unused.[30] It was clear that even in this sector, in which many Indonesians envisaged an expression of indigenous enterprise, demand for capital and credit was limited. The rate at which traditional modes of production could supply the increased volume of administrative, technical, and entrepreneurial skills to complement capital and credit was once again overestimated.*

The Urgency Industrialization Plan in the sphere of large-scale industry was even more disappointing. Rapid development of this sector was viewed as a first, quick attack on the problem of Indonesia's misshapen economic structure. It called for the rapid building of a number of sizable industrial establishments, some to process raw materials for export, others to provide materials for domestic construction, still others to provide a variety of outputs for domestic consumption.

The majority of the projects did not go beyond the planning stage.[31] Projects actually undertaken encountered frequent delays. In the few enterprises which were completed, the government's capacity to provide managers to operate the firms economically was quickly exhausted. In spite of fairly large outlays for financing, industrial output continued to languish. The main intent of these plans—replacing foreign entrepreneurs with Indonesians—led only to less effective entrepreneurship in the nontraditional sector of the economy.

This suggestive Indonesian experience emphasizes that capital requirements cannot be measured solely in physical terms. The conclusion seems inescapable that Indonesia's greatest short-run requirement is investment in human capital—education, technical training, perhaps even institutional change—to provide the conditions under which

*On the other hand, Surjo Sediono, an official in the Ministry of Economic Affairs, has pointed out to the author that recent surveys reveal that the programs undertaken several years ago are now (1958) producing significant output results. This seems to confirm the conclusion that entrepreneurial bottlenecks limit the rate at which capital goods and credit can be absorbed and the speed with which they can be brought to fruition as productive capital.

financial capital can be absorbed into the economy at rates adequate to provide increased per capita output. It would also appear that intensely nationalistic policies which isolate the minorities which now possess entrepreneurial skills are inconsistent with rapid economic development. The search for complementary agents to prosecute development has overlooked those ethnic groups which fail to meet strict Indonesian standards of nationality. If such policies continue, it is possible that relatively great financial resources may fail to provide the results which the Five Year Plan is designed to achieve. Effective use of funds mobilized for development may be frustrated by the failure to make these resources available to entrepreneurs who can employ them productively. The recent Indonesian takeover of Dutch firms as a result of the West Irian dispute is a case in point. Indonesian experience from independence to the present suggests that maintaining output in these firms during the next few years will strain Indonesia's entrepreneurial resources to the utmost. It is certain that this move in itself will be a major obstacle to realizing the present Five Year Plan by diverting Indonesia's sparse supply of managerial and technical factors from development roles to those formerly performed by Dutch entrepreneurs. The short-run bottleneck to development now, even more than during the rehabilitation years from 1950 to 1956, clearly lies in the ability to put investment resources to effective use rather than in the ability to supply them.

A Dilemma: Magnitude of the Program and Bottlenecks to Development

The magnitude of a development program appropriate to Indonesia's present capacity raises a serious dilemma for Indonesia's development planners. On the one hand, domestic pressures for economic and social change require that dramatic results be shown in raising the rate of capital formation and expanding real income. On the other hand, it appears that Indonesia has not yet established the preconditions—particularly those concerned with entrepreneurship and growing supplies of technical skills—to prosecute a plan of the required size. In the context of these basic problems, Indonesia's First Five Year Plan appears to be something less than a realistic attack upon the problem of stagnation.

In later chapters we reach the conclusion that the First Five Year Plan does not call for the degree of sacrifice which might have been feasible from the viewpoint of the economy's capacity. We conclude that the scale of the plan is smaller than a maximum effort at mobilizing financial resources could support. Our estimates of Indonesia's capital requirements point to an even more ominous conclusion: the First Five Year Plan is too small to launch cumulative growth. Indonesia must undertake to form capital at the rate of 13 per cent of net national product over the first decade of the development period if self-sustained growth is to be reached. "Savings" must also be supplied in excess of this requirement to achieve economic stability and to develop the human skills essential to economic progress. The First Five Year Plan calls for net capital formation of only 6.8 per cent during the first five years and 8.5 per cent in the second. Employing an ICOR of 3.5:1, which we believe to be as low as a developing country at Indonesia's stage may expect, the plan will scarcely maintain per capita output at postwar levels.* Under the National Planning Bureau's

*If $\Delta\gamma = \frac{S}{K}$, where $\Delta\gamma$ is the change in real income (output), S is the rate of saving, and K is the ICOR, we find that $\Delta\gamma$ works out to 1.9 while the rate of population is conservatively estimated to be 1.7.

concession that only 40 per cent of the expected small increase in per capita income be recaptured for investment, the Second Five Year Plan would also fail to provide significant increments in output per capita.

Even the modest goals of the plan may be unduly sanguine if the problem of developing entrepreneurs to use capital more productively is not attacked with realism. Such evidence as we have suggests that Indonesia, beginning independence with distinct disadvantage in this regard, has aggravated the problem by more nationalistic attitudes than she can afford. Minority groups with technical and managerial talents have been increasingly isolated from development activities, and Benteng policies have failed to fill the void because they have emphasized conditions external to skillful enterprise rather than training for entrepreneurship itself. Nowhere in the plan's program do we find adequate emphasis upon this prime prerequisite for economic growth. The expulsion of Dutch entrepreneurs and technicians suggests that rather unrealistic assumptions about Indonesian capacity for entrepreneurship persist.

With maximum efforts to break the entrepreneurial bottleneck through full utilization and development of the requisite skills—and an accelerated inflow of foreign technical aid—Indonesia might not now be capable of absorbing into productive use the capital required for development. A program of the scale necessary to achieve a take-off to sustained growth may require a preparatory stage devoted to forming these preconditions. The present study is concerned mainly with the feasibility of financing a development program adequate to achieve modest growth objectives. The foregoing discussion suggests, however, that we make no assumptions about Indonesia's present capacity to execute a development program of the rough magnitude suggested in this chapter. The chapters which follow point to the conclusion that careful planning and rigorous fiscal policy involving general domestic belt-tightening may go far toward solving the problem of financing a program of the required magnitude. It suggests nothing about Indonesia's potentiality to meet successfully the many other difficulties which are likely to arise during an attempt to convert a stagnant economy into a growing one.

Notes to Chapter 1

1. Eugene Grasberg, Indonesia's Investment Requirements, Center for International Studies, Massachusetts Institute of Technology, Cambridge, 1955, 46 pp.

2. See Appendix A, p. 371.

3. Grasberg, op. cit., p. 25.

4. Tillman Durdin, "Barter Trade Hurts Djakarta," New York Times, December 21, 1957. In mid-1958 Prime Minister Djuanda was reported to have said that regional poaching on foreign-exchange earnings had deprived Central Government of $300,000,000 (Rp. 3.4 billion). See Tillman Durdin, "Indonesia Finds Dissidence Costly," ibid., June 3, 1958, p. 52.

5. Greg MacGregor, "Indonesia Sinks to Economic Low," New York Times, August 3, 1958, p. 18.

6. In Grasberg's words, "It is difficult not to admit that by assuming as high an ICOR as in the present paper one may appear 'unduly pessimistic.' Yet the present writer refuses to be emboldened by these encouraging instances, his main reason resting on the belief that all major disappointments in history, from the construction of the tower of Babel, to the Panama Canal, to Hitler's failure to capture Moscow, were caused by shunning 'undue pessimism.'" Op. cit., p. 20. Perhaps as many failures have resulted from lack of heart to attack a problem at the outset because it has been made to look too difficult.

7. Economic Commission for Asia and the Far East, United Nations, Economic Survey of Asia and the Far East, 1954, Bangkok, 1955, p. xiv.

8. Sumitro Djojohadikusumo, "Balanced Development of Agriculture and Industry," Ekonomi dan Keuangan Indonesia, Vol. VI, July 1953, pp. 383-385.

9. This figure, for example, leads Professor Walt Rostow to results in terms of investment rates which demarcate stages of development in several empirical cases. W. W. Rostow, "The Take-Off into Self-Sustained Growth," The Economic Journal, Vol. LXVI, March 1956, pp. 34-38. This is also close to the average ICOR suggested in an empirical study of more than thirty countries by Dr. Egbert De Vries, "The Balance Between Agriculture and Industry in Economic Development," 1954 (mimeographed).

10. G. M. Meier and R. E. Baldwin, Economic Development, John Wiley & Sons, New York, 1957, p. 340.

11. Benjamin Higgins, "The Indonesian Five Year Plan: Proposals for Research," Center for International Studies, Massachusetts Institute of Technology, Cambridge, 1957, p. 9.

12. Douglas S. Paauw, "The High Cost of Political Instability in Indonesia, 1957-1958," Internationale Spectator, Vol. XII, November 1958, pp. 532-540.

13. Ibid., p. 537.

14. Such economies are defined as those "where the apparent savings and investment rates . . . have reached 10% or over. . . ." Rostow, op. cit., p. 36.

15. See Benjamin Higgins, Indonesia's Economic Stabilization and Development, Institute of Pacific Relations, New York, 1957, p. 39.

16. Report of the Bank Indonesia, 1954-1955, p. 52. The Governor of the Bank Indonesia, formerly the Java Bank, issues an annual report shortly after the end of each fiscal year in both English and Indonesian editions. In general, these annual reports are thorough and careful reviews of Indonesia's monetary and fiscal developments. They provide the best available source of data on many of the problems with which we are concerned.

17. Ibid., pp. 52-53.

18. M. D. Dris, "Taxation in Indonesia," Ekonomi dan Keuangan Indonesia, Vol. XI, August-September 1958, p. 421. Dris' study is the only general review of the Indonesian tax system made since Indonesia became independent in 1949. At the request of the Indonesian government, Mr. Dris was appointed by the United Nations Technical Assistance Administration to undertake a survey of the existing tax system and to present recommendations for improvement. Dris' final report to the Indonesian government has been published in full in the issue of Ekonomi dan Keuangan Indonesia cited. The report covers the entire tax system with the exception of foreign trade levies and excise duties.

20. Indonesia's National Planning Bureau has emphasized the importance of reducing inflationary pressures if economic development is to be seriously undertaken. In a 1955 report, the following statement is put forth: "The Five-Year Development Plan, which is now a subject of study of the Planning Bureau, would not be workable if a persistent budgetary deficit disturbing the necessary economic balance is not eliminated in a reasonable

period of time." National Planning Bureau, "Indonesia's Economic and Social Developments in 1954," Ekonomi dan Keuangan Indonesia, Vol. VIII, July 1955, p. 411.

21. National Planning Bureau, "A Study of the Indonesian Economic Development Scheme," ibid., Vol. X, September 1957, Table III, p. 622.

22. Ibid., pp. 616-617.

23. National Planning Bureau, "Indonesia's Social and Economic Developments in 1954," ibid., Vol. VIII, July 1955, p. 369.

24. Ibid.

25. The Economist Intelligence Unit, Three Monthly Economic Review of Indonesia, No. 22, October 1957, pp. 3-4, and ibid., No. 24, May 1958, p. 7.

26. Sumitro Djojohadikusumo, "The Budget and Its Implications," Ekonomi dan Keuangan Indonesia, Vol. VI, January 1953, p. 10. (Italics in original.)

27. Sumitro Djojohadikusumo, ed., "The Government's Program on Industries," ibid., Vol. VII, November 1954, p. 735.

28. As quoted in J. M. van der Kroef, "Indonesia's Economic Difficulties," Far Eastern Survey, Vol. XXIV (1955), pp. 19-20.

29. Report of the Java Bank, 1952-1953, p. 123.

30. Sumitro Djojohadikusumo, "The Government's Program on Industries," loc. cit., p. 719.

31. Ibid., pp. 705-709.

2

SAVINGS, INVESTMENT, AND INFLATION, 1951-1957

An evaluation of Indonesia's potential capacity to finance capital formation of the magnitude necessary to provide a take-off to cumulative growth should begin with a survey of pre-planning levels of savings and investment. Unfortunately, reliable estimates of savings and investment have not been published, and there is little consensus among students of the Indonesian economy as to what their value might be. Among non-Indonesian observers it has become conventional to place net investment near zero;[1] one postwar study supplied an estimate suggesting this conclusion.[2] S. Daniel Neumark, a United Nations' advisor to the National Planning Bureau, estimated gross investment in 1952 to be Rp. 4.9 billion, as compared to gross national product of Rp. 93 billion (5.3 per cent).[3] After deducting his estimate of capital consumption allowances—which Indonesia's National Planning Bureau now considers too high—Neumark's estimate for the economy's net investment works out to only Rp. 0.6 billion (less than 1 per cent of net national product).

There are a good many indications that this estimate was too low. This rate of investment would imply that Indonesia failed in those years to meet capital requirements for maintaining per capita supplies of all goods and services.[4] This conclusion is not supported by evidence on the performance of the Indonesian economy in the years immediately after independence. Agricultural output showed significant increases, and the Indonesian Planning Bureau believes that industrial output expanded as well.[5] In the words of the National Planning Bureau, "Dr. Neumark's figures would give an ICOR so low that it certainly must be considered erroneous."[6]

In conjunction with the publication of Indonesia's First Five Year Plan the Planning Bureau issued its revisions of Neumark's estimates of Indonesia's investment performance for the years 1951-1955. These estimates are presented in Table 3 (gross investment) and Table 4 (net investment).

Table 3

GROSS INVESTMENT, 1951 - 1955

(Million Rp., 1952 Prices)

	1951	1952	1953	1954	1955	1951-1955
Non-*desa* investment	5,040	6,821	6,238	5,686	5,918	
Desa investment	1,400	1,500	1,600	1,700	1,800	
Total (gross investment)	6,440	8,321	7,838	7,386	7,718	
Percentage of gross domestic product in 1952 prices	8.0	10.0	8.6	7.6	7.8	
Average percentage						8.5

Source: National Planning Bureau, "A Study of the Indonesian Economic Development Scheme," *Ekonomi dan Keuangan Indonesia*, Vol. X, September 1957, Table III, p. 622.

We must emphasize, as the Planning Bureau readily admits, that these estimates are little more than informed guesses. Our evaluation follows from the method by which they were made. The method consisted of computing total capital imports into Indonesia and adding an estimated local investment component, which averaged about 63 per cent of total investment for the period 1951-1955. It was further assumed that the result could be taken as a measure of gross investment performed by the non-desa (non-village) sector of the economy—which can be construed to be roughly coterminous with the capital-intensive sector. An independent estimate for investment accomplished at the desa level was added.* The Planning Bureau maintains that this addition corrects for the most important omission leading to underestimation in the Neumark study.

Table 4

NET INVESTMENT, 1951-1955
(Million Rp., 1952 Prices)

	1951	1952	1953	1954	1955	1951-1955
Gross investment	6,440	8,321	7,838	7,386	7,718	
Capital consumption allowances	2,463	2,496	2,730	2,910	2,952	
Net investment	3,977	5,825	5,108	4,476	4,766	
Net investment as percentage of net domestic product in 1952 prices	5.1	7.2	5.8	5.0		
Average percentage						5.6

Source: Same as for Table 3.

*The National Planning Bureau defines the desa sector as the "small agricultural sector." For consistency, we use the term desa (literally, village) sector to refer to labor-intensive agriculture and related activities. Non-desa refers to all other economic sectors, including plantation agriculture, capital-intensive industry, and government.

In presenting its revised estimates of net investment, the Planning Bureau maintained that Neumark's capital-consumption allowances were much too high. Neumark had placed them at Rp. 3.7 billion for 1951 (about 4.5 per cent of gross domestic product) and Rp. 4.3 billion for 1952 (about 4.6 per cent of gross domestic product). On purely deductive rather than statistical grounds the Planning Bureau argued that they should be reduced to 3 per cent of gross domestic product. It is doubtful that this more favorable rate of capital-consumption allowances has resulted in overestimation of net investment, however, since the Planning Bureau's estimate of gross investment appears to be at the conservative limit. Public (non-*desa*) investment is based upon Central Government accounts which fail to include public investment performed by local governments unless financed through central subsidies. Our field research suggested that considerable self-financed investment activity was occurring at the *kabupaten* level in 1953 and 1954 (see Chapter 7) and that some of this activity appeared to be occurring outside the *desa* sector as defined by the Planning Bureau. The present writer's estimate of the economy's net investment, based on Indonesian government materials and including what we considered to be a realistic local government component, placed net investment for 1953 at about Rp. 6 billion[7] (as compared to the National Planning Bureau's estimated Rp. 5.1 billion for that year). This estimate placed net investment above the Planning Bureau figure even though Neumark's higher capital consumption allowances were employed.

If the National Planning Bureau's estimates for the economy's investment performance are to be accepted as provisional bench marks for the planning of development finance, we should bear in mind that they probably underestimate the capacity of the economy to reach the capital requirements presented in Chapter 1. As the conflict between Central Government and local governments in the outlying islands heightened in 1954 and 1955, the investment activity of local governments—not reported in Central Government statistics—appears to have increased. This was clearly the case in 1956 and 1957; for the latter year Central Government investment undoubtedly fell, but there is some fragmentary evidence suggesting that this reduction may have been more than offset by increased local government investment activity in the relatively autonomous provinces.[8]

The volume and composition of Indonesia's annual capital formation during the pre-rebellion years appears to have approximated that shown in Table 5.

Table 5

NET INVESTMENT IN A TYPICAL PRE-PLAN YEAR

(Billion Rp., 1952 Value)

Public sector:	
Central Government*	1.30
Local governments†	1.25
Private sector:	
Capital-intensive sector‡	2.10
Labor-intensive sector§	1.00
TOTAL	5.65

*This estimate is consistent with Central Government (gross) investment estimated by the National Planning Bureau and with a Ministry of Finance estimate of Central Government capital formation.

†Details on which this estimate is based are given in Chapter 7.

‡This estimate is consistent with the Planning Bureau's figures for investment in the private sector (excluding the desa sector).

§This estimate, including more than the Planning Bureau's "desa sector," is based on a distinction between capital formation financed by local governments (included under the public sector) and that privately financed, which is included here. Capital formation of this amount must be estimated to account for the considerable growth of output from this sector between 1950 and 1956.

Capital formation of the amount given in Table 5 would have shown a net investment rate averaging about 6 per cent of net domestic product for the five years ending with 1955. This result approximates the Planning Bureau estimates, which show net investment averaging 5.6 per cent of net domestic product for the years 1951-1955.[9] This difference, however, has some significance since the First Five Year Plan hopes to raise net investment to 6.8 per cent of net domestic product. If annual investment rates of 6 per cent have failed to provide increased per capita income, it is doubtful that a modest increase in this rate (less than 1 per cent) will yield significant development results. Even if the Planning Bureau estimate of the rate of net investment (5.6 per cent) is accepted, doubts about the adequacy of the scale of the First Five Year Plan to provide desired results persist, as we have suggested in the previous chapter. Grasberg's estimates of capital requirements, which are the only comprehensive and careful estimates available, reveal that a slightly higher rate of capital formation is needed to allow the Indonesian economy to maintain per capita consumption. Grasberg's calculations for 1956 showed that a net investment rate of 5.8 per cent of net domestic product would maintain per capita consumption of all goods and services but would fail to correct Indonesia's persistent balance-of-payments disequilibrium and would also fail to promote greater independence of food and textile imports.[10]

It is significant that the Planning Bureau reports a somewhat lower level of capital formation for 1954 and 1955 than for 1952 and 1953. (See Table 4.) In 1954 and 1955 the rate of net investment reported (5 per cent) falls slightly below the average for the five-year period (5.6 per cent). This seems to suggest slightly decreased investment activity in the capital-intensive sector; the Planning Bureau itself reports "desa investment" at a somewhat higher level for these years. In fact, it is probable that increased investment activity in the labor-intensive sector and at the local-government level may have offset the decline in investment in the capital-intensive sector. The conclusion that emerges is a significant one. It appears that investment in the higher ICOR (capital-intensive) sector fell continuously after the relatively prosperous year 1952, supporting our argument that the development program in Indonesia—in order to reverse this trend—must soon confront the problem of increasing output in those sectors where ICORs are relatively high. Severe balance-of-payments and stability problems appear to have affected investment in these sectors adversely during 1954 and 1955, and this apparently has been true, a fortiori, in 1956 and 1957. Therefore, even though it may be realistic to credit an estimated Rp. 5.65 billion (as the economy's present level of capital formation) against the capital requirements estimated in Chapter 1, we are led to believe that developmental investment will involve a relatively high ICOR in the first years of the plan. Here, too, the evidence seems to contradict the easy assumption that development activity will be able to take advantage of an ICOR near 2:1.

Financing Investment during the Pre-Plan Years

According to the National Planning Bureau estimates, gross investment averaged Rp. 7.5 billion (8.5 per cent of gross domestic product) during the five pre-plan years, 1951 through 1955. (See Table 3.) Although this estimate—as in the case of net investment—appears to be somewhat low, our analysis will not be hampered by using these data to obtain some idea of the pattern by which (gross) investment has been financed in recent years. The problem here concerns the means by which the economy provided gross savings to finance the volume of gross investment realized.

The National Planning Bureau's results suggest that Central Government's contribution to the financing of gross investment averaged slightly over Rp. 2 billion and that the private capital-intensive sector contributed amounts averaging between Rp. 3.5 and Rp. 4 billion. The remainder—varying from Rp. 1.4 billion to Rp. 1.8 billion—was financed by the desa sector (explicitly defined as the small agricultural sector by the National Planning Bureau).[11] The data presented by the National Planning Bureau prevent analysis of financing by strict national income accounting concepts. The local government component, for example, is included in the desa rather than in the government sector.

Central Government Financing

Since 1951, financing of Central Government's contribution to gross investment has been provided mainly from inflationary sources. If net savings on government account are defined as tax and tax-like revenues minus current expenditures, the government over the period 1951-1956 engaged in a substantial amount of dissaving. In some instances, the government, through employing one devise or another, was able to reduce spending in the private sector to offset its dissaving. During 1953, when government financing of investment totaled about Rp. 1.6 billion, its cash deficit amounted to just over Rp. 3 billion. About one-seventh of this deficit (Rp. 440 million) was financed by the noninflationary method of requiring prepayments from importers.* The remainder was financed by a combination of inflationary sources: revaluation of the gold stock (Rp. 1.7 billion), borrowing from the central bank (Rp. 600 million), newly issued treasury currency (Rp. 140 million), and reductions in balances of government agencies (Rp. 143 million). In 1954, with government gross investment approximating Rp. 2 billion, the cash deficit of Rp. 3.5 billion was financed almost exclusively by borrowing from the central bank (Rp. 3.2 billion). In 1955, with government gross investment and the deficit both amounting to about Rp. 1.8 billion, the deficit was fully financed by imposition of a new kind of importers' advance payments, the deposit of Rp. 5 million by all foreign import firms.† This produced a substantial reduction in the money supply and brought temporary respite from inflationary pressures. Obviously, this measure brought relief only during the period of "prepayment"; unless the amount of prepayment deposit is increased, it cannot be further used as a source of noninflationary financing of the government deficit. In 1956 the government found itself making net refunds of prepayments to importers, and this amount (Rp. 180 million) and the full amount of the cash deficit (Rp. 2.3 billion) were financed by borrowing from the Bank Indonesia.

For the most part, therefore, both government dissaving on current account and the finance of investment required resort to inflationary finance. This has led, *pari passu*, to an increase in the money supply,[12] and increased private spending as a large part of government

*These amount to a forced loan to the government so long as a given volume of import trade is maintained.

†The 1955 deposit was tantamount to a tax on importers, refundable only if import operations were discontinued. In March 1956 this levy was extended to Indonesian importers at the lower assessment of Rp. 500,000.

expenditures generated multiplier effects not offset by taxes or other leakages.

The fundamental question in assessing the merits of deficit-financed investment involves the impact of expenditures on output. The case for inflationary finance of development is frequently based on the presumed existence of underemployed resources (disguised unemployment) in the underdeveloped economy. If these resources can be brought into productive activity through increased government demand, or can be employed more fully, deficit-financed expenditures, it is argued, may generate little inflationary pressure on prices of consumer goods. Output of goods and services—through the absorption of unemployed resources—will shortly offset increased spending.

The lack of merit of this method for financing Indonesian economic development has been adequately demonstrated by experience with deficit-financed government investment programs. The problem in Indonesia has been, and continues to be, primarily one of providing capital equipment to complement unemployed labor resources. There has been little excess capacity in readily arable land or factories capable of absorbing these resources if, in fact, they could be transferred to the capital-intensive sector. Inflation-financed government investment has therefore tended to add to aggregate demand without generating increases in output. The gestation period of much of the government investment program has been uncomfortably long as bottlenecks of engineering, planning, and administrative skills have delayed the fruition of these projects. Increased output, therefore, has been long in appearing; in some cases projects were abandoned because the government failed to provide the necessary complements of essential managerial and entrepreneurial skills.[13]

Desa Sector Financing

Financing of investment in the *desa* sector has apparently shown quite a different pattern, apart from subsidies for capital formation received from Central Government (averaging about Rp. 300 million per year). The remainder, probably averaging about one and one-third billion rupiah annually (according to National Planning Bureau estimates), was predominantly financed by local taxation, direct mobilization of labor services, or the utilization of private savings mobilized within the sector itself. Mobilization of labor services, which has been used extensively by the more autonomous local governments, serves to direct seasonally unemployed resources to capital formation activities. (See Chapter 7.) This method of financing therefore adds to both the economy's real savings and its gross investment. The impressive volume of local government capital formation financed from this source as well as private, self-financed investment in this sector is important in accounting for relative price stability in the labor-intensive sector long after price inflation had threatened productivity in the capital-intensive sector.[14]

The significance of this type of financing for a comprehensive development program is discussed in Chapter 7. It might be well to point out here, however, that financial resources which can be mobilized within the labor-intensive sector itself may fail to respond to government efforts to transfer them to the capital-intensive sector through the pull of government inflation-financed expenditures. The Indonesian case may be unique in this regard; at any rate, the usual assumptions appropriate to such transfers in advanced economies appear to be invalid. First, as we have already suggested, it is doubtful that complementary capital goods can be developed rapidly enough to make large-scale transfers feasible. Secondly, we should note that the greater part of these resources in Indonesia represents seasonal unemployment from activities within the labor-intensive sector. Transfer of these resources from the sector would tend to reduce output of food and smallholders' exports since virtually all of the sector's labor resources are devoted to primary employment during certain peak employment periods. Finally, the geographical and economic dichotomy between Java and the outlying islands poses almost insurmountable problems to sectoral transfers. By and large, since the capital-intensive sector lies outside Java, sectoral transfer will involve considerable geographical relocation. Already a labor shortage has appeared in the outlying islands, with wages and living standards being perceptibly above those on Java.[15] Limited transfer of labor resources from the labor-intensive sector has satiated demands in the capital-intensive sector on Java, where seasonal employment with a high labor turnover is characteristic of factory and estate employment conditions. Transferring disguised "dynamic" unemployment to the more capital-intensive industries on the outlying islands is, therefore, the essence of the problem, but this cannot be done either by inflationary financing or cheaply in terms of capital requirements. In addition to possible adverse effects on Javanese peasant production, a program to bring about sectoral transfers on a large scale would involve the vast investment requirements of a massive relocation effort. In this case, the argument for raising output through relatively cheap transfers of disguised unemployment to more productive occupations vanishes. Indonesian experience with solving either population or productivity problems through relocation programs has been disappointing.

Disguised unemployment in the static sense, i.e., underemployed labor which can be transferred to other occupations without dynamic change in agriculture itself, is not available in significant quantities on Java. In a dynamic situation, however, where agricultural reorganization was under way so that the periodically unemployed labor would not be essential to maintaining output by temporary employment during peak seasons, significant quantities of labor might be transferred out of agriculture simultaneously with raising agricultural output. It is important, therefore, that disguised unemployment in agriculture be considered in dynamic rather than static terms. When viewed this way, the case for employing surplus agricultural labor by increasing aggregate demand without providing capital for reorganizing agriculture offers little attraction as a cheap and painless way to finance development.

So long as seasonal and other types of disguised unemployment are found in Indonesia's labor-intensive sector, it appears that these resources can be best mobilized for development purposes through local government and private inducements operating within the sector itself. As economic development proceeds, entry of labor into the capital-intensive sector will take place, of course, but it is doubtful that this process can be accelerated by Central Government efforts to force such transfers through disbursing newly created funds in the capital-intensive sector. These conclusions emphasize the importance of including a relatively large local-government component (or community development program) in Indonesia's development plan. We suggest in Chapter 7 that output can be increased through local investment, particularly if it is coordinated with the central development plan. Indonesia's First Five Year Plan appears to place too little emphasis on the community development ingredient, planning for a meager Central Government expenditure of about Rp. 200 million over five years. The local counterpart which might be generated through a coordinated program is set at about 25 per cent of the total five-year outlay. This appears to be considerably less than the desa sector could mobilize in an all-out effort toward self-improvement.

Financing in the Private Sector

Description of the sources from which gross investment (averaging Rp. 3.5 to Rp. 4 billion annually) was financed in the private, capital-intensive sector presents more of a problem. Possible sources include private (reported) voluntary savings mobilized by financial institutions, inflationary credit provided by private or government banks or by the government itself (indirect finance), and nonreported savings from current or past income (direct finance). The one point on which there is relatively satisfactory evidence is that private investment was not significantly offset by voluntary savings mobilized through financial intermediaries. In 1953 such private voluntary savings represented only 2 per cent of the private sector's estimated gross investment. With less gross investment estimated, and moderate growth of voluntary savings, the ratio of such savings to the sector's gross investment rose to about 5 per cent in 1954. In 1955 this ratio was about 4 per cent.

The amounts of voluntary savings mobilized by various financial institutions in recent years are presented in Table 6. While these institutions have not shown much success in collecting loanable funds from savers, they have engaged in a substantial volume of lending operations.

Table 6

PRIVATE VOLUNTARY SAVINGS MOBILIZED BY FINANCIAL INTERMEDIARIES, 1953-1956*

(Million Rp.)

	1953	1954	1955	1956
Bank Indonesia, Bank Negara Indonesia, Bank Industri Negara, and foreign private banks	34	11	49	68
Postal savings banks and private savings banks	37	39	34	45
Cooperatives	20	55	111	127
Private Indonesian commercial banks	0	60	2	26
TOTAL	91	165	196	266

*Increases in time and savings accounts, and in cooperative capital and deposits.

Source: Based on figures given in Report of the Bank Indonesia for 1953-1954, 1954-1955, 1955-1956, and 1956-1957.

What fraction of credit extended by the banking system was used to finance investment cannot be determined, but annual statistics reporting bank loans to various industries suggest that an important part of gross investment may have been financed through bank credit. In 1955, for example, the Bank Indonesia, the Bank Negara Indonesia, the Bank Industri Negara, and seven foreign-exchange banks increased their combined loans to the private sector by about Rp. 1.3 billion.[16] Of this total, the greatest single increase (Rp. 400 million) was taken by importers. Loans to exporters increased by about Rp. 35 million—largely because they were forced to hold larger inventories. New credit extended to industrial enterprises (Rp. 182 million) was clearly devoted primarily to financing investment in such diverse undertakings as a gunny-bag mill at Surabaja, a caustic soda plant at Waru, a match factory at Medan, and several others. In the same year (1955), credit extended by the small private Indonesian banks contracted slightly, but their credit outstanding represented only 7 per cent of the total loaned by all reporting banks to the private sector. On balance, in 1955 the banking system increased lending to the private sector by about Rp. 1.2 billion while mobilizing voluntary savings of only Rp. 196 million (about one-sixth of newly extended credit). It is doubtful, however, that more than one-half of bank credit to the private sector has been used to finance capital formation. This leaves the financing of most of the private (capital-intensive) sector's gross investment unaccounted for. Gross investment is estimated to have been about Rp. 3.5 to Rp. 4 billion, while indirect bank financing of capital formation appears to have been well below Rp. 1 billion, of which only a small part represented voluntary savings mobilized by banks.

The remainder must have been financed by a combination of nonreported business or personal savings, "political credits" to "Benteng" and government-sponsored firms, credit extended through nonbank channels, and foreign sources. For the more prosperous foreign firms—particularly the petroleum companies—internal savings and funds from abroad were apparently the most important sources of finance;[17] for others, it appears that current internal savings were unavailable for financing investment as rising domestic costs of production and relatively weak export markets threatened profits. This appears to have been true of the agricultural estates, largely owned by the Dutch before 1958.

This situation reflects financing problems common to many underdeveloped countries. In the first place, it suggests a low ratio of intermediary financing to the total finance of capital formation. To employ Raymond Goldsmith's terms, it also reveals a bias in favor of direct (nonintermediary) finance and therefore a small share of financial intermediaries in a low "financial interrelations relation ratio."[18] Yet evidence on financing economic development in advanced western countries has suggested that financial mediation has been an important concomitant of economic growth.[19] Restricted access to intermediary financing of investment tends to limit private investment to older and stronger firms and, frequently, to foreign firms with external facilities for financing (for example, supplied by parent companies). Secondly, the failure of intermediaries to mobilize personal voluntary savings to significantly offset their credit provision raises the danger of generating inflationary pressures through the financial system, particularly if commercial banks have, as in Indonesia, a tendency to extend credit without close scrutiny of the end uses to which it will be put. In the following chapter the point is made, with reference to Indonesia, that it is doubtful that commercial-bank credit creation is offset to any significant extent by hoards.

Savings, Investment, and Inflation

The impact of the pre-plan pattern of savings and investment can be most effectively evaluated from the perspective of all the forces operating to change the level of aggregate demand. The former Governor of the Bank Indonesia frequently alleged that the government deficit had been the greatest source of inflationary pressures during the post-independence years.[20] To assess the accuracy of this common presumption, the effects of government finance, the private credit-savings relationship, and the balance of payments on aggregate demand should be considered.

Table 7

GOVERNMENT EXPENDITURES, REVENUE, AND DEFICITS, 1952-1956

(Billion Rp.)

Year	Expenditures Reported	Revenue Reported	Actual Revenue	Budgetary Deficit	Inflationary Deficit
1952	13.5	9.2	7.9	4.3	5.6
1953	12.0	9.7	9.5	2.3	2.5
1954	12.0	8.4	8.6	3.6	3.4
1955	12.4	10.3	9.9	2.1	2.5
1956	18.0	15.7	14.0	2.3	4.0

Source: Reported expenditures and revenue and the budgetary deficit are from Report of the Bank Indonesia for 1952-1953 through 1956-1957. Figures for later years are given in Appendix I, Table I-1. For method of deriving actual revenue and inflationary deficit, see text.

Table 7 compares the budget deficit (1952-1956) as reported by the Indonesian government with what might be termed the "inflationary deficit." The latter concept eliminates from government revenues those sources of finance which are inflationary in nature (e.g., profits from the revaluation of the gold stock) and adds to revenues those which are similar to taxes in their effect on aggregate demand (e.g., importers' advance payments). This method results in relatively great differences in the estimated magnitude of the two concepts of the government deficit for 1952 and 1956.

The data in Table 7 can be used to give a rough approximation of the impact of the government's fiscal policy upon aggregate demand. Changes in government expenditures and tax receipts have direct and induced effects upon aggregate demand. Changes in government expenditures, a component of total spending, raise or lower aggregate demand directly, but they also affect the level of private expenditures by altering producers' receipts. Increased government expenditures, for example, have expansionary effects upon aggregate demand through adding to demand for goods and services (for collective consumption) and, in addition, through inducing new private expenditures from the increased income generated (multiplier effects). The expansionary effects will depend on the magnitude of leakages from the newly generated income; the increase in aggregate demand will equal the change in government spending multiplied by the reciprocal of all leakages from the new income.

Similarly, changes in tax receipts have both direct and induced effects upon the value of aggregate demand. Increased tax receipts reduce income available to producers for allocation to other sectors. Reductions in tax collections raise producers' receipts and consumers' disposable income. The magnitude of the effects of the changes upon aggregate demand depends upon the size of leakages from income affected by tax changes. The higher the private sector's propensity to leak income which would remain in private hands were it not for changes in tax collections, the less deflationary will be tax increases. A greater part of the new income captured by taxation merely replaces private leakages where the value of the marginal propensity to leak income is relatively large than where it is small. It follows that tax reductions will tend to be less inflationary where the leakages in the private sector are relatively great since a relatively larger part of the increased private income resulting from the tax reduction will not be spent. By contraries, a relatively high propensity to consume and relatively small leakages from new income in the private sector will lead to more deflationary effects from tax increases and more inflationary effects from tax reductions.

The effect of changes in government spending must be evaluated, therefore, in conjunction with changes (or the lack of changes) in tax receipts. The direct and induced effects of such changes upon aggregate demand may be summarized as follows:

$$\Delta Y = \Delta E\left(\frac{1}{1 - D}\right) - \Delta T\left(\frac{D}{1 - D}\right), \text{ where}$$

ΔY represents the change in aggregate demand <u>resulting from changes in fiscal policy</u>

ΔE represents the change in government expenditures

ΔT represents the change in tax receipts

D represents the marginal propensity to spend (domesestically) in the nongovernment sectors

$1-D$ represents total leakages from new income (i.e., the marginal propensity to leak income by savings, tax payments from newly generated income and imports)

The pertinent variables for which empirical values must be estimated are the marginal propensity to spend from income changes (D) and its converse, the marginal propensity to leak income from demand for domestic goods and services (1-D). Income arising from new expenditures may leak off to new private savings, to larger tax payments, or to increased import spending. Indonesian experience in the postwar period suggests that neither tax payments nor imports showed any significant response to increments in gross national product.

The nature of the tax structure and import policy is such that these leakages fail to change significantly with changes in gross national product. Hence these leakages are assumed to be zero. Private savings remain as the only significant leakage from increments in gross national product; evidence on the empirical value of this variable in Indonesia, however, is scanty. Reported private savings mobilized by intermediaries have shown little response to the growth of aggregate demand. Between 1953 and 1955 gross national product rose by about Rp. 37 billion while savings reported by banks increased by only Rp. 100 million. Savings in the form of cash hoards may have risen during this period, but, even if all of the newly created money were held as hoards, increments in savings in this form would have represented only one-seventh of the growth of gross national product between 1951 and 1955. Increments in personal savings appeared to be held mainly in the form of real assets—primarily consumer goods—but this process fails to increase the economy's supply of aggregate real savings.[21] We conclude that estimating the marginal propensity to save at 1/5 would be the maximum value we can assign to this variable.

In the formula above, therefore, the marginal propensity to spend would be given a value of 4/5, with leakages from gross national product changes of only 1/5. Private savings are the only leakage; changes in import spending and tax payments are taken as 0.

Applying these values to the variables D and 1-D, we would find that the expenditure multiplier would work out to 5 while the tax multiplier would be 4. If new government expenditures involved leakages from the domestic income stream, the balanced-budget multiplier would be less than unity, the value suggested by our results. In the Indonesian setting, however, we find no evidence suggesting a marginal propensity to leak government expenditures to imports or to noncurrent demand for domestic goods. The expansionary effects of government expenditures, even when matched by an equal increase in tax receipts, are therefore assumed to be unity. Where not offset by tax receipts, the effect of increased government expenditures upon aggregate demand would tend to have the full multiplier effect of 5, as our assumptions imply. We assume that the multiplier effects of changing expenditures and tax receipts work themselves out within a year, since the progression will have relatively little effect after the several income periods occurring within a single year.

Table 8

EFFECTS OF CENTRAL GOVERNMENT FINANCE ON AGGREGATE DEMAND, 1952-1956

(Billion Rp.)

Year	ΔE	ΔT	ΔY
1952	+ 4.4	- 2.4	+ 31.6
1953	- 1.5	+ 1.6	- 13.9
1954	0.0	- 0.9	+ 3.6
1955	+ 0.4	+ 1.3	- 3.2
1956	+ 5.6	+ 4.1	+ 11.6

Source: See Table 7.

Table 8 shows the effects of government finance on aggregate demand as measured under these assumptions. Over the 1952-1956 period the impact of the government budget was largely inflationary, adding a total of Rp. 46.8 billion to aggregate demand in 1952, 1954, and 1956 and reducing it by a total of Rp. 17.1 billion in 1953 and 1955. For the period as a whole, government finance led to an average annual increase in aggregate demand of about Rp. 6 billion.

In view of the government's close relationship to the Indonesian banking system, the government's impact upon the generation of inflationary pressures is also reflected by the growth of bank credit. So far as data are available, we can compare the growth of bank credit to private and semigovernmental institutions with the banking system's mobilization of voluntary savings. Although there may not be close correlation between these data and private savings and investment, this method provides a rough estimate of the private sector's addition to spending by credit creation. Perhaps it can be best assumed that the remainder of investment was offset by _ex ante_ savings by one of the patterns of finance suggested above. Under this assumption, which is justified by Indonesia's pre-plan experience during 1951-1956, bank credit and banked savings become the significant indicators of changes in the savings-investment relationship. A summary of changes in credit extension by the banking system (ΔL) and voluntary savings mobilized by banks (ΔSv) and their effect upon aggregate demand ($\Delta \gamma$) is presented in Table 9. The change in aggregate demand is estimated as

$$\Delta Y = \Delta L \left(\frac{1}{1 - D}\right) - \Delta Sv \left(\frac{D}{1 - D}\right), \text{ with D}$$

having the same value as above, i.e., 4/5.

Assuming that nonbank-financed investment was just offset by unreported savings, Table 9 reveals that the failure of bank mobilization of voluntary savings to keep pace with the growth of bank credit exerted a continuous impetus to the expansion of aggregate demand from 1952 to 1956. In 1955, for example, when government finance reduced aggregate demand by an estimated Rp. 3.2 billion, the growth of private bank credit provided a countervailing force in the amount of Rp. 5.2 billion. During the years 1952-1956, it led to an average annual increase in aggregate demand of approximately Rp. 3.5 billion. Estimates of increments in credit creation are conservative since they are taken from reported figures. "Political credits," which are alleged to have been important during this period,[22] have not been included. Such credits represent provision of funds by government or semigovernment financial agencies to favored Indonesian entrepreneurs. Needless to say, estimation of their quantitative significance is impossible. It has been alleged that new credit-creating institutions were organized for this purpose—the Bank Umum Nasional may be cited as an example—and that such institutions added one more source to a vast complex of banks devoted primarily to inflationary financing of rising private expenditures.

Table 9

EFFECTS OF BANK CREDIT AND VOLUNTARY BANKED SAVINGS ON AGGREGATE DEMAND
1952 - 1956

(Million Rp.)

Year	ΔL	ΔSv	$\Delta \gamma$
1952	+ 650	+ 17	+ 3,182
1953	+ 447	+ 90	+ 1,875
1954	+ 589	+ 165	+ 2,258
1955	+ 1,202	+ 196	+ 5,226
1956	+ 1,163	+ 266	+ 4,751

Sources: Data are compilations for all credit institutions for which statistics were reported in the annual editions of the Report of the Bank Indonesia. These include the Bank Indonesia, Bank Industri Negara, Bank Negara Indonesia, seven foreign-exchange banks, Bank Rakjat Indonesia, Jajasan Kredit, *desa* banks, twenty (largest) private Indonesian banks, postal savings banks, private savings banks, and cooperatives.

To complete the picture of forces operating to change the level of aggregate demand, we must also consider Indonesia's balance-of-payments situation during the pre-plan years. Data relevant to evaluating the impact of foreign trade are presented in Table 10. To get an accurate picture of this impact during the period, we include the years 1950 and 1951, when the balance of payments gave a great boost to aggregate demand, and, along with government finance, started the new Indonesian Republic along the path of inflation. In 1948 and 1949 the Indonesian balance of payments showed relatively large deficits on current account (about Rp. 0.8 billion against total foreign payments of about Rp. 2.0 billion in 1949). This condition was reversed in 1950, the first year of Indonesian independence, when the current account produced a surplus of approximately Rp. 1.3 billion.

The effects of balance-of-payments stimuli on changes in aggregate demand, presented in Table 10, are computed under the same assumptions made for government finance and private credit. Here the change in aggregate demand ($\Delta\gamma$) is measured as:

$$\Delta\gamma = \Delta EX \left(\frac{1}{1 - D}\right) - \Delta IM \left(\frac{D}{1 - D}\right).$$

There is some question as to what balance-of-payments variables should be used to measure EX and IM. We have chosen to use total current expenditures abroad for the value of EX and total current receipts from abroad for the value of IM. The major difference—in the Indonesian case—between this choice and employing merchandise exports and merchandise imports as measures of EX and IM is the relatively large amount of investment income paid by Indonesia to foreigners. These payments are similar to payments for other current items inasmuch as they represent a leakage from current Indonesian income to expenditure abroad, and thus they may be construed to have the same downward multiplier through induced effects on consumption spending as expenditures for imported goods and services.

Table 10

EFFECTS OF BALANCE OF PAYMENTS ON AGGREGATE DEMAND, 1950 - 1956

(Billion Rp.)

Year	Δ EX	Δ IM	ΔY
1950*	+ 3.9	+ 1.8	+ 12.3
1951*	+ 4.8	+ 4.9	+ 4.4
1952†	+ 1.8	+ 5.1	- 11.4
1953	- 1.6	- 3.4	+ 5.6
1954	+ .6	- .2	+ 3.8
1955	+ .9	- .7	+ 7.3
1956	- .3	+ 2.6	- 11.9

*Rupiah valuations of foreign trade for 1950 and 1951 are based on the effective foreign-exchange rate of Rp. 7.60 = U.S. $1.00 rather than the "official" rate of Rp. 3.80 = U.S. $1.00. In these years, export proceeds were earned at the rate of Rp. 11.40 = U.S. $1.00. Of this amount, however, Rp. 3.80 went to the government as a de facto tax on exports through the government's use of a foreign-exchange certificate system. Imports were paid for at the rate of Rp. 7.60 = U.S. $1.00. Thus, to accurately assess the expenditures multiplier, we must use the rate actually received by exporters (Rp. 760 = U.S. $100), and, to measure the effects of the import leakage, we must employ the actual rupiah rate paid for foreign currencies (Rp. 7.60 = U.S. $1.00).

†Beginning in early 1952, the government officially devalued the rupiah to Rp. 11.40 = U.S. $1.00 and abandoned the foreign-exchange certificate system. Beginning with 1952, therefore, this rate is employed for the rupiah valuation of both imports and exports.

Sources: Data are from balance-of-payments statistics published in annual editions of the Report of the Bank Indonesia.

The results in Table 10 reveal that the balance-of-payments changes exerted inflationary pressures on the Indonesian economy throughout the post-independence years with the exception of 1952 and 1956. In 1950 and 1951 these pressures were particularly strong, and in 1950 they were reinforced by an inflationary government deficit of approximately Rp. 1.7 billion,[23] with both expenditures and tax revenues showing large increases. In 1951, however, the government budgetary results showed a surplus of approximately Rp. 1.2 billion. Both expenditures and tax revenues appear to have been above 1950 values, but tax yields rose somewhat more than expenditures. Although the available data do not permit an estimation of the government's quantitative impact on aggregate demand in these years, it seems safe to conclude that the inflationary pressures generated by the balance of payments were not greatly mitigated by government finance in 1951 and in 1950 were considerably aggravated. Thus by 1952, the year in which our estimates of inflationary pressures generated by the various forces at work begin, the inflationary process was already under way.

The various forces leading to expansion of aggregate demand in Indonesia may now be combined to provide an estimate of total inflationary pressures during the period 1952-1956. This is done in Table 11.

Table 11

SUMMARY OF THE EFFECTS OF GOVERNMENT FINANCE, BANK CREDIT, AND THE BALANCE OF PAYMENTS ON AGGREGATE DEMAND, 1952-1956

Year	Government Finance (Billion Rp.)	Bank Credit (Billion Rp.)	Balance of Payments (Billion Rp.)	Total (Billion Rp.)	Percentage Change in Aggregate Demand*
1952	+ 31.6	+ 3.2	- 11.4	+ 23.4	+ 29.0
1953	- 13.9	+ 1.9	+ 5.6	- 6.4	- 6.0
1954	+ 3.6	+ 2.3	+ 3.8	+ 9.7	+ 9.0
1955	- 3.2	+ 5.2	+ 7.3	+ 9.3	+ 8.0
1956	+ 11.6	+ 4.8	- 11.9	+ 4.5	+ 4.0

*Based on the National Planning Bureau's estimate of the value of gross domestic product in 1952 (Rp. 81 billion).

Sources: Col. 1 taken from Table 8, Col. 2 from Table 9, and Col. 3 from Table 10.

The results from summating the effects of changes in government finance, inflationary (bank) financing of private investment, and the balance of payments are the same as those that would be provided by the use of a general formula compressing the various factors into form.* Such a general formula might be written:

$$\Delta Y = \left(\Delta E + \Delta I + \Delta EX\right)\left(\frac{1}{1 - D}\right) - \left(\Delta T + \Delta S + \Delta IM\right)\left(\frac{D}{1 - D}\right)$$

We note that Δ L and Δ Sv are used instead of Δ I and Δ S on the assumption that the latter variables are the best measures of changes in the value of investment expenditures and *ex ante* savings. This involves the assumption that, since nonintermediary financed investment was offset by nonbanked savings, this part of the savings-investment relationship caused no change in aggregate demand. This assumption implies that the effect of changes in the total savings-investment relationship upon aggregate demand can be measured by the relationship of changes in intermediary credit (Δ L) relative to changes in savings mobilized by intermediaries (Δ Sv).

The results show that government finance was the dominant source of inflationary pressures, although it did exert a deflationary impact in 1953 and 1955. Inflationary pressures were consistently aggravated by bank financing of investment. Over the five-year period, the balance of payments exerted a slight deflationary impact, but it served to reduce aggregate demand in the years when the government's impact upon the expansion of aggregate demand was strongest (1952 and 1956).† On

*Using the formula given for 1952, for example, we find the numerical values as follows: (4.4 + 0.65 + 1.8) X 5 — (-2.4 + 0.17 + 5.1) X 4 = 22.7. Differences from the result in Table 11 are caused by rounding figures.

†This should not be construed to imply that balance-of-payments variables behave independently of the other variables. Had it not been for government deficit financing, the balance of payments presumably would have exerted a greater and more consistently deflationary force upon aggregate demand.

the whole, aggregate demand rose year by year with the exception of 1953, when the combined forces produced a short-lived respite from inflationary pressures.

Aggregate Supply

The conclusion from the above analysis is that upward pressures on aggregate demand were greatest just after the transfer of sovereignty to the Indonesian Republic (1950-1952)—but continued to be exerted with considerable force in the three years just before the Five Year Plan was announced. Comparison of this conclusion with limited data on the behavior of aggregate supply yields interesting results.

Unfortunately, complete data on aggregate supply are not available. Indices of the physical volume of output have not been constructed, and the Planning Bureau's estimates of the value of gross domestic product in constant dollars involve so much extrapolation that we cannot trace the growth of output by this series. In the absence of aggregative data, we resort to the use of physical volume of output of the most important food crops and the volume of imports of consumer goods and raw materials. Combined, these series comprise the most important sources of supplies of consumer and capital goods. This method, however, omits supplies of domestically produced manufactures; but data are not available to furnish the basis for satisfactory measurement of changes in this component of total supply. No doubt, some expansion of output from this sector was achieved during the pre-plan period, but it appears that this had no significant effect on providing net increases in aggregate supply. Licensed capacity has grown somewhat in some local manufacturing industries while falling in others.

Supplies of Food

Data on the physical volume of output of Indonesia's six most important food crops are presented in Table 12. Output increased substantially between 1951 and 1954. In 1955, 1956, and 1957, however, output was below the record level of 1954. This supports our contention that the limit for expanding output by capital-cheap projects—even in agriculture—has apparently been reached. During the years of rising output of food crops, imports of rice were reduced substantially below the high levels of 1950-1952. By 1955, however, maintenance of domestic supplies required drawing down inventories of the Food Foundation (JUBM) by almost 400,000 tons. As a consequence, rice imports rose from 125,000 tons in 1955 to a new high of over 800,000 tons in 1956. Despite these measures, the prices of foodstuffs rose dramatically throughout Indonesia in 1955, 1956, and 1957, as shown in Table 13.

Table 12

OUTPUT OF SIX MAJOR FOOD CROPS,* 1951 - 1957

(Million Tons)

Year	Volume of Output	Percentage Change
1951	17.5	
1952	18.7	+ 7.0
1953	20.1	+ 7.0
1954	22.6	+ 10.2
1955	21.0	- 6.6
1956	21.5	+ 2.4
1957	22.3	+ 3.7

*The crops included are rice, maize, cassava, batata roots, groundnuts, and soybeans. See Appendix I, Table I-20 for breakdown by crop.

Sources: Data are from annual editions of the *Report of the Bank Indonesia*.

During the years of rising food output, on the other hand, prices of foodstuffs remained remarkably stable. After virtually doubling in the first two years of Indonesian independence,[24] there was little change in food prices between 1951 and 1954. The expansion of food output obviously absorbed much of the increase in aggregate demand during these years. However, it appears doubtful that Indonesia can look forward to recurrence of this success without relatively great increases in investment in the agricultural sector. Data on the behavior of food prices for 1951 through 1958 are presented in Table 13.

Table 13

INDICES OF FOOD PRICES, 1951-1958*

(1953 = 100, except for Makassar and Pontianak)

	Twelve Foodstuffs	Nineteen Foodstuffs			
Year	Countryside of Java	Djakarta	Makassar (Celebes)	Medan (Sumatra)	Pontianak (Borneo)
1951	92	89	86	103	113
1952	117	94	87	96	117
1953	100	100	87	100	114
1954	97	106	94	111	120
1955	127	141	135	167	171
1956	153	161	161	168	186
1957	160	177	169	165	...
1958	244	258	232	259	304

*See also Appendix I, Table I-21.

Sources: Report of the Bank Indonesia for 1956-1957 through 1958-1959.

Supplies of Imports

The Indonesian government has vacillated between rigorous import controls to protect its gold and foreign-exchange reserves and allowing severe drains on these reserves to counteract domestic inflationary pressures. Supplies of imported goods for consumer-goods markets have consequently fluctuated within rather wide margins. Data on the physical volume of imports destined for consumer-goods markets are presented in Table 14.

Table 14

IMPORTS OF CONSUMER GOODS, RAW MATERIALS, AND CAPITAL GOODS, 1951-1958*

(Thousand Tons)

Year	Consumer Goods	Raw Materials	Capital Goods	Total
1951	895	2,376	154	3,425
1952	1,313	3,240	196	4,749
1953	732	3,282	138	4,152
1954	583	3,190	125	3,898
1955	444	4,096	127	4,667
1956	1,292	4,386	172	5,850
1957	927	5,371	180	6,478
1958	875	2,515	117	3,507

*For value of imports, see Appendix I, Table I-16.

Sources: Annual editions of the Report of the Bank Indonesia, Appendices.

Much of the increase in the two years of relatively large consumer-goods import volumes (1952 and 1956) can be accounted for by disproportionately large imports of foodstuffs, particularly rice. In 1956, for example, imports of rice rose by about 650,000 tons, representing an increase in expenditure on rice imports of over Rp. 1 billion. Price inflation has been fought in the years of relatively great volumes of imports, therefore, primarily by increasing supplies of food at the cost of dangerously large reductions in Indonesia's monetary reserves.

Table 15

WHOLESALE PRICE INDICES OF IMPORTED GOODS, 1951-1958

(1953 = 100)

Year	Forty-four Import Commodities	Six Foodstuffs	Ten Textiles	Thirteen Chemicals
1951	99	67	109	99
1952	94	84	89	90
1953	100	100	100	100
1954	109	110	110	109
1955	145	144	169	151
1956	136	146	118	137
1957	160	178	137	141
1958	247	244	248	208

Sources: Report of the Bank Indonesia for 1956-1957 through 1958-1959.

Despite these measures, wholesale prices of imported goods—which represent the most important source of supply for many raw materials and finished goods essential to subsistence—have shown substantial rises since 1953. (See Table 15.) Prices of these goods showed alarming increases in 1955, a symptom of inflationary pressures which induced the government to relax import restrictions in 1956. While price inflation was successfully restrained by this step in 1956, foreign-exchange reserves had become so depleted that Indonesia's capacity to contain inflationary pressures by a liberal import policy had been virtually exhausted. We might also note that the situation in 1956 was eased by the import of 175,000 tons of rice (of a total 250,000 granted) from the United States under a surplus agricultural commodity agreement. All of this suggests that the Indonesian economy has reached a point where further expansion of aggregate demand will produce greater inflationary pressures on prices than those generated in the period before announcement of the Five Year Plan, a situation which emphasizes the necessity for providing for the finance of development from noninflationary sources.

Implications for Financing Economic Development

In summary, the period since independence (December 1949) has been one of relatively constant inflationary pressures inducing a general upward trend in prices. By the end of 1950, prices had already been doubled by increased aggregate demand generated by a dramatic change in the balance of payments from a current account deficit to a large surplus. This force continued throughout 1951, and inflationary pressures were accelerated by the continuous growth of bank credit made available to the private sector. In 1951 the government budget showed a fortuitous but relatively small surplus, whereas in 1950 it showed a deficit. Indonesia began its independence, therefore, with inflationary pressures on prices not offset to any significant extent by taxation or voluntary savings. Although the years since 1952 have been a period of retrenchment accompanied by stringent balance-of-payments controls, the government has failed to maintain price stability as repressed aggregate demand could scarcely be contained in 1955 and 1956. In the setting of a negligible domestic industrial base, and approaching the short-run capacity of agricultural output, aggregate demand has spilled over to the import-goods markets in ever greater volume. In 1955 these forces threatened to produce open price inflation, but they were restrained (in 1956) by the government's willingness to use a large part of its meager gold and foreign-exchange reserves to enhance domestic supplies. Continued expansion of aggregate demand, therefore, will tend to produce speedy and vigorous price responses, as evidence on price behavior during 1957 demonstrated.[25] If domestic economic stability is not to be sacrificed completely, financing economic development over the next several years will require abandonment of inflationary sources.

Moreover, it is clear that even the repressed price inflation of the pre-plan period has had adverse effects upon economic development. In the capital-intensive sector of the economy there have been persistent demands for increased wages. Man-hours lost during strikes chiefly concerning the wage-price issue, totaling less than 1 million in 1952, reached 5 million in 1953, about 2.4 million in 1954, 4.1 million in 1955, 7 million in 1956, and 8 million in 1957.[26] Wages in the capital-intensive sector increased by approximately 20 per cent in estate agriculture between 1954 and 1957 and by even larger percentages in other industries.[27] Despite the failure of wages to keep pace with domestic price rises, increased wage costs have been an important deterrent to the expansion of export earnings.[28] Export industries have become increasingly unprofitable, and neither the volume nor value of exports increased significantly between 1953 and 1956. Foreign enterprise has hesitated to expand the size of its investments in this context of constantly rising domestic costs of production, and it is in difficulty for precisely this reason.[29] In the face of flagging export earnings, the government turned in succession to reduction of export taxes, offering export premiums which allowed the exporter to obtain greater rupiah proceeds than sale of foreign exchange at the official rate provided, and, in 1957, to a comprehensive export certificate system tantamount to devaluation. These efforts have apparently failed to counter the inevitably unfavorable effects of domestic price inflation on export earnings.[30]

Inflation during these years has also affected the volume and direction of private investment. The Planning Bureau's figures suggest that gross private investment in the capital-intensive sector fell both in absolute amount and as a percentage of gross domestic product between 1952 and 1956. Officials of the Bank Indonesia have frequently noted an increased tendency to employ liquid funds for realizing short-term gains from inflation.[31] This is an inevitable symptom of inflation, particularly in underdeveloped countries where the risks of new productive investment are great. There can be little doubt that the last several years of Indonesian inflation, beginning perhaps in 1953 or 1954, have led to a substantial amount of misallocation of investment resources as they have been channeled to financing inventory hoards and speculative activity rather than to capital formation.

Inflation in Indonesia has further hampered economic development by unloosing balance-of-payments forces which have depleted foreign-exchange and gold reserves to dangerously low levels. In limiting the growth of export earnings while stimulating government and private demand for imports, inflation prompted the government to countenance severe reductions in gold and foreign-exchange holdings in an effort to restrain the upsurge of consumer-goods prices. Since 1952 the government has vacillated between exchange stringency—with consequent rising prices—and relative leniency to gain temporary price stability through the import of a greater amount of goods than current foreign-exchange earnings allowed. During 1956 and 1957, domestic price inflation was repressed by permitting foreign reserves to fall far below the legal cover ratio (20 per cent) for obligations of the central bank. Gold and foreign-exchange reserves, as measured for legal cover purposes, stood at Rp. 2.9 billion at the end of 1955, providing a cover ratio of 29 per cent.[32] By the end of 1956, reserves had fallen to Rp. 2.4 billion, lowering the cover ratio to 22 per cent.[33] At mid-year 1957, reserves totaled Rp. 1.8 billion and the cover ratio fell to the unprecedented low of 13 per cent.[34] By early 1958 it had fallen to 11.6 per cent, and a year later it was under 8 per cent.[35]

In assessing the implications of this unfavorable trend for the finance of economic development, the former Governor of the Bank Indonesia expressed his concern in these terms:

> At the end of 1956 there were no indications that the fall of foreign exchange reserves could be halted in the first months of 1957. Moreover, the events at the end of 1956 in the various regions of Sumatera and Sulawesi will certainly cause a further dwindling of the foreign exchange receipts of the country in 1957.
>
> . . . . . .
>
> In view of the above my considered opinion is that at the present stage the implementation of development projects either of the Government or private enterprise, requiring long term expenditure, for the time being must be postponed unless there are special additional sources made available for this purpose.
>
> Meanwhile, retrenchment of foreign exchange expenditures has its limits. Either to meet minimum needs of consumer goods or to supply badly needed raw materials, auxiliary goods or capital goods, such in order to keep the existing production machinery running, a minimum outlay of foreign exchange is necessary, which minimum cannot be lowered without disturbing the internal economic situation.
>
> . . . . . .
>
> . . . Retrenchment must not be limited to foreign exchange expenditure only, but must also go hand in hand with an endeavor to reduce the money circulation in the country. . . . In view of the fact that the increase of the money supply up to now was caused chiefly by the Government budget deficits, retrenchment of Government expenditure and/or increase of Government revenue are the foremost requirements for halting, or at least moderating the inflationary trends.[36]

Indonesia has now reached the point where restoration of economic stability has become sine qua non for effectively launching its development program. For this reason we have included elimination of the government deficit as one of the country's capital requirements for economic growth. In this context, the search for sources from which development may be financed over the short run must be limited to noninflationary domestic sources or external capital.

Notes to Chapter 2

1. For example, the Economic Commission for Asia and the Far East reports that "capital formation has been negligible in recent years." ECAFE, United Nations, Economic Survey of Asia and the Far East, 1954, Bangkok, 1955, p. xiv. Charles P. Kindleberger cites an estimate which places net investment at 0.5 per cent of net national product. Economic Development, McGraw-Hill, New York, 1958, p. 189.

2. S. Daniel Neumark, "The National Income of Indonesia," Ekonomi dan Keuangan Indonesia, Vol. VII, June 1954, pp. 348-391.

3. Ibid., Table III, p. 356.

4. See Eugene Grasberg, Indonesia's Investment Requirements, Center for International Studies, Massachusetts Institute of Technology, Cambridge, 1955, Table 6, p. 29.

5. National Planning Bureau, "Indonesia's Economic Developments, 1953," Ekonomi dan Keuangan Indonesia, Vol. VII, July 1954, pp. 410, 414-416, and "A Study of the Indonesian Economic Development Scheme," ibid., Vol. X, September 1957, pp. 611-613.

6. Ibid., p. 619.

7. Douglas S. Paauw, "Financing Economic Development in Indonesia," Economic Development and Cultural Change, Vol. IV, No. 2 (January 1956), pp. 174-175.

8. See, e.g., Tillman Durdin, "Barter Trade Hurts Djakarta," New York Times, December 21, 1957.

9. National Planning Bureau annual figures show this percentage at 5.1 for 1951, 7.2 for 1952, 5.8 for 1953, 5.0 for 1954, and about 5.0 for 1955. "A Study of the Indonesian Economic Development Scheme," loc. cit., Table III, p. 622.

10. Grasberg, op. cit., pp. 21-25. (Maintaining per capita consumption of all goods and services includes Grasberg's objectives 1, 2, and 3 detailed in Chapter 1.)

11. National Planning Bureau, "A Study of the Indonesian Economic Development Scheme," loc. cit., p. 619 and Table III, p. 622.

12. Between 1950 and 1955, the money supply virtually trebled, with the greatest percentage increases occurring in the later years. Report of the Bank Indonesia, 1955-1956, pp. 18-19.

13. Douglas S. Paauw, "The High Cost of Political Instability in Indonesia, 1957-1958," Internationale Spectator, Vol. XII, November 1958, pp. 532-540.

14. It was stated in the Report of the Bank Indonesia, 1954-1955 (pp. 13-14) that:

"To begin with there is the problem of the rise in the cost of living. Statistically, two spheres are to be distinguished, viz. the towns and the countryside. The family budgets in these two spheres differ; apart from rice, which plays an important role in both budgets, the urban sphere is not homogenous in so far as it falls apart into an Indonesian and non-Indonesian part, the latter group outweighing the other as regards its dependence on import goods.

"With respect to the development during the year under review, it must be considered fortunate that the available price index numbers for foodstuffs in the countryside were fairly stable. Price index numbers of rice did not deteriorate (1938 = 100, December 1953: 4,043, December 1954: 3,886). Other foodstuffs too, such as maize, coconut oil, salt, ground nuts, etc., remained on the same level. Meat and fish rose, but on the whole it can be stated that as far as foodstuffs are concerned, the cost of living index remained stationary.

"This does not apply to the towns, where price index numbers of nineteen foodstuffs rose some hundreds of points (300 to 500) from the end-1953 level. Cost of living index numbers for civil servants and unskilled labour were also up (civil servant: January 1950 = 100, December 1953: 238, December 1954: 272.5; unskilled labor: July 1938 = 100, December 1953: 2,421, December 1954: 2,672)."

15. Report of the Bank Indonesia, 1956-1957, p. 17.

16. Report of the Bank Indonesia, 1955-1956, p. 78-79.

17. Benjamin Higgins and Others, STANVAC in Indonesia ("United States Business Performance Abroad"), National Planning Association, Washington, D. C., 1957, pp. 100-101.

18. See Raymond W. Goldsmith, "Financial Structure and Economic Growth in Advanced Countries" in Capital Formation and Economic Growth, National Bureau of Economic Research, Princeton University Press, Princeton, 1956, pp. 113-160.

19. Simon Kuznets, "International Differences in Capital Formation and Financing," *ibid.*, pp. 52-59.

20. See *Report of the Bank Indonesia, 1955-1956*, p. 15, and *Report of the Bank Indonesia, 1956-1957*, pp. 11-14.

21. See Chapter 3.

22. *Report of the Bank Indonesia, 1956-1957*, p. 19.

23. This figure is estimated from the increase in total government debt in 1950. See *Report of the Bank Indonesia, 1953-1954*, Table 15, p. 60.

24. *Report of the Java Bank, 1951-1952*, pp. 75-76. An independent cost-of-living index shows a rise of 68 per cent between June 1950 and August 1951. Economic Commission for Asia and the Far East, United Nations, *Mobilization of Domestic Capital: Report and Documents of the First Working Party of Experts*, Bangkok, 1952, p. 45.

25. The Economist Intelligence Unit, *Three Monthly Economic Review of Indonesia*, No. 22, October 1957, Summary.

26. *Report of the Bank Indonesia, 1957-1958*, Table 94, p. 205.

27. *Report of the Bank Indonesia, 1956-1957*, pp. 183-184, and *Report of the Bank Indonesia, 1957-1958*, pp. 200-202.

28. *Report of the Bank Indonesia, 1954-1955*, pp. 14-15; *Report of the Bank Indonesia, 1956-1957*, p. 184; *Report of the Bank Indonesia, 1957-1958*, pp. 200-202.

29. The Economist Intelligence Unit, *Three Monthly Economic Review of Indonesia*, No. 22, October 1957, p. 6.

30. *Report of the Bank Indonesia, 1955-1956*, pp. 16-17, and The Economist Intelligence Unit, *Three Monthly Economic Review of Indonesia*, No. 22, October 1957, pp. 3-4.

31. *Report of the Bank Indonesia, 1953-1954*, pp. 27-28, and *Report of the Bank Indonesia, 1954-1955*, p. 13.

32. *Bank Indonesia Bulletin*, No. 11, Fourth Quarter, 1956, Appendix B.

33. *Ibid*.

34. *Bank Indonesia Bulletin*, No. 12, First and Second Quarters, 1957, Appendix B.

35. Abridged balance sheets of the Bank Indonesia (weekly).

36. *Report of the Bank Indonesia, 1956-1957*, pp. 103-104.

3

FINANCIAL INTERMEDIARIES AND THE SUPPLY OF SAVINGS

Voluntary Savings and Economic Development

Economists who have studied the problem of economic development usually conclude that voluntary domestic savings, indirectly supplied through intermediaries, cannot go far toward financing the capital requirements for raising output per capita.[1] This conclusion is considered to be particularly valid for the early stages of development, during which the rate of net capital formation must be doubled or trebled if self-sustained growth is to be achieved. In this chapter we examine some of the general factors limiting the growth of voluntary savings and the prospects for increasing voluntary savings in Indonesia.

Voluntary savings, from the point of view of the individual spending unit, refer to that part of current income which is not spent as payments for factors of production, consumer goods, and taxes or allocated as unilateral transfers. The spending unit which abstains from such allocations of its current income may do so either to defer spending until a later economic period or to use savings to finance investment. In the former case, voluntary savings lead to the acquisition of financial assets (or possibly hoards); in the latter case, voluntary savings lead to the acquisition of real assets in the form of productive capital.

It is not inevitable, therefore, that all voluntary savings supplied by individual spending units will materialize as investment in productive capital. Savings are automatically channeled to capital formation only where the saver and investor are the same spending unit and saving is explicitly undertaken to finance investment during the current economic period. This process has come to be known as self-financing or internal financing of capital formation.*

Where capital formation is not self-financed, however, there arises the problem of "finance" proper—the transfer of voluntary savings from saver to investor. It is important to emphasize that the financial process involves more than the transfer of voluntary savings from "surplus spending units" to investors. These funds may also be transferred to "deficit spending units" to finance expenditures on consumer goods in excess of current income (consumer dissaving).[2] The transfer of voluntary savings among individual spending units may involve either direct finance or indirect finance. Direct finance occurs if the surplus spending unit makes its voluntary savings directly available to borrowers by absorbing their direct debt. Indirect finance requires the intervention of a financial intermediary which obtains voluntary savings from surplus spending units in exchange for its own direct debt and distributes these funds to deficit spending units in exchange for their direct debt.[3]

The distinction between direct and indirect finance has special relevance for financial aspects of underdeveloped countries. A significant part of the voluntary savings of surplus spending units is directly transferred to finance dissaving of consumer spending units. In many

*Financing of capital formation may also occur by liquidation of the spending unit's stock of financial assets. In this case, however, such dissaving must be offset by voluntary saving by other spending units which acquire the financial assets released.

underdeveloped countries, a noninstitutionalized, unorganized money market provides the mechanism through which voluntary savings of upper-income spending units flow directly to finance consumer dissaving by lower-income groups. In this case voluntary savings performed by individual spending units are offset by dissaving of other (consuming) units, and the volume of savings which would otherwise have been available to finance capital formation is, pari passu, reduced.

If voluntary savings of individual spending units are not directly transferred to deficit spending units, they may either be hoarded or made available to financial intermediaries. If they are hoarded as cash and not offset by newly created credit or money, producers will find that they cannot make planned inventory liquidations at existing prices. In this case voluntary savings have been offset by involuntary additions to stocks of goods held over from one economic period to the next. This can scarcely be described as developmental capital formation since the involuntary addition to stocks is likely to lead to a contraction of gross national product in succeeding economic periods. Whether or not commercial bank loans to investors to offset such hoarding should be described as a part of the role of intermediaries (as Gurley and Shaw contend), we see here that commercial banks may play an important function in transferring to the finance of developmental capital formation those funds which otherwise would remain as hoarded voluntary savings, offset by involuntary inventory accumulation.

Although voluntary savings held as cash hoards are as deflationary as savings mobilized by intermediaries in their effect upon aggregate demand so long as they remain hoarded, this is not equally true of voluntary savings hoarded in other forms. In many underdeveloped countries, voluntary savings to be held over time are typically stored in such valuable and highly liquid assets as jewelry, precious metals, real estate, and foreign exchange. The conversion from monetary savings to savings hoarded in these forms represents a transfer payment from the saver to the seller of the asset, assuming that the asset was not produced during the period in which the saving occurred. In the typical situation, such assets are put up for sale to allow the seller to consume in excess of current income. Since real estate (including land) and hoards of jewelry and precious metals tend to be sold, therefore, to allow the individual who has saved in the past to dissave in the present, new savings hoarded in these forms tend to be offset by dissaving of other consumers.[4] This also appears to be true for foreign-exchange hoards withheld from export earnings in previous economic periods. In the situation where newly generated foreign-exchange earnings are hoarded, the deflationary effect of the local proceeds not being spent is nullified by the withholding of foreign exchange from financing the import of goods, which in itself is inflationary.

Voluntary savings which are hoarded may also become tied up in increased holdings of previously or currently produced consumer goods—rice, textiles, livestock, etc. If the consumer goods acquired represent stocks from past production previously hoarded by others, the argument is much the same as in the case where saving is embodied in jewelry, precious metals, or real estate. The transfer of funds to those liquidating such hoards is likely to lead to expenditures for consumption. When hoards are built up in the form of currently produced consumer goods, what may represent personal savings of one group of consumers is made available for consumer spending by others. In addition, this form of hoarding is inflationary from the supply side since it reduces the volume of consumer goods available for current consumption.

Finally, voluntary savings of surplus spending units may be supplied to financial intermediaries in exchange for their indirect debt (such as time and savings accounts, saving and loan shares). Financial intermediaries may be successful in collecting voluntary savings, however, only to loan these funds to finance consumption expenditures of deficit spending units. In this case we again observe that saving by one group (surplus spending units) is offset by dissaving of others (deficit consumer spending units) and that, to the extent that this occurs, the economy's savings available to finance capital formation have not increased.

It appears that the objective of increasing significantly the volume of voluntary savings to finance capital formation involves <u>both</u> increasing supplies of loanable funds <u>and</u> preventing their diversion to non-developmental uses. It is not so much a problem of drawing into the financial system funds which might otherwise be hoarded as cash, since financial claims on resources can be created by commercial banks to offset cash hoards. On the other hand, where the voluntary savings supplied by individual spending units are directly transferred to borrowers, public policy has virtually no means of influencing the allocation of loanable funds between deficit consumer units and investors. If, however, loanable funds can be garnered by financial intermediaries, rather than being directly distributed by savers, monetary policy may be employed to alter the relative shares distributed to finance consumption and investment. In most underdeveloped countries, solution to this perplexing financial problem involves extending the scope of the organized money market (commercial banks and all financial intermediaries) while circumscribing the scope of the unorganized money market. The obstacles to progress in this direction appear to be deeply rooted in social and cultural factors, although one particularly significant variable, the magnitude of the interest rate spread between the two sectors of the money market, may be responsive to monetary policy.

In most underdeveloped countries the volume of voluntary savings supplied from current income is small; moreover, financial institutions are unsuccessful in mobilizing and transferring savings to investors. Both factors are related to the low levels of productivity in such economies, with consequent low per capita income and consumption levels. Most consumer spending units must spend virtually all their current income on consumption to provide even a minimum subsistence standard. Yet, characteristically, not all personal incomes are low. Some individuals, at least, receive real incomes adequate to provide consumption expenditures for a comfortable standard of living and a margin for voluntary saving as well. Unequal income distribution may or may not produce much personal saving. Prewar studies of income distribution in Indonesia showed significant inequalities in income distribution[5] and small aggregate voluntary savings. In Japan, however, unequal distribution of income contributed greatly to the economy's ability to save for financing economic development throughout the "take-off" stage.[6] Conditions in a developing (or take-off) economy—Japan in the period 1900-1930—and those in an economy in an earlier development stage—Indonesia today—differ; and these differences are paramount in explaining different rates of voluntary savings. In predevelopment stages many of the patterns of traditional society persist, and these tend to reduce the economy's propensity to save. In the first place, upper-income groups assign considerable prestige value to conspicuous consumption, and there is a strong tendency for upper-income groups to spend the greater part of their incomes on consumer goods and services. In underdeveloped countries today this propensity seems to be reinforced by what Ragnar Nurkse has termed the "international demonstration effect," inducing all levels of income recipients to attempt to emulate standards of consumption in economically advanced societies.[7] Thus in the Philippines, despite great disparities in the distribution of income and wealth, the rate of saving and investment is very low relative to national income.[8]

One finds similar problems impeding the flow of individual savings from upper incomes to the finance of capital formation. The general pressure toward consumption in excess of income among the lower-income groups results in high rates of return on short-term loans to consumers and traders. Savings from upper-income groups are often made available to meet consumption needs of low-income groups without going through banking intermediaries. Such phenomena as pawnshops, the landlord who loans to his tenants during the growing season, and the unorganized money market in general are symptomatic of societies which channel the savings of one group to finance consumer expenditures of others. Since the total supply of loanable funds is small and consumer demand for credit is great, rates of return may be as high as 50-100 per cent per annum, or more, for consumer and trade credit while rates for longer-term investment loans are typically considerably less.

Thus, if voluntary savings from upper-income groups are to contribute to the finance of capital formation, it is important that they be mobilized by intermediaries—perhaps the government—capable of making them available to investors rather than consumers. In these conditions, increasing the aggregate volume of voluntary savings to finance economic development is tantamount to enforcing general reductions in consumption among those consuming units which habitually dissave.

If real income is growing, however, this result may be achieved by holding consumption near existing levels. Channeling voluntary savings to capital formation, therefore, may differ little from taxation in its effect upon consumption.

Finally, there are more general social and political forces in many underdeveloped countries which also tend to circumscribe the scope of voluntary savings in financing development. In seeking to emulate economic values of Western countries or to free themselves from the heritage of a colonial past, many underdeveloped countries have striven to achieve a more egalitarian distribution of real income. Redistribution of income through fiscal processes, social legislation, and labor union activities—frequently backed by government policy—have all had their place in reducing inequalities in income distribution. Although upper incomes may have been high relative to average incomes, their aggregate amount has usually been a relatively small share of national income. By and large, consumption levels of the lower-income groups are not significantly raised by redistribution, while the (voluntary) saving potential of these economies may be reduced by partly eliminating upper-income groups. Redistributive policies also tend to discourage investment incentives through high and graduated income and profits tax rates which may also discourage voluntary savings.

These remarks bring us to the consideration of a hypothesis which relates an economy's level of voluntary savings to its distribution of income in a rather unique way. W. Arthur Lewis suggests that the ratio of voluntary savings to national income is a function not just of inequality of income distribution but of inequality of a particular kind.[9] Lewis maintains that voluntary savings become a significantly large share of national income only where inequality of income distribution is such that the entrepreneurial profits are a relatively large share of national income.* Lewis believes that, if unequal distribution of income exists and the society's upper incomes accrue to landlords or traders, the volume of voluntary savings will be small since such groups continue to adhere to the values of their traditional society and use their incomes for conspicuous consumption and other purposes which deter capital formation. Therefore, despite unequal distribution of income in underdeveloped countries, profits, interest, and rental incomes as a whole tend to be a much smaller share of national income than in advanced economies. A study comparing these distributive shares as a percentage of national income in Indonesia and the United States seems to confirm this hypothesis. Profits, interest, and rental incomes represented about 24.5 per cent of the national income in the United States but only 11 per cent in Indonesia.[10] Indonesian data were based on a prewar year when the Dutch colonial government was in power and the redistributive policies of the new sovereign state had not yet taken effect. The presumption is that profits, interest, and rents would now comprise a lower percentage of national income than in 1939. However, it is not certain that this is true. Redistributive policies have been put into effect almost exclusively in the modern, Western sector of the economy, but these policies have been tempered by the Benteng program, which has sought to replace Western enterprise by Indonesian enterprise. Evidence suggests that property incomes and trade profits

*This appears to be a restatement, perhaps a refinement, of the classical hypothesis about saving. Moses Abramovitz believes that a proposition to the following effect is derivable from classical theory: "Capital formation, as a proportion of national product, tends to increase as the proportion of income going to profits rises." (National Bureau of Economic Research, Capital Formation and Economic Growth, p. 665.) Lewis' refinement might then consist of his emphasis on "capitalistic" or entrepreneurial profits. Presumably his statement also involves some verification through extensive empirical research.

have risen in the labor-intensive sector, and this too may have offset the effect of redistribution in the capital-intensive sector.*

On the other hand, in the Philippines it is clear that the share of entrepreneurial and property income is extraordinarily high—some 56 per cent—and still savings and investment are low. It should be emphasized, however, that this may not contradict Lewis' hypothesis since these can hardly be called "capitalistic profits." They are essentially returns based on positions of economic power in something less than a dynamic capitalistic society.

The social and political context of some newly independent countries such as Indonesia is hostile to the accumulation of capitalistic profits of the kind that played an important role in financing economic growth in the West. This fact does not lead to the conclusion that economic development will not occur; it does suggest, however, that the pattern of financing capital formation will probably be different if development is to occur. The scope of voluntary savings may be less significant, but this does not imply that the role of voluntary savings can be completely ignored. Even though the state may become the major source of financing development, mobilization of savings by intermediaries can play an important supporting role by redirecting loanable funds from consumer dissaving and low productivity investments to developmental uses. Mobilization of small savings from the agricultural sector, for example, might add to the scale of development expenditures which can be financed by noninflationary methods if this sector cannot be reached by taxation. Collection of small voluntary savings amounting to only 1 or 2 per cent of national income might well prove to be the critical margin in financing the take-off

*See Chapter 5.

to economic growth. Taxes are never popular, and it is desirable to do everything possible to encourage people in underdeveloped areas to save a larger share of their incomes—voluntarily.

Financial Intermediaries and Voluntary Savings in Indonesia

Despite a long history of colonial efforts to channel voluntary savings into financial institutions, credit extension in Indonesia has not been significantly offset by banked savings. We have shown that private investment has been financed primarily by inflationary bank credit or methods which have nothing to do with financial intermediaries. Frequently, the ability to invest depends on access to internal savings or other means of self-financing. Only a small part of bank credit finds its way to financing investment. Such voluntary savings as occur tend to remain outside the banking system and eventually flow through the unorganized money market, thus permitting dissaving by lower-income groups. This process fails to increase the economy's supply of real savings.

It is clear that the problem of mobilizing voluntary savings in Indonesia is not one of a shortage of financial institutions. Indonesia is plagued, if anything, by excessive proliferation of banking institutions, resulting in considerable duplication of lending functions and credit extension with little coordinated monetary control. The financial system includes a core of government financial institutions, a network of foreign banks, and a small but growing number of private Indonesian banks.*

*This is not the place to undertake a detailed review of financial institutions in Indonesia. The interested reader may refer to C. F. Scheffer, Het Bankwezen in Indonesië Sedert het Uitbreken van de Tweede Wereldoorlog (Banking in Indonesia since the Outbreak of the Second World War), Djakarta, 1952, or to the same author's Financieele Instelligen (Financial Institutions), Djakarta, 1955.

The government banks include the Bank Indonesia, the Bank Industri Negara, the Bank Negara Indonesia, the Bank Rakjat Indonesia, and specialized governmental lending agencies (Bank Desa, Lumbung Desa, and Jajasan Kredit), all almost exclusively financed by funds allocated through the government budget. There is some specialization of function among these governmental institutions. The Bank Indonesia has been the central bank since 1953. Although lending functions are eventually to be transferred to other banking institutions, it continues to do a significant amount of commercial business. Its central banking functions currently include the exclusive right to note issue and its role as the primary source of direct credit for the government.

The Bank Industri Negara is primarily concerned with extension of long-term credit to Indonesian estate agriculture, industry, and mining. The Bank Negara Indonesia specializes in the extension of credit to Indonesian exporters and importers. It has frequently been used as a source of finance to enable the government to carry out its Benteng policies.* The Bank Rakjat Indonesia, which was established in 1946 to succeed the Dutch colonial Algemene Volkscrediet Bank, was originally intended to replace the Dutch institution in extending credit primarily in the rural sector. However, its function was redefined in 1951; since that time it has sought to extend credit to medium-sized and small commercial and industrial firms. Between 1951 and 1957 the percentage of this bank's total credit offerings extended in the rural sector fell from 49 to 9 per cent, while the percentage extended to medium-sized and small commercial and industrial concerns rose from 43 to 77 per cent.[11]

*These policies are designed to promote the handling of export and import business by Indonesian nationals. Special licensing and credit arrangements are offered to encourage this development.

Both the desa banks and the desa lumbungs have been revitalized since 1952. The desa banks are primarily concerned with extending small monetary loans to agriculturalists; the desa lumbungs are concerned with extending rice loans to the rural sector. The Jajasan Kredit (Credit Foundation) is essentially a guarantor agency. It provides credit guarantees for approved enterprises which are unable to provide collateral for ordinary commercial bank loans. Guarantees are provided primarily for credits obtained from the Bank Negara Indonesia and the Bank Rakjat Indonesia. In addition to these agencies with commercial banking functions, the government operates a postal savings bank, Bank Tabungan Pos, and a state pawn shop service. The postal savings bank, which is a continuation of the original Dutch institution, has had some success in collecting small-scale deposits throughout Indonesia. The state pawnshop service continues to expand gradually in terms of both the number of pawnshops in existence and the total amount of loans outstanding. All of the governmental financial institutions have local offices throughout the archipelago.

Lack of coordination in the operations of the governmental financial institutions has been intensified by the entry of several government ministries into the credit field. In a statement on the government's credit policy, former Minister of Economic Affairs Iskaq pointed out that his Ministry granted credits to small firms in several areas of enterprise.[12] Such credits are administered through a number of specialized agencies, including Jajasan Kredit, Djawatan Koperasi (Department for Cooperatives), the Crediet Industri Ketjil (Small Industries Credit Bureau), Jajasan Fonds Keradjinan (Office for Handicrafts Credits), and the Bank Rakjat Indonesia (Indonesian People's Bank). Other ministries have felt obliged to follow this lead. The Ministry of Agriculture grants credits through the Kantor Gerakan Tani (Office for Peasant Movement) and the

Jajasan Perkebunan Rakjat (Smallholders Bureau); the Ministry of Internal Affairs performs a similar function through the Biro Rekonstruksi Nasional (Bureau of National Reconstruction); and the Ministry of Labor has its own credit agency in the Djawatan Penempatan Tenaga (Labor Exchange Office). The fact that these agencies engage only in the extension of credit rather than in the collection of resources from which credit may be extended underscores the necessity for simplifying the whole structure of government credit operations if monetary controls are to contribute to the finance of development.

There are seven important foreign private banks in Indonesia which in 1959 had still escaped full nationalization by the government in the anti-Dutch campaign that began in December 1957. These foreign banks have provided banking services for the foreign community and have been primarily concerned with the financing of foreign enterprise. Along with the government financial institutions, they dominate the banking business in the country. At the end of 1957 the foreign and government banks had outstanding credits amounting to Rp. 25,462 million while private Indonesian banks had only Rp. 846 million outstanding. The emergence of private banks, the number of which is rapidly growing, is predominantly a postwar phenomenon. Their credit has been largely extended to small exporters (in Sumatra) and to small traders (in Java), although in 1956 their loans to small-scale industry rose substantially.

The final component of the financial system in Indonesia is the stock exchange in Djakarta, which began business on June 4, 1952. It has provided facilities for turnover of the securities outstanding. However, domestic entrepreneurs have not used the stock exchange to float new issues; the Bank Industri Negara has offered a few issues to nonresidents holding blocked accounts.[13] The Governor of the Bank Indonesia described the activities of the stock exchange in these terms:

> Unfortunately it must be admitted the stock exchange business here in Indonesia is still of little significance. . . . This state of affairs must be attributed in large measure to the public's general unfamiliarity with the possibilities of the stock exchange, and to the great inclination to invest savings in real estate and movables.[14]

The credits extended to the private sector by some of the important institutions in this complex financial system are given in Tables 16 and 17.

Table 16

CREDIT OUTSTANDING:
BANK INDONESIA, BANK NEGARA INDONESIA,
BANK INDUSTRI NEGARA, AND FOREIGN PRIVATE BANKS
JANUARY 1953, DECEMBER 1953 - 1956
(Million Rp.)

	Jan. 1953	Dec. 1953	Dec. 1954	Dec. 1955	Dec. 1956*
Semigovernment enterprises	438.8	162	321	613	455
Autonomous bodies	0.3				
Banks and credit institutions	130.6	50	60	41	55
Insurance companies and savings banks	3.9	7	4	17	16
Rice mills	6.1	7	8	4	4
Trade in domestic products	52.8	55	103	83	83
Exporters	221.1	257	359	390	375
Importers	527.5	516	457	867	1,367
Sugar plantations	487.8	490	444	364	318
Other plantations	184.9	219	156	187	241
Industrial enterprises	149.9	239	366	302	354
Storage and transport enterprises	98.1	111	127	44	69
Other enterprises	84.2	130	239	423	463
Individuals	15.1	15	16	67	125
Total	2,401.1	2,258	2,660	3,402	3,925

*For 1956 the figures omit loans extended by the Bank Industri Negara.

Sources: Data are from annual editions of the *Report of the Bank Indonesia.*

The data in Table 16 indicate that approximately one-half the credit extended by the government banking complex and the large foreign banks flows to semigovernment enterprises and the trading sector of the economy. Similarly, over two-thirds of the credit extended by Indonesian private banks has been absorbed by the trade sector (Table 17). Agricultural plantations, the other important consumer of organized credit, rely heavily upon the resources of the foreign banking system. Such credit extension to the private sector has been completely overshadowed by the Bank Indonesia's holding of government debt. For example, at the end of 1956, government indebtedness to the Bank Indonesia stood at Rp. 10.3 billion, while all other bank credit totaled Rp. 3.9 billion.[15]

Table 17

CREDIT OUTSTANDING:

TWENTY INDONESIAN PRIVATE BANKS

1953 - 1957*

(Thousand Rp.)

	1953	1954	1955	1956	1957
Trade	75,727	114,966	101,943	317,755	294,343
Industry	15,156	30,221	42,250	101,196	243,862
Transportation	3,936	4,347	6,011	6,438	16,815
Estate agriculture	3,163	9,430	10,911	7,423	13,329
Individuals	2,823	17,200	9,682	23,719	22,486
Sundry	1,246	23,039	10,833	5,645	81,703
Total	102,051	199,203	181,630	462,176	672,538

*Figures refer to December 31 of each year.

Sources: Report of the Bank Indonesia for 1954-1955 through 1958-1959.

The Unorganized Sector of the Money Market

The foregoing description would be incomplete without some reference to the unorganized money market. One of the distinct features of the credit system in Indonesia is the wide range of both interest costs and terms under which credit is extended. The important differences are those between the organized market we have described above and the unorganized sources, consisting mainly of firms and individuals who extend credit as an adjunct to other activities. Despite the establishment of many government credit agencies, small producers and traders (particularly retailers) are still forced to rely on the unorganized sector of the market for short-term credit.* Credit facilities made available by the government (e.g., the Bank Rakjat Indonesia) are impractical when ready access to credit is required. Processing of loan applications by the government credit agencies is a slow, cumbersome procedure, and risks of rejection are great. Furthermore, strict collateral requirements are maintained unless credit is extended for political reasons, which is rarely true for small-scale borrowing. Similarly, the standards demanded by private foreign and Indonesian banks cannot be met by most small borrowers. The guarantor provision of Jajasan Kredit is also highly selective. The small industrialist or trader lacking personal sources of finance turns, therefore, to private lenders. Interest rates on credit from this source range from 2 to 10 per cent per month, with the rate charged depending on informal conditions surrounding the

*Alice Dewey finds in the area which she studied intensively only two "sources of new capital" available to small-scale retailers (bakuls): private moneylenders and the government's market (pasar) banks. She finds the former to have declined in importance as a source of trade credit. ("The Market," manuscript prepared for the "Modjokuto" series to be published by the Free Press, Glencoe, Illinois.)

loan—personal contacts, prestige, and status. Since there is little flow of financial resources between the organized and unorganized money markets, a discontinuous interest rate structure emerges. Interest rates on loans extended through the government banks and the private banking system tend to be relatively low since these loans are offered primarily to the best credit risks. Interest rates demanded and obtained by private lenders are several times as high. Credit is not available on terms between these extremes.

These symptoms of Indonesia's undeveloped credit system have significant bearing on the prospects for mobilizing savings through public and private intermediaries or security markets. Loanable funds provided by surplus spending units may be loaned out through the informal money market at highly remunerative rates of interest. Since the existing financial institutions do not mobilize savings on a large scale, their resources are inadequate to provide credit on a scale adequate to force these rates down. The net effect is that savings loaned in the informal sector are associated with a high rate of return. To the extent that high interest rates stimulate voluntary savings, these savings tend to be diverted to the unorganized sector of the market. Current supplies of voluntary savings tend to flow to uses not consistent with developmental objectives. In short, credit extended from noninflationary sources—voluntary savings—tends to be allocated in large part for nondevelopment uses while credit extended from inflationary sources—the banking system—is restricted to prime borrowers or those with political advantages. Hence it is important that efforts be made to channel the resources now dissipated through the unorganized sector of the money market to the organized sector, where the allocation of loanable funds can be made subject to control by monetary authorities.

Increasing Bank Mobilization of Voluntary Savings

Voluntary savings mobilized by financial intermediaries are defined here as claims of depositors on these institutions in the form of time and savings deposits. The failure of Indonesian financial institutions to mobilize loanable funds can be demonstrated by comparing their indebtedness to suppliers of loanable funds with the total money supply. The comparative figures through 1956 are given in Table 18.

Table 18

TOTAL MONEY SUPPLY AND VOLUNTARY SAVINGS MOBILIZED BY INTERMEDIARIES, 1951, 1953-1956

(Million Rp.)

	1951	1953	1954	1955	1956
Time and savings deposits:					
Combined figures (all major banks)	95	119	153	212	180
Private Indonesian commercial banks	12	15	74	75	115
Postal savings banks and private savings banks	77	141	180	214	259
Total	184	275	407	501	554
Money supply:					
Currency	3,328	5,218	7,474	8,647	9,372
Demand deposits	1,706	2,269	3,643	3,587	4,021
Total	5,034	7,487	11,117	12,234	13,393
Time and savings deposits as per cent of money supply	3.6%	3.7%	3.7%	4.2%	4.1%

Sources: Data are from annual editions of the _Report of the Bank Indonesia_.

Only the postal savings banks have shown progress in accumulating savings; however, their total savings accounts were only Rp. 225 million in 1956.

The volume of voluntary savings mobilized by Indonesian intermediaries is small even when compared to that of other underdeveloped countries. As computed from Table 18, mobilized savings are about 4 per cent of the money supply. In recent years they have been nearly 30 per cent in India (as an example of an underdeveloped country) and about that same percentage in the United States. The Indonesian proportion has remained relatively constant over the period observed in spite of efforts to increase voluntary savings. Increases in banked savings have been unimpressive because they have been offset by rapid expansion of the total money supply. Even in absolute terms, voluntary savings grew from Rp. 174 million in 1951 to only Rp. 540 million in 1956. Annual increases have not offset a significant fraction of investment expenditures, as we have already pointed out.

These figures suggest that these institutions are not discharging the intermediary function on a significant scale, a problem underlined by the fact that Indonesian banks have not been able to dispose of their capital stock by sales to the public but have had to rely on government capital provision. The Governor of the Bank Indonesia referred to the problem in these terms:

> In general, however, I have to state that insuffcent attention has been devoted to what I have described above as the first essential—sufficient capital of their own and private balances. There was still too persistent an inclination to open up banking and credit businesses with capital which had been advanced by the Government or the Central Bank. Attempts to attract credit balances from the private individual were not sufficiently fostered; instead, the chief inclination has been to try and obtain government deposits.

> My own view is that this tendency is to be regretted, because it is alien to the standards of a sound banking system, which stands or falls according to the contribution of the bank's own capital and the attraction of credit balances. Also, in my opinion, the attraction of giro [clearing] balances and money deposits from third parties by the private Indonesian banks is an absolutely essential first step towards building up of capital funds in the Indonesian community. The Indonesian banks will have to prove their social function and their usefulness by being in a position to inspire public confidence and attract money from third parties; not, however, by lending money,—which some obviously regard as their main object,—from funds provided by the Government or by the Central Bank. By so doing, they would in the end become mere branch offices of the Government or the Central Bank. At the same time, every attention must of course be given to the establishment of a well-equipped and efficiently functioning administration.[16]

In short, practically all of the funds which are available to the indigenous Indonesian banking system are obtained from government subscription to capital, government advances or deposits, and advances from the Bank Indonesia. Capital subscription in the case of the government banks has been almost exclusively provided by the government. In addition, the government has deposited its own funds or authorized the Bank Indonesia to deposit funds in the government financial institutions. It is these funds from a combination of government sources which for the most part provide even the basic working capital for Indonesian banking operations. These institutions have failed to mobilize either capital or deposits from the private sector of the economy.

It should also be pointed out that the ratio of demand deposits to total money supply is considerably lower than in advanced countries. In fact, this ratio has fallen during the past few years, indicating a growing preference for liquidity and perhaps the reduced scope of

Western enterprise.* The ratio of demand deposits to total money supply fell from 49 per cent at the end of 1947 to 41 per cent at the end of 1950. By the end of 1951 it had fallen to 34 per cent, after which time it gradually fell to 30 per cent, where it has remained since late 1955. In part, this trend reflects the fact that money newly generated through the government deficit is ordinarily put into circulation as cash rather than through deposit currency. More basically, however, it reflects the lack of acceptance of deposit money as a means of payment and other general impediments to the use of deposit money in an underdeveloped country. (Any foreigner who has visited Indonesia finds himself tempted to hold currency rather than demand deposits because inefficient management causes delays in making bank deposits and withdrawing currency.)

Tax enforcement also has conflicted with efforts to stimulate the growth of bank deposits. As the new Indonesian government has become more firmly established, enforcement of direct taxes has been increasingly tightened. To a large extent, taxation of the upper-income groups has been based on visible evidences of wealth, and bank accounts have been used as one of the most accessible indicators. Firms liable to taxation are not required by law to register with tax authorities. The administrative staff available to check reported statements of income and assets is inadequate to enforce the accuracy of such statements. Frequently, accounts held at government and private banks have been used as a time-saving method to estimate current income and assets for both income and capital assets taxes. As this policy has become more

*This situation is probably of significance to those who prefer to include demand deposits in the volume of voluntary savings mobilized by financial intermediaries.

generally employed by the tax authorities, upper-income groups have tended to shy away from holding financial assets in the form of bank deposits.*

The greatest deterrent to more extensive mobilization of savings by the banking system, however, appears to be the more attractive rates of return offered in the unorganized credit market. Petty lenders are found throughout Indonesia, and no amount of propaganda would induce them to abandon their profitable business. It appears unlikely that this source of savings can be tapped for economic development until the pronounced spread between interest rates is greatly reduced. Short of this, perhaps the only feasible solution would be placing restrictions upon such credit activities by strict licensing requirements, but it is doubtful that the Indonesian government would be able to cope with the administrative demands of such a system during the development period.

There may also be obstacles to mobilizing voluntary savings resulting from traditional customs of hoarding. So long as funds remain hoarded as cash, they have the same effect of reducing aggregate demand as they would if mobilized by banks and used to reduce credit from inflationary sources. The problem in Indonesia is more intractable, however; although hoarding is a significant social phenomenon, hoarded voluntary savings are not ordinarily held in the form of currency but in the form of jewelry, precious metals, or other physical assets. In the urban sector this may reflect the recent history of price instability; in the rural sector it probably reflects basic cultural

*In August 1958 the Ministry of Finance was reported to be drafting a bill on bank secrecy. According to the Antara report, "as a first step, the Finance Minister has instructed tax collectors not to ask for the list of banks' clients for taxation purposes." (Antara [New York edition], August 22, 1958, p. 3.)

biases.* One student of Indonesian society puts the matter as follows:

> The average Javanese seldom has much cash on hand. Money is not banked nor is it usually "hidden away under the mattress," so to speak. . . . Instead, the average Javanese buys something with his money. If it is a large amount he buys a cow or a goat or perhaps just a chicken. These goods are then considered to be potential sources of cash to be sold as the need arises. . . . Capital stored in this way is seen as largely static, not as an investment which is expected to yield interest, except perhaps in the case of land. . . . The object bought is primarily a way of saving one's cash, and in this view a gold bracelet is equal to a pair of lambs. . . . The jewelry, livestock, etc. owned by a Javanese family are a potential source of cash, and when the need arises the family sells these things. . . . I seldom heard of anyone selling such things in order to get capital to be invested in business. In fact, the Javanese, as a rule, dislike to put their own money into business ventures; they would much rather work with borrowed capital.[17]

Apart from the direct flow of voluntary savings to the unorganized sector of the money market for high rates of return, voluntary savings do not arise from interest-earning motivation, and, hence, they tend to become embodied in noninterest-earning real assets. It is, of course, possible that hoards of real assets may produce lucrative profits in periods of inflation, but this motive does not appear to be germane to saving in traditional Indonesian society. The opposite is perhaps more true. There appears to be common fear of loss of value from holding currency or banked savings in contrast to a general belief that real assets can be turned over easily and without loss of value. This condition underscores the importance of maintaining price stability if prevalent preconceptions are to be dispelled in an effort to increase

*The intensive "Modjokuto" study by an interdisciplinary group of Center for International Studies social scientists consistently emphasizes these limitations to increasing voluntary savings.

mobilization of voluntary savings by intermediaries. It also suggests that ready access to pawnshops, which insure transferability and liquidity of noncash hoards, may conflict with the objective of increasing banked savings.

The nub of the matter, therefore, consists of capturing savings which now flow to the unorganized sector or to noncash hoards. Perhaps this cannot be done by enhancing incentives for voluntary saving; taxation may be the only effective method. In Indonesia it appears that motivations to save in monetary form for reasons other than extending credit at high rates of return are few. Relatively high time preferences and heavy discount of the future are characteristic of underdeveloped economies; these lead to a high propensity to consume. The inducement to save for old age or emergencies is reduced by the ability to finance these needs through the family or community, and these communal values are still dominant throughout most of Indonesia. Where savings are made for these motives they tend to flow to hoards rather than to intermediaries.

Our review of Indonesia's financial system suggests that prospects for financing economic development through mobilization of voluntary savings are not favorable. Although there is a multiplicity of financial institutions in Indonesia, demand for credit is far from satisfied. The formal banking system has done little more than add to the supply of credit made available to semigovernment institutions and large exporters and importers in the capital-intensive sector. Existing financial institutions, both public and private, have not been effective in mobilizing savings to offset the growth of bank credit. Resources from which credit has been extended to the private sector have increasingly been obtained from inflationary sources provided by the government.

Meanwhile, the credit needs most closely related to economic development, i.e., long-term credit for investment purposes, have gone unsatisfied.

From the viewpoint of financing economic development, it is important that the banking system be encouraged to provide an increasing supply of real savings which can be transferred to investors, public or private. A large part of real savings supplied by surplus spending units may be dissipated to finance consumption where, as in Indonesia, the banking system fails to mobilize voluntary savings. Again, voluntary savings may fail to finance capital formation where, as in Indonesia, the greater part of bank credit is not made available to investors. Nor does an abundant supply of financial institutions with adequate credit-creating powers insure an increase in real savings. It may merely lead to an expansion of aggregate demand and hence to inflation. We have already observed that bank credit has become an increasingly important source of inflationary pressures in Indonesia.

Control of Credit

Measures to increase the volume of real savings for the finance of capital formation should encompass efforts to increase voluntary savings as well as efforts to allocate loanable funds so that voluntary savings will be channeled to investment rather than consumption spending. The latter requires the assertion of monetary control over the volume and qualities of credit extended by the banking system. However, during recent years Indonesia has sought an increase in the number of banks and the volume of credit almost as a goal in itself. In addition, there has been the paramount objective of financing Indonesian entrepreneurs, particularly in the trading sector, to replace foreign enterprise. Political credits to private Indonesians under the nationalistic mandate of Benteng policies have aggravated uncritical expansion of bank credit. If financing capital formation is to be enhanced, these funds must be allocated on the basis of sound development criteria, and the entire banking complex must be brought under the control of Indonesia's monetary authority—the Monetary Board and the Bank Indonesia.

Since 1955 Indonesia has begun to take tentative steps toward the assertion of control over the banking system. In January 1955 the government issued an ordinance delegating new monetary powers to the Bank Indonesia, the Ministry of Finance, and the Monetary Board.[18] In addition to requiring specified minimum amounts of paid-up capital for bank licensing by the Ministry of Finance, this ordinance required full reporting of bank activities to the Bank Indonesia. The most important provision of the ordinance (Article 9) granted to the Bank Indonesia potentially great powers of credit control, including limitation of the quantity of credit which individual banks may extend, restrictions upon particular kinds of credit, and the setting of minimum and maximum interest rates charged. Credit may be limited by requiring that a part of "the liquid resources of every credit institution be deposited with the [central] Bank, be invested in treasury bills, or be otherwise tied up."[19]

The problem in Indonesia is that such controls have different effects on the stronger well-established foreign banks and the relatively weak newly formed Indonesian banks. The requirement that banks provide a minimum amount of paid-up capital (Rp. 2.5 million for commercial banks) before being licensed suggests the nature of this problem. While foreign banks had no difficulty meeting the requirement, 65 per cent of the Indonesian-owned banks (59 of a total of 91 in 1956) had failed to muster paid-up capital of the required amount by mid-1957.[20] Most were granted a temporary (two-year) license to continue business under the authority of the ordinance which allowed the Ministry of Finance to grant exceptions. If, after the two-year period, capital deficiency persisted, further extension might be granted by the Monetary Board. In the meantime, these banks have continued to operate by virtue of government financial assistance,[21] a situation which implies that their resources continue to be provided primarily from inflationary sources.

The assertion of monetary control affects both foreign and Indonesian banks, while indigenous bankers protest that only foreign banks should be strictly regulated if Indonesia is to free herself from foreign economic domination. The private Indonesian banking association (Perbana) has explicitly called for this philosophy of regulation as well as greater assistance to Indonesian banks.[22] In the prevailing anti-foreign climate in Indonesia, monetary control over the Indonesian-owned component of the banking system is not likely to be vigorous. On the other hand, the amount of private credit supplied by these banks has increased considerably. The problem is aggravated by the fact that many government financial institutions, which have similarly increased in importance as sources of inflationary credit, lie outside the scope of central bank monetary control, allied as they are with particular ministries of the government.

The main practical import of the 1955 ordinance has been selective regulation of credit extended to importers.[23] When importers' prepayment requirements (rupiah cost plus import surcharges) were raised to 100 per cent in September 1955, importers' demand for bank credit to finance this prepayment threatened bank liquidity. The Bank

Indonesia undertook to rediscount importers' notes up to 40 per cent of prepayment for foreign banks and 50 per cent for Indonesian banks. Since that time credit policy has mainly consisted of varying the percentage of prepayment indebtedness which can be discounted. In 1956 the percentage was changed from 40 to 20 and finally to 0 for foreign banks, and from 50 to 40 to 30 for Indonesian banks. In early 1956, moreover, the Bank Indonesia ordered banks to cease granting post-import credits to importers since such credits were used to finance increased inventories of imported goods for speculation.[24]

In March 1957 the Monetary Board (consisting of the Minister of Finance, the Minister of Economic Affairs, and the Governor of the Bank Indonesia) issued a decree designed to further enhance monetary control. This decree restrained commercial and savings banks from engaging in trading activities and virtually all other nonbanking enterprises. The former Governor of the Bank Indonesia suggests that the purpose of this provision was to prevent the entry of banks into risky business ventures which would endanger bank liquidity and lessen the protection of bank creditors.[25] Since the Bank Indonesia does not have qualified personnel to enforce this provision, it has had to rely on bank cooperation in submitting complete and accurate reports.[26] The same decree also announced limitations on long-term credit extension. Credit with terms exceeding one year may be granted only if "paid-up capital plus free reserves" exceeds the "determined minimum working capital" of Rp. 2.5 million, and such credit may not exceed 10 per cent of paid-up capital plus free reserves.[27] What the import of this decree will be still remains to be seen.

In May 1957 the Bank Indonesia took further advantage of the regulatory powers conferred by the 1955 ordinance by establishing minimum reserve requirements. Commercial banks with demand liabilities over Rp. 75 million were required to deposit with the Bank Indonesia cash reserves equal to 20 per cent of such liabilities. In addition, a secondary reserve of 10 per cent of demand liabilities must be held in the form of treasury bills. Limitation of the supply of these bills, therefore, may conceivably become a device to exert quantitative control over credit. Experience elsewhere, however, suggests that similar reserve provisions have been effective in limiting credit extension only where they have been combined with budgetary and debt-management policies which have sought to restrict the volume of reserve-eligible assets.[28] In the setting of budgetary disequilibrium and pressures of legal limitation on borrowing from the central bank such as exist in Indonesia today, the reserve requirement may succeed only in placing a larger part of the government debt with commercial banks. This has happened in a number of countries which have resorted to this device.[29] In fact, one authority on the subject concludes that, "experience with this instrument has served to highlight the vital importance of reinforcing credit policy by appropriate budget and debt-management policies."[30]

Thus monetary control has not progressed beyond the most elementary stage in Indonesia. The Bank Indonesia Act of 1953, which defined this bank as the central bank, virtually gave carte blanche powers to the Monetary Board in the field of credit control (Article 22). The Bank Indonesia is charged with responsibility of carrying out monetary policy determined by the Monetary Board. The legal basis for monetary control apparently exists, but, apart from limitation of credit to importers, real force had not yet been exerted through either quantitative or selective controls by late 1958. It is too early, however, to evaluate the impact of the new reserve provisions.

The inflationary effects of bank credit during the pre-plan period suggest that effective quantitative controls should become an important adjunct of plans to finance development, and that selective controls over consumer, speculative, and other types of unproductive credit may also be necessary. Further, the present trend toward the growth of a highly decentralized system of small weak banks should be halted. This trend has placed the new and government subbanks outside Bank Indonesia supervision; and continuation of this policy will inevitably reduce prospects for the emergence of forceful monetary control. Effectiveness of monetary policy tends to vary inversely with the number of banks controlled, particularly in nationalistic underdeveloped countries where new banks, however weak and inflationary, are viewed as symbols of displacing foreign economic control.

Measures to Increase Savings

Initiative for expanding the amount of capital and loanable funds supplied by the public to financial institutions does not rest primarily with these institutions. Success in increasing the flow of voluntary savings to intermediaries depends more on gradual social change which may promote the habit of holding liquid assets in the form of bank liabilities.[31] In the meantime, certain negative and positive inducements to promote increased bank mobilization of savings may be helpful. The Central Import Office began requiring in 1955 that importers submit a document verifying a statement of their current account with the banks, to demonstrate that their financial position justified the issuance of an import permit of the size which they are seeking. The intention of this regulation was to prevent Indonesian nationals, who have special privileges in obtaining import permits, from reselling the permits to other importers. This provision could be extended to promote the habit of holding indirect liabilities of banks by requiring that a certain composition of time and demand deposits exists before the applicant be given an import permit.

Another step might consist of attempts to remove the obstacles to deposits outlined above. If it is true that the major obstacle to increasing bank holdings of deposits is fear of disclosure of one's assets to tax authorities, it might be worth while to declare assets held in banks outside the scope of investigation by tax authorities. A substitute, from the tax administration point of view, would be to require that taxpayers submit statements of their current and fixed assets. Intentional misrepresentation could then be punishable by law. Again, if it is true that a fear of loss of value resulting from holding one's assets in the form of time deposits is a major deterrent to the deposit habit, the banking system as a whole might experiment with some system of tying the value of time deposits to the value of a number of basic commodities. Experience elsewhere with the use of this type of parity deposits has suggested that this device is extremely effective in increasing the amounts of time deposits.

An interesting experiment undertaken by the provincial government of Central Sumatra might be generalized to promote savings habits through the use of time or savings deposits. Bank collection of savings from current income to provide a basis for credit extension has been greatly facilitated by establishing premiums in the form of savings deposits for prompt payment of loans. If repayment and interest payments are made on time, the borrower from desa lumbungs receives half of the interest payments as savings deposits at these banks. Provincial officials have reported that this system has been effective both in preventing defaulting on loan payments, thus reducing administrative costs by more than the costs of the premiums, and in substantially increasing the amounts of savings deposits held by the desa lumbungs.

In the early stages of Indonesian economic development, however, efforts to increase the supply of savings made available to orthodox Western-type intermediaries may well be frustrated by the social and cultural obstacles to which we have referred. Policies to increase voluntary saving might better promote the growth of indigenous institutions* which appear to be moving in the direction of performing functions similar to indirect finance through banking intermediaries. Such institutions are found in many underdeveloped countries. In Indonesia they have proliferated almost directly with the monetization of the labor-intensive sector of the economy and have "become more and more specifically economic rather than diffusely social institutions."[32] These indigenous institutions in Indonesia, and elsewhere, may be best termed "rotating credit associations," as Geertz has described them. They consist of "a lump sum composed of fixed contributions from each member," which is "distributed, at fixed intervals and as a whole, to each member of the association in turn."[33] Geertz believes that these institutions, known on Java as arisans (literally, cooperative endeavor), may perform an important role in combining local popular appeal with the sort of saving process required for financing development. He also contends that they may become an educational mechanism and operate to restrict consumption.[34]

*The institutions discussed here are, strictly speaking, not components of the unorganized money market discussed earlier. They represent organized credit institutions earning rates of interest considerably below those received by individual lenders in the less organized part of the market.

Among Indonesians arisan membership is "praised as a good way to save money. If one has a little cash one will certainly spend it; but if one deposits it in an arisan, one can build it up into a sizable sum."[35] Geertz believes that their success is based on the preservation of local social values, mixed with special attractions which represent inducements to save in the particular social setting in which the arisan functions. In the urban arisans in East Java, for example, the order in which the individual member receives the rotating fund is determined by lot, and here this gambling aspect has central importance.[36] While saving through the arisan is ordinarily done to finance anticipated consumption expenditures, particularly communal feasts (slametans), it is also used to provide trade capital. In this connection, Alice Dewey noted a rather untypical Javanese penchant to keep such payments up to date, which is in marked contrast to the more usual tendency to procrastinate in discharging financial obligations. She found the trade arisan to be "a reliable source of capital for people who participate in them."[37]

Geertz believes that these local institutions for saving could be oriented more specifically to the finance of economic development by taxation of the proceeds and by organizing pools for the purchase of capital goods.[38] Since these institutions are very popular among Indonesians, Geertz doubts that moderate taxation would discourage them. He also feels that these traditional institutions might successfully be infused with patriotic motivations—such as "national reconstruction"—with positive results.

Government efforts to promote the development of arisans for mobilizing savings for capital investment might yield significant results. A program combining contributions to a rotating fund with eventual acquisition of a capital good—delivered and demonstrated by a government office—could produce important leverage effects on transferring voluntary savings from inflationary hoarding to direct investment in capital goods for raising productivity in such forms as agricultural machinery, machines for cottage industry, or raw materials in scarce supply. We have already noted that personal savings tend to flow directly to unproductive uses or to hoards in Indonesia; much of these savings are supplied by producers (traders and small-scale manufacturers, for example) who might respond to the incentives provided by a program designed to offer them capital goods by what amounts to installment buying. For some members the capital good would be made available before their contributions had been made; for others, only after most payments had been completed. If the funds were disbursed by lot, however, all members would be given a chance to acquire the end result of their saving before actual saving took place.

The significance of the arisan as a potential instrument for the mobilization of savings, as Geertz points out, lies in the fact that it is a "trusted and popular economic institution in the eyes of the average Indonesian. He feels that he understands it, that it is relatively safe to put his money into, and that it is a workable device for enabling him to reach goals he could not otherwise reach."[39] It is, therefore, an instrument which, if intelligently and vigorously promoted, might successfully strike at the most serious limitations to increasing voluntary savings in Indonesia, those imbedded in traditional mores. In addition, the institutions of this type might also serve as a steppingstone to the development of more highly rationalized financial intermediaries as habits of saving for monetary gain become more generally established.

Conclusions: Prospects for Mobilizing Voluntary Savings

Indonesian experience suggests that there are severe limitations to the extent to which the supply of voluntary savings may be expanded to finance development. Where voluntary abstinence from consumption is undertaken, the resulting accumulations of liquid funds tend to flow mainly to the unorganized money market, where they are reloaned for consumption or other nondevelopment purposes, or to the acquisition of hoards. Evidence some years ago suggested that hoarding was becoming a more general phenomenon in Indonesian society.[40] Government stabilization policies and restrictions upon the supply of many types of imported goods on which funds might otherwise have been spent encouraged the growth of monetary hoards. Saving in cash hoards was apparently increased by restrictions on spending, but those savings were more than offset by dissaving in other sectors. This pattern of offsetting cash hoards failed to increase the rate of capital formation.

The appearance of active inflationary tendencies after 1955 showed that government deficit financing (dissaving) based on this type of forced saving tended to aggravate price instability and shift hoarding patterns to more inflationary kinds. Restrictive import policies and deficit financing produced sharp price rises, jeopardizing the value of money hoards. This, in turn, triggered a general flight from monetary hoards to commodities, real property, and foreign exchange, putting further pressure on domestic price levels and the black market foreign-exchange rate. This experience suggests that mobilization of hoards either through financial intermediaries or through public bond sales might have been a more satisfactory method of offsetting government deficit spending. Neither bank savings nor government bonds can be readily converted into hoards of commodities or foreign exchange.

Prospects for mobilizing monetary hoards through either public or private efforts, however, involve overcoming the obstacles we have discussed. Beyond these issues, it is also important to observe that liquidity preference itself is related to the whole constellation of government financial policies and the tenacity with which these policies are pursued. The desire to hold assets in highly liquid form—such as cash hoards—is based upon the fear that the pace of inflation may accelerate. Cash balances are held as the most ready means of transferring to commodity hoards should the value of money decline precipitously. When controls begin to slip, as they frequently do in underdeveloped countries, this conversion inevitably takes place at a rapid pace—as it has in Indonesia. One might even conclude that government deficit financing and stabilization policies have retarded the growth of voluntary savings.

All of this suggests that a government cannot seriously consider promoting the growth of voluntary bank savings or its own public bond sales while failing to maintain relative price stability. Until the basic deterrents to parting with the high liquidity of cash hoards and the safety of noncash hoards are overcome by curbing inflationary pressures, therefore, prospects for mobilizing voluntary savings through either public or private methods will continue to be unfavorable.

The Indonesian government has not attempted to sell bonds to the Indonesian public since a forced loan in 1950, when there was no question of voluntary subscription.* This lack of precedent will further

*The Bank Industri Negara has sold several issues to foreigners with blocked rupiah accounts.

hamper efforts to mobilize private voluntary savings for a development program. Much has been written about the means by which public bond sales may be stimulated in underdeveloped countries.[41] In the opinion of the author, the most basic factor related to the success of such efforts in Indonesia—assuming there are savings to be tapped—will be the degree of popular confidence in the government and its ability to maintain a reasonable degree of economic stability. If such confidence can be diffused, customary incentives to increase public bond sales—increased yields, lottery features, tax concessions, and others—may prove to be effective in promoting the finance of economic development by public mobilization of voluntary savings through sale of government securities.

Notes to Chapter 3

1. See Charles P. Kindleberger, Economic Development, McGraw-Hill, New York, 1958, p. 198.

2. The terms "surplus spending units" and "deficit spending units" are taken from J. G. Gurley and E. S. Shaw, "Financial Aspects of Economic Development," American Economic Review, Vol. XLV, No. 4 (1958), pp. 515-538. Surplus spending units are defined as those which spend less than current income and thus supply loanable funds; deficit spending units as those which spend more than current income and thus demand loanable funds.

3. Ibid., pp. 518-519.

4. See W. O. Thweatt, "Economic Growth and Distribution in the Middle East," American Journal of Economics and Sociology, January 1957.

5. J. J. Polak, The National Income of the Netherlands Indies, 1921-1939, Institute of Pacific Relations, New York, 1942, pp. 64-66.

6. William W. Lockwood, The Economic Development of Japan, Growth and Structural Change, 1868-1938, Princeton University Press, Princeton, 1954, pp. 278-280.

7. Ragnar Nurkse, Problems of Capital Formation in Underdeveloped Countries, Basil Blackwell, Oxford, 1953, pp. 57-70.

8. See Benjamin Higgins, "Development Problems in the Philippines: A Comparison with Indonesia," Far Eastern Survey, Vol. XXVI, No. 11 (1957), pp. 161-169.

9. W. Arthur Lewis, The Theory of Economic Growth, Richard D. Irwin, Homewood, Illinois, 1955, pp. 225-244.

10. Charles Wolf, Jr., "Economic Development and Reform in South and Southeast Asia," Far Eastern Quarterly, Vol. XII, No. 1 (1952), pp. 29-30.

11. Report of the Bank Indonesia, 1956-1957, Table 24, p. 92, and Report of the Bank Indonesia, 1957-1958, Table 24, p. 102.

12. Antara (New York edition), November 1, 1954.

13. Report of the Bank Indonesia, 1956-1957, p. 99.

14. Report of the Bank Indonesia, 1953-1954, p. 75.

15. Report of the Bank Indonesia, 1956-1957, Appendix E.

16. Report of the Java Bank, 1952-1953, p. 78.

17. Alice Dewey, "The Market," manuscript prepared for the "Modjokuto" series to be published by The Free Press, Glencoe, Illinois.

18. Report of the Bank Indonesia, 1954-1955, Appendix F, pp. 191-195.

19. Ibid., p. 194.

20. Report of the Bank Indonesia, 1956-1957, p. 82.

21. Ibid., p. 83.

22. Report of the Bank Indonesia, 1955-1956, p. 83.

23. Ibid., pp. 75-76, and Report of the Bank Indonesia, 1956-1957, pp. 84-87.

24. Ibid., p. 85.

25. Ibid., pp. 83-84.

26. Ibid., p. 84.

27. Ibid., Appendix G, p. 225.

28. Peter G. Fousek, Foreign Central Banking: The Instruments of Monetary Policy, Federal Reserve Bank of New York, New York, 1957, p. 68.

29. Ibid., p. 64.

30. Ibid., p. 68.

31. See Clifford Geertz, Jr., "The Rotating Credit Association: An Instrument for Development," Center for International Studies, Massachusetts Institute of Technology, Cambridge, November 1956 (hectograph), pp. 2-3. "It would seem that an effort to change the [savings-income] ratio would demand an effort to change the general pattern of mores and social structure. The main efforts along these lines so far have been of two general sorts: propaganda drives asking individuals to save through buying government securities or the setting up of Western-type savings institutions: banks, savings cooperatives, and the like. Neither of these efforts has been wholly ineffective but both of them have tended to be disappointing: the first because deep-rooted customs yield very little to official sponsored exhortations and the second because the impersonality, complexity, and foreignness

of the mode of operation of such 'capitalist' institutions tend to make traditionalistic peasants, small traders, and civil servants suspicious of them."

32. Ibid., p. 12.

33. Ibid., p. 5.

34. Ibid., p. 3.

35. Ibid., p. 14.

36. Ibid., pp. 13-14.

37. Dewey, op. cit., p. 143.

38. Geertz, op. cit., p. 46.

39. Ibid., p. 50.

40. National Planning Bureau, "Indonesia's Economic and Social Development in 1954," Ekonomi dan Keuangan Indonesia, Vol. VIII, July 1955, pp. 360-361.

41. See, for example, Part B of Economic Commission for Asia and the Far East, United Nations, Mobilization of Domestic Capital: Report and Documents of the First Working Party of Experts, Bangkok, 1952.

4

THE INDONESIAN TAX SYSTEM

Domestic financing of economic development requires either the transfer of spending from traditional nondevelopmental patterns of investment to developmental activities or increased total savings (including taxes) and investment (public and private). When total output remains relatively constant over time, an economy can generate a higher level of total saving only by reducing its existing level of consumption. If previously idle factors of production are used, of course, investment can take place without either a reduction in consumption or inflation.

Conditions in underdeveloped countries tend to limit both increases in voluntary savings and their investment in developmental undertakings. Domestic enterprise is devoted more to operating than to expanding the existing productive machinery. Aggregate real demand remains fairly constant and there is little incentive to expand the supply of goods. As a consequence, incentives to save among the upper-income group are not adequate either to restrain their own consumption or to deter the channeling of their savings to financing consumption of other groups. We have seen in the previous chapter that prospects for increasing voluntary savings in Indonesia are not promising.

Persistence of stagnation with low rates of saving and investment suggests that collective thrift[1] will have to be imposed by central and local governments to raise the economy's rate of investment without inflation. Only the state and its subsidiary levels of government appear to be capable of increasing real savings in the early stages of development. Increasing government savings, however, requires the pursuit of vigorous fiscal policies designed to reduce current expenditures and—even more important—to produce greater revenues from taxation. In most underdeveloped countries this would require a thorough reorganization of the tax system and the difficult task of trimming traditional expenditures. We should also warn that, although a larger volume of savings is necessary, accomplishing that objective may not be sufficient to insure a "take-off" to economic growth. Whether or not savings produced by government fiscal processes will fructify as output-increasing investment depends on the success of the state in transferring the resources made available to public or private entrepreneurs who are able and willing to employ them productively.

Unfortunately, fiscal systems, as well as private institutions to mobilize savings, are characteristically inefficient in underdeveloped countries. Reluctance to tackle the great challenge of fiscal improvement has led many countries to show a preference for inflationary finance, which experience in Indonesia and elsewhere suggests tends to be self-defeating. This leaves taxation as the only alternative for accomplishing collective thrift on the scale required to produce increased output per capita.

Tax financing of economic development is a controversial issue among economists and other students of economic growth. Some writers have contended that there is no economic case for employing the fiscal system to raise the rate of savings in underdeveloped countries. For example, in a recent book, Bauer and Yamey have set forth the view that this recommendation stems from the political positions of students of economic development, and that it has not been supported by economic analysis.[2] They go on to argue that compulsory public saving through taxation may also be self-defeating because it has unfavorable effects on private saving and investment.

The charge made by Bauer and Yamey seems to reverse the truth. Those who oppose fiscal financing of development overlook the more important realities in which the underdeveloped economy operates. Private saving and investment rates are typically so low that they fail to provide capital formation for economic growth. Stimulants to increase these rates are likely to be unsuccessful unless the whole cultural and social milieu surrounding economic activity is transformed. An important part of the transformation represents forming overhead capital which does not provide returns which can be appropriated by private investors. In this situation, the only hope of encouraging growth lies in the changes which a small group of government planners may be able to initiate. The case for government planning and the use of compulsory public saving, therefore, rests upon both social and economic analysis. The alternative of sparking the process of economic growth in underdeveloped countries by hoping for more vigorous private enterprise has the weight of history against it. Unless conditions for growth are changed by government action, stagnation is likely to continue. Alternative sources for financing economic development, too, show little promise for supporting greater capital formation. This places the onus of sparking the process upon the government.

It does not follow, however, that government economic planning and public saving should be viewed as panaceas which will transform a stagnant economy into a growing one with little domestic effort and with no prospects of failure. Success of these methods requires an intelligent group of planners and sophisticated use of the powers which they may be able to mobilize. Policies may well be designed to promote the growth of private savings and investment by providing conditions conducive to their growth. They may also be designed to encourage the growth of public enterprise at the expense of the private sector. The mixture of public and private enterprise has little to do with economic planning or compulsory public saving; it is more likely to reflect the values of a particular society. The important point is that a particular a priori bias should not be applied to all societies by students of economic development. The view that the finance of economic development should be left to private enterprise at all stages of development in all societies strikes the author as an example of this kind of unfortunate bias.

Our study of Indonesian savings and investment suggests that these general conclusions have considerable relevance for the present Indonesian situation. Collective thrift compelled by taxation is the only means by which Indonesia can hope to provide substantially greater real savings, at least during the foreseeable short-run period of establishing preconditions for economic growth. Private voluntary savings have failed to provide adequate resources to maintain the existing level of output per capita. Increasing voluntary savings will require institutional and cultural changes on so comprehensive a scale that this method of finance is more likely to be a result of economic development than a cause.

Inflationary finance of investment in both the public and private sectors has interfered with economic development by jeopardizing economic stability. Indonesia must now face the task of adapting her fiscal system to the finance of economic development, or she will find the problem of coping with inflation replacing economic development as the primary long-run economic challenge. Even during the years since the First Five Year Plan was announced, this danger has become more real.

Yet Indonesia's capacity to finance economic development by taxation is an unknown quantity. The Indonesian government began independent rule with a cumbersome tax system inherited from the Dutch and forged during several centuries of colonialism. Lacking information about the burden of this colonial tax system upon the economy and its effects on domestic economic activity, the new government continued the system, merely making minor changes in tax rates and coverage when it seemed important to do so. Much has been said about tax reform in Indonesia, but little has been done.

An evaluation of Indonesia's capacity to finance economic development by taxation must therefore begin with a brief history of Indonesia's tax structure. This history is presented in this chapter. In Chapter 5 we shall attempt to give a rough approximation of the distribution of the government's tax burden between the economy's two major sectors (the labor-intensive and the capital-intensive sectors). Changes in tax rates and changing emphases within the tax structure inherited from colonialism appear to have produced important effects in the burden borne by these major sectors, and these effects cannot be overlooked in a study concerned with increasing real savings to finance development.

A further problem concerns the effect of taxation upon private incentives; this problem is explored in Chapter 6. Our study, however, must also inquire into the contributions which might be made by local (noncentral) government finance. In decentralized Indonesia, these sources of real savings appear to have particular significance. The potential role of local finance is examined in Chapter 7.

Historical Review of the Tax Structure

A general picture of the pattern of government nonloan income, contrasting the prewar with the postwar period, is presented in Table 19. The data for the pre-World War II period were published as final results for the years 1929-1939; for the postwar period, satisfactory data are available for the years since 1951. Data are not available for the war years, and figures for the immediate postwar years were omitted because of doubts as to their accuracy.

These data show that there have been important changes in the composition of government revenues since the transfer of sovereignty to the Indonesian Republic. Before the war, government enterprises of all types—including fiscal monopolies—contributed a significant share of total government revenue, but this has not been true in the years since independence. In 1929, before the world depression reached Indonesia, profits from government activities contributed as much as 28 per cent of total revenues; during the depression they averaged about 12 per cent of the total until 1939, when they showed a slight improvement (14 per cent). Since independence, however, income from government enterprises has been relatively unimportant. It reached a maximum contribution of 3 per cent of total nonloan income in 1952, but it has averaged only approximately 1 per cent. These results are suggestive in view of the Indonesian government's attempts to expand the public sector of the economy. The number of government enterprises has actually increased, but in the years since independence government enterprises have been plagued by problems of rehabilitation after a decade of capital erosion. Independence and the departure of Dutch civilians produced a severe shortage of administrators and technicians. Generally, therefore, government enterprises have been operated with little efficiency in recent years. The experience of these years suggests, incidentally, that public entrepreneurship may not be the most effective means of using increased real savings for economic development.

As revenues from government enterprises have fallen as a percentage of total government receipts, so income from taxes has risen. Taxes have provided well over 90 per cent of total nonloan income since 1951;* in 1929 they contributed 64 per cent and in 1939, 77 per cent.

Greater reliance on taxation as a source of government finance is one of the most important long-run developments in the Indonesian fiscal system. The trend which was apparent from 1929 to 1939 and between 1939 and the postwar period is a continuation of a general pattern away from the assessments of a colonial government upon the labor-intensive sector of the economy. The underlying trend has been away from direct labor and commodity levies designed to produce export income for the colonial government toward a more progressive tax system reaching the profits of investors in the modern, or capital-intensive, sector of the economy. A Dutch authority on the Indonesian tax system has divided Indonesia's tax history under Dutch colonial administration into four major periods.[3] The first period covers the years

*In 1953, government "income from miscellaneous sources" was unusually large because of profits from revaluation of the gold stock. In 1956 and 1957 these sources included relatively large amounts that did not represent government income from domestic sources.

Table 19

TOTAL CENTRAL GOVERNMENT INCOME*

1929 - 1939, 1951 - 1958

(Prewar: Million NEI Guilders; Postwar: Million Rp.)

Year	Taxes	Fiscal Monopolies	Government Enterprises	Miscellaneous	Total
1929	344	34	112	34	524
1930	313	34	62	31	440
1931	284	28	40	28	380
1932	228	23	14	17	282
1933	208	21	11	17	257
1934	222	21	6	18	267
1935	229	19	16	19	283
1936	261	18	17	25	321
1937	285	17	35	30	367
1938	291	15	32	39	377
1939	300	15	39	35	389
1951	9,968		131	204	10,303
1952	9,037		293	354	9,684
1953	8,415		205	1,087	9,707
1954	7,871		61	535	8,467
1955	9,747		98	462	10,307
1956	13,450		476	1,807	15,733
1957	15,235		355	1,283	16,873
1958	17,722		141	1,793	19,656

*Government income is defined to exclude proceeds from borrowing.

Sources: Data for the prewar period are from the following government publications: Statistische Jaaroverzicht van Nederlandsch - Indië (Statistical Abstract of the Netherlands Indies), Tien Begrootingen met den Volksraad (Ten Budgets with the People's Council), Het Tweede Tiental Begrootingen met den Volksraad (The Second Decade of Budgets with the People's Council), and annual issues of Bijlagen, Handelingen, Nederlandsch-Indië Volksraad. Data for the postwar period are from annual editions of the Report of the Bank Indonesia. For postwar breakdown by source, see Appendix I, Table I-2.

when the Dutch East Indian Company had exclusive economic access to the Dutch East Indies (1620-1800). During this period, taxes played a very minor role in Indonesian finance, government income being largely limited to relatively light taxes on commercial profits. However, the company imposed heavy levies on the native population through the "quota and supply" system. Through this system, combined with indirect rule, the company introduced export crops and obtained the greater part of the yields of these crops as tribute from the Regents in local control.

The second period (1800-1870), which ended with the opening of Indonesia to private capital, began with reliance on land taxation (*landrente* and *verponding*), introduced by Raffles, the brilliant but controversial British colonial administrator during the Napoleonic Wars (1811-1816). By 1830 the Dutch found that this system of taxation, combined with a new pattern of government expenditures (inherited from the British), produced fiscal difficulties and mounting colonial debt. This situation prompted the introduction in 1830 of the "culture system," under which land revenue in cash was replaced by collections of produce in kind (primarily export crops) as tribute. The government also enforced the compulsory sale at low prices to government collection agencies of export crops above the amounts of tribute. An adjunct to this system was compulsory labor on government plantations at rates of pay low enough to allow high profits from cultivation. This system proved so lucrative that Dutch private enterprise agitated for adoption of a policy which would permit private investment in Indonesian plantations. After twenty years of intensive home polemics on the issue, the "liberal system," which allowed private capital to enter Indonesia, became a reality in 1870.

After this historic reversal, private enterprise began to assume the dominant role in plantation production. Private planters took over the plantations formerly managed by the government and added many of their own. Private enterprise, it has been argued, tended to be more oppressive than state enterprise,[4] but the government followed a policy of protecting the population against the inroads of foreign enterprise. The Agrarian Law of 1870, for example, made it impossible for planters to purchase village land or to use it in any way other than on the basis of annual lease. Waste land, however, could be obtained from the government on long-term lease.

With the entry of private enterprise the government once again came to be financed primarily by taxes during the third period (1870-1920). The scope of taxes began to include foreign enterprises, which became subject to enterprise and business license fees. Prins argues that the tax burden began to shift from land toward the capital-intensive sector after 1920 (in his fourth period, 1920-1949). However, it appears that this trend was well under way much earlier than 1920, and that it was accelerated by the introduction of the so-called "ethical policy" in the first decade of the 20th century. In 1867 land taxes contributed 49 per cent of total tax revenues; in 1877, 46 per cent; in 1887, 43 per cent; and in 1897, 33 per cent. The percentage contributed by land revenues had fallen to 20 per cent by 1920 and to 11 per cent by 1929.

Colonial taxation in Indonesia has frequently been regarded as a device for imperialistic exploitation. During the period when the "culture system" was in force (1830-1861) this may have been true. The government set up an extensive system of state plantations and processing firms which recruited labor and raw materials from the populace through a compulsory system.[5] These operations resulted in vast profits;

but "the confusion of trading profits and taxes and of commercial and administrative expenditure was too complex to unravel."[6] It is clear, however, that in addition to profits from these operations, substantial increases in tax revenues took place, although in theory direct contributions to government enterprises were to have replaced taxation. Testifying to the lucrative nature of the "culture system," the colonial administration initiated in 1831 a colonial contribution to the mother country's finances. The greater part of such contributions was drawn from profits of the colonial government's enterprises, but in the last years of the "culture system" finance was partially from taxation. The contributions, which continued until 1878, did not, for the most part, arise from legitimate claims on the Netherlands East Indian Treasury. Of a total amount of f. 832.4 million* transferred from the Netherlands Indies to the Netherlands between 1831 and 1877, only f. 20.9 million represented service charges on Dutch loans.[7]

All this indicates an extremely regressive system of taxation which was supporting the administration of the colonial government and financing transfers to the mother country. The burden was borne mainly by the traditional, labor-intensive sector of the economy and consisted of a combination of compulsory labor services, providing land for government-sponsored products, and land taxation. One-fifth of the cultivated land was to be devoted to production of export crops for the government. In reality, government officials often pre-empted a much higher percentage.[8]

This historical background has considerable relevance for financing modern economic development. The most onerous kind of colonial

*The florin (Dutch, <u>Florijn</u>) is used interchangeably with the guilder (Dutch, <u>Gulden</u>).

taxation has been construed to be taxation of the traditional labor-intensive sector. The opening of Indonesia to private enterprise in the late nineteenth century led to a gradual abandonment of corvée levies on the traditional sector, and during the early part of the twentieth century land taxation came to be replaced by other revenues. Independence brought swift repeal of the land tax, but the persistence of attitudes associating central taxation of the labor-intensive sector with colonial exploitation has greatly hampered the Indonesian Republic in developing a national tax system to meet the problems brought by independence.

The trend away from the nineteenth century pattern of tax and corvée exploitation of the labor-intensive sector is shown in Tables 20 and 21. Gradually, new taxes and profits from modern government enterprises replaced income from the "culture system" type of profits from exporting agricultural products and fiscal monopolies. In 1867 income from the sale of export products produced by forced labor accounted for 50 per cent of government income. Fiscal monopolies, which sold essential goods to Indonesians, contributed another 18 per cent. However, government monopoly of export products came to be increasingly challenged by private enterprise; by 1897 only 11 per cent of government income came from this source. Moreover, government requisitioning of labor was reduced; by 1913 virtually all labor in government enterprises was hired at market rates. Meanwhile, the tax structure, too, became less oriented toward the labor-intensive sector. Table 21 shows that land taxes gave way to customs duties, excise duties, and income taxes. In 1928 land taxation yielded only 10 per cent of total tax revenues, compared to about 40 per cent in 1897 and 25 per cent in 1913.

Table 20

GROWTH OF NET GOVERNMENT INCOME BY MAJOR TYPES OF REVENUE

SELECTED YEARS, 1867-1932

(Million Florin)

	Actuals					Percentage				
Revenue	1867	1897	1913	1928	1932	1867	1897	1913	1928	1932
Taxation	25.5	52.9	102.8	361.1	228.3	33	58	54	66	75
Products	38.5	10.6	33.8	54.1	9.9	50	11	18	10	3
Monopolies	14.1	24.5	35.5	51.2	26.2	18	27	19	9	9
Enterprises	-0.8	3.7	11.0	50.3	21.7	-1	4	6	9	7
Miscellaneous			6.8	34.4	17.1			3	6	6
Total	77.3	91.7	189.9	551.1	303.2	100	100	100	100	100

Source: J. S. Furnivall, Netherlands India: A Study of Plural Economy, Cambridge University Press, Cambridge, 1939, p. 341.

Table 21

TAX STRUCTURE

SELECTED YEARS, 1867-1928

(Million Florin)

Tax	Actuals				Percentage			
	1867	1897	1913	1928	1867	1897	1913	1928
Land revenue and poll tax	12.6	20.8	25.2	36.5	49	39	25	10
Income tax and surtax, etc.			10.9	114.0			11	32
Customs and excise duties	7.6	15.8	39.7	142.2	30	30	39	39
Other taxes	5.3	16.3	27.0	68.4	21	31	25	19
Total	25.5	52.9	102.8	361.1	100	100	100	100

Source: Same as Table 20.

Growth of Government Expenditures and Revenues

Table 22 shows the growth of government expenditures and nonloan income relative to gross product. Expenditures of the Netherlands East Indies government averaged about 13 per cent of gross product during the 1930's, and expenditures of the Indonesian Republic averaged about the same percentage in the five years shown (1951-1955). However, both expenditures and revenues fell consistently after the prosperous tax years of 1951 and 1952. Despite the upward revision of tax rates after 1952, government revenues failed to keep pace with the growth of gross product. During this period government expenditures were held in check by legal limitation on the amount of deficit which could be financed through the central bank. As price inflation proceeded, the real value of government expenditures fell considerably below the postwar high achieved in 1952. Thus the Indonesian government failed to transfer a larger share of gross product to the public sector even though "socialistic" development of the economy was adopted as a major national goal. Although the government's claim on gross product fell from 15 per cent of the total in 1952 to 10 per cent in 1955, much of the government's expenditures had to be financed by inflationary means. Tax and tax-like revenues fell from 14 per cent of gross product in 1951 to a postwar low of 8 per cent in 1955. (M. D. Dris estimates this per cent to have been 7.5 in 1955.[9])

The failure of tax revenues to keep pace with the growth of gross product in the years after 1952 suggests a major weakness of the Indonesian fiscal system from the standpoints of both stability and development. Oriented toward the foreign trade sector of the economy, the tax system is incapable of capturing a significant share of increments in domestic income which does not flow through the foreign-trade sector. Government revenues as a percentage of gross product have shown a tendency to rise only when world demand for Indonesian exports produces sharply rising values of the country's foreign trade. The secondary domestic price and income rises generated by these external stimuli are, for the greater part, beyond the reach of Indonesia's present tax structure. Similarly, the tax system fails to capture even a proportionate share of the increments in the money or real income resulting from such stimuli.

Table 22

GOVERNMENT EXPENDITURES AND REVENUE
RELATIVE TO GROSS NATIONAL PRODUCT
1929, 1939, 1951 - 1955

Year	(1) Gross Product*†	(2) Government Expenditures*	(3) (2) as Per Cent of (1)	(4) Government Revenue*	(5) (4) as Per Cent of (1)
1929	4,971	515	10	524	11
1939	2,933	389	13	389	13
1951	74,200	9,200	12	10,303	14
1952	86,000	13,100	15	9,684	11
1953	85,400	11,900	14	9,707	11
1954	88,900	12,000	13	8,500	10
1955	122,600	12,400	10	10,300	8

*Millions of guilders (prewar) and millions of rupiah (postwar).

†Prewar figures are gross national product; postwar figures are gross <u>domestic</u> product.

Sources: For Col. 1 see J. J. Polak, "Het National Inkomen van Nederlandsch Indië, 1921-1939" (The National Income of the Netherlands Indies, 1921-1939), reprinted from <u>Statistische en Econometrische Onderzeokingen</u>, Vol. IV (1947); S. Daniel Neumark, "The National Income of Indonesia, 1951-1952," <u>Ekonomi dan Keuangan Indonesia</u>, Vol. VII, June 1954, pp. 345-391; and National Planning Bureau, "A Study of the Indonesian Economic Development Scheme," <u>Ekonomi dan Keuangan Indonesia</u>, Vol. X, September 1957, Table 1, p. 614. Cols. 2 and 4, same as Table 19.

This leads us to suggest a hypothesis, which we shall seek to support in later chapters, of the economy's taxable capacity and the distribution of its fiscal burden. All evidence points to the conclusion that limits to the government's ability to mobilize a larger share of national income for the public sector are set by administrative and political barriers rather than by the economy's taxable capacity. A corollary to this conclusion is that the problem of increasing real savings for financing development may be more tractable than a superficial study of the country's capabilities might suggest.

The nub of the fiscal problem in Indonesia is that the new nation inherited a system which was designed to meet the minimum requirements of colonial control. We have seen that the use of fiscal devices to provide exportable profits for the mother country was replaced during the nineteenth century by a system under which profits were taken primarily by private enterprise with a modicum of state participation. Thus, although Indonesia was ruled by a modern Western country, she was not the beneficiary of a domestic fiscal system adequate to provide resources for supporting the growth of an independent government seeking, in addition to ruling, to promote the growth of the economy and the welfare of the domestic population. It may fairly be said that Indonesia began independence with a fiscal system which, like the economy she inherited from colonialism, was underdeveloped. The fiscal performance of the prewar colonial government and that of the new state appear to be typical of underdeveloped countries. A student of Latin America has observed that "the share of the government sector in the gross national product varies between 10 and 16 per cent of gross national product" in the underdeveloped countries with which he has been concerned.[10]

The Tax Structure

A general picture of the structure of the Indonesian tax system, 1939 and 1951-1957, is presented in Table 23. Data are presented in greater detail in Appendix B. The broadest generalization that can be made from these data is that the trends under way during the colonial era have continued well into the post-World War II period. The preponderant burden of taxation, it appears, has continued to shift toward the more Westernized capital-intensive sectors of the economy. (The full import of this shift will be analyzed in the next chapter, where the question of the tax burden is discussed in detail.)

Table 23

MAJOR TAX YIELDS AS PERCENTAGE OF TOTAL TAX REVENUES 1939, 1951 - 1957

Kind of Taxation	1939	1951	1952	1953	1954	1955	1956	1957
Business income	12	7	10	13	18	19	12	10
Personal income	21	6	9	11	14	13	11	12
Consumption	24	17	20	24	30	26	21	23
Export	7	55	43	12	7	8	3	12
Import	20	15	16	39	29	32	51	41
Land	7							

Sources: Percentages for 1939 and 1951-1955 are taken from the data given in Appendix B. 1956 and 1957 figures are based on results reported in _Report of the Bank Indonesia, 1956-1957_, p. 77, and _Report of the Bank Indonesia, 1957-1958_, p. 87.

Export and Import Taxes

The most remarkable shift is the considerably greater reliance on export and import duties. In 1951 and 1952, aided by a boom in world prices for Indonesia's exports, duties on foreign trade contributed 70 and 59 per cent, respectively, to total government tax receipts. In 1953, when a shift from export to import taxation took place, these levies comprised 51 per cent of total revenues. In 1955, after considerable readjustment of the tax structure, they produced 40 per cent of the total, rising to 54 per cent in 1956 and 53 per cent in 1957. These levies on foreign trade are considerably above the 27 per cent contributed by this source in 1939.

The commanding position of customs duties in the revenue structure throughout 1951 and 1952 was primarily a result of a system of general export taxation carried out by means of a multiple exchange rate policy. By employing foreign-exchange certificates and simultaneously depreciating the rupiah, the government was able to capture one-third of domestic earnings arising from exports. The export rate was held 33 1/3 per cent below the effective import rate, the difference accruing to the government as an export tax. Exporters, for example, received Rp. 7.60 for each U.S. $1.00 earned, while importers purchased U.S. dollars at the rate of Rp. 11.40 = U.S. $1.00. This system was begun in March 1950 and discontinued in February 1952, when the government became aware of the adverse effects of heavy export taxation upon incentives in the export industries. The great yields produced by this device, as well as by other types of export taxation during the period 1950-1952, resulted from high world prices for Indonesia's exports caused by the expansion in stockpiling of basic materials by Western countries during the Korean war.

When the export-certificate system was abolished in 1952, the government imposed a series of new export duties on a number of commodities for which world demand was considered to be relatively strong.

It was hoped that these duties would partially offset the anticipated loss of revenues from abandoning the previous system. The newly imposed export duties, with rates varying from 15 to 25 per cent of the value of "strong" and "medium-strong" exports, were additional to basic export duties then in effect on all commodities, some at specific and some at ad valorem rates. The general rate of this basic duty was 8 per cent, with special rates in force for commodities such as tin (Rp. 3.50 per 100 kilograms) and forest products (5 per cent ad valorem). Reduction of or exemption from the basic export tax rate could be granted by the Ministry of Finance for one-year periods, and, with the weakening of export markets in the years after 1952, such reductions were granted to many export industries. The additional export duties were gradually abandoned, and by 1953 the government began experimenting with other methods to stimulate exports.

From October 1953 to May 1955 several rather ineffective devices were tried. Most important among them was an "export inducement measure" (_Bukti Indusement_) which gave exporters of certain products—primarily smallholders—"a freely negotiable claim to foreign exchange for imports for a percentage varying from 6 to 10 of the official equivalent of the yield in currency."[11] In October 1955 export duties on most products were lowered or abolished and rupiah premiums (from 5 to 10 per cent) on foreign-exchange earnings were allowed for a number of export products. In early 1956 the premiums were raised for some goods to as much as 25 per cent, the premium depending on the classification of the good as "weak" or "strong" in export markets. In September 1956 a new export certificate system (_Bukti Pendorong Ekspor_) was introduced. This system applied to all exports with the exception of petroleum, tin, and sugar. Exporters were granted foreign-exchange certificates (varying from 2 to 20 per cent of the f.o.b. value). The certificates, entitling the bearer to the specified amount of foreign exchange, could be sold on the free market, where rupiah values of foreign exchange were considerably greater than the official rate. Such certificates were required for the purchase of a limited number of import goods, thus assuring their profitable sale.

This system, however, was short lived. In June 1957 it was replaced by the introduction of a general export-certificate plan (Bukti Ekspor, or B.E.) which allowed greater rupiah proceeds to exporters while also imposing a new export tax. All foreign-exchange recipients are given export certificates in the amount of the official rupiah value of their foreign-exchange earnings. The certificates are sold to importers, who must supply export certificates for all foreign purchases (excepting only the petroleum companies). The selling price tended to rise, pari passu, with domestic price level increases until it was stabilized at 332 per cent of the official rupiah value in April 1958.[12] The exporter, however, is obliged to remit 20 per cent of these proceeds to the government as an export tax. With the imposition of this tax, all other export duties were temporarily abandoned. The net effect of this measure was to increase rupiah proceeds from export operations by amounts varying from 60 to 75 per cent, depending on previous tax and export-certificate arrangements for particular classes of exports. Since the export-certificate system was accompanied by a reduction in import surcharges, the gains to exporters are tantamount to government subsidy by allowing a larger share of rupiah proceeds from foreign-exchange sales to flow to exporters. When it became clear that exports were not responding to this stimulus for political reasons, the price of the B.E. certificates was frozen.

Indonesian experience with replacing earnings from the foreign-exchange certificate system by additional export duties was disappointing, to say the least. In 1952 revenues from these new duties was Rp. 600 million below the estimate of the Ministry of Finance. By 1953 export duties yielded only Rp. 1 billion as compared to Rp. 5.5 billion in 1951. By 1954 the government had probably become a net subsidizer of exports, and by 1956 the government was prepared to sacrifice a part of its scarce foreign exchange to encourage exports. Until 1957, export taxation was abandoned in favor of new levies upon imports. In that year, however, the imposition of a general 20 per cent tax on rupiah proceeds from export earnings once again raised export taxation to an important position in the revenue structure. This was accompanied by concessions which gave exporters a greater share of the rupiah proceeds obtained through the sale of certificates on the "free market." The net effect was a slight decline in import surcharge yields, which was more than offset by increased revenues from export taxation. These increases, as well as the greater gains accruing to exporters, came from rising import-good prices.[13]

The shift toward heavier import taxation was begun in August 1952, when imports were divided into four "lists" for tax purposes. List A bore no duty, List B required payment of 100 per cent duty, List C 200 per cent, and List D detailed prohibited imports (e.g., air conditioners). However, since 86 per cent of the value of imports remained on the free list and 12 per cent on List B, this schedule of duties was relatively ineffective as a revenue producer. During 1953 real teeth were put into the policy to tax imports more heavily under a system of "import surcharges." The duty-free list was reduced to approximately 50 per cent of imports, comprising essential foodstuffs and textiles as well as raw materials and capital goods for economic development. A new list was added, carrying a surcharge duty of 33 1/3 per cent and comprising items for which local demand was considered to be inelastic and goods which, it was believed, could be produced shortly in Indonesia. Semiluxuries carried a 100 per cent surcharge; luxury goods either bore a 200 per cent duty or were prohibited. By 1953 the new schedule of import surcharges alone produced revenues amounting to Rp. 1,914 million (23 per cent of total tax receipts).

In addition to its obviously lucrative revenue-producing impact, the import surcharge system, in conjunction with an import quota system, eased the strain on Indonesia's dwindling gold and foreign-exchange holdings. In 1954, when those reserves fell below the specified legal cover minimum, however, import quotas were drastically reduced, producing severe reductions in supplies and allowing sellers to raise prices to consumers by amounts exceeding import taxes. These policies caused extreme stringency both among government servants and businessmen and among other urban groups who are dependent on imported goods to maintain their customary standard of consumption.

During 1955 and 1956 the system of import surcharges was substantially revised. The Harahap Cabinet, which came to power in the summer of 1955, undertook to dispense with the quota system by raising import surcharges in an effort to reduce demand for imports. It also swept away a maze of special foreign-exchange arrangements designed to encourage exports or to discourage imports but which had degenerated into a system of special political privileges. Excepting a limited number of indispensable goods, the 1955 revision reclassified imports into four categories, ranging from "essential goods" to "super-luxury goods," bearing surcharges of 50 per cent, 100 per cent, 200 per cent, and

400 per cent of their import value. Import demand, however, was not reduced by the higher import surcharges, which led to a severe drain on Indonesia's foreign-exchange reserves in 1956 and, incidentally, produced revenues from import surcharges of Rp. 5 billion in that year compared to Rp. 1.8 billion in 1955. By August 1956 the strain on reserves had become so great that the issuance of import licenses was temporarily discontinued while the exchange control system was re-evaluated.

In September 1956 a complex multiple exchange rate system was introduced. Import goods were classified into nine categories, with surcharges varying from 0 to 400 per cent. Essentially this meant that goods defined as most essential could be purchased at the official exchange rate (Rp. 11.40 = U.S. $1.00) while other goods were to be purchased at progressively less favorable rupiah rates varying from Rp. 14.25 per U.S. $1.00 (Category 2) to Rp. 57.00 per U.S. $1.00 (Category 9).

This system was made more complex by the simultaneous introduction of foreign-exchange certificates, intended to stimulate exports and discourage certain categories of imports. Certain goods in Categories 3 to 9 were designated as goods to be financed with export certificates; they were originally defined as goods "sufficiently produced" in Indonesia and luxury items.[14] Importers of such goods were required to purchase export certificates at the going market rate and were also subject to an import surcharge slightly below the rate for goods not requiring export certificates (for Category 9 goods, for example, 300 per cent rather than 400 per cent). Exporters were given certificates up to specified percentages of their foreign-exchange earnings, the percentage (varying from 2 to 20) depending on the estimated market strength of the export product concerned. This complex system, too, failed to achieve the desired restriction of imports, and in April 1957 all imports were again temporarily halted. During the period of its brief existence this system substantially increased yields from import taxation.

In June 1957 the new Djuanda Cabinet introduced its version of exchange controls. This system, which was still in force in April 1959, is also a combination of import surcharges and export certificates. The number of categories of imports with differing surcharge rates was reduced to 6, with rates varying from 0 to 175 per cent. Goods exempted from the surcharge (Category 1) include a very limited number of "highly essentials" such as rice, raw cotton, and academic books and publications. All imports, with the exception of those covered in special agreements with the petroleum companies, required the purchase of export certificates. Exporters are given certificates for the full rupiah value of the foreign-exchange earnings surrendered; they are then entitled to sell these certificates on the export-certificate exchange. Selling rates at first varied between 205 and 232 per cent of the face value of the certificates,[15] but eventually they were frozen at 332 per cent. The imposition of a new export tax on all commodity and invisible exports, however, reduces the proceeds to exporters by 20 per cent.

The importer, therefore, begins by purchasing an export certificate at roughly twice the official exchange rate. Twenty per cent of the rupiah proceeds accrues to the government, the remainder to exporters. If the imported goods are in Categories 2-6, however, the importer must also pay a surcharge on the going market price of the export certificate. For goods in Category 4, for example, the surcharge is

100 per cent.* In this case, the importer would be obliged to purchase U.S. dollars, for example, by acquiring export certificates at roughly the rate of Rp. 37.85 to U.S. $1.00. In addition, he would be obliged to pay an import surcharge of an equivalent amount (Rp. 37.85 per U.S. $1.00), making the effective rupiah rate Rp. 75.70 per U.S. $1.00 as compared to an official rate of Rp. 11.40. The maximum rate (for Category 6 goods) would be approximately Rp. 104.00 per U.S. $1.00. This represents an extreme degree of multiple-rate structure, with the differential between the official and the effective rates accruing primarily to the government or to the exporter, depending on the surcharge rate. As the system has worked out, the rupiah proceeds are almost divided evenly where the import surcharge rate is 50 per cent (Category 3). Where the rate is higher, the government is the more important beneficiary; where lower, the exporter reaps the greater advantage. Experience since 1957 suggests that the system tended to raise revenues from foreign-exchange levies, but at the cost of generating great upward pressure on the domestic price level. Its impact upon correcting balance-of-payments disequilibrium has apparently been marginal.

The revenues derived from the import surcharge system, as the name implies, are duties additional to a basic import rate structure. The basic Indonesian import tariff is based on ad valorem rates of duty varying among three classes of commodities: raw materials and basic foodstuffs

*The surcharges, by category, are as follows:

Category	Surcharge (TPI) Rate	Category	Surcharge (TPI) Rate
1. Highly essentials	0	4. Semi-essentials	100
2. Essentials	20	5. Semi-essentials	140
3. Essentials	50	6. Luxuries	175

(9 per cent), essential consumer goods and capital goods (18 per cent), and nonessential products and luxuries (20 per cent). These basic import duties alone produced revenues totaling Rp. 1,283 million in 1953, Rp. 995 million in 1954, Rp. 1,105 million in 1955, Rp. 1,872 million in 1956, and Rp. 1,785 million in 1957. All import duties combined contributed as much as 39 per cent of total tax collections in 1953 but fell to about 30 per cent in 1954 and 1955. In 1956, however, they produced just over 50 per cent of the total tax yield, falling back to 41 per cent in 1957. Export duties yielded 12 per cent of the total in 1953, falling progressively to only 3 per cent in 1956. In 1957, following the imposition of the new export tax in June, their contribution rose to 12 per cent of total tax revenues.

Taxes on Consumption

A trend away from land taxation and toward taxation of consumers by means of excise duties was already apparent toward the end of the colonial period. That trend has continued in the Republican period, but the relative position of consumption taxation has been maintained only by the imposition of general sales taxation and steeper excise tax rates. In 1929 land taxes and other direct levies on rural income comprised about 11 per cent of total tax receipts; their contribution to the total fell to 7 per cent by 1939. On the other hand, taxes on consumption (the slaughter tax and excise duties) rose from 15 per cent of the total in 1929 to 24 per cent in 1939. In recent years contributions from the land and rural income taxes have been insignificant, while revenues from consumption taxes averaged 22 per cent of the tax yield in the period 1951-1957.

Indonesia's first experiment with general sales taxation was the turnover tax introduced in January 1951. Although it was limited primarily to imported goods and levied at a rate of only 2.5 per cent on each turnover, it produced over Rp. 500 million in 1951. However, after much criticism by domestic businessmen it was replaced in October 1951 by the sales tax, a tax assessed against goods distributed by importers and domestic manufacturers at rates of 5 per cent or 10 per cent ad valorem, depending on whether the good was classified as a necessity or luxury. Basic necessities were exempted. In 1952 and 1953, the first two full years of its force, the sales tax yielded over Rp. 600 million annually, approximately one-third of the revenues from all taxes upon consumption. Its annual yield remained near this level until 1956, when it produced almost Rp. 1 billion. That increase, however, resulted from rising wholesale prices rather than higher rates.

The greatest share of revenues from consumption taxation—more than two-thirds in the past few years—has been produced by a pattern of excise taxation which has a relatively long history in colonial finance. The tobacco excise has been by far the largest revenue producer, yielding in 1955 Rp. 1,027 million of the Rp. 1,830 million derived from excises. Apart from tobacco, excise duties are levied on a specific rather than on an ad valorem basis. Since 1954 practically all excise duties levied at specific rates have been periodically increased. Consumer goods now subject to excise taxation include tobacco, distilled liquor, beer, sugar, petroleum, and petroleum products.

Business and Personal Income Taxation*

Direct taxation primarily takes the form of taxation of personal and business incomes earned in the capital-intensive sector of the economy.

*For details of the present regulations concerning these taxes and recommendations for their improvement, see the 1958 report of the U.N. Technical Assistance Mission written by M. D. Dris, "Taxation in Indonesia," Ekonomi dan Keuangan Indonesia, Vol. XI, August-September 1958.

Income earned in the rural (or non-Western) sector of the economy was explicitly exempted from income and wage taxation during the Dutch colonial period; income taxation was enforced in the agricultural sector of the economy only where Western property titles existed, i.e., on Western agricultural estates. Agricultural income was reached by land taxation, but revenues from this source declined sharply in the last decades of Dutch control. Shortly after the transfer of sovereignty, Indonesia repealed the land tax and substituted for it a rural income tax designed to extend income taxation to sectors not reached during the colonial period. This extension has been carried out unevenly in Indonesia; on Java colonial-type land taxation has continued, since the administrative structure for collecting such taxation through local officials still remains intact. In some of the outlying islands the rural income tax has been weakly enforced through a combination of central and local government authorities. This is particularly true in areas such as Sumatra, where land taxation did not really have a firm hold during the Dutch period. (See Chapter 7.)

By and large, however, the Indonesian government has not been able to muster the administrative resources to extend direct income taxation to the rural sector of the economy. Income taxation falls primarily on the capital-intensive sector, and even relatively high incomes in the rural sector escape income taxation. Moreover, in the capital-intensive sector, where rates are much higher than they were during the prewar period, yields have shown no great improvement. The number of assessments fell steadily between 1952 and 1955.[16] Taxation of personal incomes contributed 21 per cent of total tax revenues in 1939 but contributed only 6 per cent of the total in 1951. Since 1952, personal income taxation has produced about 11 per cent of the tax yield. Although we do not know precisely what has happened to taxable income in the capital-intensive sector, it appears that Indonesians—as compared to foreigners—are now earning a considerably higher share of this sector's upper incomes than in the pre-independence period.

Indonesian personal income taxation is assessed at relatively high and steeply progesssive rates as compared with the rates in effect during the Dutch colonial period. Personal income is subject to either the wage tax or the income tax. Since 1952 the effective rate of the wage tax has been somewhat below that of the income tax; thus income earned as wages bears a somewhat lower tax rate than income from other sources. The marginal rates of the wage tax begin at 3 per cent on incomes below Rp. 5,000 (apparently raised to Rp. 6,000 in 1958) and rises to 15 per cent on wage incomes above Rp. 30,000. For income taxation effective rates begin at slightly more than 3 per cent, rising to 55 per cent on Rp. 300,000. Above this amount a marginal rate of 75 per cent is assessed against each additional Rp. 100 received. These rates compare with a spread in effective rates in 1939 from 3 per cent to a maximum of 22 per cent of assessed income. Tax reductions are given for dependents. Income of Rp. 5,000 bears a rate of slightly more than 3 per cent if the taxpayer has no dependents; this rate falls to 2.7 per cent with one dependent and to 1.6 per cent with four dependents.

There are special problems in collecting income taxes in a country where the standards of literacy, bookkeeping, and record maintenance are generally low. For these reasons, the wage tax, which is collected from employees by withholding, tends to be more effectively enforced than the personal income tax, and enforcement of the personal income tax leaves much to be desired. The taxpayer does not ordinarily submit statements of his income; rather, assessment of income is largely the responsibility of the tax authorities. Frequently this becomes little more than a guessing game, with the taxpayer ingeniously attempting to obscure the size and, often, diverse components of his total income. This situation, aggravated by a shortage of tax collectors, whose salaries are notoriously low, breeds laxity in the enforcement of personal income taxes and encourages outright evasion. Hence the cost of tax administration relative to yield is high under this system of collection and considerably less where the withholding device is utilized (as in the case of the wages tax).

There is also evidence that the high marginal rates effective in the upper-income brackets encourage evasion. The high tax rates applicable in these brackets frequently discourage the incentive to strive for higher levels of income unless evasion is possible. The obvious conclusion suggested is that lower tax rates in the higher income brackets might produce more revenues by making evasion less profitable.

These and other administrative problems have prevented the government from extending the scope of direct taxation. Since independence direct income taxation has produced a considerably smaller percentage of the total tax yield than in the decade 1929-1939. If export and import duties are considered indirect taxes upon ultimate consumers, we find that indirect taxes produced about three-fourths of total tax revenues during the period 1951-1957. To the average Indonesian taxpayer, therefore, Central Government tax burden has been felt largely in the form of "hidden taxes." This situation tends to obscure the impact of the tax burden by preserving a "monetary illusion," since the taxpayer's purchasing power is not reduced by taxation of his income. But indirect taxes reduce purchasing power through increasing the prices of goods on which the taxpayer spends his income.

The shift in the Indonesian tax structure toward the capital-intensive sector of the economy was given a major boost in 1925 when a tax on income profits (company tax) was introduced.* This tax is levied against the net profits of limited liability companies and other specified forms of business organization (e.g., limited partnerships, cooperatives, and mutual insurance companies). The company tax applies uniformly to foreign and domestic enterprises operating in Indonesia. Producing 15 per cent of total tax income in 1929, its yield fell to 12 per cent in 1939. In the years since independence, revenues from the company tax increased each year until 1956, when they fell sharply. In 1951 it produced Rp. 655 million, about 7 per cent of the total tax yield, substantially more than its yield of Rp. 275 million in 1950. In 1953, revenues from this source rose to Rp. 1,083 million, almost 13 per cent of total tax receipts; and in 1955 to Rp. 1,804 million, 19 per cent of the total. In 1956, however, results were disappointing. Revenues fell to Rp. 1,569 million, representing only 12 per cent of the tax yield. In 1957, company tax yields failed to improve. Despite considerable price inflation, they fell to just over 10 per cent of total tax receipts.

The company tax has been enforced at increasingly high rates since its introduction, both during the colonial period and since independence. Originally levied at an effective rate (base tax plus surtax) of 12.5 per cent of net profits, it was raised to 14 per cent in 1931 and further raised to 20 per cent in 1933. In 1939 the surtax was again increased, resulting in an effective rate of 25 per cent; in the following year the

*For details of the present regulations concerning this tax and recommendations for improvement, see the 1958 report by Dris, <u>loc. cit.</u>

effective rate was raised to 40 per cent, where it remained until a graduated rate was adopted by the Republic beginning with the fiscal year 1951. With the exception of newly established firms, the company tax since 1951 has been collected at rates ranging from 40 per cent on net profits below Rp. 500,000 to 52.5 per cent of profits above Rp. 2,500,000.* New firms established since January 1, 1950 and earning net profits less than Rp. 500,000 are taxed at progressive rates varying from 25 per cent to 40 per cent during their first five years.

Other Taxes

The major taxes described above have contributed over 95 per cent of total tax revenues in the period since 1951. The present tax structure also includes a relatively large variety of minor taxes, many continuing from the colonial period, which produce insignificant yields but harass both the taxpayer and the revenue collector. It appears that most of them have little more than a nuisance meaning to the taxpayer since their rates are extremely low. Their administration diverts the attention of tax authorities from enforcement of more lucrative revenue producers. Moreover, their fiscal contribution has declined since prewar years. The household tax (*personeele belasting*), for example, contributed over 1 per cent of total revenues in 1929 and 1939, but its yield for the years 1953-1955 was less than one-fifth of 1 per cent of

*Between these limits, the company tax rates and their percentages are as follows:

From Rp.	To Rp.	Per Cent
500,000	1,000,000	42.5
1,000,000	1,500,000	45.0
1,500,000	2,000,000	47.5
2,000,000	2,500,000	50.0

total taxes collected. In the prewar period this tax was levied against many forms of personal property as well as imputed rental value for homes; at present it is assessed exclusively against certain types of transportation facilities. Other minor taxes, some requiring considerable administration, include the restaurant tax ("reconstruction tax"), the capital assets tax (vermogens belasting), the urban real estate tax (verponding), the radio tax, the vehicle tax, stamp duties, and numerous other transaction levies, all of which contribute a total of less than 1 per cent of total revenues.

The complexity and diversity of Indonesia's present tax structure clearly have much to do with the efficiency of tax administration as a whole. Taxes are too numerous and their regulations too complex to make it feasible for the government to effectively reach all of the tax base which is nominally subject to taxation. Hence much of the economy's taxable capacity, in some cases representing personal incomes substantially above subsistence levels of consumption, is not reached by the present pattern of taxation. All this accounts, too, for the fact that duties on foreign trade have contributed an increasingly large share of total revenues. These duties require relatively little administration; problems of collection are eased by the fact that the flow which is taxed is both highly localized and—apart from smuggling—readily identifiable. The problem of administration, therefore, accounts for the increased shift toward taxation of the capital-intensive sector during the Republican period. Central Government administration in Indonesia tends to be primarily an urban phenomenon, radiating out from the capital, Djakarta, with ever-decreasing scope and effectiveness. Despite the limitation of administration in the provinces, Central Government has striven for greater centralization of fiscal responsibilities than the Dutch had found convenient. Since the transfer of sovereignty to the Republic, there has been no legal delegation of fiscal functions to the local levels of government. Central Government has chosen to assume responsibility for financing much of local expenditures through central subsidization since it has not delegated revenue sources to provinces and lower levels of administration. The unresolved conflict of interests between Central Government and local levels has interfered with the ability of Central Government to enlist the support of local officials in its revenue-collecting functions as the Dutch had done. In the provinces outside Java there is considerable resistance to Central Government efforts to dominate revenue sources. (In a later chapter we shall argue that a workable division of tax bases between Central Government and localities would enhance the revenue-producing capabilities at local levels of government.)

Notes to Chapter 4

1. This is Ragnar Nurkse's apt term for savings forced by government fiscal policy. See Ragnar Nurkse, Problems of Capital Formation in Underdeveloped Countries, Basil Blackwell, Oxford, 1953.

2. P. T. Bauer and B. S. Yamey, The Economics of Underdeveloped Countries, Cambridge University Press, Cambridge, 1957, Ch. 13.

3. W. F. Prins, Het Belastingrecht van Indonesia (The Tax Laws of Indonesia), Groningen, Netherlands, 1951, Ch. 2, "Beknopte Geschiedenis van het Belasting Stensel" (A Brief History of the Tax System).

4. J. S. Furnivall, Colonial Policy and Practise, Cambridge University Press, Cambridge, 1948, p. 223.

5. J. S. Furnivall, Netherlands India: A Study of Plural Economy, Cambridge University Press, Cambridge, 1939, p. 118.

6. Ibid., p. 132.

7. Ibid., p. 211.

8. Ibid., p. 137.

9. M. D. Dris, "Taxation in Indonesia," Ekonomi dan Keuangan Indonesia, Vol. XI, August-September 1958, p. 421.

10. John H. Adler, quoted in H. P. Wald and J. N. Froomkin, Agricultural Taxation and Economic Development, Harvard Law School, Cambridge, 1954, p. 67.

11. Report of the Bank Indonesia, 1953-1954, p. 92.

12. Bank Indonesia Bulletin, No. 15, First and Second Quarters, 1958.

13. Bank Indonesia Bulletin, No. 13, Third Quarter, 1957, p. 24.

14. Report of the Bank Indonesia, 1956-1957, p. 126.

15. Bank Indonesia Bulletin, No. 12, First and Second Quarters, 1957, p. 20.

16. To quote the Dris study: ". . . the number of persons liable to income tax declined steadily from 1952 to 1955 (incomes over Rp. 5,000: 227,950 in 1955 against 286,362 in 1952; incomes below Rp. 5,000: 2,119,784 in 1955 against 2,743,848 in 1952). It would seem, however, that this decline is abnormal, for even if reliefs and/or tax rates were adjusted to the cost of living during that period, incomes in industry and trade, like wages, have probably followed a similar trend. It would seem therefore that if the Administration had sufficient qualified staff and could apply more effective control, there would be a great improvement in tax returns from self-employed persons." Dris, loc. cit., pp. 434-435.

5

THE TAX BURDEN AND TAXABLE CAPACITY

Thorough analysis of the tax burden and taxable capacity in underdeveloped countries is not a conspicuous feature of the existing literature on financing economic development. The scarcity of such analysis is the result of lack of data rather than conscious or unconscious oversight by economists. Accurate information on the size of national income and its distribution is rare indeed. Without such data, it is difficult to obtain a picture of the distribution of the tax burden among the various income groups. Evidence relating to the many qualitative conditions which affect the shifting and incidence of taxes is also sparce. These very real obstacles to thorough analysis have deterred economists from making even a reconnaissance attack on some of the basic problems relating to financing economic development through the fiscal system.

Preliminary consideration of the tax burden and taxable capacity can provide important insights into the general question of financing economic development in Indonesia. Although a detailed analysis of the distribution of income and of the tax burden among groups or narrow sectors cannot be made, it is possible to provide a rough picture of the relative taxable capacity in the two major sectors of the economy. Prewar studies of national income and the tax burden shed some light on the problem. By some refinements in the prewar studies, we can attempt a comparison of the Indonesian tax burden and taxable capacity toward the end of colonial control (1939) and in 1952. Estimates are also possible for the tax burden in 1954 and 1956 and for an earlier year (1929).

Data are inadequate for a comprehensive study of taxable capacity. Postwar national income statistics are based upon data collected by S. Daniel Neumark for the years 1951 and 1952.[1] Neumark's estimates are presented as domestic product by industrial origin, but sector accounts were not derived. Extrapolations from Neumark's data have been supplied by the National Planning Bureau for later years, but these estimates are presented only as aggregates with no industrial breakdown.[2]

The analysis in this chapter, therefore, focuses upon a comparison of the prewar tax burden with that in 1952. Sectoral distribution of national income cannot be obtained from the Planning Bureau estimates for later years. However, we do provide rough estimates for the distribution of the tax burden between the economy's major sectors for 1954 and 1956, and we see no significant change from 1952. On the other hand, there is evidence suggesting that those forces which were producing changes in the sectoral composition of domestic product and income between 1939 and 1952 have produced similar changes since 1952.* This suggests that the conclusions drawn for 1952 will have continued relevance for financing economic development in the immediate future.

*The Planning Bureau's estimates for investment (presented in Chapter 2) show that annual investment continued to increase in the labor-intensive sector after 1952 while falling in the capital-intensive sector.

The Two-Sector Model of the Indonesian Economy

The basic method we have used is to analyze the distribution of national income and the tax burden between the two major economic sectors of the Indonesian economy. The dichotomy between a capital-intensive, technologically advanced sector on the one hand and a labor-intensive, technologically retarded sector on the other is so pronounced that the same tax devices produce significantly different yields in the two sectors. Our analysis attempts to show the relationship between the government's tax burden and taxable capacity in these sectors during the last decade of the colonial period and the results of applying essentially the same tax structure, with some changes in rates, in the changed conditions in which the Indonesian economy operated in 1952.

In Indonesia, as in other underdeveloped countries, the sharp dichotomy between labor-intensive and capital-intensive sectors emerged as a result of the society's limited exposure to Western techniques of production. The Western impact failed to generate technological change—with accompanying changes in social and cultural parameters—throughout the society. The result is the rather striking phenomenon, described as "technological dualism," which is analyzed in the Introduction to this volume. It is precisely this "dualism" which development planning seeks to eliminate by changing production functions throughout the economy.

For purposes of our analysis, the scope of each of the sectors must be defined with some precision. The labor-intensive sector includes all of the nonmarket economy, production of food crops for the market, smallholders' production of agricultural export crops, and small-scale cottage industry. It also includes labor and materials supplied to the capital-intensive sector (e.g., plantation agriculture, mining, and manufacturing) by those productive factors to which these activities are subsidiary occupations (i.e., factors which find their main employment in the labor-intensive sector). Similarly, all trading activities carried on within the sector itself are construed to belong to this sector; inter-sectoral trade is allocated on the basis of the trader's primary orientation. Thus trade concerned with the outward flow of goods from the labor-intensive sector is included in that sector's scope, and the flow of goods from the capital-intensive to the labor-intensive sector is excluded.

The remaining economic activity takes place within the capital-intensive sector. This sector, therefore, includes noncottage manufacturing activity, with the exception of wages paid to the rural sector; mining and plantation agriculture, with a similar deduction; and that part of trade and transport not allocated to the labor-intensive sector.[3]

There are aspects of this analytical division of the Indonesian economy which merit emphasis. Most significant, perhaps, is the fact that incomes in the form of capitalistic profits are found predominantly in the capital-intensive sector. Similarly, techniques of production in this sector are more advanced, being the products of either Western imitation or import. In this sector, too, foreign ownership of capital goods and foreign management of enterprise have been dominant, although the role of the foreigner has been consistently reduced by nationalistic policies during the past several years. The scope of foreign enterprise in this sector will be further lessened by the recent expulsion of Dutch nationals. In the prewar period, however, capital-intensive enterprises, particularly mining, plantation agriculture, and manufacturing, were almost exclusively owned and operated by foreign enterprise* or by the colonial government.

These facts permit the use of Dutch colonial studies for our analysis of the tax burden for the years 1929 and 1939. Colonial economic statistics distinguished between the economic activity of Indonesians and non-Indonesians, and estimates of both income distribution and the tax burden were presented in terms of this ethnic distinction. For the prewar period the Indonesian sector can be equated with the labor-intensive sector, and the foreign sector can be equated with the capital-intensive sector. This procedure presents conceptual problems in analyzing that part of national income and the tax burden which arose from Indonesian labor participation in the capital-intensive sector of the economy, and thus introduces some fuzziness into the analysis for the interwar period; for the postwar year 1952, our stricter definitions have been employed.

In estimating the distribution of tax burden between sectors during the prewar period we have relied heavily upon the results of a study by Götzen,[4] with refinements required by our definitions. Götzen worked with statistical data provided by two studies of the impact of the tax system on the Indonesian population.[5] Those sources were employed by Götzen to obtain the incidence and distribution of particular taxes among Indonesian and non-Indonesian groups, although in a number of cases he made completely independent estimates. Since Meyer-Ranneft and Huender's study was concerned with Java and Madura and van Ginkel's with the Outer Islands (Sumatra, Borneo, Celebes, etc.), all the ratios used by Götzen are weighted averages between this geographical dichotomy.

*Colonial statistics defined non-Indonesian minority groups (e.g., the Chinese) as foreigners.

Allocation of the central government's total tax burden in the two sectors requires rather detailed study of the nature and impact of each particular tax and of the changes in tax enforcement that occurred between 1929 and 1952. This information and the reasoning behind each ratio for allocating the tax burden between sectors is presented in Appendix C. The assumptions about tax shifting implicit in our analysis will be examined in detail in the next chapter.

Distribution of the Tax Burden and Taxable Capacity Between Sectors

Summary results of the analysis of the sectoral distribution of Central Government's tax burden are given in Table 24. Our analysis underlines the persistence of a historical trend away from taxation of the labor-intensive sector, the contribution of which to total tax revenues fell from 43 per cent in 1929 to 40 per cent in 1939 and to 36 per cent in 1952.

Table 24

DISTRIBUTION OF THE INDONESIAN TAX BURDEN*

1929, 1939, 1952

	1929		1939		1952	
	Capital-Intensive Sector	Labor-Intensive Sector	Capital-Intensive Sector	Labor-Intensive Sector	Capital-Intensive Sector	Labor-Intensive Sector
Percentage of tax burden	57	43	60	40	64	36

*These are summary results of the distribution of the tax burden between sectors. Detailed results for each year are presented in Appendix C, Table C-2.

Table 25

INDONESIAN INCOME BY INDUSTRIES, 1939

Industry	Million Guilders: Java and Madura	Million Guilders: Outer Provinces	Million Guilders: Netherlands Indies	Per Cent of Total Income: Java and Madura	Per Cent of Total Income: Outer Provinces	Per Cent of Total Income: Netherlands Indies	From Labor-Intensive Sector: Per Cent	From Labor-Intensive Sector: Million Guilders
1. Foodcrops	518	258	776	39.7	36.0	38.4	100	776
2. Export crops	31	127	158	2.4	17.7	7.8	100	158
3. Livestock products	46	21	67	3.5	2.9	3.3	100	67
4. Poultry	25	11	36	1.9	1.5	1.8	100	36
5. Fisheries	10	7	17	0.8	1.0	0.8	100	17
6. Forestry	5	8	13	0.4	1.1	0.6	100	13
7. Plantations and mines (wages)	78	73	151	6.0	10.2	7.5	100	151
8. Plantations and mines (rent)	22		22	1.7		1.1	100	22
9. Manufacturing	225	75	300	17.2	10.5	14.9	90	270
10. Government	98	54	152	7.5	7.5	7.5	66	101
11. Trade	105	30	135	8.0	4.2	6.7	80	108
12. Communications	21	8	29	1.6	1.1	1.4		
13. Servants	35	11	46	2.7	1.5	2.3	50	23
14. House rent	70	30	100	5.4	4.2	4.9	80	80
15. Professions	16	4	20	1.2	0.6	1.0		
Total	1,305	717	2,022	100.0	100.0	100.0	av. = 90	1,822

Source: For national income data, see J. J. Polak, The National Income of the Netherlands Indies, 1921-1939, Institute of Pacific Relations, New York, 1942.

The significance of this trend in the distribution of the tax burden for the finance of economic development requires analysis of the growth of national income and changes in its sectoral distribution over the same period. We now turn to a discussion of this subject.

Data for the size and composition of national income in 1939 are taken from J. J. Polak's study, The National Income of the Netherlands Indies, 1921-1939. Income was computed for the three ethnic groups, Indonesians, Europeans, and foreign Asiatics, with government export income treated as a fourth category. The income produced by these groups for 1939 was reported as follows (million NEI guilders):

Indonesians	2,022
Europeans	371
Foreign Asiatics	292
Government Export Income	38
Nonresidents	210
Total	2,933

A breakdown by industrial origin was computed only for the ethnic group Indonesians, since income arising from the other groups was based on income tax data. The composition of national income among the Indonesian group is given in Table 25.

Assuming that all European income was produced in the capital-intensive sector and allocating income of "foreign Asiatics" between the two sectors, income produced in the labor-intensive sector in 1939 is estimated to be 1,987 million guilders,* or 68 per cent of the total national income as computed by Polak.

National income data for 1952 are drawn from Neumark's study of Indonesia's national income. The distribution of income between the

*1,822 million guilders from the Indonesian group and 165 million guilders from the "foreign Asiatics" sector.

economy's two major sectors has been made on the basis of data obtained from the Central Bureau of Statistics. These results are shown in Table 26.

Table 26

THE NATIONAL INCOME OF INDONESIA BY INDUSTRIAL ORIGIN, 1952

	Total * (Thousand Rp.)	Labor-Intensive Sector Per Cent	Labor-Intensive Sector Thousand Rp.
Agriculture			
Peasant food crops	30,054,093	100.0	30,054,093
Peasant export crops	7,649,639	100.0	7,649,639
Estate crops	2,823,171	10.0	282,317
Livestock	3,132,190	100.0	3,132,190
Fisheries	2,687,666	100.0	2,687,666
Forestry	1,245,412	100.0	1,245,412
Total agriculture	47,592,171		45,051,317
Less indirect tax adjustment	-1,507,000	93.0	-1,401,510
Net agriculture	46,085,171		43,649,807
Mining	1,846,193	10.0	184,619
Industry	6,700,000	50.0	3,350,000
Transport and communications	2,491,801		
Trade, banking, and insurance	10,942,700	varies	6,586,043
Hotels, restaurants, and catering	224,000		
Entertainment industries	168,000		
Private building and construction	945,000	33.3	315,000
Rent	5,300,000	80.0	4,240,000
Free professions	500,000		
Domestic service	550,000	50.0	275,000
Central Government, including defense	4,054,956	66.7	2,703,304
Local government	1,249,800	66.7	833,200
Government income from property, excluding estates	581,300		
NET DOMESTIC PRODUCT AT FACTOR COST	81,638,921		62,136,973

*S. Daniel Neumark, "The National Income of Indonesia," Ekonomi dan Keuangan Indonesia, Vol. VII, June 1954, Table 1, p. 354.

The results of Polak and Neumark are not strictly comparable because of Polak's emphasis upon ethnic groups and because of other methodological differences between the two authors. Nevertheless, a comparison of the results of the sectoral distribution of national income for 1939 and 1952, as estimated here, yields a rough approximation of certain basic changes which occurred between the end of colonial rule and the first several years of Indonesian independence.

In 1952, 76 per cent of total national income as computed by Neumark originated in the labor-intensive sector; the amount from this sector in 1939 had been 68 per cent. It is our opinion that this significant shift resulted in part from structural changes in the economy induced by the declining role of foreigners who contributed skills and capital to the capital-intensive sector. This is tantamount to arguing that the Indonesian economy showed retrogression (in terms of extending the scope of the capital-intensive sector) during the domestic political turmoil which characterized most of the period 1939-1952. In the years since independence, Indonesian development activity, as pointed out in Chapter 1, has been effective in raising output mainly in the labor-intensive sector of the economy. In the capital-intensive sector the Indonesian government's primary concern has been transferring ownership of enterprise from foreign to Indonesian nationals. On balance, the result of this policy has probably been a net reduction of capital facilities in this sector, at least outside the petroleum industry. Essentially the same conclusions are suggested by data on the growth of Indonesia's national income published in 1957 by the National Planning Bureau.[6] These data show that between 1951 and 1955 net domestic product in constant rupiah grew at an annual rate of 4-5 per cent (depending on 1952 or 1955 value of the rupiah). Most of that increase, however, was accounted for by growth of output in agriculture, for which the National Planning Bureau made independent estimates. Growth of nonagricultural output was estimated by extrapolation from Neumark's figures, and what growth was reported here may have been overestimated by this device. The Planning Bureau estimates that income from agriculture represented 53.3 per cent of net domestic product in 1951, 58 per cent in 1954, and 56 per cent in 1955 (a bad harvest year). These figures suggest that the rate of growth in the labor-intensive sector has continued to outpace that in the capital-intensive sector since 1952. Our allocation of income between the two sectors for 1952 (see Table 26) shows that 95 per cent of agricultural income arose from the labor-intensive sector and that agricultural employment accounted for 80 per cent of this sector's income. (See Appendix C.) While the margin of error in the estimate which describes this shift in quantitative terms between 1939 and 1952 may be large, it is quite clear that a shift in the distribution of income between these sectors has taken place, and recent evidence suggests that this shift has continued.

We are now in a position to relate the tax burden in each sector to its taxable capacity (in terms of income or product). The first and most obvious conclusion that emerges from the analysis is that the tax burden fell predominantly upon the smaller of the two sectors. In 1952 the capital-intensive sector, which produced 24 per cent of the economy's income, bore 64 per cent of the central government tax burden, whereas the labor-intensive sector bore 36 per cent of the tax burden while receiving 76 per cent of national income. The argument may be put even more strongly by comparing the share of sectoral income withdrawn by direct taxation. If export taxes are included as direct taxes,* we find

*This procedure is justified by conclusions from our analysis of incidence of export taxes in Indonesia. See Chapter 6.

that direct taxation withdrew about 22 per cent of income from the capital-intensive sector but less than 4 per cent from the labor-intensive sector in 1952. (See Table 27.) Direct taxation, as defined in Table 27, produced almost two-thirds of Central Government tax yields in that year. The addition of indirect taxation, which was borne relatively equally by the two sectors, therefore, would not alter this result significantly. Since indirect taxes have been eliminated from the national income aggregate which we used, they were omitted in this calculation.

Table 27

RATIO OF DIRECT TAXES TO SECTORAL INCOME,* 1952

	Capital-Intensive Sector	Labor-Intensive Sector
Direct taxes (thousand Rp.):		
Income	1,700,700	26,200
Wealth and property	42,700	2,200
Export	2,457,400	1,443,300
Total	4,200,800	1,471,700
Income (thousand Rp.)	19,501,989	62,136,732
Direct taxes as per cent of income	21.5%	3.7%

*Data on direct taxes and their sectoral distribution are from Appendix C, Table C-2. Elaboration of methodology for sectoral allocation is also furnished in Appendix C.

The differing tax burdens between the two basic sectors are indicative of the fact that post-World War II taxation in Indonesia has been enforced with considerable vigor in the capital-intensive sector while the labor-intensive sector has received less emphasis. The problem of generalizing the scope of the central government tax administration by enforcing existing tax laws in the labor-intensive sector has not yet been squarely faced.

Our analysis can be carried further only by using less satisfactory statistical data than we have relied on up to this point. The questions which are most germane to our general theme are those concerned with the income of spending units and the tax burden per spending unit among various income groups and between sectors. As a result of limitations of data, we can suggest tentative evidence on these questions only by the broad sectors we have considered in our analysis.

Estimates of employment by occupational breakdown are available for 1950 and 1953.[7] The data for 1950 are more useful for our purposes since they are presented in more detail, with explanatory information for allocating employment between the two sectors. By applying our definitions of the capital-intensive and labor-intensive sectors, we arrive at the employment breakdown presented in Appendix C, Table C-3. The use of 1950 data involves the assumption that there were no significant changes in sectoral employment between that year and 1952.

The 1950 data placed total employment at 26 million out of a total 1950 population of about 75 million. This works out to the percentage of gainfully employed (34 per cent) reported in the last complete census—taken in 1930. Of the 26,000,000 employed, our estimate of sectoral employment places 20,262,500 in the labor-intensive sector (about 78 per cent) and only 5,737,500 (about 22 per cent) in the capital-intensive sector. This estimate of employment distribution provides the basis for presenting a rough approximation of income and tax burden per gainfully employed in the two sectors. Such estimates for 1952 are given in Tables 28 and 29.

Table 28 shows the total tax burden relative to sector income and income per gainfully employed. The table is purely illustrative since indirect taxes are included in the total tax burden but excluded from sector income (using the concept of national income at factor cost). No great violence is done to logic, however, since the indirect tax burden falls rather evenly upon the two sectors. The results thus obtained are suggestive. Although income per gainfully employed was only slightly greater in the capital-intensive sector than in the labor-intensive sector (Rp. 3,399 compared to Rp. 3,067), the total tax burden per gainfully employed was about six times greater in the capital-intensive sector. Total taxes were about 30 per cent of income per employed laborer in the capital-intensive sector in contrast to about 5 per cent in the labor-intensive sector.

Table 28

INCOME AND TOTAL TAX BURDEN PER GAINFULLY EMPLOYED, BY SECTOR, 1952*

	Capital-Intensive Sector	Labor-Intensive Sector
Income (million Rp.)	19,502	62,137
Total tax burden (million Rp.)	5,744	3,246
Gainfully employed	5,737,500	20,262,500
Income per gainfully employed (Rp.)	3,399	3,067
Total tax burden per gainfully employed (Rp.)	1,001	160
Tax burden as per cent of income	29%	5%

*For methodology, see text.

Strictly speaking, the ratio of direct tax payments to national income at factor cost is more significant. For the Indonesian economy as a whole in 1952 this was approximately 7 per cent; i.e., about 7 per cent of national income at factor cost was captured by direct taxation. Table 29, however, shows that this direct tax burden was levied mainly upon the capital-intensive sector. In this sector, the average direct tax burden upon income per worker of Rp. 3,399 was Rp. 750, leaving disposable income per gainfully employed of Rp. 2,649. In the labor-intensive sector, the average direct tax payment was only Rp. 73, leaving disposable income per gainfully employed of Rp. 2,994 from the Rp. 3,067 earned per worker.

Table 29

INCOME AND DIRECT TAX BURDEN PER GAINFULLY EMPLOYED, BY SECTOR, 1952*

	Capital-Intensive Sector	Labor-Intensive Sector
Income (million Rp.)	19,502.0	62,137.0
Direct tax burden (million Rp.)	4,200.8	1,471.7
Gainfully employed (thousands)	5,737.5	20,262.5
Income per gainfully employed (Rp.)	3,399.0	3,067.0
Direct tax burden per gainfully employed (Rp.)	750.0	73.0
Direct tax burden as per cent of employed	18.7%	2.4%

*For methodology, see text.

To summarize the results of our analysis, income per worker in the capital-intensive sector appeared to be only slightly greater than in the labor-intensive sector. However, as a result of great disparities in the direct tax burden between sectors, disposable income per worker was about Rp. 3,000 in the labor-intensive sector compared to about Rp. 2,650 in the other sector.

The income figures present a rather paradoxical result. A priori, we should have expected considerably higher income per laborer in the capital-intensive sector. By definition, capital investment per worker is greater in this sector and more modern techniques of production are employed than in the labor-intensive sector. We should expect to find a higher capital-output ratio. A labor-output ratio which is not significantly below that in the labor-intensive sector presents conceptual difficulties, suggesting that greater capital per worker has not been effective in raising productivity of labor, the goal of economic development.

The paradox suggested by our analysis reflects the political and social conditions which have surrounded Indonesian economic activity during the post-independence years. Prior to independence, the capital-intensive sector had been virtually identical with the foreign-owned and -operated sector of the economy. Data from the colonial period, in fact, substantiate this point and also suggest a considerably greater disparity between income per worker in the two sectors than found for 1952.[8] After independence, however, the capital-intensive sector became less productive as Dutch technicians and entrepreneurs left Indonesia and Indonesian management began to replace foreigners. The value of capital stock may have fallen somewhat in this sector as the Dutch attempted to liquidate past investment, and plant and equipment were frequently left idle. In some industries, at least, replacement of depreciating facilities was not possible, and, if operation continued, the capital-labor ratio tended to fall. We have already noted in earlier chapters that entrepreneurial and technical bottlenecks delayed new capital formation from reaching productive operation, prolonging the gestation period of new Indonesian investment. Squatters have reduced the effective area of Sumatran plantations; and labor legislation, together with union activity, has resulted in the retention of redundant workers in foreign enterprises.

Under such conditions the higher capital-labor ratio in the capital-intensive sector did not raise output per gainfully employed much above that in more labor-intensive occupations. It seems likely, however, that the figure of 20,262,500 persons "gainfully occupied" in this sector greatly underestimates the numbers actually engaged on a part-time basis, in view of the use of women and children during planting and harvesting seasons.

The relatively high tax burden in the capital-intensive sector may itself have diminished the productivity of this sector. There is evidence that some agricultural plantations have operated at less than full capacity and failed to reach prewar output levels because of high profit taxation, rising costs of production, and other factors.[9] Economic development requires more than capital formation; it also requires conditions under which capital-intensive industries may operate profitably.

Meanwhile, Indonesian independence appears to have stimulated the growth of output in the labor-intensive sector, particularly in the early years, so that the gap between the productivity of labor in the two sectors has been further narrowed. Government policies to raise output in this sector were more effective than their counterpart in the capital-intensive sector, as pointed out in Chapter 1. Government efforts to inject capital, fertilizer, and improved techniques into agriculture were accompanied by vigorous efforts within the desa sector itself, as the National Planning Bureau's statistics on capital formation suggest. The growth of local development programs, in part aimed at raising agricultural productivity, have been an important feature of Indonesia since independence. These forces have led to the interesting paradox that the labor-intensive sector has tended to be dynamic while the capital-intensive sector has tended to stagnate. It is essential that the growth of the capital-intensive sector and its productivity accelerate if economic development is to occur.

The Sectoral Distribution of the Tax Burden, 1952-1956

In the opening pages of this chapter we indicated that the year 1952 provides the most satisfactory basis for a study of the tax burden during the postwar period. National income data adaptable to our analysis are available for 1952 but not for later years. We have argued above that it is doubtful that the distribution of income between the capital-intensive and the labor-intensive sectors has been reversed since 1952. Rather, it appears that the trend toward a shift in the distribution of income in favor of the labor-intensive sector has continued. It is now necessary to raise the question of whether or not the allocation of Central Government's tax burden between these same sectors has followed the pattern described for 1952.

As pointed out in the preceding chapter, there have been several shifts in the structure of taxation over the period 1952 to 1956. These

Those changes are shown in Table 30, which presents yields from major taxes. Such taxes produced well over 90 per cent of total tax yields for the years shown—1952, 1954, and 1956. For the period 1952-1956 as a whole the only change of great significance was the replacement of losses from export taxation, which produced 43 per cent of total tax revenues in the favorable export year, 1952, by heavy levies upon imports. By 1956 such levies produced slightly more than half of total tax yields, again emphasizing the strong propensity in an underdeveloped economy with a relatively large foreign-trade sector to levy an important share of its total tax burden upon this sector, where ease of collection is enhanced by relatively complete exchange control. Incidentally, it should be pointed out here that the assumption of autonomy by the outlying provinces will reduce the ability of Central Government to draw a disproportionately large percentage of its tax yield from the foreign-trade sector in the immediate future. Preliminary results for 1958 testify to this fact.[10] Until the problem of national unity is resolved, there are likely to be larger government deficits and efforts to contract government expenditures. We should expect, therefore, that financing of economic development will be severely hampered, if not completely abandoned.

During the year 1954 the tax structure was in transition from one primarily oriented toward export taxation to one emphasizing import duties. Although import surcharges with high percentage rates were assessed against many categories of goods, their yield still failed to match revenues from the foreign-trade sector during the years of export boom and high export taxation. Efforts were made to increase the scope of the business income tax through more general enforcement, and excise tax rates were raised. This action produced a temporary shift from dominant reliance upon revenues from foreign trade (36 per cent of the total in 1954 compared to 59 per cent in 1952). With revisions in the import surcharge and export-certificate systems in 1955 and 1956, yields from the foreign-trade sector again began to climb, reaching 40 per cent of the total tax yield in 1955 and 54 per cent in 1956.

Table 30

MAJOR SOURCES OF TAX REVENUES, 1952, 1954, 1956

Tax	1952		1954		1956	
	Million Rupiah	Per Cent of Total	Million Rupiah	Per Cent of Total	Million Rupiah	Per Cent of Total
Business income	896	10	1,330	18	1,569	12
Personal income	648	7	805	11	1,169	9
Sales	628	7	611	7	942	7
Excise	1,075	12	1,593	21	1,877	14
Export	3,901	43	544	7	424	3
Import	1,443	16	2,174	29	6,857	51
Total of all taxes*	9,037		7,511		13,450	

*Only major taxes are included in this table; the total given includes all tax receipts. The major taxes listed contributed 95 per cent of total tax revenues in 1952, 93 per cent in 1954, and 96 per cent in 1956.

Sources: Data are from sources cited in Appendix C.

It is interesting to observe that these variations in the tax structure produced virtually no change in the allocation of Central Government's tax burden between the capital-intensive and labor-intensive sectors of the economy. This result, after all, was to be expected since Central Government was bent upon increasing revenues from its existing tax

Table 31

SECTORAL ALLOCATION OF MAJOR TAXES

1954, 1956

A. 1954

Type of Tax	Amount of Tax in Million Rupiah	Capital-Intensive Sector		Labor-Intensive Sector	
		Per Cent	Million Rupiah	Per Cent	Million Rupiah
Business income	1,330	100	1,330		
Personal income	805	100	805		
Sales	611	50	305	50	305
Excise	1,593	20	319	80	1,274
Export	544	63	443	37	101
Import	2,174	67	1,450	33	725
Total	7,057		4,652		2,405
Per Cent of Total		66		34	

B. 1956

Type of Tax	Amount of Tax in Million Rupiah	Capital-Intensive Sector		Labor-Intensive Sector	
		Per Cent	Million Rupiah	Per Cent	Million Rupiah
Business income	1,569	100	1,569		
Personal income	1,169	100	1,169		
Sales	942	50	471	50	471
Excise	1,877	20	375	80	1,502
Export	424	63	267	37	157
Import	6,857	67	4,571	33	2,286
Total	12,838		8,422		4,416
Per Cent of Total		66		34	

structure, which was predominantly concerned with the capital-intensive sector of the economy. There has been no serious effort to increase tax yields or to free Central Government from primary reliance upon foreign-trade levies by broadening the scope of its tax structure to more effectively reach the large share of national income produced and distributed in the labor-intensive sector of the economy.

Our estimate of the allocation of the major taxes between the two sectors for the years 1954 and 1956 is presented in Table 31. The ratios for allocating these taxes between sectors are assumed to have remained the same as those employed for 1952, with the exception of import duties. Business and personal income taxes have continued to be enforced almost exclusively in the capital-intensive sector. There are no apparent reasons for changing the ratios used for sales and excise taxation. Similarly, a study of 1954 and 1956 export statistics suggests the same relative composition of exports as for 1952. However, significant changes have taken place in import taxation, as noted in Chapter 4. Semiluxury goods, luxury goods, and even raw materials for the capital-intensive sector of the economy bore the major share of the burden of import surcharges. These surcharges produced the greatest part of import tax yields in both 1954 and 1956 (55 per cent in 1954 and 72 per cent in 1956), whereas the qualities of import goods consumed by the labor-intensive sector, by and large, bore little or no surcharge duty and lower basic duty rates. Accordingly, we have changed the ratios for allocating the burden of import taxes between sectors from the equal distribution estimated for 1952 (50 per cent to each) to 66 2/3 per cent for the capital-intensive sector and 33 1/3 per cent for the labor-intensive sector for 1954 and 1956.[11]

Under these assumptions, we reach the rather puzzling result shown in Table 31. Despite relatively great changes in the composition of revenues produced by its major taxes between 1952 and later years, Central Government distributed its tax burden between the capital-intensive and labor-intensive sectors in the same ratio. Our analysis suggested that 64 per cent of the tax burden was borne by the capital-intensive sector in 1952, and that in 1954 and 1956 the share of the tax burden borne by this sector rose slightly to 66 per cent.

Taxable Capacity and Economic Development

The results of our somewhat tedious analysis of the bisectoral burden of Central Government taxation may now be related to our main theme—the problem of financing economic development. The results suggest, first of all, that the capital-intensive sector of the economy bears a relatively high tax burden in terms of aggregate and per capita income and that we should not expect to find in this sector significant margins which could be channeled to the finance of development. In this regard, some further points should be noted. Tax revenues are collected from the capital-intensive sector through a combination of fiscal devices which reach several strata of society as well as a wide range of economic functions. Nevertheless, the tax structure in this sector possesses a high degree of progressivity and is effective in reaching high incomes produced by modern industrial enterprise and trade. Taxes upon consumers include both the regressive type, exemplified by the general sales taxes and excises upon articles of daily use, and the more progressive levies upon the consumption of imported goods. Consumption taxation, however, represents less than 30 per cent of the total tax yield in this sector. For the remainder, the government tax burden falls mainly upon trade and enterprise and personal incomes received in these activities. The capital-intensive sector's share of export taxation, the leading revenue producer in 1952, was contributed largely by modern enterprise—plantations, the oil industry, manufacturing firms, and their marketing channels. We find a tax structure in this sector which takes advantage of unequal income distribution resulting from an anomalous mixture of modern techniques and unskilled and semiskilled labor. The relatively high burden of taxation borne by this sector raises questions of taxation and incentives examined in Chapter 6.

The burden of taxation in the labor-intensive sector of the economy is quite a different matter. The two striking differences from the capital-intensive sector relate to: (1) the considerably lower ratio of taxes to income, both aggregate and per worker,* and (2) the lack of progressivity of tax structure. Both factors are related to the lack of enforcement of the more progressive tax devices. Personal and business income taxes are almost completely neglected, and a limited degree of progressivity is provided only by export taxation and varying duties on the consumption of imported goods. In contrast to the capital-intensive sector, consumption taxation of all types produced almost one-half of revenues in this sector.

A sector's taxable capacity depends not only on its aggregate income but also on the distribution of income within the sector. Paradoxically, for reasons discussed above, income per worker (and perhaps even per capita) appears to be only slightly lower in the labor-intensive sector. Unfortunately, there are no figures on the distribution of income

*In 1952 we found the ratio of the total tax burden per employed worker to be only 5 per cent. This compares with a land tax burden of 10.5 per cent on agricultural incomes during the 1920's. (J. W. Meyer-Ranneft and W. Huender, Onderzoek naar den Belastingdruk op de Inlandsche Bevolking [An Inquiry Concerning the Tax Burden upon the Native Population], Landsdrukkerij, Weltevreden, 1926, p. 41.)

by income groups. The available information suggests that the average peasant is better off than his counterpart in the capital-intensive sector—the unskilled laborer. Considerable disparity of income distribution exists within both sectors. Industrial capitalists have much higher incomes than their employees. But in the labor-intensive sector, too, the upper-income groups, comprised of landlords, traders, lenders, and merchant-employers, receive a disproportionate share of total sectoral income.[12] While the industrial capitalists, by and large, are subject to high tax rates, and enforcement is more feasible in the capital-intensive sector, landlords, lenders, and other upper-income groups in the labor-intensive sector escape from taxation at high and progressive rates.

Our analysis of the tax burden and the accumulating evidence on unequal income distribution in the labor-intensive sector suggests, therefore, that extension of the enforcement of tax devices now employed in the capital-intensive sector to the other sector would yield substantial increases in tax revenues. If, for example, the upper-income groups in the labor-intensive sector received one-fourth of that sector's income, a tax burden upon these groups equal to that borne in the capital-intensive sector would have produced just short of Rp. 5 billion in additional yields in 1952. Tax revenues would have been raised by more than 50 per cent, and the ratio of tax revenues to national income would have been raised from 10 to 15 per cent. Further additions to revenues might well be feasible by more general taxation of the sector as a whole, i.e., by finding administrable and politically acceptable tax devices to reach income groups below the top fourth.

Thus the problem of enlarging the scope of the fiscal system to finance a development program in Indonesia, as in many other countries, is one of more effectively taxing incomes in the labor-intensive sector. However, economic analysis which suggests the existence of taxable capacity is quite another thing from demonstrating feasibility of increasing tax yields in a particular society at a particular time. Indonesia emerged from 350 years of Dutch rule in 1949 with fiscal institutions designed to support the particular form of colonial policy known as "indirect rule." The dramatic shifts in the structure of taxation discussed in Chapter 4 were responses to the broader shifts of colonial policy from the levying of direct economic burdens upon the Indonesian populace in the labor-intensive sector to molding the economy into an adjunct of the metropolitan country. Under the latter system, indirect rule sought to preserve order and security by allowing local autonomy in fiscal and administrative matters, with a minimum of Dutch supervision. A larger and larger share of revenues produced in relatively autonomous localities was retained for local administration. Statistically, this development was reflected in the reduction of the importance of land taxes in the revenue accounts of Central Government. In this setting, therefore, the precedent of raising revenues from the labor-intensive sector for Central Government purposes became relatively weak, and rural taxation came to be identified almost exclusively with the support of local expenditures. Central Government efforts to tax the labor-intensive sector inevitably produced more than the usual amount of local friction; and, strangely enough, Central Government land taxation in particular came to be viewed as a colonial device.

The patterns of colonial taxation just prior to independence produced a cadre of tax administrators who were concerned either with administering taxation in the capital-intensive sector, on which Central Government came to rely, or with supervising local taxation and claiming a small share for Central Government. As a consequence, newly independent Indonesia possesses virtually no Central Government tax administrators who have the will or experience to enforce stricter taxation in the labor-intensive sector.

It is equally important to note that the colonial system produced strong psychological attitudes which have hampered Central Government efforts to garner an increased amount of tax revenues from the labor-intensive sector. Local autonomy has always been a characteristic of Indonesian society, and it was fostered by the policies of indirect rule. Central Government taxes were viewed as capricious devices to capture a share of the local product for colonial purposes, and the revolution brought an unfortunate popular belief that such levies would end rather than be increased. Fundamentally, such attitudes reflect a lack of social integration on the broader levels of society. Since there is little recognition of the benefits that may result from Central Government activities, evidence for sacrifice through taxation is seen only in expenditures at local levels of government. Thus the government's efforts to arouse popular enthusiasm for its development program encounter local attitudes which impede financing a higher level of developmental expenditures through Central Government fiscal processes.

It seems quite clear, therefore, that translating the tax capacity of the labor-intensive sector into administratively and politically feasible measures for raising tax collection involves greater local government responsibility for both collecting and spending revenues. The community development sector of the Five Year Plan affords one opportunity for associating higher taxes—in money, effort, or in kind—with greater local benefits of government activity. To tap fully the potential financial resources of the rural economy, however, local government must probably assume responsibility for other development projects as well. This problem is discussed in Chapter 7.

Notes to Chapter 5

1. S. Daniel Neumark, "The National Income of Indonesia, 1951-1952," Ekonomi dan Keuangan Indonesia, Vol. VII, June 1954, pp. 348-391.

2. National Planning Bureau, "A Study of the Indonesian Economic Development Scheme," Ekonomi dan Keuangan Indonesia, Vol. X, September 1957, pp. 611-614.

3. A rather similar two-sector model of the underdeveloped economy is presented by S. P. Schatz in "Inflation in Underdeveloped Countries," American Economic Review, Vol. XLVII, No. 5 (September 1957), pp. 573-577.

4. L. Götzen, "Volksinkomen en Belasting" (National Income and Taxes), Koloniale Studiën, Vol. 17 (1933), pp. 449-484.

5. J. W. Meyer-Ranneft and W. Huender, Onderzoek naar den Belastingdruk op de Inlandsche Bevolking (An Inquiry Concerning the Tax Burden upon the Native Population), Weltevreden, 1926, and van Ginkel, Verslag van den Economischen Toestand en den Belastingdruk met Betrekking tot de Inlandsche Bevolking (Report on the Economic Situation and the Tax Burden with Reference to the Native Population), Weltevreden, 1929.

6. National Planning Bureau, loc. cit., pp. 611-613.

7. The estimates to which we refer were based upon surveys by the Indonesian Ministry of Economic Affairs. They were embodied in a United Nations report and are presented in the following source, from which they were taken: Human Relations Area Files, Inc., Yale University, Indonesia, Vol. III, Table I, p. 870.

8. J. J. Polak, The National Income of the Netherlands Indies, 1921-1939, Institute of Pacific Relations, New York, 1942, esp. Table 15.1, p. 59.

9. See Report of the Java Bank, 1951-1952, pp. 151-153.

10. Report of the Bank Indonesia, 1958-1959, p. 101.

11. Support for the validity of this ratio is given by discussion in the Report of the Bank Indonesia, 1954-1955, pp. 13-14.

12. There is a growing body of evidence which documents this general situation. See, for example, H. Ten Dam, Desa Tjibodas, Bogor, Indonesia, 1951, and R. A. Adiwilaga, Desa Tjipomakolan, Bandung, Indonesia, 1953. Both studies were translated into Dutch and reproduced by the Institute for the Tropics, University of Amsterdam.

6

TAX POLICY AND ECONOMIC INCENTIVES

A government in search of fiscal resources to finance a development program cannot concentrate solely on maximizing revenues if private enterprise is to play a significant role in economic development. In Indonesia the government is regarded as the prime mover in the dynamics of growth but not as the sole entrepreneur. The First Five Year Plan explicitly limits responsibility of the government for development, recognizing that the government is unable to administer the dominant part of the industrial and trading sectors, let alone agriculture. While all major political parties nominally endorse increasing socialization of the economy, no major party calls for early extension of public enterprise to the lion's share of production. Hence the effect of the government's development program and its financing on the private sector are matters of considerable importance.

We have already noted that financing development may have disincentive effects on production and investment, and that such effects will vary with the pattern of financing.

We have also shown that inflationary finance provides no easy solution to the incentive problem. The only course that can be recommended is the selective use of taxation with an eye to its effects on incentives.

Such selection requires knowledge of the many complex relationships in the economy, and empirical studies are among the scarcest of resources in underdeveloped countries. Yet a little knowledge is better than none, and an inventory of what is known about incentive effects of taxation may suggest some tentative conclusions and point to priorities for further research.

The incidence or burden of a particular tax may vary among societies; taxes may be borne at point of impact in one society and shifted elsewhere in another. Reaction may vary with the values or economic conditions of the community. In the United States a tax on the output of a small-scale farmer may cause him to work less; in Indonesia it may spur him to greater effort. Some Dutch writers have contended that taxes on the smallholders' output call forth greater effort and output; supply curves of effort and output are said to be backward sloping.[1]

This chapter is concerned with the incentive effects of Indonesia's three important types of taxation—taxes on foreign trade, income taxes, and consumption taxes. In recent years these taxes have produced more than 95 per cent of Central Government tax revenues. The questions in which we are interested are: (1) Where does the burden (incidence) of these taxes tend to fall? (2) What effects are they likely to produce on incentives to work, save, and assume the risks of investment?

In Chapter 5 we attempted to allocate the burden of Indonesian taxes between the two major sectors in the economy. The results of that calculation, however, have little value for studying the effect of particular taxes upon incentives. We must now identify more carefully the economic function upon which the burden of each tax is likely to fall, given Indonesian conditions. In either sector of the economy the tax may fall upon any of a number of functions—enterprise, exchange, or consumption—and the effect of the tax on incentives will vary with the point of its incidence. The problem is complicated by the fact that each of these functions includes a variety of activities, some contributing more to development of the economy than others. Enterprise includes not only activities of industrial and plantation entrepreneurs in the capital-intensive sector but also the entrepreneurial activities of the small agricultural and the small-scale industrial producer and the landlord* in the labor-intensive sector. Similarly, exchange refers to the large trading houses in the industrial sector as well as to the middleman who collects agricultural exports from the rural sector and who distributes consumer goods in return. Finally, consumers too fall into a number of groups, depending on the level of their income and their spending patterns. The discussion which follows seeks to analyze incentive effects among the variety of economic activities upon which taxes may fall.

Export Taxation

In the year 1952, which served as the basis for our first estimate of the sectoral distribution of the Indonesian tax burden, export taxes were the major revenue producer. In that year levies upon exporters provided 43 per cent of total tax income, considerably below the record postwar level of 55 per cent in 1951. In later years, however, revenues from this source fell drastically, comprising only 12 per cent of the total in 1953 and 3 per cent in 1956. (See Table 23.) The main factor behind this dramatic shift away from export taxation was

*Landlord enterprise is here defined to include all of the economic activities of the upper-income, landed group in the rural sector whether they consist of land ownership and renting, merchant-employer operations, or lending.

the fall in world prices for Indonesia's major exports after 1951. The course of this price trend is shown in Table 32.

Table 32

INDEX OF EXPORT PRICES, 1950-1956

(1950 = 100)

Export	1950	1951	1952	1953	1954	1955	1956
Rubber	100	172	110	79	73	115	104
Copra	100	124	75	95	87	76	75
Petroleum products	100	113	100	86	94	92	88
Tin ore	100	162	153	155	113	120	128
Average (all exports)	100	144	102	90	86	98	92

Sources: Report of the Java Bank, 1952-1953, Table 34, p. 106; Report of the Bank Indonesia, 1955-1956, Table 39, p. 110; and Report of the Bank Indonesia, 1956-1957, Table 43, p. 124.

The loss of revenues from export taxation caused a fall in the absolute amount of government tax receipts. The decline in the ratio of tax revenues to national income was greater since both domestic output and prices continued to rise during 1952 and 1953. Total tax revenues in 1953 were Rp. 1.5 billion below 1951, and the ratio of taxes to gross national product fell from 14 per cent in 1951 to 11 per cent in 1952 and 1953. In part, however, other taxes were raised or enforced more stringently to compensate for the loss of export-tax receipts. Import duties were revised upward through the introduction of the import surcharge system in 1952, raising their contribution to total revenues from 15 per cent in 1951 to 39 per cent in 1953. Increased revenues from business income taxes and consumption duties also showed small gains.

It is important to observe, therefore, that the structure of the Indonesian tax system shows considerable response to the level of world prices for its exports. Export taxation may have been effective in channeling a part of 1950-1952 windfall profits from export trade to the government, but it also affected the distribution of the tax burden among economic functions, which is the problem that concerns us here.

The gradual abandonment of export taxation in the years since 1952 should not suggest that an evaluation of its incentive effects is unimportant. The financing of economic development requires careful scrutiny of all tax sources, and periods of rising world prices for primary products will very likely lead to the resurgence of export-tax devices. As a matter of fact, the export-certificate system introduced in June 1957, while granting greater rupiah proceeds to exporters, imposed a 20 per cent tax on those proceeds. It would be misleading to conclude, therefore, that export taxation has become obsolete in Indonesia simply because conditions for producing attractive yields have been unfavorable since 1952. Our analysis will necessarily focus on the years 1950-1952, when export taxes occupied a major place in Indonesia's tax structure.

Export taxes have been widely used by developing countries to enlarge the scope of government expenditures and to provide the financing of development itself. Yet there is no general analysis of the incidence or incentive effects of these taxes in the literature, nor can there be without reference to the specific conditions in which export trade is carried on within a particular country.

The conditions in Indonesian export markets vary in accordance with the types of goods exported and with the world demand for the country's exports.* Despite these variations, a limited number of models of the pattern of export trade have fairly general validity throughout fluctuations in the export market. Indeed, three such models seem to cover most of the cases cited in the available literature: export of smallholders' agricultural output or the products of small-scale industry through a middleman system; export of the output from plantations, mines, and modern industry through private marketing channels; and export through government marketing boards or other Central Government marketing facilities.†

It is important to emphasize at the outset that each major sector of the economy has its own export channel. Both agricultural and industrial exports from the labor-intensive sector are marketed largely through the domestic middleman system. Copra, which is marketed through the government-sponsored Copra Foundation (Jajasan Kopra), is the obvious exception. The industrial sector, on the other hand, shows a high degree of vertical integration within firms, and export channels are characteristically an adjunct of the firm itself or are provided by agents of the firm. Similarly, the public sector provides its own export outlets or closely supervises the operations of agents to whom this function has been delegated.

*M. D. Dris, the United Nations' tax expert who studied the Indonesian tax system, seems to be pointing to this problem: "Export duties, owing to the special way in which they are levied, can hardly be put in either category [direct or indirect taxes]; they in no way affect the Indonesian consumer and can only be considered as a direct levy on the exporter if the state of world markets was [sic] such as to oblige him to meet them himself." (M. D. Dris, "Taxation in Indonesia," Ekonomi dan Keuangan Indonesia, Vol. XI, August-September 1958, p. 422.) The problem is that this approach leaves the incidence of export taxes unexplained.

†This classification obviously omits exporting through cooperative marketing channels. The Urgency Industrialization Plan (1951-1955) sought to strengthen this device, but its role continues to be marginal in significance.

Table 33

EXPORTS FROM THE MAJOR SECTORS, 1950 AND 1951

	Volume (Thousand Tons)		Percentage Increase in Volume	Value (Million Rp.)	
	1950	1951		1950	1951
Products mainly from Western industries and estates* (excluding petroleum)	7,079	7,247	2	1,445	2,180
Products mainly of indigenous origin†	1,127	1,366	21	1,434	2,368

*Capital-intensive sector.

†Labor-intensive sector.

Source: Report of the Java Bank, 1951-1952, Table 36, p. 122, and Table 37, p. 123.

Private export activities show significant variations over the course of cycles in world prices for Indonesian exports. Since Westernized firms in the capital-intensive sector, whether plantation, factory, or mine, tend to market a fairly constant share of output in the export market, such firms are specialized in export activity and commit resources more or less permanently to production for export. The labor-intensive sector, on the other hand, tends to expand its participation in the export market when world prices allow greater returns to factors of production. In other words, the agricultural laborer considers his labor (and other resources) as factors which can be shifted between production for export and production for domestic consumption; whereas Westernized industry is relatively capital intensive, and the limits to expanding its capacity are more circumscribed. The volume of exports from this sector shows less response to world price changes. Thus the importance of exports to total income tends to show more variation in the labor-intensive than in the capital-intensive sector. A corollary of this proposition is that windfall profits from world price rises tend to be more important in the labor-intensive sector than an average ratio of its exports to sectoral income would suggest. Empirical evidence on the behavior of exports from the two sectors during the prosperous export years is presented in Table 33. Three basic models follow:

Model I: Export through a middleman system. The small-scale Indonesian producer, whether agricultural or industrial, typically markets his output through a middleman system which has tentacles throughout Indonesia. The middleman may be either a local trader or a representative of a large trading firm. In either case he sells goods destined for export to specialized export firms, which may provide extensive credit and transport assistance to the middleman who actually provides the marketing outlets for the smallholder or the cottage industrialist.

The actual relationship between the final exporter, the middleman, and the original producer of export products, therefore, may take any of the following forms:

1. The final exporter may dominate the whole process in bargaining strength by having a monopsonistic position, extending capital and credit for marketing functions or controlling the supply of producer goods which the middleman characteristically distributes.

2. The middleman may achieve significant bargaining strength in his own right either through monopsonistic power of his own or by accumulation of adequate capital to establish his independence vis-à-vis relatively large and specialized export and import concerns.

3. It is conceivable that smallholders may be able to develop some degree of bargaining strength of their own if they do not face a monopsonistic market. In the areas easily accessible to cities where foreign trading operations are located, individual smallholders may fçce a market where some degree of competition exists on the buying as well as on the selling side. In periods of high world prices for primary products it is conceivable that a sellers' market might arise in a market characterized by substantial degrees of competition on both sides. The normal tendency toward oligopsonistic price fixing may be frustrated by the lure of high profits, and the supply price may edge upward as a result of competitive bidding for the limited supply available in a given area.

In the actual conditions which exist in Indonesia, however, Case 3 is rarely found. The producer in the rural sector seldom has access to his own transport facilities and hence has little opportunity to move his products to market centers. Marketing structures with a substantial degree of oligopsony, if not monopsony, are typical in the export of products from the rural sector.

Whether the middleman is backed by larger trading concerns (Case 1) or operates with his own capital (Case 2), there is little difference in the result. In either case bargaining strength is weighted in favor of the buyer of export products. Supply price is held near the original producer's cost of production, and the differential between domestic supply price and what is earned on the world market represents, in part, returns from monopsonistic or oligopsonistic positions. Windfall profits, accruing from rising world prices, tend to flow to traders rather than to producers. Margins between supply price offered by middlemen and world market prices show a relatively large spread since costs of production are low, particularly those of smallholders' agricultural exports. Characteristically, they are well below costs of production for similar qualities of goods produced by agricultural estates.[2]

During the 1950-1951 boom in world prices for primary products a local fiscal office in Sumatra made an attempt to evaluate the economic effect of the export tax on rubber.* The results provide empirical support for our analysis. Prices offered original producers of rubber showed little increase even though world market prices virtually doubled. Increases of 2 or 3 per cent in the middleman's buying price were adequate to call forth substantial increases in supply. The middleman network and the export houses which it supplied were the primary beneficiaries of rising world prices.

The burden of increased export taxation in this situation—amounting, in Indonesia, to more than one-third of gross export earnings during the boom—fell upon the trading sector. The tax could not be shifted forward to the world market since price was determined by external factors; neither could it be shifted backward since supply price was held near cost of production by imperfections in the market structure. The burden of export taxation, therefore, tended to fall upon windfall or monopoly profits resulting from positions of bargaining strength in the market. In these conditions, export taxation had little effect upon production incentives of the original producer; and, even though the total burden upon the trading sector may have approximated 50 per cent of gross profits, there appears to have been little effect on incentives among traders. Of course, if export taxation had been assessed at even higher rates, approximating or exceeding trading profits,

*The results of this study were given to the present writer during an interview in 1954. They have not been published.

disincentive effects might have appeared. The middleman might then have attempted to shift part of the tax back to the original producer, inducing the smallholder to revert to cultivation of rice rather than tapping rubber trees.

It is safe to conclude that during periods of high prices for Indonesia's exports moderately high export taxes can be effective in channeling windfall or monopoly profits to the government without disincentive effects so long as tax rates do not wipe out such profits completely. But in periods of falling prices export taxation may produce disincentive effects in either the trading sector or, if successful efforts are made to shift the tax backward, among the original producers. It should be remembered, however, that these conclusions are relevant only where Model I is applicable. Export taxation is likely to produce quite different incentive effects in the capital-intensive sector, where the marketing structure is better described by Model II.

Model II: Exports by plantations, extractive industries, and industrial firms. Although smallholders' exports rose relative to those from Western-type industries during the 1950–1951 boom, the value of exports from the capital-intensive sector was almost as great as smallholders' exports in 1951 (Rp. 2.2 billion as compared to Rp. 2.4 billion). Demand conditions provided a sellers' market, allowing ready disposal of the lower-quality goods (particularly in the case of rubber) supplied by smallholders, but industries described by Model II continued to play an important role in producing the economy's foreign-exchange earnings. Marketing and supply conditions in these industries, however, suggest that the incentive effects of export taxation were more deleterious.

The major characteristic of the marketing process in this model is that the firms included here do not rely on the native middleman network. Agricultural estates are frequently subsidiaries of larger concerns which provide transport and marketing facilities. In some cases, either they are able to provide their own transport and marketing services or they have adequate bargaining strength to obtain these services at costs which contain few or no monopsonistic or oligopsonistic elements. Where marketing services are subcontracted, they are ordinarily provided by Western firms engaged in domestic and foreign trading rather than by the Indonesian middleman system.

The costs of production of firms in Model II are considerably more complex than in Model I. Labor costs, while absolutely higher per unit of product, are not the major component of the original producer's supply price. Costs of production include depreciation on many capital items—investment in processing plants, standardization of facilities, and scientific control of crops—as well as explicit managerial and entrepreneurial payments. Since labor costs are explicit, they are greater per unit of product. Employers face an organized labor market in which labor demands are supported by the government, a situation which has led to the inclusion in labor costs of contributions to labor welfare funds and, in some cases, outright payments for such social benefits as health and housing. Moreover, the costs include employers' contributions to the wages tax, which is enforced in the capital-intensive sector but not among smallholders. Thus production costs include more than the labor and other implicit costs in Model I. Payments must also be made for entrepreneurial skills, capital, and nonexport taxes. Benefits from large-scale organization and standardization are mainly in terms of quality rather than in terms of lower production costs.

There are also significant differences in elasticity of supply. While the original producer in Model I can shift from the production of export products to food crops with relative ease, the producer in the capital-intensive sector tends to be committed both in terms of his labor force, backed by a strong union, and by investment in plant and equipment. Postwar experience has demonstrated that supply cannot be readily expanded in periods of rising prices or readily contracted in periods of falling prices.

For these reasons, we find an entirely different picture of incidence and incentive effects of export taxation from that in Model I. Marketing structure in this model does not provide conditions for realizing monopsony-type trade profits. Original differentials between selling price and cost of production resulting from price rises therefore tend to accrue to the estates or industrial entrepreneur, and, similarly, the immediate impact of export taxation falls upon them rather than upon the trader. Moreover, the burden of taxation in all probability remains upon the entrepreneur. Forward shifting is obviously limited by determination of export prices outside the purview of the exporter; backward shifting (to labor) is hampered in these industries by a strong labor movement supported by government. Unions have in fact succeeded in obtaining wage increases and shorter hours for their members during recent years, while it is doubtful that labor productivity has kept pace with labor gains. In other words, enterprise is likely to be involved in a two-way squeeze between higher taxes and higher labor costs.

The ability to curtail production as export taxes cut into profits is limited both by labor organization and the economics of utilizing the existing plant on the scale associated with optimum costs. Moreover, the productive factors released by suspended operations cannot be readily shifted to alternative economic activity. Excessively high export taxation, therefore, may induce complete suspension of operations and may have serious disincentive effects on new and replacement investment. In Model I, severe export taxation might induce a shift of resources to other types of economic activity; here it would tend to result in underutilization of capacity and in unemployed resources.

It appears that export taxation in 1951 was reaching levels at which disincentive effects were beginning to occur in the capital-intensive sector, particularly in the case of agricultural estates. There is much evidence on the plight of these industries, suggesting that production was being cut back because of the taxes-labor cost squeeze. Evaluating the economic effects of export taxation resulting from the foreign-exchange certificate system, the former Governor of the Java Bank made the following comment:

> . . . In a country like Indonesia, where prosperity is to a great extent dependent on export possibilities, the continuance of a multiple rate system over a long period was bound in the long run to have a disastrous influence on the cultivation and production of export commodities. Experience has shown that where multiple rate systems are in use, internal prices and wages have a tendency to rise to the level of the prices of imported goods on the basis of the effective import rates, as a result of which the export trade soon gets into difficulties on account of the lower effective export rates.
>
> In Indonesia this trend was soon discernible, and it was aggravated still further by the rise in home rice prices. Various important export products, including tea and tobacco, which by virtue of the introduction of the certificate system were at first once more in a position to be produced on a reasonably profitable basis, were for the most part being worked at a loss again in the year 1951. It is true that this was largely due to the increase of wages in 1950/1951, though the demand for higher wages was partly inspired by the rise in the cost of living.

> It is apparent that the maintenance of the system in virtually unaltered form for about 2 years imposed too heavy a strain on the majority of the industries and plantations working for export.[3]

The difficulties of the export industries were aggravated by the fact that they were liable to increasingly heavy income taxation as well. During the years of the foreign-exchange certificate system, the company income tax was assessed at rates ranging from 40 to 52.2 per cent. The total tax burden for which these industries were legally liable at the time was, therefore, somewhere in the neighborhood of 70 to 80 per cent of net profits.

Model III: Export through government marketing channels.* The one commodity for which the government provides an export outlet to the private sector is copra, one of Indonesia's many agricultural exports. In 1951, copra accounted for about 10 per cent of the value of exports. In 1954, 1955, and 1956 its share fell to about 5 per cent. The Copra Foundation was created during the depression of the 1930's as a government monopsony in copra-producing areas. It aimed at building up a buffer fund to equalize payments to original producers between periods of depressed and high world prices. It has developed into an organization designed to improve the quality of copra products as well. Prices at which copra is purchased are adjusted to provide surpluses during periods of relatively high world prices, the objective being to assist the copra industry rather than to produce revenue (profits) for government account.

*The author wishes to express gratitude to Mr. R. A. Kartadjoemena, a former Indonesian Director of Revenues, for making available information used in this section.

The ratio of prices paid to the original producer of copra relative to world market prices is substantially above that prevailing before the middleman group was displaced. In a remote manner, therefore, the earnings of the foundation are a tax upon the displaced middleman group. The foundation is liable to export taxes which are paid from the spread between its buying and selling prices. Thus high export tax rates tend to divert a part of these margins to the government instead of allowing them to accrue for purposes for which the foundation operates. Production incentives might be affected adversely if buffer funds should be severely reduced or if the foundation's profits were reduced to the point where efforts to improve quantity and quality of output were hampered. There is no evidence that the high export tax rates in 1950-1952 produced such results. The experience of this marketing agency suggests that the government might be able to employ this device more widely as a source of finance if the administrative resources were available to allow efficient operation. The net effect would be a division of the present high levels of middleman profits between government and original producers, with positive, rather than negative, incentive results on output.

Marketing of products from public enterprises also falls within this model. The Indonesian government participates in the production of export goods either through wholly government-owned firms (e.g., Bangka tin mines) or through mixed public-private corporations (e.g., Billiton tin mines). Such enterprises are found primarily in the fields of mining, agricultural plantations, and transportation. All are subject to export taxation, but—as a general rule—wholly government-owned enterprise is exempt from the income tax while mixed public-private enterprise is liable.

Export marketing is carried on through government sales offices, appointed agents, or, in the case of mixed enterprise, through the private partner.* Marketing arrangements, however, have little to do with the incidence of the export tax, which can fall only on the profits of these enterprises. Viewed as additional profits taxation, these levies may indeed affect the attractiveness of private participation in mixed enterprise, and in this particular case we should expect to find much the same incentive effects as under Model II. In the case of wholly government-owned enterprises, however, production and investment decisions are determined not so much by profitability as by the Indonesian conception of the role of the government in the economy. This has been particularly true since the transfer of sovereignty, bringing with it demands for increased "Indonesianization"† of the economy—a term somewhat synonymous with nationalization. In 1954, for example, coal production was maintained at the average postwar level although exports fell sharply—by 36 per cent—and the major mines operated at a loss.

Export Taxation and Incentives: Conclusions

The taxation of exports in Indonesia emerges from this analysis as a fiscal device with rather uneven effects upon economic incentives. Regarding effects on the private sector, it seems safe to conclude that

*The Bangka tin mines, wholly government owned, sell through a government tin sales office; the Billiton Company, a mixed enterprise, markets through the private partner as does the NIAM (Netherlands Indies Petroleum Company), a government-private company. Government-owned agricultural estates either have their own sales agencies or employ private export brokers.

†This is the Indonesians' own term, used, for example, in the Report of the Bank Indonesia, 1954-1955, pp. 148-151.

taxation of this kind is likely to have a negligible impact on incentives only where the market structure is so imperfect that the tax is absorbed by middleman profits rather than being shifted backward to original producers. Even there, if rates are raised so high that middlemen's incentives begin to be affected, members of this group may be unwilling to continue collecting export products, or, if they succeed in shifting the tax backward, the original producer may shift from production of export products to other goods. That this result is likely to occur is borne out by the shift by smallholders from export crops to rice and other local goods when world prices for Indonesian exports declined after 1951.

Up to a point, therefore, export taxation may be effective in reaching middlemen profits in the rural sector without serious effects on the supply of exports. However, this result is likely only during periods of high world prices, and then only if tax rates do not exceed certain limits which cannot be clearly drawn. These taxes cannot be regarded as a satisfactory means of reaching upper incomes in the labor-intensive sector over the longer run.

In the capital-intensive sector, where the introduction of improved techniques and expanded investment is directly related to Indonesia's economic progress, there is even greater danger of disincentive effects from export taxation. Here, as we have seen from Models II and III, since export taxation tends to fall on the profits of enterprise, it must be viewed as adding to the burden of relatively higher rates of income taxation. It should be remembered that it is in this sector, too, that income taxation is enforced with considerable stringency, the total tax burden approximating one-third of the sector's income. Firms in this sector cannot easily shift to more lightly taxed sectors of the economy—those involving trade, speculation, or production for the domestic market. But in any case such shifts are undesirable in a developing country; if anything, the capital-intensive sector should be the more lightly taxed in order to encourage those firms which help to expand the country's supply of productive capital or which supply one of the country's scarcest resources—foreign exchange.

Business and Personal Income Taxation

In this section we shall consider the effects of business and personal income taxation on incentives to produce, save, and invest. Two points should be clarified at the outset. First, apart from export taxation, income taxes are the most important fiscal burden falling directly upon business enterprise. There are numerous transaction taxes for which businesses are liable, but these are assessed at such low rates that they have little effect on incentives. There is also a capital assets tax to which both individuals and nonincorporated businesses are liable. However, it is collected at nominal rates (Rp. 5 per thousand of assessed capital) and is applied only to net worth in excess of Rp. 250,000. Moreover, it cannot be regarded as capital-gains taxation since valuations are not readily revised upward in accord with general price increases. Excise duties and sales taxes are also collected from businesses, but these are readily shifted forward to consumers as they are intended to be.

It is also important to observe that taxation of business and personal income is primarily a phenomenon of the capital-intensive sector; and, since high rates are in force, these taxes are a major factor in explaining the significantly greater tax burden borne by this sector. Prima facie, therefore, the Indonesian tax system appears to weight business incentives against the capital-intensive sector. All of this quite obviously assumes that the burden of these taxes falls upon the original taxpayer—that they are not shifted to other sectors in the economy. This hypothesis requires examination.

The company tax is assessed against limited-liability companies, limited partnerships on a joint-stock basis, cooperatives, mutual insurance companies, societies and foundations not operating for the general public interest, and foreign corporations operating in Indonesia. The personal income tax is theoretically assessed against all personal income, including income from single proprietorships and dividends on stocks in limited-liability companies. Legally, therefore, there is double taxation of Indonesian income from dividends.

As a practical matter, the company tax is enforced against business enterprises which employ the most modern methods of business procedure, where accounting is adequate to provide a reasonable estimate of net profits. Such firms are predominantly foreign owned, and their production is geared primarily, but not exclusively, to the export market. For the remainder, business incomes—in domestic trade and production—fall under the scope of personal income taxation and are exempted from the company tax.

A comparison of the rates which have been in force for company and personal income taxes since 1952 shows some significant differences. Such a comparison is made in Table 34.

Although personal income tax rates are substantially below the company tax rates in the lower ranges of income (below Rp. 100,000), in the upper ranges of income, personal income tax rates exceed company tax rates by greater and greater margins as income rises.

Table 34

EFFECTIVE TAX RATES, COMPANY TAX AND PERSONAL INCOME TAX

Income (Rp.)	Company Tax Rate (Per Cent)	Personal Income Tax Rate (Per Cent)
3,000	40.0	3.0
50,000	40.0	22.0
100,000	40.0	36.0
300,000	40.0	57.5
500,000	42.5	64.0
1,000,000	45.0	70.0
2,000,000	50.0	72.5
10,000,000	52.5	74.5

Source: Ministry of Finance.

Conclusions from this comparison should be qualified, however, to take account of differences in the enforcement of the two taxes. The company tax is assessed against net profits on the basis of the accounting records of Westernized firms. Since corporations are relatively few in number, enforcement is generally effective. The personal income tax, on the other hand, which is legally applicable to all noncorporate business income, is essentially a means of extending direct taxation to traditional, non-Western business organizations. Here few records are kept and enforcement is a matter of estimating the net income by rather haphazard methods. These problems have brought a general tendency toward laxity of personal income tax enforcement coupled with widespread evasion. Thus the ratio of taxes actually collected to legal tax liability is much lower than in the case of the company tax. For this reason, the real burden of the company tax (in terms of percentage of income withdrawn) is generally higher than that of the personal income tax at all levels of income. Moreover, virtually no attempt is made to enforce personal income taxation beyond the scope of Central Government fiscal offices in larger cities.

This brings us to consideration of the shiftability of income taxes. There are important differences in the conditions of enterprise between firms which are liable to the company tax and firms which are liable to the personal income tax. Firms subject to the company tax operate mainly in the sector of the economy concerned with the export and import trades. Production is primarily oriented toward export, although many of these firms have been developing a domestic market to absorb part of their output. By and large, therefore, prices for the output of firms subject to the company tax are determined by the world market, where there is no possibility of shifting the tax forward to consumers.* Firms which market a significant share of their total output locally may be able to achieve some degree of forward shifting, since market structures are imperfect and there is little price competition among sellers. Even in this case, however, complete shifting of the tax is likely to be difficult. Part of the net profits resulting from price increases designed to cover the tax will be once again taxed away. Moreover, company tax rates in Indonesia have not been finally approved by Parliament until well after the economic period to which they apply. Tax liability is not known and final tax settlement is not made until net profits for a given year are a matter of historical record.

Nor are conditions in the Indonesian labor market conducive to backward shifting of the company tax. Corporate enterprise finds itself

*Indonesia has no exports which comprise so large a part of total world supply that prices could be influenced from the supply side of the market.

in the position of having to deal with strong labor organizations formed to raise wages in precisely those industries in which corporate organization predominates—petroleum, mining, agricultural estates, and manufacturing. Collective bargaining, supported by government labor policy, has led to frequent wage increases in corporate enterprises. In some cases, real wages have risen more rapidly than productivity, adding a second burden to high company tax rates.

In contrast, firms which are subject to personal income taxation—single proprietorships and partnerships—appear to have more opportunity for shifting. Such firms, which dominate domestic trade and small-scale domestic production, tend to view income taxation as a part of cost. Standard pricing policy consists of the addition of a profit markup to costs, and, with the income tax considered as a business cost, these firms tend to shift the tax plus the markup on to consumers. In other words, higher income taxes may stimulate entrepreneurs to exploit their monopoly power more fully.

Domestic markets in Indonesia are notoriously imperfect, and oligopolistic price fixing appears to be almost universal.[5] A Dutch study in 1940 suggests that prices were determined by the cost-plus method, and that competition was inadequate to establish even rough equivalence between price and cost.[6] In such conditions, the income tax on business profits from domestic firms would tend to be shifted forward to consumers. The net result might well be overshifting, i.e., the resulting increase in prices exceeds the amount of tax imposed. If indeed the tax is considered to be an item of cost and is shifted forward to consumers on a cost-plus basis, the net profits of the firm might be reduced by shifting where demand is relatively elastic. A study of this phenomenon in Latin America suggested that "the average businessman presumably does not make too great an effort to discover the new price at which profits (after the imposition of a tax) will be maximized."[7] Market and enterprise conditions in Indonesia suggest a similar situation. If this phenomenon is characteristic, we believe that the incentive effects of personal income taxation on enterprise would be unimportant even where overshifting of the tax actually reduced net profits.

Backward shifting, too, appears to be more possible for firms subject to the personal income tax. In most activities dominated by noncorporate enterprise, unionization has proceeded slowly. Here the entrepreneur typically deals with laborers on the basis of traditional, or even paternalistic, relationships, with bargaining strength clearly on the side of enterprise. The feasibility of backward shifting, however, may be limited by conditions emerging from this type of labor market. Wage rates tend to be held at relatively low levels by market forces, and there may be little margin for wage reductions to allow shifting.

Conditions for tax shifting in Indonesia suggest that income taxation, too, may have different incentive effects in different sectors. Profit incentives, the ultimate determinant of the allocation of resources among alternative uses, appear to be more seriously affected by the company tax than by personal income taxation. The company tax which is borne by the capital-intensive sector is strictly enforced, and market conditions allow little opportunity for shifting. However, there is no evidence that profit rates are higher in those industries dominated by the corporate form of enterprise than elsewhere. In fact, what evidence we have on profit rates suggests the opposite.[8] On these grounds, we conclude that direct income taxation tends to weight profit incentives against capital-intensive industries in the modern sector (where the company tax is enforced) and in favor of less highly organized businesses operating in traditional trades and industries. It should also be noted that strict enforcement of the company tax and double taxation of dividend income discriminate against the corporate form of business enterprise, and this may be one of the factors which has impeded the development of the domestic security market. Tax rates themselves discriminate against corporate enterprise in the lower ranges of income, and rather loose enforcement of the personal income tax against business leads to the same result for higher incomes. Of course, for foreign enterprises tax laws in the home country as well as in Indonesia are important. For American firms, for example, Indonesian corporation income taxes matter little since they may be deducted from American corporation income tax liability, and there is no great difference in tax rates.

There is, however, a broader question related to the incentive effects of income taxation in an underdeveloped country: To what extent and how does taxation affect the whole range of economic enterprise? Does the fiscal system tend to induce a flow of resources from relatively unproductive activities to more productive ones? Economic development requires the shifting of resources from less to more productive activities, a process which may be affected one way or the other by taxation. Taxation of income and profits has special importance since it affects the allocation of productive resources among alternative uses.

The essence of the incentive problem in developing countries is that the society should reward entrepreneurs commensurately with their contribution to development itself, but in many countries, including Indonesia, traditional patterns of reward tend to do just the opposite. Profits flow to those groups which have maneuvered themselves into monopoly or quasi-monopoly positions of control in trade, ownership of land, and other nondevelopmental roles in the traditional society; and these ventures attract the use of the society's relatively scarce supply of capital, enterprise, and other resources. Indonesian society continues to follow its traditional orbit in the rural, labor-intensive sector of the economy. Hence, traditional and nondevelopmental activities are mainly found in this sector. If the present pattern of incentives is to be altered by fiscal powers, therefore, direct taxation of enterprise should be enforced with greater vigor in the labor-intensive sector.

Among the traditional roles which contribute little to development of the economy while earning relatively high rewards, speculation deserves emphasis. Shortages of goods and generally rising price levels stimulate the flow of scarce resources to speculation in real estate and commodities without involving the commitment of funds to capital investment. Such activities, organized on a personal basis and providing tax collectors with little evidence of net worth or income, have been notoriously successful in escaping income taxation in Indonesia. It is precisely these activities, therefore, which are encouraged by the present pattern of income taxation and its enforcement. In this situation, selective income taxation seems to be called for as a device to promote development by directing the flow of savings and investment to more productive activities. Capital-gains taxation, property taxation, and taxes on inventories should be viewed as alternative ways through which income from speculation might be reached. In net result, such devices would have the same significance as income taxes; they might, however, be specifically designed to reach tax sources which escape the present income tax, thereby not only providing additional financing for development but, in all probability, also stimulating the flow of private investment to more productive activities.

In addition to the effects of business and income taxation upon general determinants of investment and resource allocation, other incentive effects are felt through the provisions under which income taxation is enforced. These provisions include both the average and marginal rates which are in force as well as the allowances for depletion and tax abatement for one purpose or another. The structure of rates, as we have seen, discriminates against firms subject to the personal income tax only after relatively high levels of income have been reached; actually, loose enforcement of this tax probably compensates for this factor. The company tax itself discriminates against firms of larger size. Rates vary from 40 per cent on net profits of less than Rp. 500,000 to 52.5 per cent on profits exceeding Rp. 2,500,000. Since the tax is assessed simply on the basis of the level of net profits without reference to rate of return on investment, size itself is penalized. The problem is that relatively large profits are more a function of the technical requirements of production (large-scale operations) than of high rates of return on capital. Since larger firms tend to have a relatively higher capital-labor ratio, the present corporation tax tends to discourage capital-intensive production.

We suggested in earlier chapters that the productivity of the capital-intensive sector as a whole has fallen since the colonial period. Independence brought nationalistic policies which were designed to restrict the profitability of the foreign-owned share of the capital-intensive sector and to transfer ownership to Indonesians. Productivity has fallen in the foreign firms, with some exceptions, because of labor difficulties, import and other restrictions, and the seizure of plantation land by squatters. In firms newly transferred to Indonesian ownership, productivity has suffered at the hands of inept management, and a shortage of technical skills has frequently led to inefficient utilization of capital facilities, particularly those of larger scale with relatively complex technology. In discriminating against such firms, the company tax has hampered attempts to raise the productivity of the capital-intensive sector. Yet this sector is the major producer of foreign exchange, and Indonesia's ability to provide capital goods for development—or to replace imports—depends on the growth and productivity of this sector. Improving conditions both for profitable production in the capital-intensive sector and for its growth should be regarded as Indonesia's most urgent short-run development objective. Whatever can be done to relieve the unfavorable effects of high, discriminatory taxation upon this sector merits high priority in tax reform for economic development.

Disincentive effects on the volume of business savings and investment may occur either through reducing the capacity to invest by reducing savings (the disposable-income effect) or by adversely affecting the prospective rate of profit on new or replacement investment. It is quite clear that Indonesian income and profits taxation is levied at rates which could produce effects of this nature, particularly for Indonesian-owned firms. Where tax shifting is severely circumscribed and tax enforcement is relatively strict, which is generally true in the capital-intensive sector, the capacity to invest may be significantly reduced. Access to market sources of finance is limited by deficiencies in the money market (described in Chapter 3) and high interest costs. Internal savings are the main source of finance, and tax rates averaging near 50 per cent of net profits obviously reduce the capacity to accumulate business savings for capital investment.

Most of the firms against which the company tax is levied, however, are foreign owned. The fact that such firms have access to home financing places them in a favorable position relative to domestic enterprise. Nevertheless, heavy profits taxation may have some importance in reducing the attractiveness of foreign investment in Indonesia. Foreign decisions to invest or not to invest are influenced by a wide variety of political, social, and economic factors, and the role of taxation might easily be given unjustified importance. There are, however, some important tax considerations. The company tax is only one of several taxes borne by foreign enterprise in Indonesia. The total tax burden, which is considerably in excess of the company tax rates, places Indonesia among those countries now levying the highest tax burden upon foreign enterprise.

Some of the provisions of the company tax mitigate to some extent the disincentive effects of the existing high and progressive rates of profits taxation. Losses incurred in a given fiscal year may be deducted from profits during the following five years, but such deductions must be made as rapidly as profits in subsequent years permit. Losses cannot, therefore, be averaged over a period of years. In other countries with high rates of profits taxation, averaging losses with profits over a period of years has been used to offset disincentive effects on producers with heavy risks. The risk factor is particularly great in Indonesia, where much of production is presently oriented toward foreign markets showing wide price fluctuations frequently occurring in short periods of time.

A new depreciation decree applicable to the company tax was announced by the Ministry of Finance in 1953. It was hoped that this decree would encourage new investment by providing flexible depreciation arrangements permitting companies undertaking new investment to reduce their tax liability during a three-year period following the new investment. Expenditures for investment may be depreciated for tax purposes at any rate the investing firm chooses during the first three years after such expenditures are made. If larger profits are expected in the future, depreciation deductions may be deferred. If accelerated depreciation or deferment is not desired, or if full value is not depreciated within the specified three-year period, depreciation deductions follow a prescribed fixed depreciation schedule which varies with the nature of the investment.

Another provision permits firms proposing to undertake new investments in a given fiscal period to claim depreciation allowances for the proposed investment in the fiscal period prior to that in which the investment is actually undertaken. A firm earning large profits in a given fiscal year can avoid paying the company tax on a part of these profits if it declares its intention to invest funds in the next fiscal period. Investment is rather liberally construed in the 1953 regulations, although no legal definition is given. "It is our purpose that no attempt be made," the 1953 decree declares, "to give a legal connotation to the term 'investment,' since in the present condition [of the Indonesian economy] nearly all expenditures for fixed and working capital in the next several years can be expected to stimulate the increase of Indonesian productive capacity." The only exceptions explicitly made by the decree concern expenditures for purchasing existing productive assets from other owners, and expenditures for "luxuries" which do not lead to the expansion of productive capacity.

The positive effects of these provisions on savings and investment may partially offset the disincentive results of high rates of profits and income taxation. It is not clear to what extent these provisions have actually been used to reduce tax liability. Since the advantages are available only to corporate enterprise, they may tend to compensate both for the fact that the company tax is more strictly enforced and for whatever disincentive effects it may have.

Taxes on Consumption*

Since 1952, taxes falling upon consumers have come to play an increasingly significant role in Indonesian fiscal policy. In other primary-producing countries, too, there has been a tendency to shift from taxation of the export sector to taxes on domestic and imported consumer goods as export earnings have declined. In some quarters it has been urged that consumption taxation generally and taxation of imported commodities in particular must bear a large share of the burden of financing development to avoid disincentive effects upon domestic productive enterprise. The difficulty with this argument—in addition to failing to discriminate between productive and unproductive enterprise—is that it overlooks the probability that taxes falling upon consumers may also involve disincentive results. It strikes us as important, therefore, to inquire briefly into the relationship between consumption taxation and economic incentives.

In 1951, export taxation was the main device by which the Indonesian government sought to reach windfall profits resulting from the export boom. In that year import duties were relatively low,† and their yield was only 15 per cent of total tax revenues. They were not designed to influence the composition of imports or to husband the economy's foreign-exchange resources for reserve and developmental purposes. Following the introduction of the import surcharge system in

*Import taxes are construed to be similar to excise taxes in nature and are included in this discussion of taxes on consumption. In the case of import duties on raw materials, the price of the final consumer good has tended to reflect the amount of duty.

† The basic import tariff rates have remained at the rates in effect in 1951: 9 per cent ad valorem for raw materials and semimanufactured goods, 18 per cent for ordinary consumer goods, and 20 per cent for luxury goods.

1952, however, import taxation contributed 39 per cent of the total tax yield in 1953.[9] Similarly, the yield from sales and excise taxation comprised 16.5 per cent of the total in 1951 but rose to 24 per cent in 1953. Thus, if import duties fell primarily upon consumers, as we argue below, levies upon consumers rose from 31.5 per cent of the total tax burden in 1951 to 63 per cent in 1953. Further increases in the rates of these taxes raised their yield to 72 per cent of the total in 1956.

Since 1951, conditions in Indonesia appear to have been conducive to a high degree of forward shifting. Chronic inflationary pressures and the government's program of import stringency have created a sellers' market for consumer goods, particularly those of foreign origin. Demand for imported goods and for many domestic products as well has been relatively inelastic. In the setting of the high-unit-profit mentality prevailing among Indonesian businessmen, and the oligopolistic structure of markets described in the preceding sections, the new levies have been borne largely, if not entirely, by consumers.

The importance of imported consumer goods deserves special emphasis. Foreign markets are virtually the sole source of supply for a wide range of manufactured consumer goods, from bicycles to canned foods. Although much has been written about the nonmonetary sector of underdeveloped countries, markets are extremely significant in distributing imported goods throughout every area of Indonesia. It is important to recognize the incentive aspects of this phenomenon. Perhaps too much attention has been given to the undesirable consequences of the "demonstration effect" in raising consumption, which allegedly threatens domestic financing of development. From our observation in Indonesia, it appears that the lure of foreign patterns of consumption is equally important in calling forth more effort from Indonesian labor and enterprise.

Imported goods have become both a symbol of and an incentive to progress and improvement. Many are themselves means to economic development; for example, mobility of labor has been vastly improved by access to imported bicycles and motor scooters, to say nothing of automobiles.

During the years of retrenchment since 1952, however, foreign exchange has been rationed among imported goods with little regard for these values. Except for a short period under the Harahap government in 1956, the main factor limiting domestic consumption of foreign goods has not been the import surcharge but, rather, the supplies of foreign exchange made available by the government.[10] In this way, the strongest type of sellers' market has been created, as it were, by fiat, and full shifting of the import surcharge to consumers is an inevitable result of competitive consumer bidding for goods in short supply.

It is difficult to provide empirical evidence of forward shifting of import surcharges by tracing price rises of imported goods. A good many of the items in the Central Bureau of Statistics' index of wholesale prices of 44 imported goods are in the category of essential goods on which no import surcharge was imposed. This index, however, rose from an average of 2,314 in 1952 (with 1938 = 100) to 2,461 in 1953; 2,693 in 1954; and 3,559 in 1955. Even goods on the free list have shown substantial price rises, since exchange rationing and a quota system have accompanied the surcharge system. The domestic retail price of powdered milk, an item on the free list, rose from Rp. 3.75 per can in August 1952 to Rp. 7.40 eight months later (April 1953).[11] This evidence suggests two points which deserve our attention: (1) the government import policy caused market conditions conducive to forward shifting of whatever surcharge might be imposed; (2) the policy also resulted in rising consumer-goods prices, even where no surcharge was collected by the government, through providing conditions under which sellers could earn windfall profits resulting from artificial scarcities. The underlying scarcity of foreign exchange and import control programs has, therefore, tended to redistribute real income from consumers to the middleman class, while the structural change in the tax system has also shifted the tax burden against consumers in favor of traders and speculators.

It should be noted that the import surcharge system has become more general and that the progressivity of rates has been increased.* When the system was adopted in 1952, as much as 86 per cent of the value of imports remained on the free list and surcharges were levied largely against the most obvious luxury goods. In January 1953 imports were reclassified so that 50 per cent remained on the free list, with 30 per cent placed on the list (B-1) bearing a surcharge of 33 1/3 per cent ad valorem and the remaining 20 per cent on lists (B-2 and C) carrying surcharges of 100 and 200 per cent. With these changes, many commodities consumed at all levels of income, including such items as paper, stationery, cosmetics, and soaps, became liable to surcharge duties of 33 1/3 per cent or 100 per cent.

In 1956, import surcharges were raised still further. A 25 or 50 per cent surcharge was imposed on essential commodities; semi-essential goods bore a surcharge of 75 or 100 per cent. The surcharge rate on luxuries was set at 150 or 200 per cent, and the rate on super-luxuries at 400 per cent. At the discretion of the Monetary Board, rice, yarn, raw cotton, airplane fuel, and textbooks could be altogether exempted from import surcharges. Perhaps less than 20 per cent of imports remained in the exempted categories.

*A brief history of the system of import taxation is given in Chapter 4, pp. 215ff.

In June 1957 the system was considerably altered by the general introduction of export certificates, which had been required for some commodities after the 1956 revision. Exporters receive export certificates in the amount of the official rupiah value (Rp. 11.40 = U.S. $1.00) of their foreign-exchange earnings. Importers (who possess import licenses) must purchase export certificates on the free market as their source of foreign exchange. Export certificate prices to the importer varied until they were frozen at a maximum of 332 per cent of their face value by action of the Monetary Board in April 1958. The exporter pays a 20 per cent tax on proceeds and retains the remainder. The importer must also pay specified surcharges on the going market rate of export certificates. The surcharge rates vary from 0 to 175 per cent for six categories of import goods. Exceptions from surcharge levies have been further restricted so that virtually all foreign purchases must now be financed with export certificates. (For an elaboration of this system, see Chapter 4.)

The net effect of this revision was to raise the rupiah cost of almost all imported goods to at least more than double the official exchange rate. Most of the proceeds (80 per cent) from the increase accrues to the exporter. In addition, however, the government levies an import surcharge upon this free market rate. The rupiah cost of most imported goods has been greatly increased, but the exporter now realizes a significant part of the differential between official rates and effective import rates. In July 1957 the government allowed revaluation of goods held in inventory which had been imported prior to the introduction of the new system. This caused price increases of 50 per cent for the majority of imported commodities.[12] According to the Bank Indonesia's Research Department, this provided the impetus for a renewed price spiral for all goods, including those produced domestically.[13]

There is every probability that the surcharge system and its many modifications have placed imported goods of the incentive type beyond the means of most income groups. It is clear that contraction of supply and shifting of the tax—the net effects of the import surcharge system—eliminate some consumers from the market. This effect is shown in the following diagram, which pictures the result of the imposition of an import surcharge on an incentive good.

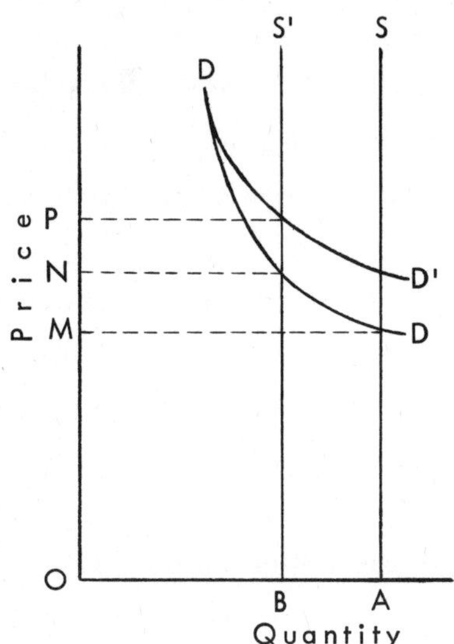

Note: The demand curve (DD) is drawn to show greater price elasticity in the lower price ranges (where demand of lower-income groups is reflected) and almost complete price inelasticity in the upper price ranges. Supply is assumed to be completely inelastic, S representing supply before introduction of the surcharge, S' representing supply after the imposition of surcharges and quotas. The price rise resulting from this reduction in supply is sufficient to allow considerable forward shifting of the surcharge. DD' represents the position of the demand curve after the incentive effect has operated to increase income among buyers excluded by price N.

In this case, one that is commonly found in Indonesia, the imposition of an import surcharge will tend to have adverse incentive effects upon the supply of effort and upon risk-taking in productive sectors of the economy. Consumers in the lower-income range (BA) have been eliminated from the market through the price rise (MN) resulting from reduced supply. If the commodity is highly valued, the low-income consumer may increase his income by accepting more employment in an attempt to obtain the good at the new price. This will cause a shift in the demand curve as shown (to position DD'), which will induce a further price rise (to P), again placing the good beyond the reach of the low-income consumer, causing him to reduce his supply of effort originally exerted for the objective of obtaining the particular incentive good. A corollary of this argument is that imported goods have come to be less widely distributed as import taxation has become more severe. Increasingly, their distribution has been restricted to foreigners and high-income Indonesians with Western patterns of consumption—both mainly in the capital-intensive sector. The 1957 revision eased the impact of import taxes on those paid in foreign currencies, since foreigners are now given export certificates for their official currency conversions.

Progressivity in rate structure is also found in Indonesian sales and excise taxes. A general sales tax has been in force since 1951, with rates of 5 per cent on goods classified as necessities and 10 per cent on those classified as luxuries. Primary foodstuffs, notably rice, and other essential goods are exempt from the tax. Excise duties are levied against alcoholic beverages (including both distilled liquors and beer), sugar, tobacco, and petroleum products. Of these, only sugar and tobacco are generally consumed by lower-income groups; however, lower rates are levied against domestically produced tobacco products. Similarly, sugar manufactured without the aid of machinery (i.e., that produced by traditional methods) is exempt from excise duty.

Excepting the probable disincentive effects of import surcharges, therefore, Indonesian consumption taxes have probably not had serious economic repercussions upon lower-income groups. The incentive effects of these taxes upon middle- and even relatively high-income groups in the capital-intensive sector is quite another matter, and the main shortcomings of consumption taxation probably lie here. High rates of consumption taxes on goods consumed by these groups have added to the burden of relatively high income taxation in this sector. Disincentive effects are felt particularly among Westernized businessmen and civil servants, who not only have a good part of their income taxed away through income taxation but also bear a large tax component in the prices of goods which are standard items in their pattern of consumption. The real problem is that goods which are defined as luxuries in tax legislation are in fact essentials in the standard of living of Westernized groups in the capital-intensive sector—imported Western-style clothing being the most obvious example.* One of the most dramatic results of this situation has been the efflux of foreign advisers (particularly Europeans), who have found it difficult to maintain conventional standards of living in Indonesia.

Consumption taxation levied under a progressive rate schedule as defined in Indonesia fails to discriminate among sources of income. It has raised the cost of production[14] and cost of living for the small entrepreneur engaged in productive activity. Accordingly, it tends to have disincentive effects both upon the supply of savings actually designed for productive investment and upon the supply of effort. Import tariffs, excise duties, and sales taxes are levied on goods which constitute both business costs and ingredients of the conventional urban standard of living. This conclusion is supported by the fact that demand for goods subject to import surcharges has been so inelastic that these levies have produced unexpectedly large revenues. Full forward shifting of

*Such clothing bears a 100 per cent ad valorem basic import duty plus a 10 per cent sales tax and import surcharges.

the tax suggests that these revenues have come from consumers' incomes, but mainly from those in the capital-intensive sector, where the burden of other taxes is relatively great. Pressures on wages and export prices are inevitable.

This conclusion could, of course, be reached for any tax levied by the government; the point made here is that consumption taxes fall indiscriminately upon those who might otherwise make productive use of their savings and upon those who clearly would not. Lack of selectivity is germane to tax policy in an underdeveloped country since a tax of this type, falling upon the nascent middle- and upper-income groups in the capital-intensive sector, may discourage the development of precisely the type of activity which would promote the growth of output.

Notes to Chapter 6

1. This is a recurring theme among writers subscribing to the "dualistic theory." Its leading exponent, Dr. Boeke, puts the matter succinctly: "This inverse elasticity of supply should be noted as one of the essential differences between Western and Eastern economics." J. H. Boeke, Economics and Economic Policy of Dual Societies as Exemplified by Indonesia, Institute of Pacific Relations, New York, 1954, p. 40.

2. The conclusion emerges clearly for the case of rubber, for example, from the data made available by P. T. Bauer's study, The Rubber Industry: A Study in Competition and Monopoly, published for the London School of Economics and Political Science, Cambridge, Mass., 1948, pp. 114-115 and 270.

3. Report of the Java Bank, 1951-1952, pp. 109-110.

4. Report of the Bank Indonesia, 1954-1955, p. 145.

5. Bureau of Foreign and Domestic Commerce, U.S. Department of Commerce, Indonesia: Summary of Basic Economic Information, August 1952.

6. G. Abeln, "Beteekenis van de Industriële Ontwikkeling voor het Conjunctureverloop" (The Implications of the Industrial Situation for the Business Cycle), Industrie in Nederlandsch-Indië (Industry in Netherlands Indies), Economic Weekly for Indonesia, Special Issue (May 1941), Batavia, pp. 25-32.

7. J. H. Adler, E. R. Schlessinger, and E. C. Olson, Public Finance and Economic Development in Guatemala, Stanford University Press, Stanford, 1953, p. 109.

8. H. J. van Oorschot, "Difficulties of Postwar Industrial Development," Economic Review of Indonesia, Vol. III, October, November, December 1949, pp. 116-119.

9. The surcharge rate represents a tax assessed as a certain percentage of the rupiah wholesale value of import goods. For further explanation of the details of this system and the surcharge rates, see Benjamin H. Higgins, "The Rationale of Import Surcharges," Ekonomi dan Keuangan Indonesia, Vol. VI (1953), pp. 228-236.

10. For a fuller discussion of import surcharge policy, see Benjamin H. Higgins, Indonesia's Economic Stabilization and Development, Institute of Pacific Relations, New York, 1957.

11. Central Bureau of Statistics, Statistical Abstract, 1955, p. 72.

12. Bank Indonesia Bulletin, No. 13, Third Quarter, 1957, p. 24.

13. Ibid.

14. Costs of production appear to have been affected by the inclusion of many capital and technical items on relatively high import surcharge lists. The reactions of small firms to the imposition of levies on these goods were sharp and critical. The leading Chinese newspaper, for example, made the following comment: "In reviewing the new list, one wonders why such materials as hoes, building materials, technical appliances, industrial chemicals, certain raw materials, etc. are made more expensive. Are they not designed to raise production?" (Keng Po, February 2, 1953.) Similarly, the system has produced pressures on wages, particularly in the capital-intensive sector, as suggested in Chapter 2.

7

THE ROLE OF LOCAL FINANCE*

Our discussion up to this point has dealt mainly with the role of Central Government in financing Indonesian economic development. Given the political and social framework discussed in the Introduction, and the factors outlined at the end of the previous chapter, it is clear that the potential role of local finance should also receive serious consideration. Indeed, the success of domestic financing of economic development in Indonesia will depend in large measure upon taking full advantage of the resources that can be mobilized through local fiscal processes.

The contribution of local finance to Indonesian economic development has not received much attention. During the Dutch period, lack of concern for local finance was perhaps an inevitable consequence of colonial rule which had little concern for development of the economy as a whole. Investigations of local finance were chiefly concerned with the extent to which local taxes added to the burden which the colonial government imposed upon the indigenous population.[1] The scope and importance of local finance continued to grow, however, as

*Much of the material in this chapter originally appeared in my article entitled "The Case for Decentralized Financing of Economic Development in Indonesia," Far Eastern Quarterly, Vol. XV, November 1955.

the Netherlands East Indies government responded to Indonesian demands for greater local autonomy. In 1904 an ordinance which authorized the formation of local councils to levy taxes for the support of local development projects provided a great stimulus to the local financing of community-development investment activity (such as "water supplies, slaughter houses, markets, public baths, cemeteries, irrigation works, drains, sewers, drainage of waterlogged lands").[2] The ordinance applied primarily to Java and Madura; on the Outer Islands considerable autonomy already existed through the device of "Native States," which were given almost complete local autonomy in political and fiscal matters and were ruled by native princes loyal to the colonial government—although the colonial government collected certain of its indirect taxes. As a result, the total tax burden per capita in the Native States was found to be the lowest in Java, but it is suggested below that the Native States were capable of financing more local capital formation than the directly governed territories. The difference in the central tax burden between the two types of regions apparently was large enough to allow a lower total (central <u>and</u> local) tax burden in the autonomous regions even though their tax systems produced more local resources for financing local capital-formation projects.

The importance of that state of affairs for present Indonesian development planning lies in the fact that local fiscal autonomy led to a relatively high rate of locally financed investment. Furthermore, it paved the way for the evolution of attitudes toward central and local taxation which have greatly influenced the postwar realities in which economic development must be financed in Indonesia.

Data are not available to provide a satisfactory estimate of the significance of total local government investment during the last decade of colonial rule. Although investment expenditures of the Native States were reported, there are no reports for the directly governed territories. A comparison of investment in the Native States with colonial government investment, however, underlines the prewar importance of local finance. Such a comparison is made in Table 35.

Table 35

GOVERNMENT INVESTMENT, 1935-1938

(Thousand NEI Guilders)

Year	Central	Native States	Total	Native States as Per Cent of Total
1935	3,057	2,570	5,627	46
1936	4,628	3,680	8,308	44
1937	11,405	4,693	16,098	29
1938	9,282	5,507	14,789	37
Average				39

Source: Data obtained from Ministry of Finance, Nederlandsch-Indië, Het Tweede Tiental Begrootingen met den Volksraad (The Second Decade of People's Councils' Budgets), Dept. van Financien, Batavia, 1938; and annual editions of Statistische Jaaroverzicht van Nederlandsch-Indië, published by the Dutch colonial government's Central Bureau of Statistics.

The data in Table 35 indicate that the Native States alone contributed a significant share of the total investment realized through government accounts—an average of almost 40 per cent of total colonial and Native States government investment during the period 1935-1938. If the capital formation of nonautonomous local governments were added, the local government component would be somewhat higher.* It should

*Nonautonomous regions were directly governed by the central colonial government; they did, however, possess some fiscal functions of their own.

be understood, however, that Indonesia shared the world depression of those years, and that the colonial government's ability and willingness to finance capital formation were considerably less than they had been a decade earlier, while this was not equally true for local governments. This suggests, incidentally, that local government investment expenditures were less sensitive to cyclical fluctuations. Investment expenditures of the Native States were ordinarily a substantially greater percentage of their total budgetary outlays than in those of the colonial government. In 1938, for example, capital formation accounted for 15 per cent of total Native States expenditures but only slightly more than 1 per cent of colonial government expenditures.[3] A related point of significance is that local government capital formation was necessarily financed by local government savings while colonial government investment was often financed by borrowing.

The ability of local governments to finance capital formation during the colonial period was facilitated by their access to compulsory labor services (Heerendiensten) for local public works. In 1938 the monetary equivalent of the compulsory labor services that were recruited by the Native States was 4,932,000 guilders; and investment was reported at 5,507,000 guilders.* In the same year compulsory labor services valued at 5,468,000 guilders were mobilized by the directly governed territories, suggesting that in these localities, too, considerable investment activity was taking place. Although the means through which labor services are mobilized have become less compulsory, this method of financing investment has continued to be of importance since independence.

*Labor services have been converted to monetary terms by using the money-payment equivalent required to redeem labor services into cash payments.

Thus it may be stated that local governments in Indonesia have a history of a relatively great degree of fiscal autonomy involving responsibility for local developmental activities. It is also clear that these governments have a tradition of rather vigorous fiscal policy capable of supporting significant amounts of local capital formation.

Despite the lack of published information on postwar local finance in Indonesia and its contribution to Indonesian economic development,* there are unmistakable evidences that developmental investment has continued to be undertaken by local governments. Numerous observers have returned from localities throughout Indonesia impressed with local fervor for prosecuting both output-increasing and welfare-type investment. In the provinces outside Java there is a strong urge for local autonomy both in government functions generally and in the fiscal process in particular, an urge dramatically expressed in vigorous efforts to provide local improvements from resources available to the political subdivisions. Considerable attention has been given to the problem of delegating political and economic functions to local levels of government, but delay in introducing a workable division of authority has brought conflicting tendencies toward centralization and local autonomy. On Java, where Central Government control has consistently been relatively firm, domination of local fiscal processes by Central Government has tended to stifle the local urge for development throughout the period since the transfer of sovereignty to Indonesia in late 1949. In the outlying provinces, where interest in local improvement is strong, attempts at Central Government domination of local functions continually produced friction, leading to increased independence from

*In the past few years, however, Indonesian newspapers have carried accounts of local development activities. These reports reflect rising popular interest in the scope and importance of local governments in economic development.

Central Government control until 1956, when several localities virtually established their independence from Central Government jurisdiction. Even during the years before the open break,* local disaffection prevented coordination between central and local developmental activities and led to a lack of awareness in Djakarta of the contribution which local finance could make to effective planning for Indonesian economic development.

The operating assumption in Djakarta had been that local finance—both on the expenditure and on the revenue side—had been almost completely inoperative after the Dutch relinquished control over the archipelago. It was assumed that the local financial offices had not reclaimed their financial functions, pending the government's clarification of the distribution of revenue sources and proceeds between central and local authorities. Demarcation of these functions was implicitly called for in the Constitution of 1950, and it has been the subject of study by a continuing committee (the Nasrun Committee). The view that local levels of government were inactive in fiscal operations was unequivocally put forth in the Karakacheff report on the Indonesian budget system:

> It may be stated that the general budget of the Central Government includes practically all expenditures of the local authorities. Most of them have no receipts of their own. The few existing taxes in certain of them, such as entertainment tax or dog tax in Djakarta Raya, are rather insignificant. Thus the grants of Central Government cover almost the totality of expenditures of the local authorities.[4]

The 1953-1954 Report of the Bank Indonesia expressed a similar view of local finance:

*See Introduction.

Pending the issue of legal regulations governing the financial relationship between Central Government and daerahs [autonomous regions], in recent years practically all taxation has been incorporated in the budget of the Central Government.[5]

Gradually, Central Government has begun to show some awareness of local fiscal processes. The Dris report data on the income and expenditures of local governments, obtained from Central Government sources, are presented in Table 36.

Table 36

INCOME AND EXPENDITURES OF THE REGIONAL OR LOCAL COMMUNITIES, 1952-1956

(Million Rp.)

Year	Expenditures	Gross Totals Local or Regional Resources	Grants from Central Government
1952	2,014.0	200.0*	1,887.0
1953	2,130.0	340.0	1,836.0
1954	2,733.0	377.7	2,355.0
1955	2,719.0*	429.0	1,775.0†
1956	?	?	3,120.0

*Estimated.

†Exclusive of capital expenditures.

Source: M. D. Dris, "Taxation in Indonesia," Ekonomi dan Keuangan Indonesia, Vol. XI, August-September 1958, p. 408.

The evidence presented in this chapter suggests that these estimates greatly underrate the extent to which local governments have actually succeeded in financing expenditures from local resources. Furthermore, it is our impression that the Dris report minimizes the extent to which the collection apparatus has been maintained and improved in the Outer Islands, and that it overrates the collection capacity of Central Government.[6]

During the transition years 1953–1956 the Indonesia project of the Center for International Studies, Massachusetts Institute of Technology, conducted studies of local fiscal activities both on Java and in the outlying provinces. That research, as well as observation and discussions with other observers, indicated that the views accepted by Indonesian officials were at least partially wrong. Local governments not only continued to exist; in many areas they performed important financial and economic functions. It should be pointed out, however, that the effectiveness and scope of the financial offices in the areas nearest Djakarta (e.g., West Java) were the most limited. Here the influence of Central Government, which attempted to compress all fiscal and economic functions within its budget, was the greatest; and local governments became dependent upon Central Government resources. Proximity of these areas to the seat of Central Government has no doubt led to the currency of the mistaken views described above. In reality, the degree of local fiscal activity and local initiative in financing economic development has tended to vary almost directly with distance from Djakarta.

Intensive research conducted by the author on both Java and Sumatra provided a contrast between local governments whose finance was dominated by Central Government and those with some degree of fiscal autonomy. The results of these studies compare the pre-1956 situation in West Java with that in the province of Central Sumatra. The results given below are based on discussions with local financial officials in Bandung, the capital of the province of West Java, and in Bukkittingi and Padang, both sites of administrative offices for Central Sumatra. It was clear from this investigation that the structure of West Javanese local finance reflected the proximity of the province to Djakarta, and that local finance in Central Sumatra and the attitudes of the province's officials reflected resistance to Djakarta's attempts at centralization, as well as a strong propensity for local independence in fiscal matters. The effects of this basic difference in orientation are shown in the patterns of local revenues and expenditures.

The Structure of Local Finance Prior to Rebellion

In the period before the breakdown of Central Government authority in the Outer Islands after 1956, local financial operations were carried on at three levels of administration—*desa* (village), *kabupaten* (district), and province—in both West Java and Central Sumatra.* Cities (*kota*

*These levels of local government were provided by the Territorial Government Law of 1948. To a certain extent they were further endorsed in 1956 legislation dealing with the structure of local government. However, the 1956 legislation provided for a change in terminology, referring to the three levels as Level I, Level II, and Level III. It has also recognized the great diversity of basic local organizations in Indonesia by making Level III organization optional if its functions could be amalgamated and discharged at a higher level.

The province is the level of administration just below Central Government's Ministry of Interior. Prior to the 1956 legislation, the province was headed by the governor, an appointee of Central Government; the 1956 legislation provided that the top official (*Kepala Daerah*) be elected by the representative council of the province (an elected body) and confirmed by the president. The *kabupaten*, prior to 1956, was to be headed by an official selected by Central Government from a list submitted by the *kabupaten*'s representative assembly. In practice, the chief administrative official has been the *Bupati* (regent of the district), a traditional Central Government official. Thus at the first two levels of local government, the 1948 law produced some autonomy through the establishment of representative councils, but Central Government continued to hold tight reins through appointed officials. The extent of such Central Government besar) in each province formed separate fiscal administrative units similar to the kabupaten in level of jurisdiction. Legally, each level of local government was responsible for supervising fiscal administration of the level below it. However, supervision of village finance by the kabupaten was more meaningful in Central Sumatra than in West Java. In Central Sumatra, villages were in fact required to submit their budgets to the kabupaten above them for approval and forwarding to the province and to the Central Government. This system was in effective operation in 1954. In West Java, on the other hand, villages failed to draft budgets for transmission to the higher levels of government.

Desa Finance

Since village budgets are not published, satisfactory information on desa finance could not be obtained for West Java. It was apparent, however, that the village was responsible for the maintenance of some local capital facilities such as roads, bridges, and public buildings,

---

appointment power, with attendant control in local government, was the essence of the controversy prior to the 1956 legislation.

The desa was specified as the lowest administrative unit by the 1948 law. Here, too, the law called for representative councils and appointment of the top official from a list of candidates submitted by the head of the province. This provision has been ignored and the village has continued to be headed by the traditional lurah on Java and the kepala negeri in Sumatra. These local officials have, however, been subject to strict control of Central Government through its chain of local officials (wedanas and tjamats).

This hierarchy of local government exists side by side with another—existing mainly in East Indonesia—in which there has been only one level of local government dealing with Central Government. These independent regions have, by and large, managed to maintain greater local autonomy than those described above. The problem of local autonomy and central-local relationships is fully discussed in John D. Legge, Problems of Regional Autonomy in Contemporary Indonesia, Modern Indonesia Project, Southeast Asia Program, Department of Far Eastern Studies, Cornell University, Ithaca, 1957, and in Robert Jay's forthcoming volume on local government in the "Modjokuto" series, to be published by the Free Press, Glencoe, Illinois.

which were financed in part by local recruitment of labor services, thus obviating the necessity for monetary tax collections. Yet financing of village expenditures was provided mainly by Central Government subsidies, which in 1954 and 1955 provided about Rp. 100,000 for each village on Java and Madura, totaling about Rp. 2 billion on these islands alone.[7]

In Central Sumatra village budgets (numbering 1,200) were regularly transmitted to the kabupaten. Their compilation, analysis, and approval were delayed as the province awaited Central Government action in confirming provincial and kabupaten jurisdiction over the budgets as well as underwriting the costs of printing and compiling them. Hence no aggregative statistics on village finance in Central Sumatra were available, although certain generalizations about village finance in this area were made on the basis of the submitted budgets. The budgets provided for the mobilization of both monetary and nonmonetary resources. Current expenditures requiring payment in monetary terms were estimated, and the estimates were used as a basis for allotting the head tax among the village inhabitants. Additional monetary income was frequently obtained from local levies such as the pasar (market) tax, the slaughter tax, taxes on forestry products and coastal fishing, and harbor fees, despite continual controversy between Central Government fiscal representatives and local authorities over the proceeds from such levies.

Investment and capital-maintenance projects which could be carried out with little more than labor resources, including construction of schools, irrigation works, and roads, were supported primarily by local mobilization of voluntary labor contributions. The capital equipment for such projects was ordinarily obtained from the province or Central

Government as subsidy to the village. It was my impression that substantial net investment was taking place in such projects even at the village level in Central Sumatra, where there appeared to be considerably more drive for improvement than in West Java.

The leading item of expenditure in the village budget in Central Sumatra was for construction and maintenance of the primary schools (*sekolah rakja'*), which was estimated to comprise about 60 per cent of the total. Local interest in providing educational facilities in Central Sumatra appeared to have reduced the cost of education as a provincial undertaking. Expenditures for education absorbed less than 40 per cent of the Central Sumatran provincial outlays while they absorbed at least 60 per cent of provincial outlays in West Java, where there was less interest in undertaking such expenditures at the village level.

Kabupaten Finance

On the *kabupaten* level of administration there were also significant differences in local finance between the two provinces surveyed. At this level, too, the greater dependence of local levels of government in West Java on Central Government support was apparent. In Central Sumatra, Central Government financial assistance was not used to finance current administrative expenditures; subsidies were received only for assistance in construction of roads, and were equal to approximately 20 per cent of total *kabupaten* income. In West Java, however, Central Government subsidies supported more than two-thirds of current expenditures. Here government subsidy comprised about three-fourths of the combined (current and capital) budget.

The assumption was easily made in West Java that Central Government was responsible for providing all the fiscal resources for supporting the capital budget of the kabupaten (as well as a substantial share of the current budget). Yet it was felt that this dependence on Central Government subsidy restricted kabupaten investment. This impression was confirmed by observation in Central Sumatra, where both the initiative for undertaking investment projects and the means to support them were sought locally. Here capital expenditures comprised a considerably larger share of the total budget than in West Java, and local officials were preoccupied with drafting new development plans and implementing them locally. Mobilization of resources to finance the projects appeared to place no great strain on the local economy. This suggests that resources out of which local investment projects may be financed lie near the local administrative level and can be effectively mobilized there. Sumatran fiscal authorities argued that strict adherence to Central Government policy would have greatly limited the scale of the kabupaten investment program; hence, they defied a Ministry of Interior dictum that all local investment projects should receive both Central Government approval and financing. In West Java, where this principle was taken seriously, the complaint was made that capital expenditures did not represent as large a share of the total budget as in the prewar era.* Local authorities doubted that net capital formation was being achieved, while in those areas on Java with less Central Government domination and in the Outer Islands there was unmistakable evidence of positive capital formation at the kabupaten level.

The proximity of the West Java provincial seat to Djakarta and the consequent close identification with Central Government finance may

*In fact, officials concerned with kabupaten finance pointed out that in the prewar period about 70 per cent of kabupaten expenditures were capital-producing in nature; since independence this percentage has declined to about 40 per cent.

not be the only factors in the loss of fiscal autonomy in kabupaten finance and the relatively low rate of local capital formation. Several other factors should be weighed and investigated. First, there is evidence that per capita incomes in Sumatra are substantially above those on Java because of the more favorable resources-population ratio in Sumatra. A second factor is the distribution of income. The evidence suggests that income is distributed more unequally in West Java than in Central Sumatra, particularly in the rural sector.

The preliminary results of a number of studies have indicated that the rural tenancy problem is more serious in West Java than in other areas of Indonesia. A strong landlord-rentier class has emerged since the end of World War II, and there has been a significant shift in the distribution of rural incomes in the direction of such upper-income groups. Our discussion in the preceding chapter suggests, further, that such shifts have not been followed by compensating changes in the tax structure. Rural taxation, as it has been enforced on Java, is particularly incapable of reaching increments in incomes accruing to these groups. Since local finance in Indonesia is in large part based on the rural sector, the changes in the composition and size of rural income may account for differences in local finance as well as for the presumption that there was greater capacity to finance local development expenditures in Central Sumatra than in West Java.

Kabupaten income in both West Java and Central Sumatra varied greatly by locality within the two provinces. Since Central Government failed to resolve the problem of fiscal interrelationship among the various levels of government, there were no accepted or formally authorized sources of kabupaten income. Fiscal authorities in Central Sumatra were making efforts to follow the postwar shifts in the size and distribution of incomes in their province. In West Java the structure of kabupaten levies, although extremely diverse and complex, remained quite similar to that during the Dutch colonial period, comprising a few traditionally local taxes, a large number of "retributions,"* and a limited amount of poaching on what Central Government regarded as its revenue sources.[9] In Central Sumatra, local fiscal authorities had by 1953 escaped the strait jacket of Dutch colonial tradition and had added new levies, while continuing to collect most of the traditional local taxes and retributions. New sources of revenue included kabupaten duty on rubber exports from the eastern part of the province to Singapore (the largest single revenue producer in that area), levies on incomes from mines, duties on forest products, and receipts from kabupaten-operated enterprises. Hence there was an effort in this area to exploit the new tax base produced by increased local incomes and greater exports. It should be pointed out, however, that this effort usually produced conflict with Central Government authorities since Central Government tax devices, rather than new methods, were adopted to reach the new sources of revenue.

Provincial Finance

In both Central Sumatra and West Java provincial expenditures were financed almost exclusively by Central Government subsidy before the conflicts of 1956-1958.[10] The province of Central Sumatra had no legal revenue sources of its own although provincial officials were

*Retributions are conceived of as payments for specific government services and, hence, are distinguished from taxes. In West Java they include levies on the construction of new buildings, on legal contracts, on reproductions of legal documents by the government, on inspection of meat and animals for slaughtering, on pasars, on trash removal, on public sales of sea produce, and on parking places for public vehicles.

responsible for collecting certain types of taxes and remitting the proceeds to Central Government offices. In West Java a few insignificant revenue sources still belonged to the province: income from lease of public lands, resale of provincial stocks of goods, and surtaxes on two Central Government taxes (urban real estate tax and household tax). In 1953 locally collected revenues contributed only Rp. 4,500,000 to a total provincial budget of Rp. 225,000,000 (2 per cent).[11]

In 1954 capital expenditures comprised only 9 per cent of budgeted expenditures in West Java, while estimated investment expenditures comprised about 40 per cent of provincial outlays in Central Sumatra,* a result which shows the force of historical precedent on fiscal performance at the local level. Where the precedent of autonomy is great, as in Central Sumatra, the local fiscal processes tend to be more vigorous, both in financing investment and in supporting general local expenditures through local fiscal processes. Expenditures on education absorbed almost 60 per cent of provincial expenditures in West Java and only about 40 per cent in Central Sumatra, largely the result of greater fiscal autonomy at the subprovincial levels of government in Central Sumatra and greater interest in providing educational facilities at the lower levels of government. Local fiscal autonomy apparently resulted in more scope for expenditures on public health in Central Sumatra, where they were 17 per cent of the budget as against only 2 per cent in West Java. In Central Sumatra this expenditure consisted primarily of new medical installations—hospitals, clinics, and medical equipment—and as such represented predominantly investment expenditure.

Judging from newspaper reports, the seizure of fiscal autonomy by local units greatly spurred local expenditures for economic development.

*These data are from the budgets drafted by the provincial governments.

In Central Sumatra, for example, where fiscal autonomy was asserted in 1956 and continued throughout 1957, considerable progress was reported. According to the Djakarta daily, Pedoman, Colonel Husein, Chairman of the Benteng Council, reported that Central Sumatra expenditures increased from Rp. 196 million in 1956 (when Central Government subsidization of the provincial budget still existed) to Rp. 411 million in 1957.[12] Expenditures for "development activities" rose from Rp. 34 million in 1956 to Rp. 175 million in 1957. Another newspaper source reported that expenditures for construction (one item of capital formation) rose from Rp. 13 million in 1956 to Rp. 114 million in 1957.[13] The newspaper account emphasized that this progress should partially be ascribed to the increased amount of voluntary labor services mobilized through the gotong rojong (mutual assistance) system.

Similarly, in the North Celebes area, where virtual autonomy existed during 1957, an extensive new development program financed mainly by voluntary labor mobilization was reported in many newspaper accounts. One account described an extensive highway and construction program which yielded impressive results during 1957.[14] The point was made that the program was financed primarily by gotong rojong subscriptions of labor services, with some monetary allocations from local governments.

Such reports were representative of many which have come from areas where some degree of local autonomy was achieved as a result of the challenges to Central Government authority. A consistent strain of emphasis is placed upon the importance of freedom from central prerogative to approve or disapprove local projects if such undertakings are to flourish. A related point which is repeatedly made is that local sacrifice for development activities varies inversely with the degree of dependence upon Central Government subsidy for financing local projects. The issue at stake is whether or not local units wield the power of decision in choosing, financing, and prosecuting local development activities. Where this power clearly rests with local units, local governments are willing to provide financing. Where it is lacking, there is a strong tendency to acquiesce in Central Government prosecution of all aspects of capital formation, including its financing.

The Role of Central Government Fiscal Offices in Local Finance*

It is impossible to draw a complete picture of local finance without reference to the role of Central Government fiscal offices and their relationship to local fiscal systems. The tax impact of Central Government in areas outside larger cities was felt almost exclusively through those offices. Moreover, the problem of intergovernmental fiscal relationships arose mainly from the play of forces that shaped their role in localities. It is particularly important to review this role briefly since those offices represented Central Government's sole direct fiscal access to the rural sector, where we have discovered the greatest potential tax capacity from which tax resources for financing economic development may be mobilized.

Central Government fiscal offices outside Djakarta were the local representatives of the Ministry of Finance; as such they should be distinguished from the local fiscal operations described in the first part of this chapter. They collected a substantial part of Central Government

*The organizational structure of this part of the tax service and the responsibilities of district offices are described in M. D. Dris, "Taxation in Indonesia," _Ekonomi dan Keuangan Indonesia_, Vol. XI, August-September 1958, pp. 430-435.

revenues, since, although they did not collect customs duties, which are Indonesia's most important revenue producers, other taxes of major importance were assigned to their administration. The most important single revenue producer under their jurisdiction was the company tax, followed in the order of their importance by the income tax on individuals, the wages tax, and the sales tax. They were also responsible for collecting taxes of lesser importance, including the urban real estate tax, duties on property transfers, the stamp tax, the capital-assets tax, the vehicle tax, the reconstruction tax, and the tax on private property.

A general lack of clearly differentiated responsibility between the Central Government fiscal offices and local government tax officials has been one of the major problems in the Indonesian tax system. Legally there are virtually no sources of tax income available to local governments. All tax collection, therefore, has been a Central Government prerogative during the period since independence. In practice, however, the government has found it necessary to rely on local officials to collect a part of its tax revenues. In general, this situation has resulted in a certain amount of division of labor in tax collection, and it has led the government fiscal offices to distinguish two collection functions under their jurisdiction: first, the function of assessing and collecting certain taxes directly, and, second, the function of supervising the collection by local officials of certain taxes delegated to them. These lines of responsibility are not consistently drawn throughout Indonesia, and the division of the tax collection function reflects both precedent and the capabilities of Central Government offices in particular tax districts.

In both Central Sumatra and West Java we found Central Government tax officials protesting that they were responsible for collecting an extremely complex and diverse series of taxes. The complexity of the tax structure under their administration had adverse effects upon both local acceptance of Central Government taxation and the efficiency of administration of the tax system as a whole. The attempt to collect the total tax levy through duties on a variety of economic functions not only promoted evasion but also bred the feeling that the local fiscal process had a nuisance rather than revenue-producing quality. The conclusion that Central Government taxation would become more generally accepted if the fiscal burden were limited to two or three direct levies was inescapable. Popular resistance interfered particularly with efficient collection of the reconstruction tax, a tax on the patrons of restaurants. Because of popular feeling against this postwar tax, it was ordinarily impossible for the restaurant owner to collect it from his patrons. Hence it came to be collected as an additional business tax on the restaurateur. Since no sales records were kept, collection was usually effected through a rather arbitrary process of assessing the owner's ability to pay. Thus a difficult and costly collection process was necessary, and the reconstruction tax produced relatively small yields in the provinces studied.

In both Central Sumatra and West Java it was apparent that the diversity of Central Government taxes interfered with effective administration of the important revenue producers. Each tax for which the Central Government tax offices were responsible had its own complicated array of regulations. Since the officials were responsible for collecting a large number of minor taxes as well as the important revenue producers, they were unable to concentrate on the assessment and collection of taxes which, with sufficient effort, could have contributed considerably greater revenues. Specialization of tax collections would have required reducing the number of taxes to the few important revenue producers; tax officials in both provinces contended that simplification of the tax structure would have doubled the tax yield.

A further collection problem—one which was found to be especially serious in the Outer Islands—was the inability of Central Government tax officials to supervise collection of taxes beyond the larger cities where the tax offices were located.* In Central Sumatra and other areas where communications are still rather primitive the provincial inspectorate's control over local tax officials was limited. As a result, local tax representatives often failed to remit tax proceeds to Central Government tax offices. It was also pointed out that local tax officials were frequently reluctant to assess and collect taxes strictly. To promote more effective enforcement, government tax officials in some areas made periodic visits to the more important tax districts. A visit by the tax inspector from the Padang office in Central Sumatra to one of the larger but more remote cities in the province revealed that laxity of the local tax collector had resulted in substantial leakages

*The Dris report, published four years after our study was made, also emphasizes the significance of this problem: ". . . the [Central] Administration [of Inland Revenue] lacks two vital sections—a service responsible for inspecting the district offices at regular intervals and another responsible for collecting taxes.

"Senior officials in the technical division do in fact have authority to carry out certain tasks in the country as a whole; but the exigencies of their own office work prevent them from travelling more than occasionally and this means that the central Administration has no direct or regular contact with its district offices; the latter merely send in extremely brief monthly statistical reports, no really effective control is exercised over the internal organization of these offices, the output of their staff or the regularity of their operations. . . . This shortcoming is particularly serious in Indonesia in view of the size of the country and the widely varying economic and social conditions in different areas; it should at all costs be remedied at the earliest opportunity, and after thorough investigation, the national revenue service should propose drastic measures to clear the considerable backlog of assessments and prevent the recurrence of such a situation." (M. D. Dris, "Taxation in Indonesia," Ekonomi dan Keuangan Indonesia, Vol. XI, August-September 1958, pp. 430-431.)

in revenues. By personally enforcing the regulations of the two major taxes, the tax inspector was able to triple the Central Government tax yield in this particular area. Even on Java the lack of transportation facilities was emphasized as a major deterrent to stricter enforcement of existing tax legislation. The local representatives were not provided with the transportation to supervise adequately collection of taxes within their districts. Both in Central Sumatra and in West Java tax officials suggested that enlarging the tax cadres and equipping them more adequately with means of transport would produce high returns in terms of greater tax yields.

Such problems go far toward explaining the inability of Central Government to enforce direct taxation in the rural sector of the economy. Even where the fiscal officials made a serious attempt to carry out the administration of the many taxes under their jurisdiction they failed to reach much beyond the cities in which their offices were located. It is for these same reasons that Central Government found it necessary to delegate all or a part of the assessment and collection of revenues outside urban centers to local officials.

The second major responsibility of the Central Government tax offices, therefore, was supervision of the collection of the taxes delegated to local government officials. Potentially most important is the padjak ketjil (rural income tax). Efforts to enforce this tax in the rural sector began after 1952 but results have been disappointing. In Central Sumatra the collection of this tax was delegated completely to the local government officials; in Java, Central Government tax officers penetrated into the villages to collect the tax on incomes above a specified minimum (which varied by locality). In Central Sumatra, the Central Government office exercised only indirect supervision over the collection process. A government official was given responsibility for a particular tax district, a division of the kabupaten. Responsibility for collection fell to the kepala negeri, the local village head corresponding to the lurah on Java. This official had little motivation for accurate assessment of incomes or upward revision of tax rates, in accordance with postindependence legislation, since there was no local benefit from the revenues he collected in behalf of Central Government. Even on Java, where collection was shared with Central Government authorities, there was a tendency toward laxity in collection and assessment of the rural income tax. In East Java the income line dividing local collection and Central Government collection was Rp. 3,400; in West Java the income line was Rp. 5,000. There was a natural tendency on the part of both the taxpayer and the local tax collector (lurah) to keep the assessment within the bounds of local collection, a tendency for underassessment of rural incomes which was aggravated by the fact that in many areas on Java the lurah was allowed to retain a percentage of the tax proceeds which he collected. This amount was retained by the lurah personally rather than being used for the desa treasury.

This division of responsibility for collection of the rural income tax has been one of the basic reasons for the inefficiency of Central Government tax enforcement. The tax system has attempted to reach too far down into the structure of Indonesian society, leading to Central Government collection efforts in areas where they were inevitably ineffective. Since Central Government tax officials have been incapable of reaching the greater part of this tax base directly, they have relied upon the cooperation of local officials who have no great interest in maximizing Central Government revenues. An almost inescapable conclusion follows. It would both relieve the problem of tax administration and reduce Central Government subsidization of local governments if this particular tax were turned over to localities.

Local Finance and Economic Development

The most significant aspect of local finance for Indonesia's economic progress is the extent to which local levels of government employ their fiscal processes to undertake investment. Investigations in Central Sumatra, West Java, Jogjakarta, East Java, and Bali indicated that locally financed investment projects are of major importance to the Indonesian economy. The case for recognizing the scope of such investment activities, their nature, and their variation by area cannot be put too strongly. Effective development policy should be aimed at maximizing this type of local investment, first, to alleviate the heavy financial burden of central subsidies to local governments, and, secondly, through coordination of local efforts with the financing and execution of Central Government development efforts, to utilize local development activities for the prosecution of a program of genuinely national character.

In the period when nominal unification existed in Indonesia (1950-1956), Central Government policy tended to stifle rather than promote local initiative in undertaking and financing small-scale development projects. *Kabupaten* and provincial governments were required to obtain approval for proposed local projects from the Ministry of Interior, with the Ministry pre-empting responsibility to arrange financing. Approval ordinarily involved extended delays, causing dwindling local interest in the projects and frequently their abandonment. Governments in the outlying provinces—particularly Central Sumatra and Sulawesi, where local autonomy was greatest—assumed initiative in financing and prosecuting developmental projects within their means without awaiting government approval; but integration of those projects with larger-scale planning and the opportunity to draw on the technical assistance and general support of Central Government would have speeded their completion. Djakarta's awareness of the problems and the potentialities of mobilizing local resources for capital formation is essential to sound planning for increasing the rate of investment accomplished by all levels of government. This issue has become so important in Indonesia that, and as a first prerequisite to carrying out a program of economic development, Central Government must resolve the problems of local autonomy and delineation of fiscal processes before it can reassert general control throughout Indonesia.

Part of the problem lies in the fact that Central Government has failed both to recognize the importance of granting local autonomy and to comprehend the contribution which local fiscal processes can make to financing development by mobilizing resources beyond its reach. In Indonesia, as in other underdeveloped countries, the fiscal capacity of Central Government has been overrated and that of local governments overlooked, perhaps because of lack of information. In this sense, planning the finance of development programs may be more hampered by the shortages of statistics than by shortages of financial experts. In most studies available to the Indonesian government the assumption has been made that local expenditures are undertaken only where Central Government provides subsidies to finance them. This assumption, for example, lies behind Neumark's methodology, resulting in understatement of the investment component of national income.[15]

Analysis of the summary of local budgets issued by the Ministry of Interior for 1953 (Table 37) reveals the extent to which local capital formation is underestimated by Neumark's estimate, which was based exclusively upon Central Government statistics. The Ministry of Interior budgets for local governments are drawn up on the assumption that local governments to which Central Government subsidies are made (province, kabupaten, and kota) have no resources of their own, hence that subsidized expenditures comprise their total outlays.

Table 37

MINISTRY OF INTERIOR SUMMARY OF TOTAL BUDGETS OF LOCAL GOVERNMENTS, 1953

(Thousand Rp.)

	Province	Kabupaten	Kota	Total
Ordinary expenditures	1,116,922	369,788	120,325	1,607,035
Capital expenditures*	221,721	34,381	15,075	271,177
Subsidies to primary schools	18,086		4,288	22,374
Total	1,356,729	404,169	139,688	1,900,586

*Comprising expenditures on roads, bridges, irrigation facilities, public buildings, new classrooms and equipment for primary schools, health facilities, agricultural and veterinary facilities, and expenditures for development of inland fishing.

In the case of provinces, the finance of which is closely associated with the Ministry of Interior budget, this estimate of gross capital formation may be roughly correct; but in the case of kabupaten and kota, which in many areas have independent budgets and independent fiscal resources, both total expenditures and capital formation are grossly underestimated. *Kabupaten* capital expenditures for all Indonesia were estimated at only Rp. 34,381,000. In Central Sumatra alone, capital expenditures in 1953 were reported to total approximately Rp. 40,000,000. The Ministry of Interior estimate included no recorded capital expenditures at the *kabupaten* level for this province or for North Sumatra, South Sumatra, Kalimantan (Borneo), and Sunda Ketjil; it included only small amounts for Sulawesi (Celebes) and the Moluccas. Yet in the provinces visited by our research teams investment activities were observed to be more vigorous on the *kabupaten* than on the provincial level. The Ministry of Interior (as did Neumark) also excluded any reference to capital projects undertaken at the *desa* level. In short, although investment at the local government level is one of the most important components of investment in the economy (perhaps approaching the size of Central Government investment), its significance has not been recognized by either Central Government or its observers.

For the years prior to the assumption of autonomy by the outlying provinces, a rough estimate of net investment performed by local governments of Rp. 1.5 billion annually appears to be conservative. The Ministry of Interior reported subsidies of Rp. 271 million for new investment projects (net investment) for the year 1953. On the basis of the limited data to which we had access, it seems realistic to estimate the value of investment projects completed by local governments without the support of the Ministry at roughly four times this amount. Moreover, it appears that the amount of local capital formation could have been doubled had fiscal functions been intelligently divided among the various levels of government and if tax enforcement had been tightened.

Our emphasis upon the importance of local government investment requires a description of the process as we found it. At the lowest level of government (the desa) the greater part of the mobilization of resources did not enter the sphere of monetary calculus, although even at the desa level the economy itself was highly monetized. Labor services for the local projects were mobilized directly through the village council, which drew upon the village labor supply according to the seasonal demands of primary occupations in a given area.* Hence the monetary sector of the economy was consciously side-stepped in the mobilization of resources to provide labor for investment projects. This suggests an awareness of seasonal underemployment of labor resources and an effort to mobilize them for combination with other factors of production provided by financing through the monetary sector. Thus the labor input (which was estimated by local authorities to represent 70 per cent of total "cost") was combined with material and equipment financed from monetary tax collections undertaken by the desa itself or, more usually, obtained from higher levels of government as subsidy. It was pointed out that skilled labor, technicians, and engineers represented the scarcest real factors. These factors, too, were economized by kabupaten and provincial governments, which shifted them among local projects according to demand. It was emphasized that the rate of local investment could be greatly accelerated if Central Government could provide an increased supply of these specialized factors to be allocated for investment activity by local governments. Foreign aid programs could contribute significantly to local investment by providing technical experts (engineers, surveyors) at provincial or

*Gotong rojong. This system of financing local projects has a long and successful history in Indonesia.

kabupaten levels of government rather than assigning them exclusively to Djakarta.

At the *kabupaten* level the process of local investment varied greatly between Java and the more autonomous outlying provinces. On Java there was a tendency to rely on Central Government financing for development projects, while responsibility for both the financing and mobilization of the real factors was largely assumed by the *kabupaten* in the Outer Islands. This situation was reflected in the efforts of the local governments outside Java to capture a part of the increments in taxable capacity which have appeared to emerge since the end of colonialism. In Central Sumatra the provincial office for *kabupaten* administration assumed responsibility for the drafting of plans for local development projects; it advised on direct recruitment of the labor supply for their implementation; and it provided technical advice to local governmental units where there was initiative for undertaking new projects. Here, too, the financing was provided partly from monetary tax collections and Central Government subsidies and partly by employment of the idle labor resources recruited by the individual *kabupaten* itself. At this level, however, the nonmonetary "financing" of development projects was considerably less than at the village level.

Much of the investment activity taking place at the local level, particularly in the outlying provinces, was supported from genuinely local resources. Financing was partly in terms of monetary tax collections (which may or may not have interfered with enlarged Central Government tax collections) and partly in terms of nonmonetized resource mobilization (which presumably did not interfere with Central Government taxation).

Centralization versus Decentralization in Financing Indonesian Economic Development

The foregoing review of the structure of local finance in Indonesia and its potential role in the development of the economy raises important questions concerning fiscal relations among the various levels of government. From the point of view of economic development, it is critical that intergovernmental relations allow each level of government to contribute the maximum in mobilizing resources from which development can be financed. It is also important that the supply of technical skills and administrative abilities available at the various levels of government be fully utilized in a program of economic development. In Indonesia, as in other underdeveloped countries, such skills and abilities are not found exclusively among Central Government officials. In fact, Indonesia possesses a vast reservoir of competent officials at the lower levels of government,* a source of abilities and skills which could contribute significantly to economic progress both in mobilizing the fiscal resources to finance development plans and in the actual implementation of such plans. Realization of the potential contribution which might be made from local resources depends on the proper balance between local autonomy and Central Government coordination in relationships among the various levels of government.

*The M.I.T. group of social scientists who completed the "Modjokuto" study in Central Java were impressed by the competence of local administrators. Dr. Clifford Geertz, returning from a field study in Bali in 1958, reported the same impression. He also found a tendency among traditional rulers to assume new economic roles, leading to a vigorous indigenous entrepreneurship. Utilizing this reserve of administrative capacity may well be Indonesia's most significant opportunity to rapidly raise its capacity to absorb as well as to mobilize capital for economic development.

Our empirical studies in Indonesia also indicate that the ultimate basis of economic development in a democratic society—individual and group initiative—is related to the degree of autonomy which localities have been able to achieve. The greatest amount of local participation in development programs was found where localities had been able to resist the attempts of Central Government to dominate their political and fiscal functions. In such areas individual and local initiative produced relatively high levels of local capital formation and rising levels of per capita income. Local autonomy preserves the link between individual sacrifice and benefit, providing the incentive for the release of new energies necessary to transform an economically stagnant society into a dynamic one.

The case for a sizable local ingredient in Indonesian economic development and its financing is a strong one. Yet local developmental activities alone cannot produce the structural changes needed to solve some of the basic economic problems of a newly independent country. A plethora of local irrigation works, transport facilities, and export processing plants cannot create an industrial structure adequate to free Indonesia from its present dependence on foreign trade for industrial imports; nor can it provide an effective take-off to cumulative economic growth. Undue emphasis on decentralized development of the type described here would not result in effective use of Indonesia's broad variety of economic resources through specialization and division of labor. The heavy investment requirements necessary to meet the more general objectives of Indonesian economic development are obviously beyond the capacities of local levels of government. Central Government alone possesses the fiscal power and financial capacity to undertake the broader type of social overhead investments which are essential to maximize the productivity of smaller-scale investments by localities and individuals.[16]

Conflicts between the central and local governments over the distribution of revenue sources, as well as in the specific role of financing economic development, became increasingly severe as the struggle for local autonomy became more general in the Outer Islands. Insecure Central Government control led to renewed efforts to centralize fiscal functions more completely. In the Outer Islands this state of affairs produced uneconomic duplication of expenditure functions, with considerable confusion as to who was responsible for financing current and developmental activities. Several levels of government participated in the support and construction of schools, hospitals, and road and irrigation facilities, while Central Government insisted on its prerogative to approve and finance such projects as far down as the _kabupaten_ level. On Java the result was excessive central control over local governments, which has blurred the relationship between local benefit and local contribution. Local autonomy over functions providing exclusively local benefits is desirable, as suggested above, since such functions can be performed more efficiently at the local level and financing can be arranged more economically through use of local resources which cannot be mobilized through Central Government fiscal processes.

The situation which prevailed in the years before the outlying provinces declared their virtual independence of Djakarta was a particularly unsuccessful combination of centralization and decentralization in reaching revenue sources. The provinces had virtually no sources of income, while _kabupaten_ and _desa_ tended to exploit any sources of revenue within their purview, regardless of Central Government efforts to tax the same sources. The effects of the multiplicity of taxation had important implications for financing economic development:

1. Central Government fiscal offices engaged in the collection of taxes for which they were not administratively suited, i.e., taxes which could have been more effectively collected by local governments. (The rural income tax and the tax on private property are notable examples.) This effort made Central Government tax administration in the provinces a cumbersome and inefficient process and was a major factor generating hostility toward Central Government.

2. Central Government interference with tax bases structurally adapted to local collection deprived local units of natural revenue sources and caused them to seek a diversity of petty and uneconomic levies to finance their expenditures, which in turn produced a pattern of local revenues yielding small income relative to costs of collection.

3. The uneconomic distribution of taxable capacity necessitated large-scale Central Government subsidization of localities, representing a heavy drain on its budget and limiting its ability to undertake the financing of a development program.* Even so, in the provinces on Java it was felt that arbitrary decisions as to the size of government subsidies to provinces and _kabupaten_ and uncertainty as to their amount limited the capacity of provincial and _kabupaten_ governments to undertake capital formation of the scope called for by local need. In short, the haphazard system of distribution of revenue sources and subsidies which emerged after independence was inadequate to support necessary

*For 1953 the Ministry of Interior reported subsidies to local governments amounting to Rp. 1.9 billion, approximately 16 per cent of total reported Central Government expenditures (Rp. 11.9 billion). By 1955 such subsidies were near Rp. 3 billion. The adverse effects of the subsidy system on financing economic development are presented in detail by the Governor of the Bank Indonesia in _Report of the Bank Indonesia, 1954-1955_, pp. 19-20.

functions of local governments. Further, a broad subsidy program, which was an inevitable consequence of that system, by its very nature implied relatively great Central Government influence over local finance and consequent loss of local autonomy.

Paradoxically, in the first years after Indonesia's independence considerable thought was given to these problems, and a governmental committee undertook to study them.* The recommendations of this committee assigned a number of taxes to local levels of government† and provided for the division of other tax revenues between central and local governments. Taxes such as the rural income tax, which are potentially the most lucrative sources of local revenues, were to be collected under Central Government supervision and the proceeds divided according to a formula which provided no link between local sacrifice and local benefit. The Nasrun study did not deal with the role of local finance in economic development and it failed to delineate the expenditure function in detail among the various levels of political administration in Indonesia. After several years before Parliament, most of the Nasrun recommendations were enacted into law in late 1956, under pressure of threats of local rebellion. The 1956 legislation‡ requires further Parliamentary action to put into effect the Nasrun proposals.

*The Nasrun Committee was appointed to study the problems of financial relations between central and local governments. Its recommendations appeared in an Indonesian document and were also presented in Indonesian and Dutch by J. de Bruine in a series of articles in Ekonomi dan Keuangan Indonesia. They are summarized and evaluated in Appendix D. The Nasrun Committee recommendations appear to have been the basis for 1956 legislation on the problem of central-local fiscal relationships. (See Appendix E.)

†The pasar (market) tax, the amusement tax, and the bicycle tax are three local taxes now in effect to be retained by local units. The urban real estate tax, the vehicle tax, the tax on consumption in restaurants, and the household property tax are examples of taxes to be transferred from Central Government.

‡A brief summary, taken from the Dris report, is presented in Appendix E.

The existing relationship between Central Government and local units limits the financing and prosecution of economic development because Central Government has attempted to go beyond the reaches of its administrative capacity on both sides of the fiscal accounts. In this volume it has been suggested that revenues could be increased if taxes which could be more efficiently collected by local administrations were transferred to local units. It has also been suggested that the rate of capital formation could be accelerated by yielding jurisdiction over local investment projects to the appropriate level of local government. At the same time, local capital formation could be increased by Central Government provision of those technical skills and materials which are most scarce. All this would involve a degree of coordination and cooperation between Central Government and local development activities which has not existed in most areas of Indonesia.

Available evidence points to the conclusion that there is significant scope for local development projects in Indonesia's total program of economic planning. The present study suggests that there are margins of taxable capacity which can be reached only through taxation at the local level. It also suggests that idle resources which cannot be mobilized through the Central Government fiscal process could be brought into the development program by local investment projects. Moreover, the psychological urge for improvement could be activated by the incentives provided by the link between sacrifice and opportunities for local benefit. Once this process was set in motion, the heavy burden of subsidies to support local current and investment functions could be gradually withdrawn from the Central Government budget, a move which would tend in itself to increase the government's capacity to finance its development plan.

Development activities which can be prosecuted from resources available to local levels of government could become an important component of Indonesia's development plan. Local investment projects could provide facilities to increase the output of food, improve local transport, and increase export earnings. In fact, the productivity of large-scale Central Government development projects—such as large-scale irrigation and power plants and national communications systems—can be maximized only if local facilities are supplied to complement such external economies. The optimum pattern of Indonesian economic development consists of a blend of centralization and decentralization in planning and execution which would fully exploit the fiscal and administrative capacities at each level of authority.

In the immediate future, restoration of national unity and prosecution of the Five Year Plan require that Central Government face and resolve the problem of its relationship with regional groups in the Outer Islands.[17] Some of those groups appear to have launched local development programs with renewed vigor, employing the revenues which formerly flowed to Djakarta for financing provincial development. Unless the pattern of national dissolution is soon reversed, Indonesian economic development over the long run will consist of a series of local plans, with Central Government planning restricted to the island of Java. This result would deprive Indonesia from realizing the most important potential gain of national economic development—regional division of labor and specialization between highly populated Java and the natural-resource-abundant Outer Islands. As economic regionalism proceeds, the possibility of establishing political unity and the feasibility of a national program designed to combine the advantages of a mixture of central and decentralized development will become more remote. Historical precedents showing the relationship between political fragmentation and the failure of plans for economic development are uncomfortably abundant. The Kuomintang government of Mainland China, for example, failed to achieve its development goals partly because it was unable to extend its fiscal and political powers beyond two or three provinces where its control was almost totalitarian.

We must emphasize, in conclusion, that solution to the problem of central-local fiscal relationships will require a broad settlement of the political problems which have plagued the Indonesian Republic since its formation. Throughout the years from 1950 to 1959 a formula to preserve both national unity and local autonomy has been sought. Understandably, Central Government has pressed for enough control at all levels of political organization to enable it to execute national decisions. The essence of the Indonesian problem, however, has been that Central Government control has been exerted by erecting a structure of government tentacles which function independently of, rather than <u>through</u>, existing (primarily traditional) local political institutions. We have seen evidence of this duality in the fiscal system; in fact, it is characteristic of all political functions. This duality has produced conflicts over a wide range of issues, making it increasingly difficult to move toward a settlement in terms of a blend of local autonomy and central authority. Prior to the breakdown of Central Government authority in the Outer Islands in 1956 and 1957, the government was able to rig control over what should constitutionally be local functions by resorting to escape clauses in the basic Territorial Government Law of 1948.[18] The unfortunate consequence of that breach of democratic intent is that it has hampered the realization of a basic settlement by arousing such fear and resentment among Indonesians in some areas that it has become difficult if not impossible to accept legitimate Central Government demands for effective unification. Contemporary Indonesian history teaches, once again, that voluntary popular support for a central government diminishes where traditional, perhaps even instinctive, local functions are arrogated by authority rather than yielded by consent. Yet voluntary and enthusiastic support for national goals is a sine qua non for successful prosecution of a development plan.

An attempt to solve the problem by legislation in 1956 failed because neither Central Government nor the local units would negotiate a basic settlement.[19] The new decentralization law which resulted from a series of conferences was hardly a compromise. Taxes to be transferred to local governments represented only 1 per cent of total Central Government tax receipts in 1956.[20] Recent events suggest that the road to national unity will be difficult;* it may be impossible to resolve the problem under the present republican form of Indonesian government. Nevertheless, constructive thinking about Indonesian development prospects requires emphasis upon the blending of central and local participation. The fact that a basic political settlement is prerequisite to a program of this nature does not invalidate the conclusions of this chapter. The writer believes that the poignant failures confronted during the short span of independence—of which political fragmentation is the greatest—may yet lead to a resurgence of national cooperation. If—as suggested here—a successful development program requires integration of the parts and the whole, economic development may become the cause around which political support for national unity can best be rallied.

*Since the rebellion was put down in 1958, guerrilla warfare and local resistance to central authority continue to plague the government in Djakarta.

Notes to Chapter 7

1. See J. W. Meyer-Ranneft and W. Huender, *Onderzoek naar den Belastingdruk op de Inlandsche Bevolking* (An Inquiry Concerning the Tax Burden upon the Native Population), Landsdrukkerij, Weltevreden, 1926.

2. Department of Agriculture, Industry and Commerce, *1930 Handbook of the Netherlands East Indies*, Buitenzorg, Java, 1930, p. 97.

3. Data are from annual editions of the *Statistische Jaaroverzicht van Nederlandsch-Indië* (Statistical Abstract of the Netherlands Indies), published by the Netherlands Indies Central Bureau of Statistics.

4. V. Karakacheff, "Notes on the Budget System of Indonesia," mimeographed manuscript, p. 2.

5. *Report of the Bank Indonesia, 1953-1954*, p. 54.

6. M. D. Dris, "Taxation in Indonesia," *Ekonomi dan Keuangan Indonesia*, Vol. XI, August-September 1958, pp. 524-525.

7. These figures are from a statement by Indonesia's former Prime Minister, Ali Sastroamidjojo, published in American Indonesian Chamber of Commerce, Inc., *Information Bulletin*, No. 402, March 1955, p. 30.

8. A former Governor of the Bank Indonesia, for example, argues that this is true. See *Report of the Bank Indonesia, 1956-1957*, p. 17.

9. This same pattern appears to have existed in East Java. See John D. Legge, *Problems of Regional Autonomy in Contemporary Indonesia*, Modern Indonesia Project, Southeast Asia Program, Department of Far Eastern Studies, Cornell University, Ithaca, 1957, p. 41.

10. The *Report of the Bank Indonesia, 1954-1955* (p. 18) quotes Ministry of Interior data showing that total *daerah* expenditures were Rp. 2,733 million, of which only Rp. 378 was financed from local resources, the remainder by Central Government subsidy. The same result is shown by evidence presented by Gerald S. Maryankov in *Decentralization in Indonesia: Legislative Aspects*, Modern Indonesia Project, Southeast Asia Program, Department of Far Eastern Studies, Cornell University, Ithaca, 1957, p. 53.

11. A similar situation is reported for East Java. In 1956, provincial levies contributed only Rp. 7 million to an expenditure of Rp. 412 million. See Legge, *op. cit.*, p. 41.

12. *Pedoman*, January 4, 1958.

13. *Mimbar Umum*, January 2, 1958, reprinting an article from *Haluan*, the Padang daily.

14. *Pikiran Rakjat* (Menado), September 21, 1957.

15. S. Daniel Neumark, "The National Income of Indonesia, 1951-1952," *Ekonomi dan Keuangan Indonesia*, Vol. VII, June 1954, pp. 357-358.

16. The ways in which the two reinforce each other are emphasized in William Lockwood's study of economic development in Japan, *The Economic Development of Japan, Growth and Structural Change, 1868–1938*, Princeton University Press, Princeton, 1954.

17. For a general review of this issue see Maryankov, *op. cit*.

18. Legge, *op. cit.*, pp. 19–21.

19. *Ibid.*, pp. 50–62.

20. Hans O. Schmitt, "The Economics of Political Disintegration in Indonesia," Ch. 4, p. 32 (unpublished manuscript).

8

A FISCAL PROGRAM FOR INDONESIA

The Indonesian government faces five major economic tasks: to unite the scattered islands in an integrated economy; to raise general productivity as a first requirement for overcoming widespread poverty; to effect the structural change necessary to relieve the chronic stress in the balance of payments; to launch a bold attack on technological dualism and its accompanying problem of low incomes and unemployment; to find productive employment for the growing population of Java. These closely interrelated tasks call for a vigorous and large-scale program of balanced growth, the major aspects of which would be: establishment of import-replacing industries in Java; development of industries processing domestic materials, mainly for export and mainly in the Outer Islands; expansion of plantation output by replanting with improved strains rather than by increasing total hectarage; and a shift to more extensive and mechanized methods of food production.

The First Plan does not provide such a program. The plan framework (see Appendix A) as accepted by Parliament postpones until the Third or Fourth Plan an effort sufficiently massive to overcome fundamental economic problems. In analyzing the plan in Chapter 1, we expressed concern that further delay in mounting an all-out attack on Indonesia's economic problems will dissipate the dynamic force infused into

Indonesian society by the revolution. Postponement has already threatened the political and social stability of the country. Our conclusion, therefore, is that every effort should be made to accelerate the expansion of developmental investment.

The Nature of the Problem

Although two somewhat different versions of the Indonesian development program have been presented,* both are conservative in planning increases in capital formation, and both make what appear to be unduly optimistic assumptions about increments in national income. In both, the ICOR for the first five-year period is placed at 2:1; but, as we have suggested, there is no reason to expect so favorable a relationship between development investment and increments in output. Both versions of the plan also project annual rates of population growth at 1.7 per cent for the first five-year period, 1.8 for the second, 1.9 for the third, and 2 for the fourth, even though 60 per cent of the projected increments in national income will be made available to consumers throughout the development program. Almost universal experience during the development process suggests, however, that rates of population growth rise more rapidly than these estimates if gains in output are made available to enhance consumption standards. Moreover, neither version of the development program provides that increased real savings above the amount required for development be mobilized to cope with the short-run problems of price and balance-of-payments instability.

*The original version was drawn up by the National Planning Bureau and submitted to Parliament. The second version was suggested in National Planning Bureau, "A Study of the Indonesian Economic Development Scheme," published in Ekonomi dan Keuangan Indonesia, Vol. X, September 1957.

There is also some ambiguity about the rate at which net investment will be expanded during each of the four Five Year Plans presented.[1] The National Planning Bureau's original projections, for example, called for net investment of 6 per cent of national income during the First Plan period but placed the net investment rate at about 8.5 per cent at the end of the period. If net investment is to rise from 6 to 8.5 per cent of national income over a five-year period, annual investment must obviously average more than the planned 6 per cent. The same confusion between average rates and those at the beginning and end of the period is evident in the investment budgets of the later Five Year Plans.

What concerns us here is that both Planning Bureau versions of the development program appear to fall far short of budgeting enough net investment to achieve a take-off to sustained growth. The original presentation of the investment budget planned for realizing a net investment rate of 8.6 per cent at the end of the first five-year period, 12 per cent at the end of the second, 16 per cent at the end of the third, and 20 per cent at the end of the fourth. The second, and presumably revised, presentation is modest in its investment goals: a net investment of 8.5 per cent of national income at the end of the first five-year period, 10.8 per cent at the end of the second, 12.6 per cent at the end of the third, 12.9 per cent at the end of the fourth, and 16.7 at the end of the fifth.[2] The major difference between the two versions is that the second is even more optimistic than the original about the ICOR relevant to later planning periods. The ICOR is not expected to rise above 3:1, which appears to be unrealistic.

A more cautious estimate of capital requirements, as presented in Chapter 1, suggests that these rates of investment will fail to provide a take-off. Moreover, rising economic expectations following independence and almost a decade of frustration appear to make a more aggressive development program necessary to promote political stability and national unity. In Chapter 1 we indicated that annual net investment of at least 13 per cent of national income will be necessary to provide steady increases in national income per capita. Clearly, such acceleration of net investment cannot be achieved in any one year, although this goal might not be too ambitious for a five year plan—commencing when a settlement is reached on the central-local government conflict.

We have emphasized that growing economic instability has aggravated the development problem. Real savings must be increased not only to finance developmental investment but also to eliminate the government deficit and to rebuild foreign-exchange reserves. If, for example, financing these stability and development objectives were spread over the next five-year period, real savings would have to increase from a rate of 6 per cent of national income to 17 per cent. In the first year, the ratio of savings to income would rise by 3 per cent, but these resources would be devoted exclusively to achieving economic stability. Later, the rate of savings would be increased by 2 per cent each year; these increments could be devoted to financing development.

A model of such a program, employing the same assumptions as those made for estimating capital requirements in Chapter 1, is presented in Table 38. The ICOR for all developmental investment is assumed to be 3.5:1, and the annual rate of population growth remains at 1.7 per cent during the first five years, when all increments in per capita income are to be reinvested. This approach to Indonesian development would require belt-tightening throughout the first five years. In the first year, consumption would have to be reduced by approximately 3 per cent, but, by the fifth year, restriction of consumption would

Table 38

INDONESIAN GROWTH MODEL, 1960 - 1970

Part A: Model of Suggested Indonesian Development Program in Annual Sequence *

Period	Year	(1) Net Savings (Per Cent of National Income)	(2) Net Investment (Per Cent of National Income)	(3) Increase in National Income (Per Cent)	(4) Increase in Population (Per Cent)	(5) Increase in National Income Per Capita (Per Cent)
	1960†	6	6	1.7	1.7	0.0
First Five Year Plan Period	1961	6	6	1.7	1.7	0.0
	1962	8	8	2.3	1.7	0.6
	1963	10	10	2.9	1.7	1.2
	1964	12	12	3.4	1.7	1.7
	1965	14	14	4.0	1.7	2.3
Second Five Year Plan Period	1966	17	17	4.9	1.7	3.2
	1967	18	18	5.1	1.8	3.3
	1968	19	19	5.4	1.9	3.5
	1969	20	20	5.7	2.0	3.7
	1970	20	20	5.7	2.0	3.7

*Assumptions: (a) ICOR equals 3.5 : 1; (b) rate of population growth rises as per capita increments in national income are made available to consumers.

†First year of domestic political stability, regardless of actual date.

Table 38 (continued)

Part B: Financial Requirements for Suggested Model (in Billion 1952 Rupiah)

		(1) National Income	(2) Increase in National Income	(3) Increase in National Income to Offset Population Growth	(4) Increase in National Income Available for Reinvestment or Increased Consumption
	1960	101.7*			
First Five Year Plan Period	1961	103.4	1.7	1.7	0.0
	1962	105.8	2.4	1.8	0.6
	1963	108.8	3.0	1.8	1.2
	1964	112.5	3.7	1.9	1.8
	1965	117.0	4.5	1.9	2.6
Second Five Year Plan Period	1966	122.7	5.7	2.0	3.7
	1967	128.9	6.2	2.2	4.0
	1968	135.9	7.0	2.4	4.6
	1969	143.6	7.7	2.7	5.0
	1970	151.8	8.2	2.9	5.3

*This figure is based on the average pre-plan (1951-1955) rates of growth. It has been assumed that national income grew at these rates from 1955 to 1958, and that during 1958 and 1959 national income failed to grow because of domestic political and economic difficulties.

Table 38 (concluded)

Part C: Growth of National Income in Suggested Model (in Billion 1952 Rupiah)

Period	Year	(1) Total Financial Requirements*	(2) Additional Annual Requirements	(3) Increase in National Income Available for Reinvestment	(4) Deficit (-) or Surplus (+) (Column 2 less Column 3)	(5) Total Financial Requirements above Reinvested Increments in National Income
	1960	6.0				6.0
First Five Year Plan Period	1961	9.3	3.3	0.0	- 3.3	9.3
	1962	11.6	2.3	0.6	- 1.7	11.0
	1963	14.1	2.5	1.2	- 1.3	12.3
	1964	16.8	2.7	1.8	- 0.9	13.2
	1965	19.9	3.1	2.6	- 0.5	13.7
Second Five Year Plan Period	1966	22.0	2.1	3.7	+ 1.6	13.7
	1967	24.5	2.5	4.0	+ 1.5	13.7
	1968	27.2	2.7	4.6	+ 1.9	13.7
	1969	30.2	3.0	5.0	+ 2.0	13.7
	1970	31.9	1.7	5.3	+ 3.6	13.7

*Total financial requirements exceed the amounts which must be mobilized as savings to finance the plan's investment. The government must, in addition, mobilize a greater volume of tax resources to eliminate inflationary pressures and to rebuild foreign-exchange reserves. These additional requirements to obtain stability are assumed to be 3 per cent of national income during the First Five Year Plan period, and 1 per cent of national income during the Second Five Year Plan. The reasoning behind these assumptions is elaborated in Chapter 1.

be less than 1 per cent. Commencing with the Third Five Year Plan period, a significant part of increased output could be made available for improving consumption standards. The great advantage of such a program would be that the take-off to sustained growth would be realized at the end of the Third Five Year Plan period and annual improvements in per capita consumption could thenceforth be provided each year. By 1970—ten years after launching the development program—increases in output would be adequate to raise real income per capita by 3.7 per cent each year despite rapid population growth. Although accelerating the climb to the take-off involves relatively great short-run sacrifice, there must be such acceleration if stagnation is to be overcome. A more leisurely pace would jeopardize the success of the whole program by failing to raise output sufficiently to keep safely ahead of population growth, in which case output gains for reinvestment to accelerate the pace of development might fail to materialize. Such a failure would undoubtedly weaken incentives to development, and the national will to achieve a take-off to economic growth might be seriously impaired.

The question of financing these requirements can be approached better through rupiah values than through investment rates. The National Planning Bureau's projections begin with an estimated pre-plan value of national income (apparently in 1952 rupiah) of Rp. 100 billion. On this basis, the First Five Year Plan calls for total investment of Rp. 30 billion, or Rp. 6 billion per year. Of this amount, however, the government is to finance only Rp. 12.5 billion, or about Rp. 2.5 billion each year. This, again, reflects the modesty of the plan; during the period 1953-1955, government investment expenditures ranged from Rp. 1.7 billion to Rp. 2.4 billion. The remainder of the plan's budgeted investment (Rp. 17.5 billion) is to be financed by the private sector. This sector's contribution, too, is not significantly above its investment performance during the years before 1956. The conclusion emerges that Central Government is slated to maintain virtually the same volume of investment financing as during the pre-1956 years, while the private sector is expected to expand slightly its contribution to development finance. We should note also that the projected volume of public capital formation will fall relative to national income if, as the Planning Bureau believes, such a low rate of capital formation will raise national income.

It appears, therefore, that Central Government has no intention of employing its fiscal powers to mobilize a significantly greater volume of real savings to enhance stability and to launch an all-out attack on the development problem. The suggestion that Central Government has failed to face the problem of financing stability and development, perhaps because of doubts about Indonesia's financial capacity, emphasizes the importance of inquiring into the financial feasibility of the program outlined here.

The growth model presented in Table 38 proposes that the sacrifice to provide a take-off to economic growth be compressed into the first five-year period.* It calls for the mobilization of greatly increased volumes of financial resources (savings and tax receipts) over this period to: (1) cope with the problem of instability resulting from budgetary disequilibrium and foreign-exchange losses; and (2) raise net investment

*Undertaking an ambitious development program of this nature would require solution to the problem of national unity discussed in Chapter 7. For purposes of exposition we assume that it might begin in 1961, and that 1960 rates of growth will be zero, an assumption suggested by failure to launch the First Five Year Plan because of unresolved basic problems of political and economic stability.

from the estimated pre-plan rate of 6 per cent of national income to 14 per cent. To accomplish these bold objectives, our analysis in Chapter 1 suggests that total financial requirements would be about 17 per cent of national income. The model provides that none of the increments in national income are to be made available to improve consumption standards during this period; all are to be reinvested to assure the feasibility of achieving the projected rates of growth. Moreover, there will be need for reductions in consumption to provide resources to reach the objectives specified. Raising the economy's rate of savings from 6 per cent to 14 per cent, in addition to coping with inflation, in five years is a major feat. Even though national income were to grow at an annual rate of 3 per cent per capita and the full increment were mobilized as savings, this would raise the rate of savings by less than 3 per cent.

The financial requirements of the suggested program are converted into rupiah values in Table 38, Part C.* In terms of constant rupiah prices, the First Five Year Plan would require raising the rupiah volume of real savings from the pre-plan amount of about Rp. 6 billion to approximately Rp. 17 billion annually. Moreover, tax receipts must be increased by about Rp. 3 billion to eliminate Central Government's inflationary impact upon the economy. If all the increments in national income can be recaptured for investment during the First Five Year Plan period, the amount of additional tax and savings resources to be mobilized would represent the difference between estimated savings in the

*Rupiah values are in terms of 1952 prices since the estimates of financial capacity discussed below are in terms of price levels existing before the post-1955 inflationary trend set in. We have noted earlier that the period 1952-1955 was one of relative price stability, compared to the immediate post-independence period and the post-1955 situation.

year preceding the plan (Rp. 6 billion) and financial requirements in the last year of the First Five Year Plan (Rp. 13.7 billion). (See Table 38, Part C, Column 5.) Thus the sacrifice required by the model could be roughly measured as Rp. 7.7 billion. The fundamental problem of financing the take-off is the mobilization of additional taxes and savings in roughly this amount from present income levels. If consumption can be reduced sufficiently by the financial and fiscal measures we have discussed, the financing of a massive assault on stagnation is assured. Again, however, a caveat must be interjected: although adequate finantial resources are a necessary condition of economic development, equally difficult problems of entrepreneurship—and many others—must be simultaneously solved.

Can the Financial Problems Be Solved?

What conclusions about the feasibility of financing a program of the magnitude proposed here can be gleaned from the present study? In general, it is our conclusion that the problem of financing economic development per se need not induce Indonesian planners to settle for a program which has little hope of providing a take-off to sustained economic growth—and the present Five Year Plans would appear to be of this nature. But a second conclusion is inescapable: the financial problem cannot be solved without a broad attack upon the existing financial and fiscal framework. It is not enough to accept existing institutions as unalterable because history has bequeathed them. Government administration in the financial field—as in all others—must be molded to promote economic growth. Moreover, the required initiative and vision still may be the scarcest of all the indispensable ingredients of a successful development program.

Our study has also suggested the directions in which financial reform must move if a greatly increased volume of real savings is to be mobilized for launching a massive attack upon economic stagnation. These conclusions are significant, if they are valid, because the limited entrepreneurial energies available to an underdeveloped country should not be wasted upon reform for the sake of reform alone. They must be employed to produce institutional changes which have the greatest marginal efficiency in terms of placing more investment resources at the disposal of a small core of entrepreneurial elite. It would be folly to bear the costs of overcoming inertia to change financial institutions where such change would contribute little toward solving the problems at hand. The specific areas in which institutional change would appear to be most essential to financing development in Indonesia emerge from the conclusions set forth in the remainder of this chapter.

Our analysis of proposals for increasing savings did not leave us very sanguine with respect to prospects for significant increases in voluntary savings. These are now at a low level—less than 5 per cent of national income. There is no lack of credit institutions; indeed, the burgeoning of such institutions threatens central bank control over the money supply. However, it is possible that improvements in the financial system could redirect savings from less to more productive uses. There is clearly a need for banking legislation which would give the central bank more effective control over the credit operations in the country as a whole. It is also possible that such devices as the premiums for savings in South Sumatra, the issuing of "tailor-made" government securities, and other measures discussed in Chapter 3 would stimulate some increase in savings. On the whole, however, it seems unwise to count on any substantial volume of increased voluntary savings apart from reinvestment of the profits of enterprise.

Perhaps current government expenditures can be reduced somewhat without a retardation of economic growth. Economies in the current budget have been under study by the Indonesian government for years. During 1953 and 1954 a "streamline committee" was assigned the task of improving the efficiency and reducing the size of the civil service. As early as 1952 Dr. Sumitro, as Minister of Finance, introduced budgetary cuts designed to reduce the civil service, army, and police. His efforts at that time were nullified, however, by withdrawal of currency from the central bank by various ministries for expenditure in the following fiscal year; at that time the administrative controls and the political situation did not permit the government to prevent such action. The Minister of Finance of the second Ali Sastroamidjojo government also drew up a plan (the Winisobo Plan) for streamlining the civil service; but reductions in army and police expenditures are difficult while insecurity prevails in some parts of the country and until some political settlement with the outlying provinces is reached. Although it appears that relatively small proportions of expenditures for army and police will be actually required in terms of internal security if national unity is achieved, security problems cannot be adequately studied by outsiders. We can only recommend that any reductions in current expenditures consonant with efficiency and security should be made.

The chronic budget deficit indicates that, even with maximum cuts in current outlays _and with_ a campaign to increase savings, the achievement of _steady_ growth will require increases in tax revenues plus foreign aid and investment approximately equal to the increase in developmental investment. The program to increase tax revenues would have two major facets: tax reform by Central Government, and devolution of fiscal powers and developmental responsibilities from Central Government to the local governments. We shall consider these two aspects of the tax program in turn.

Central Government Tax Reform

We concluded in Chapter 5 that Indonesia has untapped taxable capacity. Two things are meant by this statement. First, levels of consumption can be reduced, at least for some income groups, without serious hardship; and, second, the fiscal process could be used to redirect productive resources, especially capital and enterprise, in a manner increasing total output.

In Chapter 4 we saw that some progress has already been made in increasing the relative share of taxes in total government revenues. Whereas in 1867 taxes produced only 33 per cent of government revenues, by 1932 the figure had risen to 81 per cent. While this trend toward increased reliance on taxes for revenues has continued in the postwar period, revenues have failed to keep pace with the increase in expenditures. By 1952, government expenditures had reached 14 per cent of national income while revenues were still less than 10 per cent of national income.

In looking at the tax structure one is struck by the great importance in total revenues of the taxes falling on foreign trade. In 1952, export duties comprised 43 per cent of total revenues and import duties 15.9 per cent. Thus taxes on foreign trade constituted 59 per cent of total tax revenues in that year. In 1955, export duties had shrunk to 8 per cent of total revenues and import duties to 31.5 per cent, a total of 39.5 per cent. Collapse of the Korean war boom, a later slump in the export market, reduced rates of export duties, and improvements in collections of business and personal income taxes contributed to the decline in the relative importance of foreign trade in providing tax revenues.

Some critics have argued that even 40 per cent of tax revenues is an excessive proportion to obtain from the foreign-trade sector. However, it should be recognized that the fault in Indonesian practice lies not with the structure of the tax system but with the structure of the Indonesian economy. Let us define the gross national income (Y) as the sum of production for the foreign-trade sector (O_f) and production for the domestic market (O_d),

$$Y = O_f + O_d. \tag{1}$$

Since all taxes are derived from income, we may write:

$$T = T(Y), \tag{2}$$

where T equals total tax revenues. Assuming that taxes may be expressed as a percentage of output in each of these sectors, we may write:

$$T_t = T_1 \cdot O_f + T_2 \cdot O_d. \tag{3}$$

For our purposes we shall use the symbols in per capita terms and assume that O_d (per capita output in the domestic trading sector) is constant—which is more or less the case. Differentiating with respect to time (t),

$$\frac{dT_t}{dt} = \frac{dT_1}{dt} \cdot O_f + T_1 \frac{dO_f}{dt} + \frac{dT_2}{dt} \cdot O_d.$$

Our equation shows that it is virtually impossible to protect total revenues against fluctuations in foreign trade. Historically, T_2 (the percentage of domestic income recaptured in taxes) has gone down because of the failure of Central Government to collect income taxes in the rural (labor-intensive) sector or to reimpose land taxes. If we were to assume that T_2 is also a constant, then of course:

$$\frac{dT_t}{dt} = \frac{dT_1}{dt} \cdot O_f + T_1 \frac{dO_f}{dt} . \tag{3a}$$

In this case fluctuations in tax revenues will reflect only changes in output of the foreign-trade sector.

The dependence of tax revenues on foreign trade cannot be removed by substituting income taxes, sales taxes, or other taxes for export duties and import surcharges. So long as the variable share of income is generated in the foreign-trade sector, tax revenues are bound to fluctuate with the volume of foreign trade. In other words, the structure of outputs must be changed as a prerequisite for a significant change in the tax structure. Divorcing revenues from foreign trade will be a result of economic development, not a means of financing development. In the first phase of the development program the government must follow a course of compensatory fiscal policy to offset fluctuations in foreign trade. Such a policy includes the accumulation of foreign-exchange reserves in periods of buoyant exports in order to permit continuation of imports during periods when exports drop and government spending for development purposes is accelerated. Income and employment can be stabilized by a policy of "telescoping" the development program in periods when foreign trade is slack.

In Chapter 4 we saw that a good many "nuisance taxes," such as the slaughter, statistical, and transaction taxes, have survived from the Dutch colonial period. These taxes yield very little in revenue, and their collection is expensive for both private enterprise and the government. As a first simple step toward tax reform, the nuisance taxes could be abolished. The Dris report recommends that all of these taxes be carefully studied with a view to their modification or abolition. It suggests that the urban real estate tax (Verponding) be replaced by an improved property tax, that the tax on private possessions be abolished, and that all others be drastically changed to enhance their effectiveness.[3] It also recommends that the reconstruction tax be transferred to local authorities on the ground that this step would result in "a considerable improvement in receipts."[4]

In Chapter 4 we also noted a decline in the labor-intensive sector's share in total tax revenues, whereas taxes on industry are already high and progressive. Another conclusion was that there are limits on the amount of export duties which can be collected; in any case, when the value of exports is falling as a result of contracting world markets, increases in export duties will not lead to an increase in revenues but will act as a further discouragement to exports.

In Chapter 5 an effort was made to allocate the tax burden between the capital-intensive and the labor-intensive sectors. We saw that the rural sector's share in national income increased from about 68 per cent in 1939 to some 76 per cent in 1952, an increase which reflects primarily the growth of smallholders' production. In 1952 the industrial sector, with only 24 per cent of national income, was paying 64 per cent of total taxes, and the rural sector, with 76 per cent of national income, was paying only 36 per cent of total taxes. Despite changes in the tax structure, virtually the same situation prevailed in 1954 and 1956.

Put another way, direct Central Government tax revenues were about 4 per cent of rural income but 22 per cent of industrial income. Moreover, income distribution in the rural sector had become increasingly unequal with the growth of a new landlord class.

A similar disparity was found to exist when tax burdens are reckoned in terms of income per laborer. Total Central Government taxes represented 29 per cent of income per employed worker in the capital-intensive sector but only 5 per cent in the labor-intensive sector. The more accurate measure of direct taxes per employed laborer showed this burden to be 19 per cent of income in the capital-intensive sector compared to 2.5 per cent in the other.

The closing paragraphs of Chapter 5 made the point that, although community development projects are particularly suitable for finance by local taxation, maximizing tax revenues will probably require the allocation to local governments of other projects as well, with commensurate increases in the financial powers of local governments.

Chapter 6 analyzes the incidence of various types of taxes in an effort to ascertain their effects on incentives to work, save, and invest. Where exports take place through middlemen, as is the case with most smallholders' production, it is possible for export duties to recapture windfall profits when export prices are rising. However, if the middleman is able to pass taxes backward, export duties have a bad effect on production when prices are falling. In the industrial sector, on the other hand, backward shifting is a good deal more difficult and forward shifting is usually impossible because prices are set in the world market. Consequently, the tax is borne by the producers. Current output is difficult to reduce, especially in the case of plantations. Thus the major decision confronting entrepreneurs in the export industries is whether or not to reinvest. When profits are squeezed by rising costs and falling prices, export duties are an added deterrent to reinvestment, and they may even cause underutilization of the economy's limited industrial capacity.

Income tax rates are already so high as to have disincentive effects where the income tax law is enforced. There is also a danger that further increases in import surcharges and other semi-luxury taxes would affect supplies of labor and risk-taking, since additional effort or risk-assumption is often undertaken in hopes of improving standards of living that only imports or other luxury goods can provide. The "demonstration effect," although a nuisance from the standpoint of the balance of payments, does provide incentives for increased effort and risk-taking provided that the imports and luxury goods are available at prices that put them within the range of a majority of the local populace. Import surcharges, while necessary from the standpoint of protecting the balance of payments, may put these goods and services out of reach, with serious effects on supplies of effort and of risk-taking.

In sum, we have reached the following somewhat discouraging conclusions with regard to Central Government taxation: (1) Central Government tax revenues must be increased. (2) With the present structure of production, Central Government tax revenues cannot be totally divorced from fluctuations in foreign trade. (3) The rates of income taxation cannot be raised without risking unfavorable effects on incentives to work, save, and invest. (4) Further increases in export duties or import levies might also have unfavorable incentive effects.

There are, however, several things which Central Government can do to increase its tax revenues. First, it might introduce some or all of the self-enforcing tax system discussed in recent literature,[5] a system designed to simplify the problem of administration where—as in underdeveloped countries—inadequate bookkeeping records and lax tax morality promote evasion. The principle is that attempts to evade tax liability will automatically involve new tax liability as great as or greater than the first. Taxes can also be enforced by regulations which offer strong inducements to encourage reinvestment of profits in output-increasing capital facilities. The Indonesian tax system provides a better basis for shifting to a self-enforcing tax system than most. It already has a tax on capital; there has been experience with a turnover tax; there are legal sanctions against excessive hoarding; and the Central Bureau of Statistics has an efficient organization. Much of the information needed for enforcement of the system is already flowing to the Central Bureau of Statistics. If the government were reluctant to proceed immediately to the introduction in toto of so novel a tax system, substantial improvements in tax collections could be obtained by introducing it in part. For example, the capital tax could be made an effective instrument; a capital gains tax could be introduced; a tax on excess inventories and an expenditures tax could be established. Any one of these measures could be introduced without the other features of the self-enforcing system. Any one of them would improve tax collections. Of course, to obtain the full benefits of a self-enforcing system the whole closed system must be put into effect.

Second, the enforcement of conventional taxes could be further improved. The elimination of nuisance taxes would save a good deal of administrative time and effort, with little loss of revenue, permitting the redirection of effort to more important taxes. More attention could be devoted to recruiting a tax-enforcement cadre of the proper size, training, and experience. (M. D. Dris emphasizes the importance of this step in his report to the Indonesian government.[6]) The domestic-trade sector could be compelled to pay something closer to its fair share of total taxes by more effective licensing of all domestic traders. Such a step would also help in the establishment of the self-enforcing tax system.

Third, consumption taxes of various kinds could be made an effective substitute for a progressive income tax. (The Dris report also confirms the feasibility and importance of this recommendation.[7]) The self-enforcing system includes a general sales or turnover tax. Short of this step, a progressive sales tax might be made a productive source of revenue.

Part of the income of upper-income groups in the labor-intensive sector, particularly in rural areas (both traders and landlords), is reached through Indonesia's present pattern of indirect taxation, i.e., through taxes on imported goods and excise and sales levies on other consumer goods. There is a particular problem, however, in the fact that the pattern of spending in the labor-intensive sector is different from that in the capital-intensive sector. Imported goods are less important in the former, and a greater part of the spending of the upper-income groups in the rural sector is outside the scope of the more progressive existing taxes. Spendings on the employment of labor for personal ease and comfort (domestic services), dwellings, food, and locally produced valuables are outside the scope of existing consumption taxation. Moreover, the pattern of spending is such that much of earned income is spent on the purchase of real estate, leading to the concentration of property ownership, or on the acquisition of inventories. Purchase of land or of durable goods already in existence (jewels, gold) does not draw upon current economic resources, and funds recaptured from such spending by taxation might not reduce very much the community's aggregate level of consumption. In the Indonesian situation, however, property, inventory, and capital gains taxes would at least tap incomes of the upper-income groups in the rural sector, reducing their consumption by its effect on disposable income. It would also tend to direct their interest and energies toward means of increasing their wealth that might be more productive.

Effectively reaching the income of rentiers—landowners, lenders, and merchant-employers—through Central Government taxes presents formidable problems. In order to impose an equitable burden upon these groups, it is necessary to identify important areas of spending. It is also important that such spending be taxed without involving too great a degree of "surmise" in tax assessment.

There appear to be at least two areas of expenditures in which partial enforcement of taxation of this group could be begun—ownership of real property and expenditures on domestic services. Possession of real property cannot be readily obscured. Inheritance and gift taxes might also be added to tighten the enforcement of real property taxation and to prevent the continuing accumulation of land and real estate.

The basic defect in Indonesia's present tax system is its lack of scope. The structure of taxation as a whole is progressive, perhaps too progressive to maximize revenues for development without diluting economic incentives. But progressive levies are applied effectively only in the capital-intensive sector. In 1951 the Indonesian government provided legislation for collecting an income tax on small incomes,* but this tax has not been seriously enforced in most areas of Indonesia, particularly in the rural sector. Consideration should therefore be given to devising _other_ taxes to reach low incomes at the rates _legally_ provided in Indonesia's income tax legislation. Consumption taxation may be the most feasible means of reaching Indonesian incomes now outside the scope of Central Government taxation.

*This is the so-called "_padjak peralihan ketjil_" (literally, small-income tax) applicable to incomes below Rp. 5,000, with rates up to 3 per cent.

Present consumption taxation includes both a limited number of excise duties and a "general" sales tax levied at either 5 or 10 per cent ad valorem, depending on the classification of the good taxed—necessity or luxury. Primary foodstuffs and many other essentials are exempted. The ineffectiveness of this pattern of taxation in tapping consumer spending as a whole is demonstrated by the comparison of revenues from these taxes with total estimated consumption as given in Table 39.

Table 39

CONSUMPTION AND SALES TAX REVENUES

1. Net value of goods and services consumed, 1954-1955 (million Rp.):	
Food	50,400
Other necessities	20,850
Other goods and services	11,650
Total	82,900
2. Proceeds of sales tax, 1954 (million Rp.)	611
3. Sales tax as per cent of total consumption	.7%

Sources: Line 1: Eugene Grasberg, Indonesia's Investment Requirements, Center for International Studies, Massachusetts Institute of Technology, Cambridge, 1955, Table 4, p. 16. Line 2: Report of the Bank Indonesia, 1954-1955, Table 15, p. 67.

Grasberg's breakdown of total consumption indicates the reasons for the failure of sales taxation to produce significant amounts of revenue. Total consumption was estimated to be approximately Rp. 83 billion, of which Rp. 50 billion represented consumption of food and perhaps an additional Rp. 10 billion represented other exempted necessities. If these estimates are meaningful, over 70 per cent of total consumption was entirely exempted from the sales tax while another 12 per cent was taxed at the lower rate of 5 per cent.

If all consumption had been taxed at the rate called for by the tax on small incomes (approximately 3 per cent), revenues from sales taxation would have totaled about Rp. 2.5 billion. In short, this level of taxation of lower-income groups is consistent with the income tax rates now in the law but not enforced. Should the present degree of progressivity in sales taxation be maintained, and a rate of 3 per cent be levied on consumption not reached under the present schedule, total estimated revenues from consumption taxation would approximate about Rp. 3.5 billion. (See Table 40.)

Table 40

ESTIMATED CONSUMPTION TAX REVENUES

(Billion Rp.)

Food and other necessities (3 per cent)	1.80
Other necessities now taxed (5 per cent)	.55
Other goods and services (10 per cent)	1.20
Total	3.55

This estimate has an upward bias since services consumed cannot be taxed by sales taxation; moreover, some food and other necessities are consumed directly and do not enter trade channels. With corrections for these factors, the addition of a 3 per cent sales tax on food and necessities not now covered would yield about Rp. 2.36 billion.*

In rural areas, where tax evasion is most rampant, a tax on spending for domestic services would be a simple form of "surmise income

*The nonmarket sector is estimated at 25 per cent of total output. (Sumitro Djojohadikusumo, "The Budget and Its Implications," Ekonomi dan Keuangan Indonesia, Vol. VI, January 1953, p. 15.) The amount of nontaxable services is estimated to be Rp. 3.6 million.

tax." Observation of the pattern of spending in the rural sector strongly suggests taxes geared to the number of domestic servants, there being no better readily available index of the real income of individuals in this sector. This is particularly true since servants are associated with prestige and wealth. Enforcement will be promoted by the fact that the number and remuneration of domestic servants cannot easily be hidden from even the most superficial scrutiny of tax collectors.

Discussion of Indonesian tax reform would not be complete without reference to the tax on foreign residents. This tax, announced in late 1957 but made retroactive to January 1, 1957, imposed a heavy levy on all foreigners; rates were set at Rp. 1,000 for the head of each family, Rp. 750 for wives and adult members of a family, and Rp. 350 for children.[8] Revenue officials anticipated almost preposterous yields,[9] but the wholesale departure of Dutch nationals since December 1957 will reduce yields to a fraction of what they would otherwise have been. Its burden will fall mainly upon the Chinese minority, and it is expected that this group will make large-scale applications for citizenship. If the intent of this tax is what it appears to be on the surface—another expression of uncritical nationalistic sentiment—it should be judged on the merits of such policies. We should emphasize, however, that this tax will add to the relatively great burden already levied upon the capital-intensive sector, and that it will tend to have disincentive effects upon the entrepreneurial efforts of one of Indonesia's most dynamic economic groups.

Local Government Finance

The hope for increased tax revenues lies mainly in increased local responsibility for investment. Indonesia has a long history of local autonomy under the Dutch regime and even earlier. Although local finance is probably less important now than it was before the war, it remains more important than is commonly supposed. Net investment for developmental purposes by local governments is also of considerable significance. However, the provincial governments have no important source of revenue of their own; and the present structure of rural taxation does not recapture enough of the increases in rural incomes, especially incomes of the new rentiers.

The present system of using local tax offices to collect Central Government taxes is inefficient, the local tax offices of Central Government finding it difficult to collect effectively the wide range of taxes now imposed by the government. Since in practice the jurisdiction of the local fiscal offices of Central Government is limited to the cities in which their offices are located, they do not have the potential which local governments have for collecting in the villages. Moreover, administrative capacities as well as tax-raising potential exist at the local-government level. Thus a strong case can be made for allocating to local governments some productive taxes of a kind they can best collect, and at the same time according to the local governments responsibility for development projects of a kind that can be efficiently executed by local governments.

Ever since the decentralization-of-powers legislation of the revolutionary government in 1948, a great deal of thought has been devoted to the problems of devolution of powers, including fiscal powers. A bill for the reallocation of fiscal authority was prepared by the Djuanda government, based largely on the recommendations of the Nasrun Committee, established for the express purpose of studying central-local government financial relations. Unfortunately, these

Table 41

ESTIMATED INVESTIBLE RESOURCES FROM CHANGES IN THE INDONESIAN FISCAL SYSTEM

(Million Rp., 1952–1955 Value)

Trade licenses*	500
Capital gains taxation†	400
Reduction of subsidies to localities (increased local government taxes)‡	2,000
Increased local investment (direct labor inputs)‡	1,250
Extension of consumption taxation§	1,700
Improved enforcement of business and personal income taxes‖	1,000
Property and domestic service taxes¶	500
	7,350
Minus revenues from taxes whose abolition is suggested	- 50
Total increased yield	7,300

*This estimate is based on Neumark's estimate of trade margins for 1952. In that year, his breakdown shows income from trade in the rural sector at Rp. 9.2 million of a total of Rp. 10.7 million. Thus a trade license tax amounting to a rate of only 5.5 per cent would yield revenues of Rp. 500 million.

†This is a rough estimate of the yield of capital gains taxation employed in conjunction with income and property taxation, based on the ratio of capital gains yield relative to income taxation in the United States. The estimate takes account of the lower tax enforcement capabilities in Indonesia.

‡These estimates are based on the material in Chapter 7. As argued there, greater fiscal autonomy to local governments is required to mobilize these resources.

§The differential between our final estimate of Rp. 2,360 million and what the sales tax has yielded in recent years (in 1952–1955 rupiah value).

‖This estimate is based on data presented in Chapters 4, 5, and 7, which indicate that stricter enforcement of these taxes could be achieved by the abolition of taxes which yield little revenue but require much administrative effort (household tax, capital assets tax, restaurant tax).

¶In Chapter 5 we indicated that income in the rural sector was just over Rp. 65 billion in 1952. If, as assumed there, 25 per cent was distributed to upper-income groups, the estimated yield from these taxes appears to be conservative.

recommendations do not seem to be adequate from the standpoint of financing economic development. The formula suggested for dividing tax revenues between governments fails to provide the link between sacrifice and benefit which would maximize taxable capacity. It does not tie increased local revenues to increased local government responsibility for economic development. It is our view that if local governments were assigned the field of land taxation and given responsibility for community development projects and other projects of particular importance to the locality where they are carried out, they could replace Central Government subsidies with their own revenues to the extent of Rp. 2,000 million annually and, in addition, execute each year community development projects equivalent in value to Rp. 1,250 million. A "development tax" might also be utilized by local governments to finance their development projects. A summary of the proposed changes in the fiscal system is presented in Table 41.

Impact on Domestic Consumption

Of the total new investible resources estimated in Table 41, Rp. 6.1 billion would represent effective reductions in the level of consumer expenditures.* The remainder (Rp. 1.25 billion) would be provided from direct local mobilization of currently unemployed resources without incurring monetary taxation or monetary expenditures. Using Grasberg's estimate of the total level of consumption in 1954-1955, fiscal mobilization of resources on this scale would require a total reduction in consumption of just over 7 per cent. The assumption on which our estimate for greater fiscal revenues is built would indicate that

*At pre-rebellion level of national income, valued at 1952-1955 rupiah value.

Rp. 3,850 million of the increased tax yield would come from upper-income groups and Rp. 2,200 million from lower-income groups (the main item being the extension of the sales tax to goods consumed by lower-income groups). Much of the reduction in consumption would presumably come, therefore, from nonfood and nonessential goods, the value of which was estimated by Grasberg at Rp. 11,650 million.[10]

The development model presented in Table 38 suggests that employing the fiscal system to mobilize additional real savings on this scale would be almost adequate to finance the take-off to sustained growth.* The program suggested in connection with the model would require that these additional resources be provided over a five-year period. In other words, fiscal improvement to provide an additional Rp. 7 billion in real savings from the pre-rebellion income level could be undertaken over that period of time. The model for financing economic development also stresses another important reason for strengthening the fiscal system during the take-off period. During the first five-year period all of the income gains must be reinvested to assure reaching the desired rate of accelerating investment. Our study has shown that we cannot expect this function of recapturing output for reinvestment to be delegated to the private sector of the economy. Regardless of whether mobilized savings are made available to public or private entrepreneurs the fiscal system must enforce the necessary collective thrift. It would appear that the structural and administrative changes recommended here could be adapted to this second aspect of financing development as well as the first. In generalizing the scope of Central Government's tax

*The development model calls for increasing real savings from the pre-rebellion income level from Rp. 6 billion to Rp. 13.7 billion, an increase of Rp. 7.7 billion. The estimates in Table 41 suggest that relatively moderate fiscal changes might provide Rp. 7.3 billion.

system, and in revitalizing the fiscal role of local governments, the ability to recapture increments in national income would be greatly enhanced.

Banking Legislation

The recent introduction of a reserve requirement for commercial banks is one step in the direction of establishing central bank control over the volume and allocation of private credit. If the banking system is to play its proper part in the financing of development, however, further steps must be taken. In order to acquire more precise control of the money supply, the Bank Indonesia might extend its reserve system to incorporate a system requiring 100 per cent reserves against deposits in excess of a stipulated ceiling. Another essential step will be a reduction in the number and an increase in the strength of national banks. Former Bank Indonesia Governor Sjafruddin has himself indicated his concern over the growing number of small, weak national banks and has suggested that they might be united into a single branch banking system.[11] Judging from the experience of other countries, however, it is not necessary to go quite so far to assure a strong, flexible, and manageable banking system. The British, Canadian, and Australian models, consisting of 5 to 10 banks with branches throughout the country, would seem to be adaptable to the Indonesian situation. A simple means of compelling the amalgamation of national banks into a small number of branch banking systems would be the strict enforcement of a higher minimum capital requirement as a basis for receiving a bank charter. The present regulations grant exemptions to precisely those banks which should be made to adhere to stricter standards.

Finally, the nationalistic emphasis which has led to rather indiscriminate multiplication of government credit agencies should be abandoned. The private banking sector should be encouraged to play a more positive role in Indonesian economic development; if monetary reform measures are successful in realizing this objective, Central Government can free itself from its self-assumed obligation to provide credit. Most democratic countries have found that it is important to provide a system of checks and balances between public finance and private credit creation in the interest of allocating credit according to sound economic criteria. In this connection, we might also note that efforts should be made to foster the independent assertion of monetary control by the Bank Indonesia. There have been indications that the bank has had difficulty in exercising forceful monetary control independently from the short-run interests of the executive branch of the government.

Foreign-Exchange Policy

In 1957 the Djuanda government introduced a new foreign-exchange system which represented a considerable improvement over the previous ones. It provided that exporters be granted export-promotion certificates equal to the full foreign-exchange value of their exports and representing claims on foreign exchange for imports. The certificates could be sold in a free market, 80 per cent of the rupiah proceeds being retained, the other 20 per cent being turned over to the government as a kind of tax. The government itself would acquire its foreign exchange in the open market. At the same time the number of categories of import surcharge rates was reduced from nine to six—0, 20, 50, 100, 140, and 175 per cent, respectively. These rates were applied to the market price of imports, however, not to their price at the nominal official rate of exchange. Thus a good formerly on the 100 per cent surcharge list and costing $10.00 cost the importer Rp. 220.40; if the good remained on the 100 per cent list but the certificates were bought in the open market at Rp. 20.00 to U.S. $1.00, it would cost the importer Rp. 400.00. Rice and essential cotton textiles were on the free list; moreover, rice and possibly essential cotton textiles were to be subsidized so as to avoid any serious rise in the worker-peasant cost of living. An interesting detail of the regulations is that foreign investors and tourists were to be treated as exporters and be granted certificates in exchange for the foreign exchange they brought in.

In an effort to counteract the establishment of independent foreign-exchange systems in the dissident regions, the government set up branch offices of the Foreign Exchange Institute in Surabaya, Makassar, Bandjarmasin, Medan, Palembang, and Padang. When the conflict with these regions has been settled, and the rupiah has been stabilized for some time, the government may wish to simplify the foreign-exchange system still further. A new official rate could be established at the prevailing market rate. If necessary, the government might continue to subsidize rice and essential textiles to avoid a rise in prices of wage goods and a consequent wage-price spiral; but, by the time the rupiah is stabilized, it might be hoped that Indonesia will be self-sufficient in rice and that textile prices will have adjusted themselves to the prevailing wage and foreign-exchange rates. An official free market might be retained for some time for nonregistered capital transactions and imports of nonessential goods; foreign exchange would be made available at official rates only for essential goods and registered capital transactions. Instead of the present system of import surcharges, a single "luxury tax" on imported nonessentials might be imposed. In this manner the number of differential rates might be reduced to three or four instead of the present seven or eight.

Foreign Investment

Our studies indicated that no foreign investment law would by itself attract large quantities of private capital to Indonesia. However, since so much attention has been focused on the matter, it is just as well that there is such a law on the statute books at long last. It may not attract much capital, but the continued lack of a law had become a deterrent to foreign investment, since it was known that a law was under discussion.*

A particularly important feature of the new law is the Foreign Investment Board. It is to be hoped that the Board will have a competent secretariat. It would also be desirable to have attached to each major Indonesian embassy a representative of the Board who could provide interested persons with all the necessary information regarding investment in Indonesia. The Board, directly or through its secretariat, could then deal with all aspects of foreign enterprise in the country so that foreign investors would need to deal with only one agency of the Indonesian government. As also suggested above, in the early stages of the Board's operations it might be desirable to recruit through the Technical Assistance Administration of the United Nations one or two advisers who could interpret the laws and regulations to potential investors and explain to the Indonesian government the nature of the proposals made by the foreign enterprises.

*The Foreign Capital Investment Law as approved by the Indonesian Parliament in 1958 is presented in Appendix H.

Given the magnitude of the economic development task and the political context in which it must be solved, the Indonesian government does not face a choice of employing either domestic financing or external financing by foreign investment or foreign aid. Any hardheaded appraisal of the financial requirements for Indonesian development must lead to the conclusion that only a judicious admixture of all three sources of funds can assure a take-off into sustained economic growth. In Chapter 1, we pointed out that foreign capital and aid must play an important role in financing the foreign-exchange costs of the development program. Even when the maximum politically possible effort has been made to increase tax revenues at both the central and local government levels, and when every avenue for encouraging savings and improving allocation of credit has been explored, a substantial flow of funds must be sought from abroad. Given the existing conflicts of view toward foreign aid and foreign enterprise within Indonesia itself, it is doubtful whether a program for filling the gap from one source of foreign capital alone would be acceptable to Parliament and the people. Indeed, it seems likely that launching a take-off within the next decade will require an all-out attack on all three fronts at once.

Notes to Chapter 8

1. Benjamin Higgins, "The Indonesian Five Year Plan: Proposals for Research," Center for International Studies, Massachusetts Institute of Technology, Cambridge, 1957, p. 6.

2. National Planning Bureau, "A Study of the Indonesian Economic Development Scheme," Ekonomi dan Keuangan Indonesia, Vol. X, September 1957, pp. 630-636.

3. M. D. Dris, "Taxation in Indonesia," Ekonomi dan Keuangan Indonesia, Vol. XI, August-September 1958, pp. 430-435.

4. Ibid., p. 487.

5. For a comprehensive review of such a system, see Benjamin Higgins, "A Self-Enforcing Incentive Tax System for Underdeveloped Countries," Chapter 3 of Economic Development: Problems, Principles, and Policies, Norton, New York, 1959.

6. Dris, loc. cit., pp. 430-437.

7. "Conditions in Indonesia," the report states, "justify a fairly wide use of indirect taxes, since they can be levied and administered easily at relatively little cost, and particularly since they offer the only possibility of draining off the excess money in circulation and providing considerable revenue at short notice." Ibid., p. 422.

8. Economist Intelligence Unit, Three Monthly Economic Review of Indonesia, No. 22, 1957, p. 5.

9. One estimate placed potential yields at Rp. 9 billion annually. Ibid.

10. Eugene Grasberg, Indonesia's Investment Requirements, Center for International Studies, Massachusetts Institute of Technology, Cambridge, 1955, Table 4, p. 16.

11. Antara (New York edition), July 7, 1957, p. 2.

9

THE ROLE OF FOREIGN AID AND INVESTMENT

The previous chapters have been concerned with an evaluation of Indonesia's capacity to finance a development program adequate to reach sustained economic growth. The conclusions from this study may now be restated to indicate their implications for U.S. assistance.

First, a program adequate to provide a rapid take-off to sustained economic growth and to outstrip the expected rate of population growth would involve relatively great economic and social costs. The program could be financed only with widespread improvements in institutions to mobilize domestic savings; and, in the early stages of economic development, there is little alternative to placing the major burden of the financing upon Indonesia's fiscal system. With far-reaching changes in the fiscal system, and successful tapping of local resources through solution of the problem of local autonomy, public savings could conceivably finance the greater part of the increased capital formation necessary for economic growth. Increasing domestic savings would require a ten-year period of domestic sacrifice, but consumption of lower-income groups need not be reduced below socially desirable levels.

Second, successful mobilization of savings from all the potential domestic sources studied would fail to provide adequate financing for a development program of the required magnitude. Although the gap between over-all requirements and domestic savings would not be disconcertingly large, foreign capital would have to be attracted to fill this gap or the development effort would be likely to fail on two counts: its failure to meet minimum investment requirements, and its failure to finance the required imports of capital goods essential to carrying out the total program. Our estimates suggest that the shortfall in domestic currency would be about Rp. 2.5 billion annually and that about $200 million per year would be needed in additional foreign exchange.

Third, Indonesia is presently incapable of launching a development program of this magnitude; but, with effective action at home and aid from abroad, meeting the preconditions need not take long. Political unification and stability must be achieved, production must be raised to pre-1956 maximum levels, and price and balance-of-payments equilibrium must be at least approximated. The massive deficit in the government budget must be eliminated, the nearly depleted foreign-exchange reserves replenished, the volume of domestic output restored to post-independence record levels, and domestic capital formation maintained at least at the levels reached in the period 1951-1956. The value of export earnings yielded by this modest output target, if captured by Central Government, would at best finance minimum import requirements for consumer goods, raw materials, and capital goods. Foreign exchange necessary to rebuild national monetary reserves and, later, to meet the additional demands of the development program must, therefore, be obtained primarily from additional inflows of foreign capital.

The discussion in previous chapters has suggested that Indonesian development planners will be confronted by a short-run gap between massive capital requirements for development and the current absorptive capacity of the economy. In 1951-1952, when the Indonesian government was in a position to finance large-scale developmental investment as a result of unusually favorable export earnings which produced a large budget surplus, administrative shortages and absence of complementary skills kept real capital formation below that which could be financed. These same shortages stretched out the period between supplying financing for development projects and the flow of output from new capital facilities. That experience has led to less ambitious public investment goals, but it has also focused Indonesian attention on the necessity for increasing supplies of both skills and administrative capacity. While Indonesia's absorptive capacity (given greater political and economical stability) is undoubtedly considerably larger than it was in 1952, an expanded program of foreign technical assistance is required if the intangible bottlenecks are to be broken in time to permit the leadership to undertake a development program that can help to meet the political problems that lie ahead. Awareness of Indonesia's limited absorptive capacity, as well as uncertainties about the volume of foreign capital and technical assistance available, probably had much to do with the National Planning Bureau's recommending in 1956 a Five Year Plan which was too modest to achieve rising output per capita.

Realistic appraisal of what might be done at this stage to further the cause of Indonesian economic progress suggests that short-run priority be given to restoring price and balance-of-payments stability and expanding Indonesia's capital-absorptive capacity. A program embodying these objectives would represent a sound approach to the solution of Indonesia's longer-run problem of stagnant levels of output. If such a program took form in Indonesia and foreign assistance were sought to insure its success, the reasons for a greatly increased volume of economic aid would be compelling.

In the first stage of constructive economic planning, the needs for U.S. assistance would be considerably larger than the average annual volume provided in recent years. During the first eight years of Indonesian independence (through 1957) total U.S. aid to Indonesia was approximately $185 million, an average of about $23 million per year. In addition to about $39 million allotted through our aid program proper (International Cooperation Administration and its predecessors), the total includes Indonesian drawings of $77 million against Export-Import Bank credits and a Surplus Commodities Agreement (Public Law 480) for $68 million concluded in 1956. (See Appendix G.) In contrast to this modest volume of assistance, which has gradually grown, Indonesia's short-run additional needs require a much more significant American commitment.

The estimated 1959 budget deficit is Rp. 9 billion. The actual deficit is likely to exceed even this record high for estimated deficits. Clearly such deficits must be eliminated if stability is to be restored. U.S. commitments to provide significant amounts of aid could supply the incentive for the thorough fiscal reorganization needed to accomplish this goal. Expenditures must be reduced and tax revenues increased immediately if chaotic price behavior is to be halted. Domestic measures alone, however stringent, cannot do the job. Reductions in security expenditures—which presuppose a political settlement in the Outer Islands—are unlikely to exceed Rp. 3 billion. Restoration of political control and strict enforcement of existing taxes in previously disaffected areas may raise tax revenues enough to reduce the deficit by perhaps another Rp. 2 billion. Even the maximum feasible efforts to trim nondevelopmental expenditures and increase tax revenues are likely to leave the deficit above Rp. 3 billion for the next few years. To the degree that these deficits are offset by imports financed by foreign aid, however, they need not be inflationary. With present relative prices, imports worth $100 million would probably offset a deficit of Rp. 3 billion.

Indonesia's persistent loss of international reserves since 1951 (see Table 42) raises further problems for stabilization and development plans.

Table 42

GOLD AND FOREIGN EXCHANGE HOLDINGS, 1951-1958

(Million Rp.)

End of	Gold Holdings	Net Foreign Exchange Fund Holdings	Bank Balances Abroad	Other Foreign Exchange Holdings	Total
1951	3,309	938	1,977		6,224
1952	2,777	- 751	1,557	- 26	3,557
1953	1,688	- 924	1,263	10	2,037
1954	1,055	- 278	856	30	1,663
1955	953	483	1,236	6	2,678
1956	532	- 69	1,097	6	1,566
1957	469	- 295	1,056		1,230
1958	452	1,318	742	12	2,524

Sources: 1957-1958 and 1958-1959 editions of the Report of the Bank Indonesia.

Present reserves could be wiped out in one year of payments difficulties. At the end of 1957, gold and foreign-exchange reserves totaled less than $110 million, an amount smaller than Indonesia lost in 1956 through liberal import policies designed to restrain inflationary pressures. In early 1959, holdings were about 15 per cent of Indonesia's recent annual foreign payments on current account, scarcely adequate to provide a buffer to insure maintenance of even the present relatively low level of imports.[1] It is doubtful, therefore, that Indonesia could withstand the balance-of-payments repercussions associated with a development program, to say nothing of normal cyclical and seasonal fluctuations, with so small a buffer of international reserves.

We have argued in Chapter 1 that Indonesia's gold and foreign-exchange reserves should be replenished to something near the 1952 level ($300 million). In the short run, Indonesia's balance of payments cannot be expected to show changes which would permit rebuilding reserves quickly from normal trade and investment patterns. Indonesia may require outside assistance in the neighborhood of $120 million for this purpose. Spread over a three-year period, the requirement would be $40 million per year. The target date for bringing the budget into balance might also be set at three years, after which external assistance to provide greater price stability could be withdrawn.

For each of the three years during which the short-run program for obtaining domestic stability was in force, therefore, external resources approximating U.S. $130 million would be required for the purpose of restoring relative domestic stability alone.* With improving conditions for private foreign investment and capital assistance from other countries the United States government contribution necessary to assure success might be near $100 million. If this program were successfully carried out, economic stability should be adequate to provide favorable conditions for launching a comprehensive development program at the end of the three-year period. The fiscal reforms needed to bring the annual budget into balance could be extended during this period

*$40 million to rebuild foreign-exchange reserves over a three-year period and $90 million to provide resources to eliminate the budget deficit.

to promote the greater mobilization of public savings which, we have concluded, must serve as the financial basis of the first stage of the development program. In the present context of U.S. aid programs, assistance primarily designed to contribute to currency and foreign-exchange stabilization raises practical problems of extending such assistance. What Indonesia needs is, first, continuous injections of consumer goods to offset existing inflationary pressures, and, second, foreign exchange which could be allowed to accumulate as a buffer against short-run balance-of-payments fluctuations.

Could Indonesia effectively use $100 million in U.S. aid? Benjamin Higgins has recently argued that it could:

> Indonesia has the absorptive capacity to use effectively at least $100,000,000 per year for the next few years; half, under our commodity surplus disposal plan, to provide Java with food and textiles until the problem of providing alternative employment for Javanese peasants can be tackled; and half for highly visible "impact" projects in the outer islands. The latter would include the Asahan Valley development scheme (power, aluminum, pulp and paper, cement, rural electrification, irrigation), the Sumatran highway, the Atjeh railway, improved transport in Celebes and Borneo, land reclamation and mechanized dry-rice farming in Borneo, and the like. While these are being executed more can be planned, and possibilities for developing industries in Java to replace imports can be studied. Such a program would remove one of the major sources of dissatisfaction in the outer islands, reduce the amount of unrest in Java and start Indonesia as a whole on the road to economic development.[2]

The three-year period during which political and monetary stability would be restored must also be used to develop the absorptive capacity of the economy so that a truly large-scale development program can be begun. During this period existing productive capacity must be fully utilized. This involves little more than restoring output to the levels achieved before the domestic political turmoil of 1956-1958 occurred. With the exodus of Dutch technicians and managers in 1957 and 1958, Indonesian capacity to raise plantation output, for example, has declined. Some of these plantations—rubber, tea, coconut, and coffee—were reported in 1958 to have been idle since they were seized from the Dutch in late 1957.[3] In mid-1958 the Indonesians hoped to reach self-sufficiency in rice, which had been within their grasp a few years before. During 1958 Indonesia was forced to buy 700,000 tons of foreign rice; and eliminating this great drain on foreign exchange will require an ambitious program of planting, elimination of plant diseases, improved irrigation, and the opening of new lands, as the Indonesian leadership acknowledges.[4]

A realistic appraisal of prospects for reviving production would result in a gloomy prognosis unless foreign technical assistance and supplies of strategic developmental materials can be provided in expanded volume. The need is urgent for external assistance of these kinds, which, if successful, would undoubtedly improve the domestic political situation by reversing the trend toward economic chaos. The Indonesian public does not now expect dramatic development projects; corrective measures which would gradually restore domestic production and provide a larger flow of necessities would be likely to have the best possible political impact in the present situation.

In addition to more goods from abroad, to bring inflation under control Indonesia needs more technical and commodity assistance to restore domestic output—personnel to provide managerial and technical services to bring estates and other firms to full productive capacity, and fertilizer, raw materials, and even capital goods to expand the output of food. But Indonesia's longer run needs, mainly the development of scarce human factors to use efficiently the capital facilities provided by a development program, must not be overlooked in this quest for short-run domestic stability.

Many more technicians of all kinds—engineers, managers, public administrators, and planners—must be trained if capital is to be absorbed in sufficient volume to raise output per capita. In this role, small-scale U.S. technical assistance has been welcome and effective in the past.[5] The small past programs could provide the core for a much larger U.S. contribution to Indonesia's long-run economic development. Increasing U.S. aid of the kind extended by the International Cooperation Administration (ICA) from the 1958-1959 volume of about $7 million to about three times this amount annually would represent a promising approach to more rapid growth of Indonesia's capital-absorptive capacity.

For many years Indonesia has received external assistance for a number of major development projects which have appeared to be credit worthy by international banking standards. The technical assistance program should not be competitive with loans provided under such conditions. To the extent that Indonesian development projects now under way or planned qualify for loans from the International Bank for Reconstruction and Development, the Export-Import Bank, or similar agencies, the longer-run development problem will be eased, and the advantages flowing from the short-run program of U.S. assistance outlined here need not be threatened. Such projects must, of course, provide sufficient external financing to offset the additional domestic expenditures which might otherwise generate short-run inflationary pressures.

The volume of U.S. assistance required to promote the short-run program for Indonesian stabilization and preparation for development should, therefore, be viewed as independent of the financing of credit-worthy projects by U.S. agencies or by agencies to which the United States contributes. The annual U.S. contributions to support the three-year program proposed here are summarized in Table 43.

Table 43

SUGGESTED ANNUAL U.S. CONTRIBUTIONS TO THREE-YEAR PROGRAM OF ASSISTANCE TO INDONESIA

(Million Dollars)

Meeting foreign-exchange costs of development and offsetting budgetary deficit	$100
Improving foreign-exchange reserves	40
Expanded technical cooperation	20
Total requirements	160
Less non-U.S. assistance (including net private foreign investment)	- 60
Net U.S. assistance required	100

A U.S. assistance program of the magnitude suggested in Table 43 is considerably larger than the average annual volume granted to Indonesia in recent years. Yet it is a relatively small program on a per capita basis, and much smaller than the aid the United States has been extending to a number of other countries in the Far East. The program suggested here calls for total aid to Indonesia of approximately $100 million annually, as compared to actual aid of $8 million in 1957 and a similar amount in 1958. Considering Indonesia's population (85 million) and her raw materials base, even $100 million per year is a modest program. In 1957 ICA aid to Cambodia (population, 4 million) was $41 million, and to Laos (population, 1.5 million) was $47 million. U.S. aid administered in 1957 by ICA alone totaled $251 million in Vietnam (population, 12 million), or almost $21 per capita. In the same year ICA aid to South Korea (population, 23 million) totaled $328 million, or about $14 per capita, and to Thailand (population, 20 million) $42 million, or more than $2 per capita. U.S. aid to Indonesia of $100 million would be only $1.80 per capita.

Since U.S. funds for foreign aid are always in scarce supply, particularly those which are not related to military objectives, ICA has very limited funds for technical cooperation. For the fiscal year 1959 President Eisenhower proposed a program of $163.5 million, of which $20 million would be devoted to the United Nations Technical Assistance Program.[6] Of the remainder, only $33 million was to be allotted to the Far East. Thus little, if any, of the proposed increase in aid to Indonesia could be financed from this source. However, the Special Assistance Fund (requested amount: $212 million) and the Contingency Fund (requested amount: $200 million) might be able to absorb the costs of raising the technical assistance component of our aid to Indonesia from its 1958-1959 level of about $7 million to the $20 million suggested. This would of course leave the equally important U.S. contributions to restore economic stability to be financed from other sources.

An important part of the latter amount could be supplied in the form of surplus commodities under Public Law 480. Aid in this form would be quite appropriate for solving the Indonesian stability problem. Imports of foodstuffs and fibers would conserve foreign exchange, offset the budget deficit, and provide complementary development goods. However, expenditures financed by counterpart funds must be reduced until price and budgetary stability are achieved. This aim could be achieved by relating the finance of the development component in the Indonesian annual budget (which would be undertaken in any case) to supplies of local currency generated by the sale of U.S. surplus agricultural commodities.

Longer Run Development Assistance

An analysis of Indonesia's needs for increased supplies of external capital during the first five years of a comprehensive development program were presented in Chapter 1. We concluded that about $250 million annually would be required to meet the foreign-exchange costs of a program adequate to provide a take-off to sustained growth; part of which might be met by the growth of private foreign investment if the three-year program to achieve economic stability is successful.

If greater political stability is attained and the West responds favorably to the challenge which the present Indonesian situation offers, it is not too much to hope that private net investment and economic assistance from other Western countries and international organizations might exceed $100 million per year. This would leave a gap of $150 million in foreign-exchange requirements to be filled by U.S. aid in this second phase of the program for Indonesian stabilization and development. If U.S. assistance were to contribute to a development program, however, a larger part would have to be provided in the form of grants and loans freely available to finance capital-goods imports. Perhaps $50 million annually could be made available in the form of surplus commodity disposal in this second phase as well. The remaining $100 million should be provided in the form of grants or "soft" loans for unrestricted development use. By the time the short-run programs to enhance preconditions have run their course, Indonesia's capacity to absorb foreign capital in this amount would present no problem.

The Role of Private Foreign Investment

A determined Indonesian effort to mobilize domestic resources for development, backed by an increased foreign aid program, could probably meet the financial requirements for stabilization and growth of the economy. However, domestic sacrifice and the strains upon an already overburdened administration could be eased by an increased inflow of foreign private investment. Alternatively, greater inflows of foreign capital could accelerate the rate of growth. Private foreign investment has the added attraction of tending to raise absorptive capacity. Foreign technicians and even foreign-supported training programs frequently accompany the flow of foreign capital to underdeveloped countries.

The foreign investment bill, which lay before Parliament for several years without action, was finally accepted in September 1958.* It is reproduced below as Appendix H. It is neither the most generous nor the most hostile of the many drafts through which the bill went prior to passage by Parliament. However, there is evidence that even much more liberal foreign investment legislation may fail to promote foreign capital inflows.[7] The Indonesia Project of the Massachusetts Institute of Technology has made an effort to determine the relative importance for foreign investment in Indonesia of general attitudes of the government and people toward foreign investors, and of such things as labor

*A brief evaluation of this legislation is presented in Chapter 8.

relations, tax policy, and foreign-exchange policy. It was also hoped that some distinction could be made among various types of foreign enterprise in terms of the obstacles that seemed more important to them. For the purpose of acquiring this information, an elaborate questionnaire was prepared, and a list of firms applying for foreign exchange for profit transfers (in general, a list of all foreign enterprises in Indonesia) was provided by the Bank Indonesia. Over 100 questionnaires were distributed, but only 9 replies were received.

It is clearly impossible to derive statistical conclusions concerning foreign investment in Indonesia on the basis of the 9 replies received. However, two points brought out by the survey merit attention.

One is inherent in the very fact that only 9 questionnaires were completed and returned. When such a low response is obtained, it can be assumed that there are important underlying factors in operation. This assumption was substantiated by the follow-up conversations. Despite assurances in the letter accompanying the questionnaire that information contained in individual replies would not be made available to the Indonesian government, these conversations showed that most of the businessmen receiving the questionnaire feared that the government might in some way obtain access to their replies. Each valued his relationship with the Indonesian government and hesitated to do anything to disrupt it. In short, most of them were more concerned with their own position vis-à-vis the government than with specific policies of the government. Similarly, many of them showed little enthusiasm for any foreign investment law, however liberal. Each felt his own position with the government more secure than the position of foreign enterprise in general; and each feared that a foreign investment law applying to all foreign enterprise, and acceptable to the Parliament, would be less beneficial to him individually than the arrangements he could make with the government bilaterally.

According to the businessmen who were approached, the Indonesian atmosphere is not predisposed toward criticism of government policies affecting foreign operations. Nor is the "climate" conducive to feelings of security. The businessmen felt that they could not afford to complete the questionnaire since honest answers would imply criticism and might thus upset their already delicate positions. The insecurity reflected in such statements, and borne out by the low response, persisted even though every assurance of anonymity was given in the letter accompanying each questionnaire.

One part of the questionnaire presented a list of 36 factors which might affect foreign investment in general. The firms were asked to indicate for each factor whether it was very advantageous, neutral, disadvantageous, or very disadvantageous to their business operations.

Of these 36 factors, 5 were indicated as disadvantageous or very disadvantageous by 8 or all of the replying firms. They are:

- No. 4 Supply of trained local personnel
- No. 6 Regulations on importation of personnel from home country
- No. 14 Ability to obtain licenses to import necessary raw materials and capital goods
- No. 18 Magnitude of total tax levies on enterprise
- No. 30 High price or short supply of consumer goods customary to Western families

This particular choice seems to indicate that the 9 firms were primarily concerned with operational difficulties due to general physical and economic conditions. They did not stress difficulties due to the legislation applying specifically to foreign enterprise.

Thus the general result of the survey, inconclusive though it may have been, was to substantiate the conclusion that the factors entering into the somewhat vague concept of "climate" for foreign enterprise, including government regulations and administrative decisions, are more important than any specific piece of legislation. "Climate" is in large measure a subjective phenomenon and cannot be quickly or easily changed. Considering the political situation in Indonesia, it is extremely unlikely that the climate can be changed quickly or drastically enough to attract in the next decade large amounts of private capital.

The climate for foreign investment in Indonesia has been further impaired by anti-Dutch actions. Perhaps little can be done to overcome this damage until Indonesia's economy has become stabilized and foreign confidence in the Indonesian government has been revived by the execution of a development program that yields results in opening up new markets and private investment opportunities. In the early years of national reconstruction, development resources will probably have to come mainly from domestic sources and foreign aid. Once Indonesia achieves a take-off into economic growth, however, private foreign capital inflows may become the strategic variable determining success or failure of efforts to sustain it. India's recent development experience suggests that financial requirements, particularly foreign-exchange needs, reach their peak after considerable progress has already occurred. Whatever the political costs involved, therefore, Indonesian efforts to encourage foreign private investment will improve prospects for successfully financing an investment program large enough to assure cumulative economic growth.

Notes to Chapter 9

1. At the end of 1957 the ratio of net gold and foreign-exchange holdings to 1957 foreign payments on current account was about 12 per cent. In early 1958, as part of the Japanese reparations agreement, Indonesian trade indebtedness of $117 million was canceled, reducing the current liabilities of the Foreign Exchange Fund by this amount. The favorable effects of this factor on foreign-exchange reserves were offset by foreign-exchange losses of about $60 million in the first half of 1958. See *Bank Indonesia Bulletin*, No. 15, First and Second Quarters, 1958, p. 11.

2. Benjamin and Jean Higgins, "Indonesia: Now or Never," reprint from *Foreign Affairs*, October 1958, pp. 6-7.

3. Greg McGregor, "Indonesia Sinks to Economic Low," *New York Times*, August 3, 1958, p. 18.

4. *Ibid*.

5. The current technical cooperation program in Indonesia emphasizes technical education, and also includes funds for technical services and training in agricultural extension, industry and mining, malaria control, civil police. See *The Mutual Security Program, Fiscal Year 1958*, Government Printing Office, Washington, D.C., p. 119.

6. *The Mutual Security Program, Fiscal Year 1959, A Summary Presentation*, Government Printing Office, Washington, D.C., p. 43.

7. See E. R. Barlow and Ira T. Wender, *Foreign Investment and Taxation*, Prentice Hall, Englewood Cliffs, 1955, p. 131.

APPENDICES

APPENDIX A

SUMMARY OF THE INDONESIAN FIVE YEAR PLAN

The Indonesian Five Year Plan for economic development, covering the years 1956-1960, was presented to the Indonesian Parliament in printed form in mid-1956. The plan is in three volumes, the first presenting the proposed planning law, the second the "plan framework" and major projects,* and the third specifications of individual projects. We present here a brief summary of the main features of the second volume, the plan framework. This volume alone contains 277 pages divided into 20 chapters: introduction; population; finance; agriculture, forestry, animal husbandry, and fishing; irrigation; mineral resources; electric power; industrialization; transport and communications; manpower resources; labor relations; education; public health; social welfare; housing; community development; cooperatives; transmigration; public administration; implementation and organization.

Chapter 1: Introduction

The introductory chapter sets forth in separate paragraphs sixteen major points regarding basic assumptions and the conceptual framework within which the plan is constructed. A translation of these paragraphs follows:

1. From a practical viewpoint it is not useful to formulate an economic development plan covering more than five to ten years. It is important to

* Garis-Garis Besar Rentjana Pembangunan Lima Tahun, 1956-1960 (Framework of the Five Year Development Plan), Biro Perantjang Negara, Djakarta, 1956.

provide an analysis of the basic direction of such a plan, which may fulfill the hopes for Indonesia to develop its economy, within one generation, to a level which guarantees an increase in the standard of living for the Indonesian people at a rate common in the more developed countries. Such an analysis is presented below.

2. The plan is based partly on an analysis of the sequence of events in Indonesia over several recent years and partly on the experiences of countries with an economic structure similar to that of Indonesia. Together these studies provide a basic direction to the plan and indicate the possibilities of development. The plan framework providing this basic direction depends upon (a) basic principles and norms of a universal character, (b) the scope and nature of government responsibility, (c) the reception and attitudes of society as a whole to the government program, and the willingness of all members of society to cooperate in the execution of the plan.

3. At the present time Indonesian net savings and investment, public and private, is estimated at not less than 5 per cent of national income.

4. During the period 1951-1955, while net capital formation was some 5 to 6 per cent of national income, the annual increase in national income was about 3 per cent per year. Thus the incremental capital-output was less than 2:1.

5. A common estimate of the current rate of population growth is 1.7 per cent per year. The probability is that population growth will increase in ten or twenty years to 2 per cent per annum.

6. It is hoped that the 3 per cent annual increase in national income can be maintained during the plan period 1956-1960. With annual population growth of 1.7 per cent, the increase in national income per capita will then be 1.3 per cent per year.

7. With a marginal savings (and investment) ratio of 40 per cent, 0.52 per cent of per capita national income can be set aside each year for new capital formation.

8. With 40 per cent of the increase in national income allocated to capital formation each year, 60 per cent of the increase is available for consumption, that is, to raise living standards.

9. The 40 per cent of the rise in per capita income which is to be allocated to capital formation will not arise from a tendency for each individual to become more "savings minded" or for his "propensity to save" to become higher. It will be the result of responsible government action and measures in the fields of monetary, fiscal, and economic policy. To achieve this level of savings and investment, government measures to stabilize the economy and to create a sound monetary system are essential preconditions.

10. In 1960, at the end of the First Five Year Plan, it is hoped that the level of capital formation will reach about 8 per cent of national income. By 1965, at the end of the Second Five Year Plan, we hope capital formation will reach 12 per cent of national income, that is, double the current level. In absolute terms, the level of capital formation at the end of the Second Five Year Plan will be more than double the current level. All these figures are estimates of the minimum that we can expect to arise from the fruits of executing the Five Year Plan.

11. The incremental capital-output ratio of about 2:1 holds only for the First Five Year Plan, when new construction is limited and a large share of work and investment must go to the repair of war damage, the elimination of bottlenecks, improvements of existing plant and equipment, and improvement of production methods. The incremental capital-output ratio must be expected to rise as time goes by, eventually reaching a level of 4:1.

12. On the basis of these factors, required capital formation for twenty years and the years following is estimated. By 1975 a level of capital formation of 20 per cent of national income can be expected. It is reasonable to assume that the ICOR will then be about 4:1 and population growth 2 per cent. Thus in 1975 the increase in national income will approximate 5 per cent per year, or 3 per cent per capita.

13. At this time Indonesia will have reached "a stage of self-generating expansion." That is, the economy will have its own power and dynamic for progress and steady growth, as in the already advanced countries. After 1975, income for the entire population will double in 15 years. Income per capita will double in 24 years. Each generation will thus enjoy a rise in standard of living of 100 per cent over that of the previous generation.

14. To realize this objective, there must be a period of striving by the present generation during the next twenty years. There will indeed be some improvements in the standard of living even during this period but not to the same degree as after 1975. The present generation will only gain a glorious name as builders of Indonesia and pioneers of the prosperity and freedom of the Indonesian nation.

15. Some may feel that the twenty-year period is too long, that the masses will not be so patient in waiting for fruits of the plan. But, if we look back twenty years to 1935, we must feel that twenty years is but a moment.

16. The twenty-year period may be shortened, and the sacrifice and efforts of the present generation reduced, if outside help in realizing the plan can be obtained. But it will be a more responsible attitude not to base our hopes on such outside help. Foreign aid—if it comes—will do no harm but is better regarded as a supplement to Indonesia's own resources. We are convinced that our Five Year Development Plan can be carried out satisfactorily even without foreign aid, and this will increase the confidence of the Indonesian people in their own strength and efforts.

Chapter 2: Population

Chapter 2 presents demographic material, most of which has already been made available in one form or another.* Figures of population growth

*See, for example, the submission of the Indonesian delegation to the ECAFE conference on population at Bandung; Nathan Keyfitz, "The Population Problem in Indonesia," Ekonomi dan Keuangan Indonesia, October 1953; and Keyfitz and Widjojo, Soal-Soal Penduduk dan Pembangunan Indonesia (Population Problems and Indonesian Development), Djakarta, 1954.

between 1930 and 1955 are presented for Java and Madura, the Outer Islands, and Indonesia as a whole. Projections are made for the periods 1950–1960 on the basis of alternate assumed rates of population growth of 1.5, 1.7, and 2 per cent. There is no discussion of population policy.

Chapter 3: Financing Economic Development

The third chapter provides estimates of the financial resources available for the plan and also a sectoral breakdown of the investment budget. The total plan calls for the investment of Rp. 30 billion over the first five years,* but details of financing are presented only for the Rp. 12.5 billion to be invested by Central Government. The allocation of this Rp. 12.5 billion among categories of projects, and between rupiah and foreign-exchange resources, is shown in Table I (reproduced here on pp. 391–392). The breakdown in terms of major source is shown in Table II (reproduced here on p. 392).

Financing "through the budget" appears to mean financing by taxes. The nature of the estimated expansion of deposits as a means of finance is not clear, and there is some indication of confusion between credit expansion and increased savings. In paragraph 3 the report refers to the rates of increase in per capita deposits in Burma, Ceylon, Pakistan, and India. It is concluded that an increase in per capita deposits of 5.1 dollars per year is possible in Indonesia in the light of the expansion of deposits per capita in India of 5.6 dollars. Since the expansion of deposits depends mainly on the expansion of credit through the banking system, and in Indonesia particularly on the extent of Central Government deficit financing through the Bank Indonesia, there seems little point in setting limits to the capacity for deposit expansion. On the other hand, if the purpose is to estimate the

*Not stated in the "plan framework" but in another National Planning Bureau document, "Some Explanations of the Five Year Plan," Ekonomi dan Keuangan Indonesia, October (in Indonesian) and November (in English) 1956. In the September 1957 issue (p. 631), a new and more elaborate model was presented, calling for investment of Rp. 35.2 billion. See Appendix I, Table I-13.

expansion of credit that is possible without inflation, a more sophisticated analysis would be needed.

The report says rightly that the possibilities of financing through the securities market is limited. In paragraph 4 it is pointed out that the 3 per cent government bonds issued in 1950 are still selling at only 50 per cent of their face value, yielding about 6 per cent, and that even this figure reflects large-scale purchases by government agencies. It is hoped, however, that after the First Five Year Plan, when financial stability has been established, greater reliance can be placed on the securities market.

Very little reliance is put on foreign loans and grants, as indicated in the introductory chapter. It should be clearly understood, however, that this figure does not include foreign private investment. The report points out that in the past the main sources of foreign loans and grants have been the International Monetary Fund, the Export-Import Bank, the United Nations Specialized Agencies, ICA, Colombo Plan, and "some countries or private institutions in Western and Eastern Europe." The possibilities of a loan from the International Bank for Reconstruction and Development and of a Japanese reparations settlement are also mentioned. The readers are reminded that the possibility of attracting foreign capital is influenced by such factors as the foreign policy of the government, internal political conditions, security, the stability of the economy, and financial policy.

With respect to taxation, it is noted (paragraph 2) that the amounts allocated for development are essentially a projection of recent experience. In the budgets of 1953-1955, investment expenditures ranged from Rp. 1.7 million to Rp. 2.4 million. The necessity of keeping government investment within a limit which is possible without inflation is stressed. Completion of projects already under way and maintenance expenditures are not included in the development budget.

Chapter 4: Agriculture, Forestry, Animal Husbandry, and Fishing

This chapter presents plans consisting mainly of continued efforts along the same lines as in recent years, but with added emphasis on agricultural training at various levels. Perhaps the most successful efforts to raise output since the transfer of sovereignty have taken place in these fields.

The introductory section states that three types of projects have been assigned high priority: first, those which are clearly realizable; second, those which are badly needed; and, third, those which have already proved their worth. Considerable importance is attached to the establishment of agricultural schools. Of the total budget for agriculture it is proposed to spend Rp. 50 million for agricultural colleges, especially for the training of teachers in agriculture. Some Rp. 20 million are to be spent on courses and schools for farmers (_tanis_), especially outside Java. About Rp. 28 million are to be spent for the Office of Community Development Education. Seed selection and improved irrigation will take some Rp. 23.5 million. Fertilizer, 100 tractors, erosion control, combat of plant diseases, and experiments with new products such as cotton and ramie are other projects. Experimental plots are to be set up. The Department for Development of _Tani_ Activities will have projects for improved cooperation, for the education of _tanis_ (both men and women), for the training of farmers' youth organizations, for assistance to cooperatives, for the development of credit institutions, and for the education of employees. The Department of Plantations will also have a training program.

The situation with respect to smallholders' rubber is said to be serious, with 20 per cent of the gardens already in bad condition. Planting must be increased over a ten-year period by some 260,000 hectares. New planting should increase from 13,000 hectares in 1956 to 26,000 in 1960 and 39,000 in 1965. Expenditures on the smallholders' rubber program are to increase Rp. 26 million in 1956-1957, to Rp. 52 million in 1960-1961, and Rp. 78 million in 1964-1965.

A good deal of emphasis is put on the need for reforestation, especially in Java where the tree cover is already below the minimal safety level. It is pointed out that reforestation not only protects the land from erosion but also provides the basis for various industries such as paper, chemicals, cellulose, housing, furniture, matches, and tanning. Tractors and bulldozers are needed for this program.

In the field of animal husbandry, the emphasis will be on experimental animal imports in order to improve breeds, especially of milk cows, Arab horses, and pigs, and on improved feeding (there is insufficient pasture). Some swamps, it is said, if drained could be used for grazing cattle. The control of disease, especially of hoof-and-mouth disease, is an important part of this program.

So far as sea fishing is concerned, motorized vessels are regarded as of primary importance. Canneries are to be set up, starting with 1956. For inland fishing, the breeding of new types of fish is stressed.

The Office of Land Use Planning must decide on the proper proportions of forests and cultivated lands, the plan states, and will have projects for flood control. Increased agricultural credit is also regarded as of considerable importance. The division of the five-year budget among the various offices in the Ministry of Agriculture is presented in a table (not reproduced here).

Chapter 5: Irrigation

Irrigation is another field in which the Indonesian government has acquired substantial experience during the past few years. The irrigation program in the plan reflects this experience, giving the impression of having been carefully worked out. It is pointed out in the introduction to the chapter that the irrigation projects are regarded as multi-purpose projects, with flood control and drainage as objectives, as well as the increased production of foodstuffs. However, among the "foundations of the plan" for irrigation, the necessity of providing food for an increasing population is given a primary place. With a population growth of 1.7 per cent per year, the population by 1960 will approach 89.8 million. In 1955 the production of rice totaled 7,126,329 tons, and imports in that year amounted to 126,983 tons; total consumption thus amounted to 7,253,312 tons. Per capita consumption is 88 kilograms per year or 241 grams per day. Production of maize in 1955 was 1.9 million tons or 60 grams per person per day. The goal of the Five Year Plan is to provide 250 grams of rice and 70 grams of maize per day. Thus by 1960, when the population reaches 89.8 million, the total requirements for rice will be 8.2 million tons per year. Production of maize meanwhile must rise from 1.9 million tons in 1955 to 2.3 tons by 1960. In short, production of rice must be increased by 200,000 tons per year. These requirements can be met partly by increased production per hectare, but some expansion of the rice hectarage will also be necessary; thus new areas must be brought under irrigation.

The chapter presents a detailed list of proposed irrigation projects with a map showing their location. The allocation in terms of hectarage and rupiahs by major districts is shown in a table (not reproduced here). Less than a quarter of the hectarage, and about the same proportion of the rupiah expenditures, is allocated to Java, on which two-thirds of the total population lives. The island which is to receive the greatest attention with regard to irrigation is Sumatra, followed by Kalimantan.

Chapter 6: Mineral Resources

Indonesia has a wide variety of mineral resources, but the quality and quantity of these resources is not clearly known. Among some sectors of the Indonesian community, there is too easy an assumption that high standards of living can be reached in Indonesia simply by "developing our rich natural resources." It is probably against such extreme optimism that the caution marking this chapter of the plan is directed.

The chapter begins with a "general view" of the importance of mineral resources in the over-all plan. It points out that economic development depends on a good many things besides resources, such as the structure of the government, the political situation, the financial position. At the same time it is necessary, before constructing a development plan, to complete an inventory of mineral resources. Such an inventory must begin with a general survey of the area as a whole, and then proceed to a more detailed account of particular minerals.

The chapter proceeds to Section A, under the heading "General Problems." The section begins with a cautious statement that it is not clear to what degree "nonrenewable" resources are a prerequisite to industrialization. If industrialization is defined in the broadest sense, it may be questioned whether the presence of nonrenewable resources is essential to industrial development. The absence of certain resources can be offset by the presence of others. The most pressing need in Indonesia is to complete the technical research on mineral resources in a systematic fashion.

Paragraph 2 is concerned with "particular problems of minerals." The peculiarities which distinguish the mining industry as one with problems of its own may be briefly summarized as follows: (a) Mineral resources are fixed in their location and limited in their amounts. (b) The great bulk of minerals is hidden, and their discovery is to some extent accidental. This fact gives mineral development a speculative character, connected with a large risk in the discovery of resources, plus the chance that they will be quickly used up, for example, in the case of petroleum. (c) The difficulty of getting at the minerals increases as production continues, and the cost of production rises. (d) The majority of mineral resources last for a long time. Accordingly, the production of secondary minerals must be increased, a fact which creates a problem for the mining industry.

Paragraph 3: The Importance of Mineral Industries in General. The increased efficiency of human productive effort made possible by mineral resources results in increased purchasing power and expanding markets.

Paragraph 4: Methods of Mineral Surveys. Exploration techniques today are very refined, including geophysical, geochemical, photogeometric, photogeological, gravity and seismic methods, magnetometer work, and aerial magnetometer surveys.

Paragraph 5: Areas to Be Surveyed. It is necessary to reduce the costs of exploration by delimiting promising areas for systematic investigation. One of the most effective preliminary approaches is to use general geological data. In general, the Indonesian islands are covered with a heavy mantle of overburden. The second, more systematic phase, which includes core drilling, is also more expensive. It is worth proceeding to such intensive search only if the results of preliminary exploration are favorable.

The chapter then proceeds to a classification of the Indonesian islands according to the types of metals that are found in them. The mineral resources of Indonesia are classified into three major types: (a) those which have already been worked for several years (petroleum, coal, tin, and bauxite); (b) minerals which are now being worked only in a small way, the production of which can be expanded (gold, silver, manganese, nickel, phosphate, asphalt, sodium, and several minerals of less importance); (c) potential mineral development (the iron ores of South Sumatra, Kalimantan, and Sulawesi, the nickel ores of Sulawesi, the basic ores of Central Sumatra, and the lead, copper, and zinc of Central Java).

With respect to petroleum, the report states that the important areas in Indonesia are limited to the Sunda region, although some oil exists in West Irian and Ceram. The figures of oil production for 1954 are presented in Table 5 (not reproduced here).

Natural gas is an important by-product of the petroleum industry. At present the great bulk of it is wasted. It is currently estimated that 1,200,000 tons are lost in the production of crude oil and approximately 900,000 tons in the process of refining. Only 40,000 metric tons of natural gas are used as a source of power in the petroleum industry itself. Natural gas can be used, however, for important technical industries, such as synthetic ammonia and fertilizer. It can also be used for the generation of electric power.

So far no coking coals have been found in Indonesia, but reserves including brown coal and lignite are substantial. Of the coal mines owned by the government, Bukit Asam is the most important. In 1954 its production reached 647,100 metric tons compared with the production at Umbilon of only 78,600 metric tons. The mines in East Kalimantan yield 174,100 metric tons. The estimated reserves of bituminous coal at Bukit Asam are 60,000,000 metric tons. It is still under investigation whether this coal, together with the iron ores at Lampung, provides the basis for an iron industry. The production of the government-owned Umbilon mine is now about 80,000 tons of bituminous, noncoking coal, but the total reserves amount to some 200,000,000 metric tons and thus are greater than those at Bukit Asam. At present, these mines are operating at a loss because production is so low. Unfortunately, to get at these reserves, a mine must be built which is very deep and thus very expensive. The possibilities of increasing production from this mine are currently under investigation.

Tin production is second to petroleum in total value. The greatest porportion of Indonesian tin production comes from Bangka, the rest from Belitong and Singkep. The mines at Bangka are now government owned.* Unfortunately, world market conditions do not currently encourage expansion of tin production. Groups in Europe are interested in buying tin ore directly from Indonesia until a tin smelter can be constructed in Indonesia. So far as is known to the Department of Mines, there has been no thorough investigation of the extent of the tin concentrate reserves. The cruder concentrates are usually less than 10 per cent tin by weight. Further study

*Up to 1957 the Billiton mines on Belitong were operated by a mixed enterprise in which the Indonesian government had a majority interest. They are now a wholly Indonesian enterprise. (Ed.)

of the tin situation is necessary; new techniques such as electrostatic and electromagnetic separation processes might be applied.

Bauxite is found in the islands of Bintan, Kojam, and some of the islands of the Riau archipelago. There may also be some bauxite in Southwest Kalimantan. The exploitation of bauxite is undertaken by a Dutch firm, NIBEM, in which the Indonesian government has approximately a 20 per cent share. The bauxite ore consists of about 53 per cent alumina and 4.5 per cent silica. Reserves are estimated at 27,000,000 tons, although only 13,000,000 of these represent proven reserves.

The chapter then turns to the minerals being exploited on a small scale, beginning with gold and silver. In the prewar period, between 1900-1940, the great bulk of gold and silver came from Sumatra. It states that a new gold mine at Tjikotok-Tjirotan would be started in 1957 with financing from the Bank Industri Negara.

Manganese is found in Java, especially in West and Central Java. The major part of these reserves is being exploited by a Dutch mining concern. However, an effort to estimate the amount of manganese resources in the Djogjakarta area has been made by the National Planning Bureau in cooperation with the local government. Preliminary surveys suggest that these resources are not very large but are scattered in small clusters which are discontinuous. Reserves of some value have been found at Doi and Halmahera Selatan, which are being exploited by the local government with assistance from the Bank Industri Negara.

Most phosphates are found in Java. Van Bemmelen, in his Geology of Indonesia, states that phosphates are found in 53 different places. It is clear that the proposed double superphosphate plant in the industrial development associated with the Asahan project cannot rely on domestic raw materials alone but must continue to use imported materials.

Turning to potential mineral deposits, the chapter first refers to the survey of iron and steel possibilities being made by a German team under the direction of the National Planning Bureau. It was expected that the team would report about the middle of 1957, and that their report would provide a basis for the iron and steel project in the Five Year Plan. With regard to nickel, it is stated that the survey conducted by the J. G. White Engineers estimates capital investment requirements at Rp. 50 per kilogram of nickel produced.*

Section C deals with the economic position of mineral industries in Indonesia. The growth of investment and labor force in these industries is indicated. Output shows more expansion over prewar levels than in the case of agriculture.

Section D of the chapter is concerned with the systematic planning of exploration. Most of it, however, is concerned with exploration already completed or under way. For example, reference is made to the exploration for bauxite in Riau by NIBEM, and by the J. G. White Engineers for coking coal. (Here it is mentioned that the reports on the possibilities of using Indonesian coal for coking by the new American process of high-temperature carbonization [Disco Process] were negative.) The geologists provided under the Colombo Plan have conducted exploration for manganese in the Djogjakarta region; as yet these discoveries are not sufficiently extensive to warrant exploitation. They have also made surveys in connection with the proposed cement plant for the Medan-Toba area. Reference is also made to an expedition sent to Southeast Kalimantan to search for iron and coal, an exploration important for the proposed iron and steel projects. The section closes with a reiteration of the importance of carefully planned prospecting.

The section concerned with petroleum policy in the plan begins by pointing out that Indonesia is a country with considerable room for private investment, both national and foreign. It is suggested, however, that private

*A program of core drilling is being carried out to determine the nature and extent of copper reserves. (Ed.)

investment must be directed toward new projects. As a matter of principle, it is said that the government must create a favorable climate for private investment, both national and foreign, since the government's own capital resources are below the requirements for raising national income. Where it is clear that there is a shortage of domestic capital for investment in some field of importance in the plan, that field must be opened to foreign investment under rules stipulated in foreign investment law. The general policy on foreign investment should be stated in that law. The government is aware of the important role that has been played by the oil companies in the development of the country. Indonesia benefits from the activities of the oil companies through taxes, foreign-exchange earnings, and indirect economic contributions. Indonesia does not yet have enough capital to expand the operations of this industry. Meanwhile, domestic consumption of petroleum and petroleum products is rising at a rate of about 10 per cent per year. There is a shortage of technicians and of capital within the country to meet this expansion of consumption and to realize foreign-exchange earning potential. As a temporary policy, therefore, the government should grant exploration and development rights to private enterprises with inadequate reserves, while showing a progressive attitude toward the Indonesian economy. Stanvac is in the weakest position with respect to the extent of estimated reserves. NIAM also needs additional reserves. The petroleum policy should include Indonesianization of the exploitation of oil resources in a progressive manner. More Indonesians should take part in the responsible leadership of the oil companies. For example, in NIAM, in which the government has a 50 per cent share of ownership, the leadership is still provided by BPM [now Shell Indonesia] .

Chapter 7: Electric Power

The chapter begins with a statement of electric power production as of 1949 relative to population. It is suggested that per capita consumption in that year was perhaps the lowest in the world—4.6 kilowatt-hours in Indonesia as compared to 410 in Italy, 814 in England, 1,990 in the United States, and 3,430 in Canada. By 1954 considerable expansion had already taken place, from 387,000,000 kilowatt-hours to 812,000,000 kilowatt-hours. However, the Five Year Plan calls for considerable further expansion of electric power capacity. The Djatiluhur project will have a capacity of 100,000 kilowatts and will produce 528,000,000 kilowatt-hours per year. The Asahan project has a capacity of 102,000 kilowatts and will produce 585,000,000 kilowatt-hours per year.

Chapter 8: Industrialization

The chapter is divided into three major parts, the first dealing with priorities, the second with policies, and the third with projects. With respect to priorities, there are two major problems—a shortage of foreign exchange and a shortage of skills and expertise.

There are basic priorities (senior priorities) and secondary (junior) priorities. Among the basic priorities are, first, the need to provide for essential consumer goods in order to save foreign exchange. Of second priority are projects which will bring foreign-exchange savings or earnings—import replacers or new exports. Third come new capital investment projects which are highly efficient in terms of scarce factors.

Among "junior priorities" the production of goods and services in general consumption among the people in Indonesia comes first. Junior priority number two is that existing industries should be maintained and small industries protected and within reason assisted; the third junior priority is to make the best possible use and distribution of domestic raw materials and skills; fourth, national principle is to be fostered and training advanced; five, existing transportation routes should be exploited in the most efficient manner since new roads are expensive; six, cheapness of products is to be secured; seven, projects that come speedily to fruition should come first where possible, especially if they can earn foreign exchange.

In the industrialization chapter stress is laid on research training and credit extension. The research program includes such organizations as the Office of Industrial Research in Djakarta; the Offices of Chemical Research in Bogor, Surabaya, and Makassar; the Office of Textile Research in Bandung; the Office of Ceramics Research in Bandung; the Office of Industrial Research in Bandung; the Office of Leather Research in Djogjakarta; and the Office of Batik Research in Djogjakarta. With respect to credit, emphasis is put on the operations of the Bank Industri Negara, but mention is also made of the Bank Rakjat Indonesia, the Djawatan Perindustrian, the Jajasan Lembaga Djaminan Kredit, etc. (p. 109).

Only the industrial program of Central Government has been translated into specific projects in the plan. The whole industrial program is broken down into three categories of projects: special projects, Central Government projects, and "recommended projects" for local government and private enterprise. Of the total Central Government budget of Rp. 12.5 billion, Rp. 3,125 billion, or 25 per cent, is for industry and mining. The allocation to the industrial sector alone amounts to Rp. 2,279.5 million, or 73 per cent of the total allocation for industry and mining. The remaining Rp. 757 million is for the mining sector, with reserves of Rp. 88.5 million.

Of the allocations for industrial projects, Rp. 1,078 million are for special projects, Rp. 776.5 million for Central Government projects, and Rp. 425 million for regional projects. In terms of foreign exchange, the requirements are Rp. 735.6 million for special projects, Rp. 351.9 million for Central Government projects, and Rp. 200 million for regional projects, giving a total of Rp. 1,287,5 million, or 56 per cent of the total industrialization budget.

Special projects are very important for the country and include: (1) the Asahan complex in Sumatra, which includes the aluminum factory at Belawan, (2) a combined iron and steel project, (3) chemical industry and fertilizer industry, (4) rayon industry. The Asahan project includes the transmission of electric power, the factory for aluminum (including alumina), the factory for superphosphate fertilizer, a cement factory, harbor and transport facilities, and a pulp and paper factory (pro memoria for the time being). At the end of the Five Year Plan the electric power capacity at Asahan will be 100,000 kilowatts. The chemical industries will include caustic soda, sulfuric and other acids, ammonia, muriate fertilizer, and superphosphates. Central Government projects include such undertakings as completion of the cement plant at Gresik, construction of a cement plant at Medan, paper factories at Blabak and Toba in North Sumatra, and the like.

No detailed projects are submitted for the local government and private enterprise sectors. However, a long list of undertakings is provided, and these are divided into those recommended by Central Government, those which are considered complementary to the government sector, and others; that is, industries where there is "still an opportunity to work." These are also subdivided into industrial types such as food, beverage, and tobacco, textiles, heavy industries, clothing and apparel, and wood and furniture.

Chapter 9: Transport and Communications

A total of Rp. 3,125 million is allocated for transport and communications, of which Rp. 1,169 million will be in foreign exchange. The greater proportion of this sum is allocated to roads and bridges, with railroads second. Post, telephone, and telegraph come third, followed by shipping and harbors. It is interesting to note that of the expenditures on roads, the island which will receive the greatest share is Sumatra, with Rp. 390 million, followed by Kalimantan with Rp. 290 million. The allocation for Java, including the special district of Djogjakarta and metropolitan Djakarta, amounts to Rp. 273 million. Road equipment and the like will take Rp. 150 million of the total budget for roads.

The program for railroads is almost entirely a matter of road improvement. The rehabilitation of the important networks in Java and Sumatra will take Rp. 250 million. The plan also includes the rehabilitation of the railroad network of 164 kilometers in South Sumatra from Kertaparti to Tandjung Enim, which is important for the Bukit Asam mine. Airports and hangars for Garuda Airways will take Rp. 53.8 million. The harbor program includes a contract with a French company for enlargement of Tandjung Priok harbor, including a new tanker harbor, a third harbor of 500 meters, godowns, etc., and a 300-meter harbor for coastal vessels. Other work will be carried out at Belawan, including a new harbor, wharfs, and godowns; at Bandjarmasin, again, with a new harbor, a 200-meter wharf, godowns, etc.; and at Balikpapan, where a new landing bridge and godowns will be provided.

Chapter 10: Manpower Resources

As might be expected the program for manpower resources is concerned mainly with training. Figures are presented for the occupational breakdown for 1930 and 1953. In the latter year, some 69 per cent of the occupied population was engaged in primary production, 10.5 per cent in industry, 1.5 per cent in transport, 6.2 per cent in trade, 1 per cent in professions, 2.4 per cent in the government service, and 9.5 per cent in other occupations. Some structural change between 1930 and 1953 is indicated by these figures. There has already been a reduction in the proportion of the occupied population in the production of raw materials, and an increase in employment in industry, transport, and trade. The biggest increase seems to be in the government service.

Chapter 11: Labor Relations

This chapter contains a description of the labor legislation and regulations as they existed in 1956.

Chapter 12: Education

The chapter presents figures on the increase in the number of students from 1950 to 1955 and also a projection to 1960. The number of children attending schools is expected to increase from 10.9 million in 1956 to 13.5 million in 1960. Attention is drawn to the need for training teachers. The report of the technical education survey team is briefly summarized.

Chapter 13: Public Health

Attention is drawn to UNICEF and WHO programs against typhus, dysentery, cholera, etc.

Chapter 14: Social Welfare and Social Security

This chapter deals with both social welfare and social security. Programs on social welfare could not be considered merely as incidental efforts by private institutions of a temporary nature; all government programs which are aimed to achieve economic security, health, knowledge, welfare, and covering such fields as social security, general education, and public health are within the scope of social welfare. The role of the government in the various activities of social welfare—aid to the poor, to orphans, rehabilitation of disabled people, and so forth—under present economic conditions should be mainly directed toward efforts to improve physical capital and know-how so as to improve productivity and increase per capita income, which in turn will increase the funds available to carry out various measures in this field of social welfare. The responsibility for social welfare must be carried out by the various activities of the society; the government's responsibility in this case lies mainly in giving encouragement, stimulation, aid, and control over the activities in the society in the implementation and improvement of social welfare; the Research Institute of the Ministry of Social Affairs and various universities are carrying out research programs in this field. In the First Five Year Plan a fund totaling Rp. 12.5 million is set aside to be used primarily for consultation and research.

Social security is considered an integral part of the whole reconstruction plan, and an amount of Rp. 8.3 million is allocated to finance this program. After giving a detailed outline of the various laws and regulations concerning this subject, the various institutions set up by enterprises or by combined efforts of management and labor which are not based on labor legislation, and the various social measures concerning government officials, the chapter deals further with the social security program and its implementation. Distinction has been made between life in towns and life in rural areas. To try out a system of social security in a village community under present conditions is not yet feasible. It is recommended that the idea of gotong rojong be strengthened by way of social measures organized in the most modern way without destroying sound traditions which could serve as the basis for gotong rojong. Social security measures in towns are mainly concerned with the interests of labor, dealing with unemployment, accidents and illness because of work, old age benefits, and so forth. The implementation of such a program should be given to an autonomous agency working closely with other departments of the government and under the control of the Ministry of Labor.

In order to carry out the program, the first phase requires the training of personnel of certain groups of labor in certain specific areas, whereas broadening the program will only take place if the conditions laid down in the first phase have been met.

Chapter 15: Housing

As a consequence of World War II and the revolution, the housing situation in Indonesia is very discouraging, and it has become even worse with the exceptionally high rates of population increase and urbanization. This causes a housing situation in towns that is almost below decent human standards; in rural areas generally it is also very discouraging. It is caused not only by poverty but also by the traditional way of building houses which does not meet the basic conditions of health. This situation not only has had wide consequences in the social well-being of the people but also has affected the economic field.

Because the role of the government in the Five Year Plan is limited by budgetary considerations, the government's contribution to take positive measures in this field is very limited. An amount of Rp. 95 million has been allocated for this purpose, which covers expenses for research and technical assistance.

In the First Five Year Plan, the government will put emphasis upon research on the techniques of building houses, technical assistance, efforts to simplify administrative procedures and facilities concerning the construction of houses, encouragement to the production of building materials, and gathering information.

The finance of house construction could not possibly be assumed by the government and should be the direct responsibility of society. Because the income of the Indonesian population is low at this time, in order to cope with the financial aspect of the construction of buildings, cooperative efforts such as housing cooperatives, foundations, and the like must be encouraged, and the government should give assistance and direction; important in this respect is that the cooperative efforts must be based primarily upon the forces in society rather than be dependent upon government assistance. Housing credits must be channeled through credit institutions—banks, cooperatives, and community development organizations.

Chapter 16: Community Development

Although the plan accords considerable importance to the community development sector, there are as yet no clearly defined projects in the program, and Central Government's participation in it is limited almost entirely to provision of a central organization. The government is apparently planning to provide only Rp. 198 million over the entire five-year period for this purpose.

The introduction to the chapter stresses the need for integrated development at the community level, with cooperative efforts in such fields as health, housing, industry, agricultural improvement, and credit extension. These projects should be designed, it is stated, to produce balanced growth. The introduction does state, however, that concrete industrial and agricultural projects should have precedence over education, health, and the like. It is emphasized that the initiative for community development projects must come mainly from the villages themselves, although the cooperation of Central Government with the villages is promised.

A distinction is made between "key" projects and the "extended program." These relate to successive phases of the community development program. The basic unit for planning community development is to be the Kewedanan, a district government involving several villages. The Central Government will contribute a larger share to the extended program than to the key projects, which are to be based almost entirely on community self-help and community initiative. The plan is to begin in the first year with 16 projects in 16 "key" development or work districts. In the second year 22 district projects will be started and 10 extended-program districts will be added. In the third year there will be 28 new key district projects and 20 extended-program district projects. In the fourth year there are to be 34 key projects and 30 extended projects, and in the fifth year 40 of each.

An elaborate organization is proposed for community development. There is first of all a Central Government office or bureau comprising the Prime Minister and representatives of the various ministries and of the National Planning Bureau. This bureau will have a secretariat under a chairman and a technical board composed of the secretaries-general of the relevant ministries. Similar boards are to be established at the provincial and _kabupaten_ level, with a small secretariat and representatives of the ministries at each level.

Launching of the community development program will require training at various levels. Training programs must be set up for the secretariat, for _desa_ leaders, for various specialists, and for _desa_ school teachers.

The chapter closes with an itemization of the steps already taken. In November 1955 delegates were sent to study the community development programs of Burma, Ceylon, India, and Pakistan for a period of more than three months. In February 1956 a delegation of women was sent to Burma, India, and Pakistan. In May 1956 a nation-wide conference was held; and a temporary governmental committee on community development has been set up. Moreover, the original 16 core work districts have already been selected, and the training of 160 men from these 16 work districts has been finished. Finally, a seminar conference has been organized with 3 foreign experts in attendence.

Chapter 17: Cooperation

The chapter on cooperatives is concerned mainly with a review of developments that have taken place in the cooperative program. The number of cooperative organizations increased from 7,667 in 1952 to 11,446 in 1955, and the number of members of cooperatives from just over 1,000,000 in 1951 to 1,938,000 in 1955. No specific program or budget for cooperatives is offered in the plan. The Planning Bureau apparently regards the growth of cooperatives as part of the community development program.

Chapter 18: Transmigration

The main feature of the proposed transmigration program is its very small scale. Judging by the chapter on transmigration in the plan, the National Planning Bureau places little faith in transmigration either as a device for alleviating population pressure on Java or as a form of agricultural improvement. The total budget provided is Rp. 383 million for the five years, or approximately Rp. 75 million per year. Since the cost of transferring and settling families has been running close to Rp. 15 thousand per family, this would seem to mean that the Bureau is thinking of a program involving only 5,000 families a year, slightly less than the number of families transferred in 1955. During the first five years, the government will concentrate on two or three districts in South Sumatra as pilot-plant projects.

It is stated early in the chapter that the government wishes to encourage voluntary migration, concentrating on the improvement of roads and other supplementary activities that would assist transmigration. In hopes of encouraging further voluntary migration, the government also wishes to increase the contacts between the existing communities and the areas from which the people came. The government will administer its transmigration program on the same principles as in the community development program. The role of the government will be to move the people, clear the land, install irrigation, build roads, improve roads and bridges, and provide support for six months. Despite the small scale of the transmigration program, an elaborate organization is provided for it.

Chapter 19: Public Administration

One important condition in the implementation of a reconstruction plan is not yet fulfilled, that of the existence of an efficient governmental agency with officials with sufficient knowledge and experience. It is therefore the government's policy to try continuously to simplify the administration and the regulations, besides improving the capability of the officials.

The main problems facing the government today in public administration are those relating to:

a. setup and implementation of the budget
b. achievement of a definite division of responsibility between the various governmental functions
c. establishment of a decentralized administration
d. improvement of the efficiency of the government officials

a. Administrative problems may not be a retarding factor in finishing a project, and the proposed budget must be submitted to the Parliament on September first. Difficulties, however, such as delayed authorizations and changes in the system of carrying unspent funds to the next fiscal year, caused inaccuracies in the compilation of various ministerial budgets. The above system should be reconsidered so as to guarantee continuity in the implementation. In this respect the various regulations concerning the budget (ICW) which are out of date, and the incompetency of the administrative officials, should be taken into consideration. A state commission to consider among others the proposals of Mr. W. Karakacheff, United Nations expert, is in the process of replacing the ICW with new legislation on the budget.

b. Instability in the organizational structure of Central Government and the reorganizations that have frequently taken place in the various ministries add to administrative difficulties.

A National Committee (PANOK) to investigate the organizational setup of the ministries, established in 1952, which finished its report in 1954, proposed that changes within the ministries should be regulated by government decrees. Because some parts of Government Decree 1952 No. 20 have not yet been implemented, the consequences are: excessive differentiation, duplication, organization, and a cadre of officials which is too big and too extensive. According to this commission, if its proposals could be implemented, the budget could be reduced by Rp. 130 million.

c. A condition for local government to develop its economy is the fullest opportunity to carry out its task in this respect, organizationally as well as financially. A clear-cut division of the use of financial resources between Central Government and local governments should form the basis of the financial relationship, and draft legislation on this subject is now under consideration by the Parliament. This is also the case with draft legislation on local taxation. It is of the utmost importance to have new laws concerning the above questions.

d. In cooperation with the Ministry of Labor and the National Planning Bureau, a Work Committee on Employment Statistics has been set up headed by representatives of the Ministry of Labor. The committee calculated the total number of government employees at the end of 1953 at 1,727,548, excluding members of the armed forces.

It is doubtful whether the threefold expansion since 1940 is reduced by the additional tasks of the government. Public policy in this respect must endeavor to:

a. simplify the whole governmental administration (including local government)
b. improve skills among employees
c. give recognition to capable officials.

In order to simplify the governmental administration, opportunities must be provided to redundant employees to improve their knowledge and skill in other fields. Problems of placement should be carefully studied by a state committee, and within a limited time concrete proposals should be submitted to the government.

The over-all planning covers the following efforts:

a. long-run planning (5, 6, or 10 years)
b. local planning
c. yearly planning
d. planning policy
e. evaluation of the results
f. compilation and an analysis of statistical information.

The above measures are considered as one unity that cannot be divided into parts and should form the basis for the organizational structure.

a. Since the budget is the most important source of financing, it is necessary to consider and analyze the budget over some subsequent years. Allocation of the development funds among the various economic and social fields is based on priorities which have been decided previously. The highest organ to set up and decide upon the reconstruction plan is the Economic and Planning Council. Coordination in the preparation and implementation of the plan should be done by the National Planning Bureau on behalf of the government. Implementation of the development plan in the government sector should be done by the ministries and by agencies set up by the government primarily for that purpose.

b. Local planning. Because of inadequate information, the First Five Year Plan concerns mainly problems of national importance, looking at the country as one economic unit. But if we consider the projects in the various fields, it is clear that the plan also shows a distribution of projects over the whole Indonesian archipelago. In the future, local development must be planned accurately; in this respect the interests as well as the capability and the resources of an area should be considered carefully without losing sight of the interest of the nation as a whole.

c. The National Planning Bureau should also be an agency for the coordination and preparation of the annual plans. In this respect, we must mention the existence of the Interdepartmental Committee (PAKIN), the members of which are the Director General of the Planning Bureau as chairman and the representatives of the various ministries. This committee has the responsibility of coordinating problems in the economic and social fields and all foreign aid programs.

The various ministerial budgets concerning development projects should be submitted to the National Planning Bureau to be analyzed and discussed with the respective ministries in order to be submitted together with the ordinary budget to the Council of Ministers and Parliament.

d. Coordination between yearly policy and long-term planning could be achieved by combining the two councils, the Economic and Financial Council and the National Planning Council, into one Economic and Planing Council as declared by Government Decree 1956 No. 15.

e. The results achieved within a certain period of time can give us a picture of how far we will be able to implement the plan; on the basis of this information, further policies with regard to the various fields can be laid out and the budget for development during the following year can be determined.

f. One of the difficulties in the preparation of the First Five Year Plan was the lack of quantitative data; for the preparation of the Second and the following Five Year Plans, quantitative data should be available in sufficient volume and these data must be reliable. It is further recommended that sample surveys be used to get information in a short period, and that the statistical system be improved by broadening the statistical surveys to obtain better indications regarding various economic activities in society, especially in regard to national income and production.

Table I

THE INVESTMENT BUDGET, 1956 - 1961

(Million Rp.)

	Allocation	Domestic Currency	Foreign Exchange
I. Agriculture	1,625		
1. Agriculture	(= 13%)	1,044.0	208.0
2. Transmigration		383.0	80.0
3. Community development		198.0	40.0
		1,625.0	328.0
II. Power and irrigation	3,125		
1. Power development	(= 25%)	1,750.0	880.0
2. Irrigation		1,100.0	204.0
3. Reserves		275.0	104.0
		3,125.0	1,188.0
III. Industry and mining	3,125		
1. Special projects	(= 25%)	1,078.0	735.6
2. Central projects		776.5	351.9
3. Local gov't projects		425.0	200.0
4. Mining		757.0	442.2
5. Reserves		88.5	67.3
		3,125.0	1,797.0
IV. Transport and communications	3,125 (= 25%)		
1. Roads		1,200.0	240.0
2. Railroads		600.0	240.0

Table I (concluded)

	Allocation	Domestic Currency	Foreign Exchange
3. Post office and telegraph		495.0	230.0
4. Shipping		350.0	285.2
5. Harbors		275.0	138.0
6. Airways		100.0	27.8
7. Other		105.0	61.0
		3,125.0	1,169.0
V. Education, welfare, and information	1,500 (= 12%)		
1. Education		1,050.0	157.5
2. Health		250.0	25.0
3. Public housing		95.0	9.5
4. Labor		25.0	1.3
5. Social welfare		12.5	—
6. Information		37.5	8.7
7. Reserves		30.0	4.0
		1,500.0	206.0
TOTAL	12,500	12,500.0	4,688.0

Source: Garis-Garis Besar Rentjana Pembangunan Lima Tahun, 1956-1960 (Framework of the Five Year Development Plan).

Table II

FINANCING OF THE GOVERNMENT SECTOR, 1956 - 1960

(Million Rp.)

Year	Budget	Increase in Deposits	Bonded Securities	Total Domestic	Foreign Aid	Total
1956	1,700	—	—	1,700	200	1,900
1957	1,800	320	—	2,120	200	2,320
1958	1,900	340	100	2,340	200	2,540
1959	2,000	360	200	2,560	200	2,760
1960	2,100	380	300	2,780	200	2,980
Total	9,500	1,400	600	11,500	1,000	12,500

Source: Garis-Garis Besar Rentjana Pembangunan Lima Tahun, 1956-1960 (Framework of the Five Year Development Plan).

APPENDIX B

INDONESIAN TAX REVENUES, 1929, 1939, 1951-1957

(1929, 1939: Million NEI Guilders; 1951 – 1957: Million Rp.)

Line	Type of Tax	1929		1939		1951		1952
		Total Receipts	% of Total	Total Receipts	% of Total	Total Receipts	% of Total	Total Receipts
	Business income:							
1	Company	51.5	15.0	37.0	12.3	654.7	6.6	895.5
	Personal income:							
2	Income	54.4		36.9	12.3	529.8		647.9
3	Wage			24.8	8.3	152.2		183.5
4	Subtotal	54.4	15.8	61.7	20.6	682.0	6.8	831.4
	Wealth and property:							
5	Capital assets			1.4		7.7		11.4
6	Urban real estate	6.8		5.0		12.7		9.5
7	Vehicles			0.7		3.5		4.3
8	Household	5.2		4.0		3.4		4.0
9	Radio					11.5		16.1
10	Subtotal	12.0	3.5	11.1	3.7	38.8	0.4	45.3
	Consumption:							
11	Turnover					536.1		
12	Sales					128.2		628.4
13	Free market sales					198.1		65.8
14	Restaurant					17.2		20.2
15	Slaughter	7.0		4.1		13.5		14.7
16	Excise	43.2		68.4		746.0		1074.5
17	Subtotal	50.2	14.6	72.5	24.0	1639.1	16.4	1803.6
	Export and import duties:							
18	Export*	13.0	3.8	20.6	6.9	5429.7	54.4	3900.7
19	Import†	95.4	27.7	59.4	19.8	1451.5	14.6	1443.9
20	Subtotal	108.4	31.5	80.0	26.7	6881.2	69.0	5344.6
	Transaction taxes:							
21	Stamp	14.2		8.7		37.5		43.7
22	Property transfer	2.9		1.4		9.8		10.7
23	Permits and licenses	0.3		0.1		0.2		0.1
24	Auction	2.6		0.8		4.4		5.1
25	Lottery	1.0		0.9		4.1		5.3
26	Subtotal	21.0	6.1	11.9	4.0	56.0	0.6	64.9
27	Land	36.7	10.7	22.2	7.4			
28	Other	9.7	2.8	3.6	1.2	15.8	0.2	45.5
29	TOTAL OF ALL TAXES	343.9		300.0		9967.6		9030.8

*Including yields from foreign exchange certificates.

†Including yields from import surcharges.

‡Rounded to nearest unit.

(1929, 1939: Million NEI Guilders; 1951 - 1957: Million Rp.)

1952	1953		1954‡		1955‡		1956‡§		1957‡§		
% of Total	Total Receipts	% of Total	Total Receipts	% of Total	Total Receipts	% of Total	Total Receipts	% of Total	Total Receipts	% of Total	Line
9.9	1082.5	12.8	1330	17.7	1804	19.4	1569	11.7	1581	10.3	1
	655.3		805		945		1169		1455		2
	228.7		244		299		327		348		3
9.2	884.0	10.5	1049	14.0	1244	13.4	1496	11.0	1803	11.8	4
	10.1		8		11						5
	9.6		10		8						6
	4.4		5		5						7
	15.7		21		18						8
	18.2		23		27						9
0.5	58.0	0.7	67	0.9	69	0.7					10
											11
	633.9		611		557		942		833		12
	21.6		14		10		2		3		13
	21.5		23		25						14
	12.5		15		11						15
	1355.7		1593		1830		1877		2593		16
20.0	2045.2	24.3	2256	30.0	2433	26.0	2821	21.0	3429	22.5	17
43.2	1012.2	12.0	544	7.2	752	8.0	424	3.2	1786	11.7	18
16.0	3241.5	38.5	2174	28.9	2948	31.5	6857	51.1	6196	40.7	19
59.2	4253.7	50.6	2718	36.1	3700	39.5	7281	54.3	7982	52.4	20
	41.5		59		59						21
	10.9		12		14						22
	1.2										23
	5.5										24
	7.8										25
0.7	66.9	0.8	71	0.9	73	0.8					26
											27
0.5	16.0	0.2	20	0.3	31	0.3	283	2.0	440	2.9	28
	8406.3		7511		9354		13450		15235		29

[§]Data by detailed breakdown are not available for years after 1955.

Sources: 1929 - 1955: Ministry of Finance; 1956 and 1957: Report of the Bank Indonesia, 1957 - 1958.

APPENDIX C

DATA RELATING TO THE ALLOCATION OF TAXES BETWEEN SECTORS

1. Business income. This tax is levied on all limited liability companies, limited partnerships with share capital, other companies or associations in which capital is entirely or partly divided into shares, cooperative associations, and mutual insurance companies. In 1952, rates varied from 40 per cent on all net profits below Rp. 500,000 up to marginal rates of 52.5 per cent on net profits above Rp. 2,500,000. These rates were still in effect in June 1959.

It was assumed that the total burden of this tax fell upon the capital-intensive sector since the tax was enforced almost exclusively in this sector. Götzen's study shows a similar result. Forward shifting of the tax to consumers in the labor-intensive sector was unlikely since the tax fell predominantly upon firms producing for the export markets, the petroleum companies, for example, bearing a significant part of the total levy. Similarly, backward shifting to labor is unlikely because these firms during the postwar period have been confronted by a strong labor union organization which makes wages a matter of bilateral bargaining.

2. Personal income and wages tax. In the prewar years the personal income tax was levied against all income not subject to the business income or land taxation. It has consistently been used in conjunction with the wages tax, applying where income exceeds the amount subject to the lower rates of the wages tax. Amounts paid as wages tax are credited against the income tax liability. Since Indonesian independence, all income not subject to

the business income tax has been legally subject to the personal income tax. In 1939 the effective rates varied from 3 to 22 per cent. In 1952, effective rates began at slightly less than 3 per cent (on incomes less than Rp. 5,000) and rose to 55 per cent plus 75 per cent of each additional Rp. 100 (on incomes over Rp. 300,000). These rates were still in force in June 1959.

For 1929 the distribution of the burden between the capital-intensive and labor-intensive sectors is taken from Götzen (see note 4, Chapter 5), who arrived at his figures by applying the ratios of the assessments among the following groups: Europeans, Chinese, other foreign Asiatics, and Indonesians. For 1939 we have calculated the distribution of the burden on the basis of assessed income among the same groups. For 1952 we have assumed that all of the income tax fell in the capital-intensive sector since there was, at that time, little or no attempt to collect the income tax in the rural areas. Data from the Indonesian Ministry of Finance indicate that this assumption is justified. In 1953, when greater efforts were made to enforce the tax in the labor-intensive sector, receipts from this sector were only Rp. 66 million of a total Rp. 884 million. The problem of intersectoral shifting is avoided because of very limited enforcement of the tax on the group of traders which deals in intersectoral buying and selling.

The wages tax is levied against all wage income earned in private and public services with the exception of earnings in agriculture on land registered under Indonesian law. All estates and plantations are registered under Western law and fall under the scope of the wages tax.

During the prewar period this tax was collected at a flat 4 per cent rate. Since 1947 it has been levied at progressive rates, with a maximum marginal rate of 15 per cent. In 1952 the rates began at 3 per cent. The coverage is somewhat less complete than before the war since domestic service is no longer reached by this tax.

For 1939 we have computed the distributions on the basis of total wage income assessed in the two sectors. For 1952 we make the assumption that the same ratio holds between the two sectors, an assumption confirmed by data provided by the Indonesian Ministry of Finance.

3. Capital assets tax. This is a tax on total net worth levied on both individuals and businesses, excluding corporations. Before 1952 it was levied at low, progressive rates; since 1952 it has been collected at a rate of Rp. 5 per thousand on net worth over Rp. 250,000. It does not amount to capital-gains taxation since valuations are not readily revised in response to general price increases.

This tax is assumed to fall exclusively on the nonrural sector because of enforcement procedures.

4. Urban real estate tax. This is a tax on all real estate and property registered under Western law, which applies only to the capital-intensive sector. Property owned by Indonesians under Adat (native) law is excluded. Thus it is clear that the burden of this tax falls exclusively upon the capital-intensive sector. In the postwar period it has been levied only on reproducible property (i.e., not on land).

5. Motor vehicle tax. This tax applies only to ownership of vehicles driven by other than gasoline engines (those using kerosene, diesel fuel, or charcoal gas). Its burden is believed to fall exclusively upon the capital-intensive sector since there has been no attempt to enforce it in the labor-intensive sector.

6. Household tax. Before the war this was conceived of as a tax on use of various kinds of capital and durable goods. It included a tax on actual or imputed home rental value, household furnishings, vehicles, and horses. During the postwar period it has been impossible in practice to collect the tax on house rent and furnishings; hence the tax now amounts to a levy on certain types of transportation facilities, particularly bicycles. Götzen's ratios for the distribution of the burden between sectors have been retained.

7. Radio tax. This tax, which is levied on all radio receivers, was introduced in 1951 and has been collected as a monthly assessment of Rp. 5

per set. Ratios for its burden between the two sectors were obtained by making a slight modification of Götzen's estimate of the distribution of the household tax.

8. Sales tax. The sales tax, which is levied on all importers and manufacturers, replaced the turnover tax in October 1951. Rates are 5 per cent and 10 per cent of market value, depending on whether the good is classified as a necessity or a luxury. Since there is a certain amount of progressivity in the rate schedule, we are assuming that its burden between the two sectors was the same as that for import duties. (See note on import duties below.)

9. Free market sales tax. The free sales profits tax was adopted in 1950. It represents a levy of 95 per cent on the difference between the prevailing price of import goods sold in the domestic market and the previously controlled price, price control having been abandoned in 1950. In the post-war market conditions in Indonesia the burden of this tax has been readily shifted to consumers; accordingly, the same ratio for distribution of its burden between sectors is used as for sales and import duties.

10. Restaurant tax. Known as the "reconstruction tax," it is collected on consumption in restaurants and hotels. Since it has been enforced only in the capital-intensive sector, its burden is assigned exclusively to this sector.

11. Slaughter tax. This is a tax on butchering. Both of the studies on which Götzen relied indicate that it was borne almost exclusively by Indonesians in the labor-intensive sector, although the ratio was somewhat higher for Java and Madura than for the Outer Islands. These ratios have been retained.

12. Excise duties. The intersectoral burden of these levies is analyzed by excises on particular commodities in Table C-1; unless otherwise noted, ratios are taken from Götzen.

13. Export duties. Prior to 1940, with the exception of tin, export duties were levied exclusively on agricultural products. In 1939, receipts from

Table C-1

DISTRIBUTION OF BURDEN OF EXCISE TAXES

1929, 1939, 1952

Excise	Total	Capital-Intensive Sector %	Capital-Intensive Sector Amount	Labor-Intensive Sector %	Labor-Intensive Sector Amount
1929 (Thousand NEI Guilders and Per Cent)					
Liquor and beer	1,100	90	900	10	110
Oil (kerosene)	12,900	30	3,870	70	9,030
Gasoline	18,000	70	12,600	30	5,400
Matches	10,737	10	1,074	90	9,663
Tobacco	121	30	36	70	85
Other native excises	328	50	164	50	164
Total	43,186		18,644		24,452
1939 (Thousand NEI Guilders and Per Cent)					
Liquor and beer	1,461	90	1,315	10	146
Oil (kerosene)	11,585	30	3,476	70	8,110
Gasoline	28,429	70	19,900	30	8,529
Matches	2,372	10	237	90	2,135
Tobacco	18,188	30	5,456	70	12,732
Sugar	6,406	26	1,666	74	4,740
Total	68,441		32,050		36,392
1952 (Thousand Rupiah and Per Cent)					
Alcohol	10,622	90	9,560	10	1,062
Beer	5,835	90	5,252	10	583
Petroleum*	317,141	50	158,570	50	158,570
Tobacco	628,189	30	188,457	70	439,732
Sugar†	117,894	26	30,652	74	87,242
Total	1,079,681		392,491		687,189

*Since the amounts contributed by gasoline and kerosene are not known, an unweighted average of Götzen's percentages is used.

†The sugar excise was introduced in 1934; hence it was not included in Götzen's calculations. Our distribution is assigned on the basis of income distribution in 1939. See J. J. Polak, The National Income of the Netherlands Indies, 1921-1939, Institute of Pacific Relations, New York, 1942.

the duties on smallholders' rubber alone comprised 70 per cent of total receipts from export duties. Thus Götzen's ratio for 1929 (90 per cent falling on the labor-intensive sector) appears to be realistic, and we have adopted this ratio for 1939. Basically, the assumption behind this allocation is that the tax is not significantly shifted forward to foreign buyers, which appears to be empirically valid. The further problem is that the tax may in reality not be shifted back to the original suppliers but may be borne by middlemen. There is some evidence that this may be true. (See Chapter 6.) However, this fact has no great effect on the sectoral allocation of the tax burden since exports from the labor-intensive sector tend to flow through trade channels which are in fact part of this sector. Similarly, exports from the capital-intensive sector are handled almost exclusively through trade facilities in this sector. Thus, at whatever point incidence may fall in the producer-to-exporter chain, it can still be allocated to one or the other major sector with relative accuracy.

For 1952 we have arrived at a ratio for sectoral distribution on the basis of statistics which classify exports between (1) products mainly of Western industry and estates and (2) products mainly of indigenous origin. This breakdown is presented, for example, in the Report of the Java Bank, 1952–1953.

14. Import duties. We are using the average of Götzen's ratios for the years 1926–1932 in the absence of better data. This average indicates that approximately 50 per cent of total imports were consumed by the labor-intensive sector over the period of these years. Again the Götzen method makes a one-direction shifting assumption, positing that all import duties were shifted forward to consumers. Support for this assumption is given by imperfection in the market structure, particularly in the import-distributing trades. Moreover, there is no information available to analyze incidence more carefully through estimating elasticities of supply and demand, and our assumption is in accord with the general proposition that import duties

and consumption taxes fall primarily on the consumer in underdeveloped countries. Since the adoption of the import-surcharge system after 1952, Götzen's ratios have become less realistic; the burden of import duties has probably shifted more heavily in the direction of the capital-intensive sector. This assumption is incorporated in our estimate for the distribution of the tax burden in 1954 and 1956.

15. Transaction taxes (stamp, property transfer, permits and licenses, auction and lottery duties). These taxes, which had little more than nuisance value by 1952, contributed less than 1 per cent of total tax receipts in that year, compared with 6 per cent in 1929. (See Table C-2.) Their allocation by sector is based on Götzen's study.

16. Land taxes. Officially, these taxes were abolished in 1951, but in some areas of Indonesia—particularly Java—they continue to be collected at the low nominal rates and valuations existing in the prewar period. A part of the proceeds, collected by the local governments, is turned over to Central Government. For 1952 these receipts are listed under "receipts from abolished taxes," which totaled only Rp. 283,000. It is clear, therefore, that they had no significant bearing on the sectoral distribution of Central Government's tax burden in that year. Since 1952, however, there has been an attempt in some provinces to collect a new rural income tax in place of the land tax, but receipts to Central Government have been negligible.

Table C-2

DISTRIBUTION OF THE TAX BURDEN, BY SECTOR

1929, 1939, 1952

1929 (Million NEI Guilders and Per Cent)

Type of Tax	Amount of Tax	Capital-Intensive Sector		Labor-Intensive Sector	
		%	Amount	%	Amount
1. Income:					
Business	51.6	100.0	51.6		
Personal	54.4	68.3	37.2	31.7	17.2
2. Wealth and property:					
Urban real estate	6.8	97.0	6.6	3.0	0.2
Household	5.2	94.0	4.9	6.0	0.3
3. Consumption:					
Slaughter	7.0	20.0	1.4	80.0	5.6
Excise	43.2	*	18.7	*	24.5
4. Export and import duties:					
Export	13.0	10.0	1.3	90.0	11.7
Import	95.4	51.5	49.1	48.5	46.3
5. Transaction:					
Stamp	14.2	90.0	12.8	10.0	1.4
Property transfer	2.9	90.0	2.6	10.0	0.3
Permits, licenses, auction, lottery duties	3.9	90.0	3.5	10.0	0.4
6. Land	36.7			100.0	36.7
7. Total allocated taxes	334.3	57.0	189.7	43.0	144.6

*See Table C-1.

Table C-2 (continued)

1939 (Million NEI Guilders and Per Cent)

Type of Tax	Amount of Tax	Capital-Intensive Sector		Labor-Intensive Sector	
		%	Amount	%	Amount
1. Income:					
Business	37.0	100.0	37.0		
Personal	36.9	89.8	33.2	10.2	3.7
Wage	24.8	85.7	21.2	14.3	3.6
2. Wealth and property:					
Capital assets	1.4	100.0	1.4		
Urban real estate	5.0	97.0	4.9	3.0	0.1
Vehicles	0.7	100.0	0.7		
Household	4.0	94.0	3.7	6.0	0.3
3. Consumption:					
Slaughter	4.1	20.0	0.8	80.0	3.3
Excise	68.4	*	32.0	*	36.4
4. Export and import duties:					
Export	20.6	10.0	2.1	90.0	18.5
Import	59.4	50.0	29.7	50.0	29.7
5. Transaction:					
Stamp	8.7	90.0	7.8	10.0	0.9
Property transfer	1.4	90.0	1.3	10.0	0.1
Permits, licenses, auctions, lottery duties	1.8	90.0	1.6	10.0	0.2
6. Land	22.2			100.0	22.2
7. Total allocated taxes	296.4	60.0	177.4	40.0	119.0

*See Table C-1.

Table C-2 (concluded)

1952 (Million Rupiah and Per Cent)

Type of Tax	Amount of Tax	Capital-Intensive Sector		Labor-Intensive Sector	
		%	Amount	%	Amount
1. Income:					
Business	895.5	100.0	895.5		
Personal	647.9	100.0	647 9		
Wage	183.5	85.7	157.3	14.3	26.2
2. Wealth and property:					
Capital assets	11.4	100.0	11.4		
Urban real estate	9.1	97.0	8.8	3.0	0.3
Vehicles	4.3	100.0	4.3		
Household	4.0	94.0	3.7	6.0	0.3
Radio	16.1	90.0	14.5	10.0	1.6
3. Consumption:					
Sales	628.4	50.0	314.2	50.0	314.2
Free market sales	65.8	50.0	32.9	50.0	32.9
Restaurant	20.2	100.0	20.2		
Slaughter	14.7	20.0	2.9	80.0	11.8
Excise	1,079.5	*	392.4	*	687.1
4. Export and import duties:					
Export	3,900.7	63.0	2,457.4	37.0	1,443.3
Import	1,443.9	50.0	721.9	50.0	721.9
5. Transaction:					
Stamp	43.7	90.0	39.3	10.0	4.4
Property transfer	10.7	90.0	9.7	10.0	1.0
Permits, licenses, auctions, lottery duties	10.5	90.0	9.5	10.0	1.0
6. Total allocated taxes	8,989.9	64.0	5,743.8	36.0	3,246.0

*See Table C-1.

Table C-3

OCCUPATIONAL DISTRIBUTION, BY SECTOR, 1950*

(Thousands)

	Capital-Intensive Sector	Labor-Intensive Sector
Agriculture:		
Nonestate		15,950.0
Plantation:		
Rubber	110.0	
Tobacco		250.0
Tea	60.0	55.0
Sugar	45.0	45.0
Other	1,135.0	
Subtotal	1,350.0	16,300.0
Mining	600.0	
Manufacturing	280.0	1,720.0
Transportation	555.0	
Commerce	1,000.0	1,000.0
Professions	210.0	
Government	500.0	
Other	1,242.5	1,242.5
Total	5,737.5	20,262.5

*Source of basic employment data: Human Relations Area Files, Inc., Yale University, Indonesia, Vol. III, Table I, p. 870.

APPENDIX D

NASRUN COMMITTEE RECOMMENDATIONS ON INTERGOVERNMENTAL FISCAL RELATIONSHIPS

The Nasrun Committee was appointed to study the problems of financial relations between central and local governments in Indonesia. It is a continuing committee composed of fiscal experts from various government departments. After intensive investigation of the problems involved in the fiscal sphere of central-local relationships, the committee offered its recommendations on the matters to which it had addressed itself.

The committee concerned itself with two major problems germane to the financial relation between central and local governments: (1) the distribution of taxable resources and tax yields and (2) the allocation of equalization grants (subsidies) among the various levels of local government. The problem of division of the expenditure function has not been explicitly dealt with in the committee's recommendations.

The committee recommended a complex system which would provide for the financing of local governments by two major sources of income, one exclusively local and the other from a fund composed of part of the receipts from important Central Government taxes. Its recommendations were based on the premise that tax bases assigned to local levels of government would be inadequate to meet their income requirements; local governments were to be made permanently dependent on Central Government revenue collections for a substantial part of their support.

To provide this revenue structure for the support of local governments, the Nasrun Committee devised a system of six types of revenue to be fully or partially available to local levels of government: (1) local taxes or retributions now in existence or to be adopted in the future are to remain as special daerah taxes, exclusively for the use of local levels of government. These include present legal local taxes such as the pasar tax, the amusement tax, the bicycle, betjak, and dog taxes as well as a variety of retributions of the type referred to in the review of kabupaten finance in West Java (Chapter 7). (2) Present Central Government taxes to be transferred to the jurisdiction of localities: to provinces, the urban real estate tax (verponding), the household tax (personeele belasting), and the vehicle tax; to kabupaten, the road tax* and the copra tax.† The native real estate tax (verponding Indonesia), the slaughter tax, and the reconstruction tax‡ are to be transferred to kabupaten or kota, depending on whether the taxed instrument falls within kabupaten or kota jurisdiction. It is argued that taxes are assigned to particular levels of government to promote efficient enforcement and to prevent evasion. Taxes which require detailed knowledge of local facilities are therefore assigned to kabupaten and kota. (3) In addition, 90 per cent of the proceeds collected by Central Government from the padjak ketjil and that part of the wages tax not collected by the withholding system are to be remitted to kabupaten and kota. In addition, a general fund for support of local governments is to draw heavily upon Central Government revenues. This fund will include 90 per cent of the proceeds from the regular income tax, the regular wage tax, and the stamp tax as well as varying percentages§ from the capital assets (vermogens) tax and the company tax. (4) Similarly, a varying part of the proceeds from import duties, export duties, and excises are to be transferred to this fund. (5) Surcharges on special export duties and excises may be imposed on products

*A tax on properties fronting along roads.

†In East Indonesia, where the kabupaten level may not yet be formed, the copra tax may be claimed by local autonomies of similar level of jurisdiction.

‡A tax on restaurant consumption.

§The percentage to be allocated to this fund is to be determined each year.

produced in given areas (e.g., East Java, coffee), the proceeds of which are to be assigned to a fund to be distributed between the provinces (25 per cent) and kabupaten (75 per cent) in which these special imposts are levied. (6) Finally, the incomes of local governments will include Central Government donations, subsidies, and provisions for financing remaining deficits.

These recommendations on the division of revenue sources were accepted by the committee and apparently were the basis for Parliament's 1956 declaration of principles on the division of revenue sources. This declaration has not yet been put into effect by further legislation.* There is the further problem of working out a compromise to give local governments a share of revenues from the taxes to be defined as Central Government revenue sources. The committee proposed a set of principles to determine the distribution of the proceeds flowing into the fund under revenue types 3, 4, and 5. These principles guide the distribution of proceeds only among provinces; proposals for distribution to lower levels (kabupaten and municipalities) are yet to be made by each provincial administration and approved by Central Government. The 1956 legislation apparently follows the Nasrun proposals on the issue of distributing the yields from Central Government taxes.

The total amount of revenue made available through the fund from Central Government taxes is to be distributed each year by computing a theoretical index of deficits for the provinces by formulas including a number of factors.† The theoretical level of expenditures for each province is computed from a formula including eight factors,‡ each given a particular

*The details of the 1956 legislation are presented in Appendix E.

†To my knowledge these proposals are available only in Indonesian. This account is based on J. de Bruine, "Pembahagian Kepada Daerah daripada Bahadiannja dalam hasil Padjak Pusat" (Distribution of Central Revenues to Daerah), Ekonomi dan Keuangan Indonesia, Vol. VI, No. 6 (June 1952), pp. 361-367.

‡These eight factors and their weights are: (a) area = 1, (b) population = 4, (c) economic potential = 3, (d) educational level of the population = 5, (e) index of prices = 2, (f) extent of roads supported by Central Government = 2, (g) extent of provincial irrigation canals = 1, (h) geographic structure = 1.

weight (coefficient) for a given province and a general weight to rank its importance relative to the other factors in the formula. The theoretical level of provincial revenues is calculated by a similar formula comprising five factors,* also weighted according to their relative importance and by province. The actual (noncomputed) ratio of revenues to expenditures is then estimated for each province, and this ratio is used as a weight to obtain an index of deficits for each province. The general index can then be used to determine the share of total revenues to be allocated to individual provinces.

It is clear from de Bruine's writings and the thinking of the Nasrun Committee that the greater part of provincial, kabupaten, and kota income is expected to come from funds collected through the Central Government fiscal system. No provision is made for allocation of revenue bases to the lowest level of administration, the desa, pending their reorganization into a new administrative unit, the kota ketjil.

In addition to the funds from specific tax sources to which localities have a legitimate claim, the Nasrun Committee proposed an elaborate subsidy system. This system provides for several types of transfer payments to local governments.† The first type of transfer payment involves an element of compensation.‡ Nominally, Central Government functions which are farmed out to the administration of localities are eligible for full Central Government support. Functions which have been transferred to localities are eligible for partial or full Central Government support until the locality can provide its own financing.

*These factors are area, population, economic potential, educational level of the population, and index of prices.

†The following account is based on J. de Bruine, "Uitkeringen, Subsidies en Bijdragen aan Daerahs in het Kader van de Financieele Verhouding" (Expenditures, Subsidies, and Grants to Localities in Connection with the Financial Relationships), Ekonomi dan Keuangan Indonesia, Vol. VII, February 1954, pp. 127-129.

‡Dutch, Uitkeringen; Indonesian, Pembajaran.

Secondly, transfer payments of a short-term nature will be made on an ad rem basis. A particular daerah can qualify for such payments (subsidies)* on the basis of providing a service which has some bearing on the general welfare or on suffering a natural disaster beyond the resources of the locality. Finally, special grants† may be made to cover temporary deficits. These are viewed as emergency grants to cover fiscal adjustments until the locality can mobilize its own resources to cover the gap. Structural deficits must be corrected by structural changes in the expenditure-revenue pattern rather than by regularization of such grants.

Evaluation of the Nasrun Proposals‡

The Concept of Division of Fiscal Functions: The Nasrun Committee recommendations for the division of fiscal functions, particularly on the revenue side, are posited on the premise that substantial amounts of local government income must be collected through the Central Government fiscal system. This premise implies the further assumption that the "correct" level of local expenditures is beyond the revenue resources which can be most efficiently exploited by local collection agencies. The committee has repeatedly urged that particular taxes should be assigned to the level of administration most capable of enforcing them. Yet there has been no empirical research or theoretical inquiry into the matter of taxable capacity which could be most effectively reached through local tax administration.

The Nasrun distribution of tax bases has, in fact, neither simplified the tax structure nor attacked the problem of an extremely complex administrative problem for the tax system as a whole. Taxes which have not been lucrative revenue producers and which would be difficult to administer at

*Dutch, Subsidie; Indonesian, Subsidi.

†Dutch, Bijdragen; Indonesian, Tundjangan.

‡The 1956 legislation on central-local fiscal relationships was based upon the Nasrun proposals. An evaluation of this legislation and recommendations for improvement, taken from the Dris report, are reproduced in Appendix E.

any level of government (household, slaughter, and reconstruction taxes) have been transferred to local levels of government. On the other hand, innumerable local levies and retributions have not been abandoned. Potentially lucrative local revenue bases which have not been yielding significant revenues to Central Government have been retained for Central Government collection; the outstanding example of this category is the padjak peralihan ketjil (literally, transition small tax). As a matter of actual practice this tax is currently collected through local governments and remitted to Central Government. Our survey of local finances in West Java and Central Sumatra revealed that there is a significant amount of taxable capacity subject to this tax which is not being reached. It was repeatedly emphasized that local authorities were unwilling to maximize revenues from this source since the proceeds were to be remitted to the treasury in Djakarta.

An alternative approach would therefore assign major revenue bases to local levels of government, reducing the amounts to be transferred from Central Government resources to legitimate disaster, promotional, and deficit-covering subsidies. This approach can be defended both on equity and on economic grounds. On the ground of equity, it is questionable whether purely local-benefit-yielding expenditures should be financed from centrally collected revenues. On economic grounds, it is clear that revenue bases, such as that reached by the padjak peralihan ketjil, which lie close to local administration would produce maximum revenues if assigned to the local levels of government and related to local benefit. This would remove a major political obstacle, by which Central Government has been hamstrung, to reaching far down the scale of incomes in the rural sector. It would partially correct the unequal distribution of the total tax burden which has resulted from recent shifts in income toward the rural sector while the burden of taxation has shifted toward the capital-intensive sector.

In the Outer Islands, where the need for developmental expenditures is greatest, the shift in incomes and generally increased incomes in the rural sector have been most apparent. It was felt by local officials in Central Sumatra that assignment of taxation of rural incomes to the kabupaten and desa levels of government in these areas would go far toward financing their present levels of expenditure. Even on Java it was pointed out that the present legal rates of the income tax are not assessed against agricultural incomes. In Central Sumatra, local fiscal authorities believed that the income tax rates against agricultural incomes in particular could be increased if this tax were collected for the support of local expenditures.

Although local governments should not be prohibited from exploiting other noncentral tax bases, they should be urged to concentrate their limited administrative resources on direct levies such as the income tax. The income line dividing this tax base between Central Government and local collection could be adjusted so that primarily rural incomes fall within local jurisdiction and at a level to cover the greater part of local expenditures.

The Nasrun Formulas for Distributing Centrally Collected Revenues: If the general Nasrun recommendations are eventually implemented, the formulas for distributing the proceeds of centrally collected taxes among the provinces will be of importance since such transfers are intended to comprise a major share of income of local governments. In fact, the fallibility of any formula for computing transfers of Central Government revenues to local governments is a further reason for preserving maximum local autonomy in the matter of revenue sources.

The distribution proposals enunciated by the Nasrun Committee may be evaluated in terms of their bearing on Indonesian economic development. The major problem is that the formulas do not furnish an accurate measure of either need or ability, the two variables according to which Central Government transfers to local governments should be allocated if uniform economic development is to take place throughout Indonesia. It is particularly important that this goal be considered in light of the colonial background of the Indonesian economy. Educational, communication, health, and other essential facilities were not uniformly developed throughout the islands. The development of Java is strikingly advanced compared to that of the Outer Islands. One finds that ability (in the fiscal sense) is often least where need is greatest. Hence conscious equalization policy, based on the variation of need for these basic facilities and the varying abilities of the provinces to provide them out of their own resources, is required to correct the disparity.

The Nasrun formulas provide no direct measure of the need for such facilities or the ability to produce local resources to provide them. The variables in the formulas represent an indirect measure based on population, length of roads, educational level, economic potential, the level of prices, and other factors which do not specifically measure need or ability. The weights assigned to these factors will inevitably be arbitrary, and in some cases will reflect the opposite of need and ability. The assumption behind the selection of the variables determining the hypothetical level of expenditures is that the provinces with more developed facilities will require a higher level of expenditures to maintain them. Thus <u>need</u> in the Nasrun proposals is related to maintenance of existing facilities rather than to development of new ones. It is clear that the proposals are not intended to allocate revenues on the basis of providing a minimum standard of local facilities such as roads, schools, and police protection throughout Indonesia.

The principles behind the Nasrun distribution scheme have some merit from the incentive point of view. A higher level of local expenditures in the higher-income areas, where the educational level of the population is above the average, may provide inducements to strive for higher social and economic positions. This would seem to account for the high premium now placed on government service in Djakarta, where Central Government expenditures for the civil servant's housing and other amenities have been relatively great. However, some thought should be given to the consequences of perpetuating regional differences in economic conditions and welfare. Higher levels of local expenditures in the wealthier provinces will widen regional price and income differentials and might produce local pockets of inflation. While the goal of providing some standard level of local facilities is based on a value judgment, it is a judgment which has been generally followed by democratic countries elsewhere.

If need and ability are to be accurately measured, they should be related to estimates of specific needs and careful studies of taxable capacity. On the need side of the ledger, some standard level of minimum local facilities could be employed, and the variation in annual costs to bring all localities up to the level of these minimum standards could be estimated. For example, the local cost of providing and maintaining certain minimum room space per student in local schools, minimum teaching hours per student, and minimum supplies could be based on the variations in their present supply in given areas and the local cost of expansion of facilities. Ability, too, could be measured from direct indicators rather than by the general factors included in the Nasrun formulas. The measure of ability would ideally be based on the variation in existing taxable capacity and the present tax burden by locality.* When total financial capacity is thus estimated, it could be compared with total financial need in each province as a basis for distributing Central Government revenues. If these criteria were employed, distribution in the next several years would have to be made on the basis of virtually no knowledge of these variations, particularly on the matter of financial need.† Thus the scheme to allot substantial shares of Central Government revenues to local levels of government should be complemented by detailed studies of regional variations in financial need and ability.

The Nasrun recommendation that <u>definite</u> percentages of major Central Government revenues be assigned to the fund for localities should also be

*For example, by an estimate of the ratio of local taxes collected to per capita income.

†It is believed, however, that need and ability as used here could be more easily estimated than such intangible factors in the Nasrun formulas as economic potential, educational level, and geographic structure.

scrutinized. Yields from the major taxes* to be distributed to the provinces—the income tax, company tax, and wages tax—tend to fluctuate widely in response to changes in Indonesia's balance of payments. Varying percentages from export and import duties are also to be allocated to the provinces; while the Nasrun Committee is not specific on this point, it is probable that these percentages would actually fall in periods of budgetary stringency resulting from adverse balance-of-payments movements to which yields from these duties are particularly sensitive. Consequently, the cyclical influences in Central Government finance would be strongly transmitted to local finance. It would be preferable to base local finance more directly on the rural sector (which does not respond as directly to balance-of-payments changes) or, alternatively, to define the Central Government function as compensatory to local finance. Previous periods of deflation in Indonesia have resulted in greatly reduced subsidies to localities. These reductions have ordinarily resulted in drastic curtailment of local capital budgets, followed by cuts in current expenditures.

Adjustment through the government fiscal process could be achieved by maintaining the total of the local equalization fund at a level sufficient to meet local needs as defined above. This could be developed into an effective means of sustaining and dispersing effective demand throughout the economy in periods of domestic deflation resulting from transmitted foreign stimuli. Under the Nasrun system of equalization fund and subsidies, the compensatory mechanism could be operated through the subsidy system when fixed or falling percentages of Central Government revenues result in reduced income to localities. If the compensatory principle is explicitly recognized and employed, it could be used at the level of local finance to mobilize resources released from normal employment (as a result of cyclical forces) for developmental projects.

*90 per cent of which are to be transferred to the funds for local levels of government.

APPENDIX E

1956 LEGISLATION ON CENTRAL - LOCAL FISCAL RELATIONSHIPS*

An Act of 31 Dec. 1956 laid down regulation for allocating fiscal sources of revenue between the central Government and the regional authorities. In principle the following taxes are allocated to the regions: (a) land tax (verponding), (b) personal tax (poll tax), (c) motor-vehicle tax, (d) livestock slaughter tax, (e) reconstruction tax (on hotel and restaurant turnover), (f) tolls (on certain roads), and (g) tax on copra. Until such time as the regulation enforcing this Act is passed, 90 per cent of the revenue from the above taxes is to be allocated to the regions, starting with the 1957 financial year. In addition, the regions will receive a share of the revenue from the following taxes:

Tax on individual income Tax on wages Stamp duty Property tax (tax on inherited property) Company tax	Minimum allocation 75 per cent, maximum 90 per cent Percentage of allocation to be determined annually by Government order
Import, export and excise duties:	Percentage of allocation and bonus in favour of the producing regions, to be determined annual by government order.

So far there has been no government order taking measure to implement this Act.

*Direct quotation from M. D. Dris, "Taxation in Indonesia," Ekonomi dan Keuangan Indonesia, Vol. XI, August-September, 1958, p. 408.

APPENDIX F

EQUITABLE DISTRIBUTION OF REVENUE SOURCES BETWEEN THE CENTRAL GOVERNMENT AND THE LOCAL AUTHORITIES*

Existing Legislation

301. As was pointed out in paragraph 12, an Act of 31 December 1956 laid down rules for the distribution of revenue sources between the central Government and the autonomous regions (daerahs). The Act in question is an "umbrella" act, i.e., it lays down the general principles on which the distribution is to be based and provides that the details of the arrangement shall be embodied in government ordinances. For example, the taxes to be transferred to the regions, the designating of the regions and the period of the transfer are left to the decision of the Government (article 3). Similarly, the percentages of State taxes to be transferred to the regions are to be determined by government ordinances (articles 4 and 5) either annually and within certain limits (property tax and company tax: between 75 and 90 per cent) or for periods and within limits not laid down by law (income tax). Under article 6, the procedure for allocating State taxes among the regions is also to be determined by the Government according to such criteria as the size of the region, the number of inhabitants, its economic potentialities, population trends, cost of living, extent of the road and irrigation facilities maintained by the region and geographical classification (e.g., an island).

302. Under article 10 of the Act, an advisory commission consisting of seven members appointed by the Government is to be set up for a period of five years. Its chairman is to be one of the Government-appointed members, and its rules of procedure are to be laid down by government ordinance. This commission is to be consulted concerning the measures for giving effect to the Act, and it may, on its own initiative, submit recommendations to the Ministries of Home Affairs and Finance concerning any questions of regional finance connected with the financial relations between the central Government and the regions.

*Direct quotation from M. D. Dris, "Taxation in Indonesia," Ekonomi dan Keuangan Indonesia, Vol. XI, August-September 1958, pp. 523-527.

303. According to information obtained by the undersigned, no Government ordinance embodying regulations necessary for giving effect to the Act has so far been made. The problem of regional autonomy has, moreover, become very acute in consequence of events which have occurred in certain regions outside Java since 1956. For some months now the Government has been concentrating on this situation and, in a desire to arrive at a conciliatory solution, is said to be contemplating a conference of representatives of the central Government and the regional authorities to be held from 10 to 12 September.

Recommendations

304. It is at present uncertain what regions (provinces, districts, etc.) will be recognized as autonomous and how much autonomy will be granted to them, particularly as regards the nature and extent of the responsibilities and duties to be transferred to them by the central Government. As no specific recommendations can therefore be made concerning the criteria to be adopted for the distribution of revenue sources, nothing more than some general suggestions on the most equitable methods of distribution will be given.

305. In the first place, regional autonomy should, of course, mean an increase in the responsibilities as well as in the powers of the regional authorities. If those authorities are to be induced to use public money with prudence and moderation, they should be allowed, wherever possible, to levy, in their own territory, the taxes freely and expressly decreed with the approval of the regional assemblies in matters which are not legally and exclusively reserved for the central Government and are distinctly territorial in character. In that way, inter-regional disputes and double taxation will be avoided. Such freedom as regards taxation should be combined with respect for the general principles of national legislation and should not infringe upon the general interest. In any event, some higher authority should have the power to suspend or annual a regional decision instituting a tax that did not meet one of the above requirements. In accordance with the nature and the degree of autonomy accorded to the regions, this higher authority could be the Minister of Home Affairs or whatever minister was responsible for relations with the regions, the President of the Republic acting for the Government, or the Supreme Court acting on the application of any individual or body corporate concerned with regional taxes and including the regional authorities and the central Government.

Such an arrangement would not be entirely in line with the basic principles on which the Act of 31 December 1956 is based. It is designed to give the regions wider powers in the choice of their sources of revenue and in adapting those sources to the condition peculiar to their territory. It would probably go far towards developing a sense of financial responsibility among those who exercise regional powers.

306. As yet, many regions do not, of course, possess the administrative machinery needed for assessing and collecting taxes. Wherever necessary, the service of the State could and should, at any agreed rate of remuneration, impose and collect, on behalf of the regions, various taxes capable of producing substantial revenue, such as the tax on landed property, with the possible addition of the proposed local surtax (paragraphs 218–221); the reconstruction tax; the tax on the slaughter of livestock; the road tax (pending its abolition); entertainment, betting and lottery taxes; and so on. In addition, the State might, on behalf of the regions, collect the additional percentages to certain taxes, such as the motor-vehicle tax. To avoid practical difficulties, the regional taxes and surcharges thus collected by the State should be determined according to procedures laid down agreements of a standard type and at rates ranging between minimum and maximum levels fixed by the Government. It should be clearly understood, however, that these taxes would be levied on the authority of the region and collected on its behalf. Where the regional authorities were already responsible for the assessment and collection of certain State taxes, they would henceforth collect those taxes on their own behalf. This would be the case, for example, with the income tax as it applies to persons earning less than Rp. 5,000 (cf. paragraphs 107–109) and with the sales tax and the tax on wages below Rp. 6,000 which are collected on a flat-rate basis in respect of small-scale undertakings.

Where a region did not make adequate use of regional taxes and of the additional percentages to such taxes, i.e., where it applied rates below the minimum levels laid down by the Government or where it failed to impose some of the basic taxes, it would be excluded from any share in the joint participation fund, to which reference is made below.

307. Apart from the revenue derived from their own tax system, it would seem equitable, as provided for in the Act of 31 December 1956, that regions producing raw materials for export or general commodities subject to excise duties (such as petroleum products) should be given a special share in the export or excise duties collected on such materials and commodities. The revenue from this source should, it is felt, be allocated mainly for such regional capital expenditure as is not directly productive (e.g., education, public health, communications) and thus cannot normally be financed by loans.

308. There is the further consideration that population density, levels of living, natural resources and the degree of economic advancement vary considerably from one region to another throughout Indonesia. While some territories can, by the methods described above, obtain an appreciable

part of the revenue necessary for current administration and other expenses of a purely regional character, other territories which are naturally poorer, over-populated or economically underdeveloped will continue to be reliant on State aid to cover much of their essential expenditure. It would therefore seem that a regional joint-participation fund, maintained by contributions from the tax revenue of the State as a whole after the deductions referred to in paragraph 307 had been made, is indispensable if a certain balance between the various regions is to be achieved. This, in fact, is the object of articles 4 to 6 of the Act of 31 December 1956.

The size of these contributions would be likely to vary under the influence of various factors such as the excess of State revenue over current budgetary expenditure, on the one hand, and the excess of regional budgetary expenditure over regional minimum resources, on the other. Every year, therefore, a balance would have to be struck between national and regional needs, although the regions would have to be given some legally-established guarantee of a minimum share in State revenue (a percentage or a specified sum that would be subject to revision if the State revenue rose or fell considerably). This suggestion likewise corresponds to the provisions of articles 4 to 6 of the above-mentioned Act.

309. The allocation among the various regions of moneys from the joint-participation fund raises extremely complex and delicate problems. Article 6 of the Act of 31 December 1956 contains a number of criteria for that purpose, but, in the absence of a population census and in view of the inadequacy of statistics, most of these criteria cannot be reliably and accurately defined. As, moreover, the relative importance of each of the criteria will have to be determined arbitrarily, endless discussion and disputes can be expected to result. What is more, on account will be taken in this allocation of the amount of revenue collected by each region. Some territories might therefore benefit from State aid without exhausting their own tax resources, with the result that the amount available to other regions which are really unable to balance their budget will be correspondingly reduced.

310. In these circumstances, it is considered that the allocation of moneys to the various territories from the joint participation fund should be made annually on a more accurate and reliable basis and preferably in two stages as follows:

(a) Each region, except those which have not imposed the minimum of basic regional taxes prescribed by the Government, should receive the amount which, after deduction of its own revenue is necessary to cover ordinary expenditure, i.e., noncapital expenditure, or, in case the regional joint-participation fund is inadequate, a proportion of that amount;

(b) Each of the regions specified in sub-paragraph (a) should receive either the balance not covered by its own revenue—or possibly also by the allocation referred to in paragraph 307—which is necessary to meet capital expenditure regarded as urgent (e.g., public health, communications, irrigation, etc.), or a proportion of that balance if the assets of the fund do not permit full satisfaction of all needs.

311. The regional joint-participation fund should be administered by a council presided over by a representative of the central Government and consisting of members appointed in equal numbers by the central Government and by the regions. This council should have extensive rights of investigation and decision concerning matters that basically affect the allocation. It would, in particular, be able, when determining allocation requirements, to exclude current expenditure for which there was little or no justification and capital expenditure which up to a minimum percentage (subsequently to be determined) was not covered by other resources of the regions in question, including loans. It would, in the light of experience, make recommendations designed to improve the functioning of the fund. The chairman of the council would have power to suspend the execution of any decision regarded by him as contrary to the public interest and to notify the Government to that effect through the competent Minister (Finance, Home Affairs or of Inter-Regional Relations). Failing a government decision within, say, one month, the disputed decision would again become fully operative. Needless to say, the arrangement just described would by no means preclude the granting of extraordinary subsidies to regions in order to cover part of the cost of special or particularly important works or investments affecting not only regional development but also the national economy as a whole.

APPENDIX G

TOTAL U.S. ECONOMIC ASSISTANCE TO INDONESIA, 1950-1957

Table G-1

INTERNATIONAL COOPERATION ADMINISTRATION AID TO INDONESIA, 1950-1957

Fiscal Year	Obligations (Thousand Dollars)	Expenditures (Thousand Dollars)
1950	...	...
1951	7,973	200
1952	-1,874	5,899
1953	13,199	2,755
1954	4,357	5,337
1955	6,962	5,397
1956	10,147	7,400
1957	10,983	8,347
1958 (first half)	1,471	4,174
Total*	53,218	39,509

*Total of unrounded figures.

Source: International Cooperation Administration, Operations Report, FY 1958 Issue No. 2, p. 47.

Table G-2

SURPLUS AGRICULTURAL COMMODITY AID TO INDONESIA (UNDER PUBLIC LAW 480) THROUGH DECEMBER 1957

Fiscal Year	Thousand Dollars
1957	50,542
1958 (first half)	17,610
Total	68,152

Source: International Cooperation Administration, Counterpart Funds and ICA Foreign Currency Accounts.

Table G-3

EXPORT - IMPORT BANK LOANS TO INDONESIA, 1950 - 1957

(Thousand Dollars)

Purpose	Date	Amount	Dispensed	Out-standing
Development projects	2- 8-50	1,055	...	...
Transportation program	7-27-50	32,100	31,180	27,175
Telecommunications development	9-21-50	260	260	227
Dredging equipment, harbor construction	10-19-50	6,700	6,317	5,511
Railroad rehabilitation	11- 3-50	17,100	15,358	13,398
Aircraft and equipment	11-30-50	6,023	6,023	5,249
Electrification	1-25-51	3,586	3,582	3,123
Forest development	7-26-51	979	979	853
Marine engines	3- 6-52	1,820	1,820	1,586
Cement plant	6-24-53	14,700	11,813	10,609
Aircraft and equipment	5-17-56	7,500	...	...
Telecommunications equipment	11- 1-56	1,700	...	...
Diesel locomotive equipment	11-16-56	6,477	...	...
Aircraft and spare parts	11-22-57	1,781	...	...
Total*		101,781	77,332	67,732

*Total of unrounded figures.

Source: Export-Import Bank of Washington, Report to the Congress for the Period July-December, 1957, Government Printing Office, Washington, D.C., 1958, pp. 28-29.

APPENDIX H

FOREIGN CAPITAL INVESTMENT BILL*

The President of the Republic of Indonesia

Considering that:

In the interest of accelerating economic development in Indonesia, as well as increasing national production in order to raise the people's standard of living, capital is needed,

Capital available in Indonesia at this time is not sufficient, so that it is deemed advantageous to invite capital to be invested in Indonesia,

In order to obtain capital for national development, it is necessary to give a clear definition of the situation in order to avoid doubts on the part of foreign investors,

Considering furthermore,

Article 38, paragraphs 2 and 3, of the Indonesian Provision Constitution,

It has been decided, with the approval of Parliament, to issue a Law on Foreign Investments in Indonesia.

SECTION I
Article 1

This law interprets:

(1) Production—as any effort to produce commodities and services.
(2) Enterprise—as any combination of undertakings and/or means to produce commodities and/or services.
(3) Enterpriser—as an individual or body corporate owning an enterprise.
(4) Foreign enterpriser—as an enterpriser of non-Indonesian nationality or a legal person considered as alien by the Council, who owns

*This translation of the complete text, as passed by Parliament on September 15, 1958, was published in American Indonesian Chamber of Commerce, Inc., Information Bulletin, No. 551, October 23, 1958.

an enterpriser either wholly or partially.

(5) Council—the Council of Foreign Capital Investments, as stipulated in Article 18.

(6) Foreign capital—as capital stipulated in Article 14.

SECTION II

Article 2

Foreign capital is allowed to operate in the field of production under limitations in regard to the kinds of enterprises as stipulated in Article 3 and taking into consideration the provisions contained in Article 4.

Article 3

(1) Enterprises as follows:

- (a) Railways
- (b) Telecommunications
- (c) National shipping and government aviation
- (d) Generation of electric power
- (e) Irrigation and water supply
- (f) Manufacture of arms and ammunition
- (g) Generation of atomic energy
- (h) Mining of vital materials

are closed to foreign capital.

(2) What is stipulated in paragraph 1 shall not dimish the right of the State to employ foreign capital in the form of loans or under specific conditions.

Article 4

(1) Enterprises usually undertaken by Indonesian nationals are closed to foreign capital.

(2) The kind of enterprises as stipulated in paragraph 1 shall be determined by the Council.

(3) For specified enterprises, the territory or region for foreign capital operation shall be determined by the Council.

(4) The stipulation in paragraph 1 shall not diminish the right of the Council to regulate a method of operation similar to foreign capital, aimed at increasing the standard of and stepping up of production, in the field of enterprise mentioned.

(5) Requests for a joint operation between an enterpriser and foreign capital, on the one hand, and an enterpriser and national capital, on the other, shall be given priority.

SECTION III
Domicile
Article 5

(1) Undertakings operated wholly or for a greater portion in Indonesia as a separate unit of enterprise shall be set up as a legal body in accordance with Indonesian laws and with domicile in Indonesia.

(2) Whether an enterprise shall operate wholly or for a greater portion in Indonesia as a separate unit shall be determined by the Council.

SECTION IV
The Use of Land
Article 6

Land rights for industries:

(1) For the purpose of setting up an industrial enterprise considered important for the State, rights may be granted on land for a period of 20 years, under the name of construction rights.

(2) This 20-year period of time may be extended in consideration of the state of the enterprise.

Article 7

Land rights for large agricultural enterprises:

(1) For the purpose of large agricultural enterprises, land rights may be granted for a maximum period of 30 years, under the name of industrial rights; in specific cases, according to the nature of the crops undertaken by large agricultural enterprises concerned, industrial rights may be granted for a maximum period of 40 years.

(2) The period of time stipulated in paragraph 1 may be extended in consideration of the state of the enterprise.

Leases
Article 8

For the purpose of enterprises other than as stipulated in Article 6 and 7, the system of leases may be used for a maximum period of 10 years.

Article 9

Construction rights, industrial rights and lease rights are regulated by separate legislation.

SECTION V
Use of Manpower
Article 10

(1) The Council determines the number of foreign personnel that may be employed by each foreign enterprise.

(2) The provision in paragraph 1 contains the stipulation also regarding education and employment of Indonesian personnel and the target time when said education and employment shall be completely fulfilled.

(3) The Council exercises supervision over the methods of implementing the provisions on the basis of paragraph 2.

SECTION VI
Facilities and Guarantees
Article 11

Double taxation: Prevention of double taxation shall be undertaken as through international agreements.

Corporation Tax
Article 12

Laws and/or regulations aimed at lightening the burden of corporation taxes, the method of specific depreciation of capital goods, reduction or compensation for specific damages, exemption from the collection of stamp duties and reduction of import duties on equipment and materials needed in the enterprise may prevail also for foreign enterprises, after permission of the Council on behalf of the Government has been obtained.

Article 13

(1) To industrial enterprises a guarantee may be given, that they shall not be nationalized or changed into national ownership, during a maximum period of 20 years.

(2) The period of time stipulated in paragraph 1 shall be 30 years for large foreign agricultural enterprises.

(3) On the expiration of the period of guarantee, the question of change of ownership to national ownership may be regulated by the Council.

SECTION VII
Definition of Foreign Capital
Article 14

Foreign capital is defined as follows:

(a) Foreign exchange which does not constitute a part of the Indonesian foreign exchange reserves, and, with the permission of the authorities in Indonesia, is used for the financing of an enterprise in Indonesia.

(b) Equipment for the enterprise, including new inventions, the property of foreigners, and materials imported from outside the territory of Indonesia, as long as the equipment concerned shall not be paid for out of the Indonesian foreign exchange reserves.

(c) Part of the profits of the enterprise which, based on existing laws, are allowed to be transferred but is used for the financing of the enterprise in Indonesia.

Fixing the Size of Foreign Capital
Article 15

(1) Foreign enterprises set up after the enactment of this law shall conduct a separate administration of their foreign capital.

(2) In fixing the amount of foreign capital in an enterprise, its amount shall be that sum which remains after deduction of the amount which has been transferred through repatriation.

(3) Every year before August 1 enterprises are obligated to submit to the Council a statement of their foreign capital.

Transfers for Enterprises
Article 16

(1) Without diminishing the possibility of permits for transfers based on Article 17, and without diminishing the effects of paragraph 3 of this Article, profits of enterprises that are allowed to be transferred shall be:

(a) Profits after deduction of taxes payable in Indonesia and other obligations have been fulfilled.
(b) Costs relating to the employment of foreign personnel in the enterprise in accordance with existing regulations.

(2) Profits enumerated in paragraph 1, sub-paragraph a, shall be interpreted as profits of enterprises after deduction of all necessary costs to earn and maintain the profits concerned, including depreciation on capital goods as is customary in industry.

(3) (a) Profits may be transferred wholly, provided that the whole capital is foreign capital.
(b) In the event that enterprises are partially composed of foreign capital, profit transfers shall be allowed in accordance with the proportion between the foreign and Indonesian capital.

Transfers for Repatriation of Foreign Capital
Article 17

(1) Foreign capital may be granted permits for transfers in the original currency after the enterprises concerned have been operating for some time, in accordance with the decisions of the Council.

(2) All other transfers which are not permitted on the basis of Article 16 shall be considered as repatriation of foreign capital.

SECTION VIII
Council for Foreign Investments
Article 18

(1) Under this Act a Council for Foreign Investments shall be set up, composed of:

(a) The Minister of Industry, as Chairman and, concurrently, Member
(b) The Minister of Finance, as Vice-Chairman and, concurrently, Member
(c) The Minister of Foreign Affairs, as Member
(d) The Minister of Trade, as Member
(e) The Minister of Labor, as Member
(f) The Director-General of the State Planning Bureau, as Member
(g) The Governor of Bank Indonesia, as Member

(2) The Council shall receive its directives from the Council of Ministers, and shall be responsible to the Council of Ministers.

(3) The Council shall be assisted by a secretariat to be named by the Council.

Article 19

Without diminishing the authority of the Council as stipulated in the above Articles, the Council may determine the conditions and exercise the supervision deemed necessary to make this Act effective, insofar as such authority is not held by another agency.

SECTION IX
Provisions for Interregnum Period
Article 20

Prior to enactment of the laws stipulated in Article 9, foreign capital enterprises may be granted "erfpact" (long lease) rights, "opstal" (construction) rights and "grondhuur" (land rent) rights, in accordance with provisions in existing regulations, without prejudice to provisions regarding the periods of time stipulated in the present Act.

SECTION X
Conclusion
Article 21

This Act shall go into effect on the date of its promulgation.

In order that its contents may become generally known this Act shall be published in the State Gazette.

APPENDIX I

STATISTICAL TABLES

Note: In the following tables, ... indicates data not available; — indicates amount is nil or negligible.

LIST OF STATISTICAL TABLES

LIST OF STATISTICAL TABLES (concluded)

Table I-1

GOVERNMENT GROSS REVENUE, GROSS EXPENDITURE, AND BUDGET AND CASH DEFICITS, 1950-1959

(Billion Rp.)

Year	Gross Revenue	Gross Expenditure	Budget Deficit	Cash Deficit
1950*	7.0	8.7	- 1.7	...
1951†	11.8	10.6	+ 1.2	...
1952†	12.3	15.0	- 2.7	- 5.4
1953†	13.6	15.7	- 2.1	- 3.1
1954†	11.5	15.1	- 3.6	- 3.5
1955†	14.2	16.3	- 2.1	- 1.8
1956†	19.2	20.8	- 1.6	- 2.3
1957*	20.9	22.3	- 1.4	...
1957†	20.6	25.9	- 5.3	- 5.8
1958*	23.0	27.7	- 4.7	-10.1
1958†	20.0	29.7	- 9.7	-10.8
1959*	21.0	29.0	- 8.0	...

*Budget.

†Final.

Sources: Annual editions of the Report of the Bank Indonesia; Ministry of Finance; Bureau of Statistics.

Table I-2

GOVERNMENT NET REVENUE BY SOURCE, 1952-1959

(Million Rp.)

		Provisional Results		
		1952*	1953	1954
	A. TAXES			
	Direct taxes			
1	Personal income tax	854	884	1,049
2	Company tax	897	1,083	1,330
3	Other direct taxes	128	60	60
4	Subtotal	1,879	2,027	2,439
	Indirect taxes			
5	Turnover sales tax	628	634	611
6	Import duties	1,397	1,283	995
7	Export duties	1,819	1,013	544
8	Excise	1,096	1,355	1,593
9	Other indirect taxes	160	189	214
10	Subtotal	5,100	4,474	3,957
11	Total of A	6,979	6,501	6,396
12	B. BALANCES OF GOVERNMENT INDUSTRIES	519	205	61
	C. SUNDRIES			
13	B.E.'s†		—	—
14	Foreign exchange certificates and T.P.I. levies		1,914	1,179
15	T.P.T. levies		—	296
16	Miscellaneous		1,087	535
17	Total of C	4,712	3,001	2,010
18	TOTAL NET REVENUE	12,210	9,707	8,467

*Figures disagree with those given in the Report of the Bank Indonesia for 1954-1955, the latest edition in which 1952 figures are included.

†Export certificates.

Table I-2 (concluded)

GOVERNMENT NET REVENUE BY SOURCE, 1952-1959

(Million Rp.)

Provisional Results				Budget	
1955	1956	1957	1958	1959	
1,244	1,496	1,803	2,054	1,250	1
1,804	1,569	1,581	1,945	1,600	2
83	50	141	280	375	3
3,131	3,115	3,525	4,279	3,225	4
557	942	833	1,137	758	5
1,105	1,872	1,785	1,644	1,850	6
752	424	199	185	170	7
1,830	1,877	2,593	3,535	2,891	8
193	235	302	311	615	9
4,436	5,350	5,712	6,812	6,284	10
7,567	8,465	9,237	11,091	9,509	11
98	476	355	141	389	12
—	—	1,587	3,706	3,000	13
1,843	4,985	4,411	2,925	3,500	14
337	212	103	17	—	15
462	1,595	1,180	1,776	999	16
2,642	6,792	7,281	8,424	7,499	17
10,307	15,733	16,873	19,656	17,397	18

Sources: Report of the Bank Indonesia for 1954-1955 through 1958-1959; National Planning Bureau, Annual Report to the Economic Commission for Asia and the Far East.

Table 3

GOVERNMENT EXPENDITURES

1951 - 1959

(Million Rp.)

		High Colleges of State	Foreign Affairs	Home Affairs and Justice	Finance	Economic Affairs and Agri-culture
1951	Budget	84.8	101.6	1,039.6	953.0	896.3
	Expenditures	59.2	477.2	2,303.8	1,117.5	313.2
1952	Budget	1,272.7	105.3	2,682.8	1,099.1	2,430.4
	Expenditures	1,234.9	135.7	2,323.6	872.2	1,757.9
1953	Budget	1,094.7	96.9	1,870.6	871.9	1,960.2
	Expenditures	1,131.2	203.8	2,368.2	884.9	1,603.2
1954	Budget	1,197.1	109.2	1,921.9	1,047.7	1,306.6
	Expenditures	1,249.7	172.2	3,155.3	1,027.7	1,844.1
1955	Budget	1,170.0	92.6	2,547.6	1,209.7	1,690.5
	Expenditures	1,329.3	292.8	3,264.2	1,183.5	1,476.5
1956	Budget	1,565.8	179.6	4,134.2	1,530.6	983.9
	Expenditures	1,536.7	387.2	3,931.3	1,534.4	868.9
1957	Budget	1,799.4	218.0	4,873.7	1,340.5	815.0
	Expenditures	1,799.5	885.1	4,822.2	1,448.7	934.2
1958	Budget	2,334.0	404.8	6,137.6	1,599.0	1,697.2
	Expenditures	2,230.4	1,131.1	5,850.3	1,574.4	1,404.2
	1959 Budget	2,066.4	343.5	3,215.5	4,422.5	1,521.5

Sources: 1951, 1952, 1959: Biro Pusat Statistik, Statistik Konjunktur, July 1959, p. 107; 1953-1957: National Planning Bureau, Report on Progress

Table 3 (concluded)

GOVERNMENT EXPENDITURES

1951 - 1959

(Million Rp.)

Defense	Commu-nication and Public Works and Energy	Education and Cultural Affairs	Health	Social Affairs and Labor	Financing Service and Other	Total	
3,398.8	1,012.3	743.0	117.8	215.2	3,212.6	11,775.0	1951
3,269.0	665.8	529.6	357.4	146.7	1,385.7	10,625.1	
3,930.4	1,399.4	912.5	351.0	235.4	3,143.9	17,562.9	1952
3,032.2	1,073.5	971.8	287.2	176.4	3,160.0	15,025.4	
2,879.9	953.0	752.0	297.1	218.6	275.6	11,270.5	1953
3,875.9	1,107.8	857.5	224.5	205.2	330.5	12,792.7	
3,000.0	1,020.9	750.2	328.7	257.0	313.4	11,252.7	1954
3,327.3	1,133.3	856.1	314.0	266.0	381.9	13,727.6	
2,900.0	849.7	899.5	253.4	250.9	311.1	12,175.0	1955
3,937.5	1,029.8	975.1	314.6	274.1	384.6	14,462.0	
4,075.0	1,180.0	1,295.7	466.6	358.1	550.3	16,319.8	1956
4,378.9	1,086.4	1,138.0	472.3	328.8	552.4	16,215.3	
4,953.0	1,319.1	1,274.3	491.4	392.8	839.1	18,316.3	1957
6,055.5	1,391.1	1,408.5	515.2	410.4	841.1	20,511.5	
10,987.6	1,463.4	1,642.0	620.7	565.8	6,868.7	34,320.8	1958
11,084.6	1,294.4	1,741.7	623.8	518.2	7,859.9	35,313.0	
7,165.5	1,589.3	1,692.0	505.0	304.2	6,211.9	29,037.3	

of the Five Year Development Plan, 1956-1960, Table 66, p. 90; 1958: Report of the Bank Indonesia, 1958-1959, p. 99.

Table I-4

GOVERNMENT DEBT POSITION, 1949 - 1959

(Million Rp.)

End of	Consolidated Debt		Floating Debt	Total Debt	Movements
	External	Internal	Internal		
1949	3,882	—	3,012	6,894	+ 1,400
1950	3,792	1,540	3,302	8,634	+ 1,740
1951	4,463	1,511	1,797	7,771	- 863
1952	5,330	1,439	5,272	12,041	+ 4,270
1953	5,248	5,134	3,164	13,546	+ 1,505
1954	5,237	5,027	6,715	16,979	+ 3,433
1955	5,029	4,986	8,769	18,784	+ 1,805
1956	2,979	4,856	11,234	19,069	+ 285
1957	2,820	4,763	17,481	25,064	+ 5,995
1958	2,421	4,670	27,335	34,426	+ 9,362
1959 (June)	2,356	4,558	32,718	39,632	+ 5,206

Sources: Report of the Bank Indonesia for 1956–1957 through 1958–1959; Bank Indonesia Bulletin, No. 18, 1959.

Table I-5

MONEY SUPPLY IN INDONESIA, 1951 - 1959

(Million Rp.)

End of	Currency*	Deposit Money	Total Money	Per Cent Currency	Per Cent Deposit Money
March 1938†	240.0	180.0	420.0	57.1	42.9
December 1951	3,328.1	1,705.8	5,033.9	66.1	33.9
December 1952	4,349.2	2,254.6	6,603.8	65.9	34.1
December 1953	5,217.7	2,268.8	7,486.5	69.7	30.3
December 1954	7,473.7	3,642.8	11,116.5	67.2	32.8
December 1955	8,646.8	3,587.2	12,234.0	70.7	29.3
December 1956	9,372.4	4,021.1	13,393.5	70.0	30.0
December 1957	14,091.4	4,822.0	18,913.4	74.5	25.5
December 1958	19,871.7	9,494.5	29,366.2	67.7	32.3
June 1959	22,834.6	9,544.9	32,379.5	70.5	29.5

*Excluding cash held in bank tills and government offices.

†Estimated.

Sources: Report of the Bank Indonesia for 1956-1957 through 1958-1959; Bank Indonesia Bulletin, No. 18, 1959.

Table I-6

FACTORS IN CHANGES IN THE MONEY SUPPLY

1952 - 1959

(Million Rp.)

A. Public sector
B. Private sector
C. Foreign sector
D. Miscellaneous

	First Quarter	Second Quarter	Third Quarter	Fourth Quarter	Full Year
1952					
A.	+1,175	+1,590	+1,075	+1,825	+5,665
B.	- 239	+ 54	+ 419	+ 58	+ 292
C.	- 430	- 737	-1,171	- 892	-3,230
D.	- 253	- 123	- 716	- 89	-1,181
Total	+ 253	+ 784	- 393	+ 902	+1,546
1953					
A.	+1,075	- 398	+1,124	+ 651	+2,452
B.	- 159	+ 320	- 144	- 67	- 50
C.	- 330	- 131	- 826	- 273	-1,560
D.	- 29	+ 137	+ 108	- 136	+ 80
Total	+ 557	- 72	+ 262	+ 175	+ 922
1954					
A.	+ 783	+1,110	+ 941	+ 508	+3,342
B.	+ 212	+ 65	- 175	+ 331	+ 433
C.	- 615	- 423	+ 349	+ 420	- 269
D.	- 3	+ 76	- 141	+ 36	- 32
Total	+ 377	+ 828	+ 974	+1,295	+3,474
1955*					
A.					+1,755
B.					-1,287
C.					+1,034
D.					- 385
Total					+1,117

Table I-6

(concluded)

	First Quarter	Second Quarter	Third Quarter	Fourth Quarter	Full Year
1956					
A.	- 635	+ 465	+ 750	+ 1,687	+ 2,267
B.	+ 453	+ 398	+ 420	- 282	+ 989
C.	- 657	- 768	- 434	+ 44	- 1,815
D.	- 285	- 188	- 101	+ 292	- 282
Total	- 1,124	- 93	+ 635	+ 1,741	+ 1,159
1957					
A.	+ 878	+ 1,479	+ 897	+ 2,579	+ 5,833
B.	+ 36	+ 835	+ 1,038	+ 328	+ 2,237
C.	- 612	- 507	+ 508	- 412	- 1,023
D.	- 334	- 37	- 694	- 462	- 1,527
Total	- 32	+ 1,770	+ 1,749	+ 2,033	+ 5,520
1958					
A.	+ 2,467	+ 1,613	+ 3,049	+ 3,729	+ 10,858
B.	- 163	- 390	+ 63	- 360	- 850
C.	- 1,632	+ 731	- 518	+ 1,999	+ 580
D.	+ 33	+ 74	- 309	+ 67	- 135
Total	+ 705	+ 2,028	+ 2,285	+ 5,435	+ 10,453
1959					
A.	+ 2,062	+ 3,002			
B.	- 899	+ 730			
C.	- 64	- 1,507			
D.	- 448	+ 136			
Total	+ 651	+ 2,361			

*Quarterly figures are not available for the revised totals given here.

Sources: Report of the Bank Indonesia for 1956-1957 through 1958-1959; Bank Indonesia Bulletin, No. 18, 1959.

Table I-7

BALANCE OF PAYMENTS, 1950-1959

(Million Rp.)

	1950	1951	1952
A. Goods and services			
1. Exports and imports*	+ 954	+ 1,530	- 1,035
2. Nonmonetary gold movement (net)	—	—	+ 6
3. Foreign travel	- 33	- 26	- 106
4. Transportation	- 82	- 22	- 127
5. Insurance	- 38	- 29	- 139
6. Investment income	- 92	- 161	- 434
7. Government, not included elsewhere	- 101	- 98	- 230
8. Miscellaneous:			
a. Foreign workers / b. Other	+ 55	- 567	- 965
Total Goods and Services	+ 663	+ 627	- 3,030
B. Donations:			
9. Private / 10. Official	+ 149	—‡	+ 83
Total Current Transactions	+ 812	+ 627	- 2,947
C. Private, exclusive banks			
11. Long-term loans:			
a. Oil companies / b. Other	- 18	+ 31	- 90
12. Short-term loans	—	—	—
13. Long-term improvements			
14. Short-term improvements			
D. Government and banks			
15. Long-term loans	+ 29	- 150	+ 897
16. Short-term loans:			
a. Liabilities to IMF and IBRD / b. Other	+ 615		
17. Long-term improvements			
18. Foreign exchange holdings		+ 292	+ 2,044
19. Monetary gold holdings	+ 116	+ 269	+ 532
Total Movement of Capital, Foreign Exchange and Gold Holdings	+ 742	+ 442	+ 3,383
20. Items not included elsewhere	+ 70	+ 185	- 436

*Exports: f.o.b.; imports: c.i.f.

†Includes "other" category: 1953 = +27; 1954 = +13; 1955 = +1.

‡Owing to rounding of figures in A, donations of Rp. 1.5 million omitted.

Table I-7 (concluded)

BALANCE OF PAYMENTS, 1950-1959

(Million Rp.)

1953	1954	1955	1956	1957	1958	1st Half 1959	
							A.
+ 1,164†	+ 2,170†	+ 3,791†	+ 265	+ 1,404	+ 1,212	+ 1,297	1.
+ 5	+ 4	+ 1	+ 1	+ 1	—	—	2.
- 90	- 78	- 81	- 110	- 119	- 76	- 71	3.
- 150	- 148	- 152	- 133	- 107	- 155	- 200	4.
- 148	- 147	- 142	- 144	- 104	- 45	- 14	5.
- 621	- 1,104	- 1,231	- 727	- 968	- 783	- 497	6.
- 184	- 86	- 97	- 125	- 201	- 326	- 107	7.
							8.
- 526	- 645	- 658	- 520	- 477	- 268	- 144	a.
- 694	- 501	- 262	- 298	- 398	- 303	- 205	b.
- 1,244	- 535	+ 1,169	- 1,791	- 969	- 744	+ 59	
							B.
+ 5	+ 7	+ 4	+ 7	+ 3	+ 2	{+ 44	9.
+ 31	+ 24	+ 11	+ 10	+ 132	+ 2,150		10.
- 1,208	- 504	+ 1,184	- 1,774	- 834	+ 1,408	+ 103	
							C.
							11.
{+ 18	+ 181	+ 293	+ 26	+ 34	+ 60	{- 2	a.
	- 185	- 288	- 25	- 16	- 16		b.
- 1	- 9	+ 8	+ 9	—	—	—	12.
			—	+ 3	+ 1	—	13.
			—	+ 15	+ 9	- 1	14.
							D.
- 82	- 28	- 182	- 125	- 58	- 26	+ 464	15.
							16.
	+ 171		+ 313	—	—	{—	a.
			+ 420	+ 520	+ 86		b.
			+ 13	- 38	- 138	- 2	17.
+ 296	- 259	- 1,015	+ 691	+ 273	- 1,312	- 67	18.
+ 1,089	+ 633	+ 102	+ 421	+ 63	+ 17	- 37	19.
+ 1,320	+ 504	- 1,184	+ 1,743	+ 796	- 1,319	+ 355	
- 112			+ 31	+ 38	- 89	- 459	20.

Sources: Report of the Java Bank for 1951-1952 and 1952-1953; Report of the Bank Indonesia for 1953-1954 through 1958-1959; Bank Indonesia Bulletin, No. 18, 1959.

Table I-8

PERCENTAGE OF NATIONAL INCOME BY SECTORAL ORIGIN

1953 - 1958

Sector	1953	1954	1955	1956	1957	1958
Agriculture:						
Food	36.2	36.9	36.2	36.6	35.5	40.4
Smallholders export crops	7.9	7.9	8.0	7.1	6.5	3.6
Plantation	4.5	3.8	3.8	3.5	3.4	3.2
Livestock breeding	4.2	4.9	4.6	4.5	4.2	5.0
Fishery	3.0	2.9	2.9	2.8	2.6	3.0
Forestry	2.3	2.2	1.4	1.4	1.3	1.6
Less export tax and statistic tax	1.1	0.6	0.9	0.9	0.9	0.8
Total	56.0	58.0	56.0	55.0	52.6	56.0
Nonagriculture:						
Industry, mining, and construction	12.0	11.8	12.2	12.5	14.1	11.0
Services*	23.1	22.5	23.2	23.4	23.1	19.3
Government	7.9	7.7	8.6	9.1	10.2	13.7
Total	43.0	42.0	44.0	45.0	47.4	44.0
Total all sectors	100.0	100.0	100.0	100.0	100.0	100.0

*Transport, communications, trade, banking, etc.

Source: National Planning Bureau, Report on Progress of the Five Year Development Plan, 1956-1960, Table 78, p. 112.

Table I-9

GROSS NATIONAL PRODUCT AND NET DOMESTIC PRODUCT
1953 - 1958

(Billion Rp., 1955 Prices)

	1953	1954	1955	1956	1957	1958
Gross national product at market prices	121.0	128.5	127.9	134.5	144.7	126.8
Net domestic product at factor cost	109.1	116.7	118.9	124.5	134.5	117.1

Source: National Planning Bureau, Report on Progress of the Five Year Development Plan, 1956-1960, Table 75, p. 100.

Table I-10

FINANCING OF THE FIVE YEAR PLAN
1956 - 1958

(Million Rp.)

	1956	1957	1958	Total
Domestic financing	1,416.1	2,214.5	1,949.0	5,579.6
Foreign loans, aid, and World War II claims	401.1	422.7	1,157.4	1,981.2
Total	1,817.2	2,637.2	3,106.4	7,560.8

Source: National Planning Bureau, Report on Progress of the Five Year Development Plan, 1956-1960, Table 85, p. 133.

Table I-11

GOVERNMENT INVESTMENT, 1956-1960

(Million Rp.)

	Plan Estimate	Actual 1956	Actual 1957	Actual 1958	Actual Total
I. Agriculture:					
Agriculture (farming)	1,044.0	283.2	391.1	534.2	1,208.5
Resettlement	383.0	67.2	57.8	18.0*	143.0
Community development	198.0	—	12.4	12.6	25.0
	1,625.0	350.4	461.3	564.8	1,376.5
II. Power and irrigation:					
Construction of power installations	1,750.0	119.2	276.6	217.2	613.0
Irrigation	1,100.0	58.5	97.8	108.3	264.6
Reserve	275.0	—	—	—	—
	3,125.0	177.7	374.4	325.5	877.6
III. Industry and mining:					
Special projects	1,078.0	14.7	7.9	21.6	44.2
Central projects	776.5	215.0	248.9	36.1	500.0
Regional projects	425.0	41.4	102.7	140.3	284.4
Industrial credit	—	13.0	13.0	13.0	39.0
Research	—	21.2	24.8	6.5	52.5
Others	—	142.0*	—	—	142.0
Mining	757.0	56.2	189.7	56.2	302.1
Reserve	88.5	—	—	—	—
	3,125.0	503.5	587.0	273.7	1,364.2
IV. Transportation and communication:					
Highways	1,200.0	130.1	243.4	307.8	681.3
Railways	600.0	30.7	69.2	18.2	118.1
Communications	495.0	73.8	144.6	162.2	380.6
Shipping	350.0	—	87.5	1,050.9	1,138.4
Harbors	275.0	42.2	58.4	37.2*	137.8
Aviation	100.0	2.8	3.8	2.5	9.1
Traffic, land, river	40.0	—	—	—	—
Meteorology	15.0	0.5	1.5	1.0	3.0
Others	50.0	—	27.0	30.0	57.0
	3,125.0	280.1	635.4	1,609.8	2,525.3
V. Education, social affairs, and information:					
Education	1,050.0	256.7	286.8	89.5	633.0
Health	250.0	91.7	105.3	104.7	301.7

Table I-11 (concluded)

	Plan Estimate	Actual 1956	1957	1958	Total
V. (continued)					
Housing	95.0	8.4	8.0	5.3	21.7
Labor	25.0	2.6	5.7	4.4	12.7
Social welfare	12.5	23.0	22.0	53.7	98.7
Information	37.5	23.9	37.2	—	61.1
Reserve	30.0	—	—	—	—
Others	—	—	59.1	—	59.1
	1,500.0	406.3	524.1	257.6	1,188.0
TOTAL	12,500.0	1,718.0	2,582.2	3,031.4	7,331.6

*Actual figures for half year.

Source: National Planning Bureau, Report on Progress of the Five Year Development Plan, 1956-1960, pp. 127-128.

Table I-12

GOVERNMENT INVESTMENT SUMMARY, BY SECTOR, 1956-1958

(Million Rp.)

	Plan Estimate	Actual 1956	1957	1958	Total
I. Farming, etc.	1,625.0	350.4	461.3	564.8	1,376.5
II. Power and irrigation	3,125.0	177.7	374.4	325.5	877.6
III. Industry and mining	3,125.0	503.5	587.0	273.7	1,364.2
IV. Communication	3,125.0	280.1	635.4	1,609.8	2,525.3
V. Social affairs	1,500.0	406.3	524.1	257.6	1,188.0
TOTAL	12,500.0	1,718.0	2,582.2	3,031.4	7,331.6

Source: National Planning Bureau, Report on Progress of the Five Year Development Plan, 1956-1960, Table 84, p. 130.

Table I-13

INDONESIAN ECONOMIC DEVELOPMENT SCHEME
MODEL II*

		First Five		
		1956	1957	1958
1	Investment — million Rp.	6,000	6,500	7,100
2	Investment per capita — Rp.	71.5	76.5	82.2
3	ICOR	2:1	2:1	2:1
4	ICOR (Model I)			
5	Output increment — million Rp.	3,000	3,300	3,600
6	National income — million Rp.	103,000	106,300	109,900
7	Population — million	83.9	85.3	86.8
8	Income per capita — Rp.	1,228	1,246	1,265
9	Additional saving† — million Rp.	520	600	680
10	Increase, national income — per cent	—	—	—
11	Increase, income per capita — per cent	—	—	—
12	Investment as per cent of national income	—	—	—
13	Investment as per cent of national income (Model I)	—	—	—

*Except for ICOR, all figures refer to end of period.

†Amount saved out of income increment, assuming propensity to save is 40 per cent of per capita income increase.

Table I-13 (concluded)

INDONESIAN ECONOMIC DEVELOPMENT SCHEME

MODEL II*

Year	Plan	Plan II	Plan III	Plan IV	Plan V	
1959	1960	1961-1956	1966-1970	1971-1975	1976-1980	
7,800	7,800	13,600	20,800	30,000	44,100	1
88.6	96.0	138.7	193.1	251.8	335.9	2
2:1	2:1	2.3:1	2.6:1	3:1	3:1	3
		(2.5:1)	(3:1)	(4:1)	(4:1)	4
3,900	4,300	5,900	8,000	10,000	14,700	5
13,800	118,100	143,000	177,000	220,500	283,800	6
88.3	89.8	98.1	107.8	119.0	131.4	7
1,288	1,315	1,458	1,642	1,853	2,160	8
800	960	1,400	1,900	2,300	3,700	9
—	18	21	24	25	29	10
—	8.5	10.8	12.6	12.9	16.7	11
—	7.3	9.5	11.8	13.6	15.6	12
—	(6.0)	(8.6)	(12.0)	(16.0)	(20.0)	13

Source: National Planning Bureau, "A Study of the Indonesian Economic Development Scheme," Ekonomi dan Keuangan Indonesia, Vol. X, September 1957. Published in Indonesian in the August 1957 issue.

Table I-14

VALUE OF EXPORTS

1938, 1950-1958

(Million Rp., including revenue from export duties)

	1938	1950	1951
1. Rubber, of which:	158	1,301	2,483
a. estate rubber	(87)	(361)	(817)
b. smallholders rubber	(71)	(940)	(1,666)
2. Petroleum and petroleum products	163	560	633
3. Tin and tin ore	34	185	308
4. Copra and copra cakes	43	230	503
5. Coffee	14	118	144
6. Tea	57	57	81
7. Tobacco	39	157	103
8. Palm oil and palm kernels	19	102	139
9. Sugar	45	88	52
10. Pepper and other spices	18	1	8
11. Tapioca and tapioca products	9	13	30
12. Forest products (timber, gums, resins)	7	24	27
13. Hard rope fibers	18	12	14
14. Groundnuts and groundnut oil	4	21	23
15. Rattan	3	3	4
16. Pinang nuts	6	17	24
17. Hides and skins	4	22	26
18. Shells	1	23	18
19. Sago and sago products	1	4	6
20. Cattle	2	4	6
21. Coal	2	2	3
22. Soya beans	1	—	—
23. Other	39	95	145
24. Total†	687	3,039	4,780

*Provisional figures.

†Excluding postal parcels, passengers' goods, and ship's chandlery, and gold and silver.

Table I-14 (concluded)

VALUE OF EXPORTS

1938, 1950-1958

(Million Rp., including revenue from export duties)

1952	1953	1954	1955	1956	1957	1958*	
4,778	3,080	3,013	4,888	4,028	3,983	2,978	1.
(2,258)	(1,561)	(1,156)	(1,931)	(1,712)	(1,663)	(1,234)	a.
(2,520)	(1,519)	(1,857)	(2,957)	(2,316)	(2,320)	(1,744)	b.
2,181	2,292	2,589	2,460	2,560	3,677	3,219	2.
981	926	700	683	726	619	431	3.
641	728	657	483	513	486	239	4.
206	343	455	182	343	334	206	5.
267	267	454	355	337	340	283	6.
265	278	372	316	332	383	345	7.
346	380	347	305	347	347	314	8.
2	111	255	210	191	193	102	9.
243	206	193	158	151	177	112	10.
3	27	70	68	7	14	9	11.
59	54	66	84	60	56	47	12.
118	71	52	71	73	49	44	13.
4	38	50	12	5	14	6	14.
29	45	46	41	36	38	30	15.
35	31	34	22	39	44	22	16.
46	25	22	17	17	18	15	17.
13	15	17	14	10	7	3	18.
18	20	13	9	8	6	4	19.
20	18	9	11	6	12	9	20.
10	13	7	4	1	5	2	21.
—	10	—	—	—	—	2	22.
387	366	458	386	265	250	190	23.
10,652	9,344	9,879	10,779	10,055	11,052	8,612	24.

Sources: Report of the Java Bank for 1951-1952 and 1952-1953; Report of the Bank Indonesia for 1953-1954 through 1958-1959.

Table I-15

PER CENT OF PRINCIPAL PRODUCTS
IN THE VALUE OF EXPORTS

1928, 1938, 1950-1958

	1928	1938	1950	1951	1952	1953	1954	1955	1956	1957	1958
Rubber	17.6	22.6	43.4	51.9	46.0	33.0	30.9	46.0	40.2	36.0	34.6
Oil and oil products	9.1	23.8	18.8	13.3	19.9	24.5	26.4	22.8	25.4	33.3	37.4
Copra	6.8	5.7	7.4	10.2	5.6	7.8	6.7	4.6	4.4	4.4	2.2
Tea	6.2	8.3	3.4	2.9	2.6	2.9	4.6	3.3	3.4	3.1	3.3
Tobacco	6.1	3.9	3.3	2.2	1.9	2.9	3.8	3.0	3.3	3.5	4.0
Tin metal and ore	5.6	5.0	6.2	6.5	9.4	9.9	7.2	6.4	7.0	5.6	5.0
Palm oil and palm kernels	—	2.8	3.8	3.0	3.3	4.1	3.6	2.9	3.4	3.1	3.6
Sugar	23.8	6.5	—	—	—	1.2	2.6	2.0	1.9	1.8	1.2
Other	24.8	21.4	13.7	10.0	11.2	13.7	14.2	9.0	10.9	9.2	8.7

Sources: Report of the Java Bank for 1951-1952 and 1952-1953; Report of the Bank Indonesia for 1953-1954 through 1958-1959.

Table I-16

WEIGHTED INDEX NUMBERS OF WHOLESALE PRICES OF EIGHTEEN EXPORT PRODUCTS 1951 - MARCH 1959

(Price f.o.b., 1938 = 100)

Year		Estate Products	Farm Products	Forest Products	General
1951		724	910	1,236	847
1952		1,629	1,787	2,965	1,719
1953		1,320	1,374	3,151	1,357
1954		1,303	1,378	3,271	1,354
1955		1,598	1,760	2,566	1,696
1956		1,539	1,694	2,426	1,622
1957		1,461	1,650	2,312	1,569
1958		1,350	1,371	2,214	1,367
1959					
	January	1,441	1,489	2,245	1,476
	February	1,464	1,500	2,331	1,491
	March	1,507	1,537	2,276	1,531

Source: Central Bureau of Statistics, Monthly Survey, August 1959, p. 72.

Table I-17

VALUE OF TOTAL IMPORTS BY ECONOMIC GROUP

1938, 1951 - 1958

(Million Rp.)

Year	Consumer Goods		Raw Materials and Auxiliary Products		Capital Goods		Total
	Value	Per Cent	Value	Per Cent	Value	Per Cent	
1938	207	43.3	154	32.2	117	24.5	478
1951	1,701	51.3	1,148	34.6	469	14.1	3,318
1952	5,377	49.8	3,440	31.8	1,989	18.4	10,806
1953	3,740	43.6	3,232	37.6	1,612	18.8	8,584
1954	2,688	37.5	3,048	42.5	1,428	20.0	7,164
1955	2,137	29.8	3,760	52.4	1,284	17.8	7,181
1956	4,070	41.5	3,822	39.0	1,908	19.5	9,800
1957	2,917	31.8	4,347	47.5	1,895	20.7	9,159
1958*	1,993	33.8	2,648	44.9	1,258	21.3	5,899

*Provisional figures.

Sources: Report of the Bank Indonesia for 1954-1955 through 1958-1959.

Table I-18

INDEX NUMBERS OF IMPORTS OF INDUSTRIAL RAW MATERIALS, 1940, 1952-1958

(1950 = 100)

		1940	1952	1953	1954	1955	1956	1957	1958
Breweries:	malt (including flour and extract)	—	207	264	294	315	279	319	79
Printing works:	paper	67	102	106	111	142	163	165	114
Paint industry:	white zinc	151	74	98	66	165	103	144	100
	red lead	298	99	155	44	118	117	139	91
Weaving mills:	cotton weaving yarns	85	53	84	94	117	134	69	165
Batik works:	grey shirtings, sheetings, and supers	61	45	61	33	50	44	26	26
	bleached cambrics and shirtings	261	231	284	277	251	258	33	215
	wax (various kinds)	83	20	38	19	—	228	593	794
Kretek works:	cloves	64	57	30	70	62	117	65	76
Construction shops:	sheet iron	257	170	264	352	253	349	534	232
	bar iron	157	120	110	137	202	126	262	170
	profile iron	212	103	192	136	197	136	259	113
Building industry:	cement	111	171	137	201	244	275	217	78
Miscellaneous:	caustic soda	104	118	96	112	205	113	174	211

Sources: Report of the Bank Indonesia for 1954–1955 through 1958–1959.

Table I-19

UNWEIGHTED INDEX NUMBERS OF WHOLESALE PRICES OF FORTY-FOUR IMPORT ARTICLES AT DJAKARTA 1951 - 1958

(Importers' Selling Prices: 1938 = 100)

Year	Provisions	Textile Goods	Chemicals	Metals	Other Articles	General
1951	2,047	3,087	2,273	2,326	2,468	2,440
1952	2,552	2,519	2,077	2,364	2,058	2,314
1953	3,034	2,835	2,298	2,251	1,888	2,461
1954	3,336	3,109	2,502	2,216	2,304	2,693
1955	4,383	4,801	3,472	2,580	2,644	3,576
1956	4,449	3,344	3,143	3,029	2,674	3,328
1957	5,398	3,889	3,246	3,796	3,363	3,938
1958	7,413	7,043	4,777	5,257	5,862	6,071

Source: Central Bureau of Statistics, Monthly Survey, August 1959, p. 74.

Table I-20

RICE IMPORTS, 1953-1958

Year	Volume (Thousand Tons)	Expenditure (Million Rp.)
1953	371.5	916.2
1954	261.0	562.8
1955	127.8	248.2
1956	763.2	1,280.7
1957*	563.4	956.4
1958†	681.8	1,040.0

*Temporary figures.

†Approximate figures.

Source: National Planning Bureau, Report on Progress of the Five Year Development Plan, 1956-1960, Table 5, p. 22.

Table I-21

PRODUCTION OF ESSENTIAL FOOD CROPS, 1953-1958

(Thousand Tons)

	1953	1954	1955	1956	1957	1958*
Rice	7,031	7,530	7,216	7,309	7,443	7,613
Corn (skinned)	1,814	2,720	1,971	1,965	1,800	2,125
Tapioca (cassava root)	8,953	9,569	9,317	9,131	9,908	11,090
Sweet potatoes	2,177	2,111	1,898	2,638	2,631	2,800
Peanuts (skinned)	204	248	207	218	228	—
Beans (skinned)	306	400	346	357	327	—

*Temporary figures.

Source: National Planning Bureau, Report on Progress of the Five Year Development Plan, 1956-1960, Table 1, pp. 19-20.

Table I-22

WEIGHTED INDEX NUMBERS OF MARKET PRICES OF 19 FOOD ARTICLES AND INDEX NUMBERS OF IMPORTANT TEXTILE GOODS IN THE RURAL DISTRICTS OF JAVA AND MADURA, 1951-1959

(July 1938 = 100)

19 Food Articles			Textile Goods		
Year	Month	Average	Year	Month	Average
1951	December	4,335	1951		3,940
1952	December	3,611	1952		3,536
1953	December	3,511	1953		4,120
1954	March	3,116	1954		4,040
	June	2,690	1955		7,596
	September	3,064	1956		4,768
	December	3,334	1957	July	5,412
1955	March	3,641		August	5,880
	June	3,761		September	6,144
	September	4,391		October	6,540
	December	4,990		November	6,824
1956	March	5,582		December	7,080
	June	4,459	1958	January	7,288
	September	4,590		February	7,680
	December	4,763		March	8,292
1957	March	4,332		April	9,112
	June	4,336		May	9,024
	September	5,292		June	9,128
	December	7,901		July	9,368
1958	January	7,833		August	9,936
	February	7,806		September	10,340
	March	8,923		October	11,920
	April	7,120		November	12,572
	May	6,590		December	13,152
	June	6,792	1959	January	14,600
	July	7,077		February	15,696
	August	7,703		March	17,760
	September	8,119		April	17,608
	October	8,216		May	17,968
	November	8,230		June	28,108
	December	8,324		July	30,688

Table I-22 (concluded)

19 Food Articles (continued)

Year	Month	Average
1959	January	8,371
	February	8,344
	March	8,182
	April	7,860
	May	7,661
	June	8,097
	July	9,094

Source: Central Bureau of Statistics, Monthly Survey, August 1959, pp. 78, 80.

Table I-23

TEXTILE PRODUCTION, MAIN WEAVING MILLS, 1951-1958

Year	Mills in Operation	Yarn Used*	Sundry†	Sarongs‡	Scarves‡	Towels‡
1951	42	4,393	22,829	2,889	237	538
1952	61	6,056	29,118	3,224	113	1,863
1953	67	8,600	42,829	3,579	74	2,779
1954	65	9,195	46,144	3,925	14	2,611
1955	68	10,318	50,027	3,465	10	2,829
1956	64	10,296	52,959	3,216	1	3,020
1957	61	10,660	56,336	2,707	2	3,020
1958§	62	7,907	41,389	1,659	—	1,962

*Metric tons.

†Thousand meters.

‡Thousand pieces.

§First three quarters only.

Sources: Report of the Bank Indonesia for 1956-1957 through 1958-1959.

Table I-24

LICENSED CAPACITY OF CONTROLLED INDUSTRY

END OF 1941, 1949-1958*

	Type of Industry —Unit of Capacity	1941	1949	1950	1951
1	Printing works — 1,000 sq m printing/hr	1,761	1,819	1,977	2,177
2	Rice milling works — hp	44,170	45,677	45,984	44,824
3	Spinning mills — spindles	...	203,210	204,028	119,750
4	Weaving mills — handlooms	49,019	67,161	72,001	71,095
5	Weaving mills — machine looms	7,588	10,590	11,322	11,971
6	Knitting mills — knitting machines	120	233	257	342
7	Textile printing works — machines	—	...	...	1
8	Cigarette works — 1,000 cigarettes/minute	130	137	140	157
9	Ice works — tons/month	23,156	23,402	25,728	26,214
10	Frying pan works — tons/month	237	375	355	378
11	Rubber remilling works — 1,000 tons/year	111	135	159	162

*Licenses issued to establishments not yet erected are excluded.

†Capacity in tons during 7 work hours.

‡Number of machines.

Table I-24 (concluded)

LICENSED CAPACITY OF CONTROLLED INDUSTRY

END OF 1941, 1949-1958*

1952	1953	1954	1955	1956	1957	1958	
2,447	2,622	2,777	2,854	2,994	3,469	3,308	1
45,684	54,733	56,607	57,509	57,024	4,073[†]	4,190[†]	2
63,486	67,000	98,000	98,966	120,366	120,366	97,518	3
69,052	67,746	75,435	78,857	84,935	115,522[‡]	118,897[‡]	4
12,119	12,994	12,480	12,697	11,477	15,301[‡]	16,524[‡]	5
351	545	700	772	970	2,784	3,460	6
8	8	18	18	18	24	29	7
169	199	199	218	220	242	263	8
28,086	34,498	34,399	32,900	32,897	30,958	38,417	9
431	521	510	530	510	517	665	10
158	158	158	169	171	177	178	11

Sources: Report of the Java Bank for 1951-1952 and 1952-1953; Report of the Bank Indonesia for 1953-1954 through 1958-1959.

INDEX